THE RUSSIAN
RELIGIOUS MIND (II)
The Middle Ages
The 13th to the 15th Centuries

VOLUME FOUR
IN THE COLLECTED WORKS OF
GEORGE P. FEDOTOV

About the Author

George P. Fedotov was born in 1886 in Saratov, Russia. He began his academic life as a student of engineering but, while studying in Germany and Italy, he changed his scope of study to history. When he returned to Russia in 1914, he became Assistant Professor of European Medieval History at the University of St. Petersburg (1914-1918) and, later, Professor at the University of Saratov (1920-1922). Unable to pursue creative scholarship in Soviet Russia, Professor Fedotov left his homeland in 1925. From 1926 to 1940 he was Professor of Church History at the Russian Theological School in Paris. During this time in Paris he also worked on the journals *Sovremennyi zapiski* [*Contemporary Notes*], *Put'* [*The Way*] and *Chisla* [*Dates*]. In 1931 he co-founded the important journal *Novyi Grad* [*The New City*] which he edited until 1939. In 1941 he came to the United States where, until his death in 1951, he was Professor of Church History at St. Vladimir's Theological School.

ABOUT *THE COLLECTED WORKS* OF GEORGE P. FEDOTOV

George P. Fedotov wrote prolifically and his interests ranged over several fields of inquiry—Russian history, literature, theology, spirituality and Russian culture in general as well as political thought and the Latin West. *The Collected Works* of George P. Fedotov will be published in English and will include his numerous articles as well as his books—including reprints of those books which were already published in English.

The Russian Religious Mind (II)
The Middle Ages
The 13th to the 15th Centuries

BY

GEORGE P. FEDOTOV

Edited, With A Foreword, by John Meyendorff

VOLUME FOUR

IN THE COLLECTED WORKS OF

GEORGE P. FEDOTOV

NORDLAND PUBLISHING COMPANY

BELMONT, MASSACHUSETTS 02178

1975

BY THE SAME AUTHOR

THE COLLECTED WORKS OF GEORGE P. FEDOTOV
[Nordland Publishing Company]

Volume I — *St. Filipp: Metropolitan of Moscow*
Volume II — *A Treasury of Russian Spirituality*
Volume III — *The Russian Religious Mind (I): Kievan Christianity—
The 10th to the 13th Centuries*
Volume IV — *The Russian Religious Mind (II): The Middle Ages*
Volume V — *Peter Abelard*
[Other volumes forthcoming]

Library of Congress Catalog Card Number 75-29542
ISBN 0-913124-19-2
© Copyright 1966 by the President and Fellows of Harvard College

The Russian Religious Mind (II) is reprinted in *The Colleced Works* of
George P. Fedotov by special arrangement with Harvard University Press and
Nina Rojankovsky, Administratrix of the Estate of George P. Fedotov.

PRINTED IN THE UNITED STATES OF AMERICA

Contents

FOREWORD

"My intention is to describe the subjective side of religion as opposed to its objective side; that is, opposed to the complex of organized dogmas, sacraments, rites, liturgy, Canon Law, and so on. I am interested in man, religious man, and his attitude towards God, the world, and his fellow men; his attitude is not only emotional, but also rational and volitional, the attitude of the whole man. This wholeness of religious personality is the invisible center out of which the main phenomena not only of religious but of cultural life in general have their origin and receive their meaning . . . I do not deny the supernatural, divine character of Christianity as a religion of revelation. But I believe that its realization begins with the human response to Grace. The history of Christianity is the history of this response; its culture is the culture of this experience."

Such is G. P. Fedotov's approach to Russian history, as he himself described it, in the introduction to the first volume of *The Russian Religious Mind,* which covered the period of Kievan Christianity from the tenth to the thirteenth centuries.[1] At the time of his death in 1951, Professor Fedotov was working on the second volume of his work. It is this second volume, in some parts unfortunately incomplete, that we here present to the reader.

By understanding as he did the religious history of Russia, and by seeking, first of all, the "human response to Grace," Fedotov was in part expressing the fundamental belief of the Orthodox Christians that God acts in history with man's "cooperation," that since the moment when the Word became flesh, God's hand is essentially made present in history through those men who use freely and responsibly the

---

[1] Cambridge, Mass.: Harvard University Press, 1946, reissued 1966; Harper Torchbook (TB 70), New York, 1960.

gift of redemption. Hence, the particular role in Orthodox piety and religion of those who are called "saints," that is, those who have been recognized as having responded to God's call and have used the supernatural potentialities of the divine life given to them. It is to these people that Fedotov has given attention in his first general essay on Russian history, *Svyatye drevnei Rusi: X–XVII st.*,[2] and in a small monograph on St. Philip, Metropolitan of Moscow, *Svyatoi Filipp, Mitropolit Moskovski,*[3] a victim of Tsar Ivan IV's ferocious suppression of the opposition in the sixteenth century.

In these two works, as well as in a series of articles published in Russian periodicals, Fedotov has made a path for a literary and scholarly genre in which modern Russian religious literature is astonishingly poor: hagiography, understood neither as a mere repetition of the medieval lives of saints, in which history and legend are intermingled, nor as a negative and rationalistic "demythologizing," but as a true portrayal of men of God, standing before their Master and before their fellow men, in the entire wholeness of their religious historical personality. Fedotov was successful in this endeavor because, first of all, he was able to combine the excellent historical training that he received at the University of St. Petersburg with an ability to interpret original sources and an exceptional sensitivity to the religious life of man, and to human life in general. In his scholarly work Fedotov was always "humanistic," a lover of man or, perhaps, simply a Christian. The elaborate intricacy of historical research which, of course, he loved for itself, as does any good historian, always remained for him a means of achieving not only a better knowledge of the past but also an under-

[2] *Svyatye drevnei Rusi: X–XVII st.* (The Saints of Ancient Russia: 10th–17th Centuries), Paris: YMCA Press, 1931; reprinted South Canaan, Pa.: St. Tikhon Press, 1959.
[3] Paris: YMCA Press, 1928.

standing of the present. It was his concern of present-day Russia, his involvement in political life and in the revolutionary events of 1905 and 1917, that led him to study the past destinies of his people. It was his concern for freedom and justice, which for him were wholly based on the Gospel, that made him study the lives of those who were successful in realizing its precepts, at least partially, in the concrete historical life of the Russian people.

A concern for the religious destiny of Russia, taken as a whole, was in fact Fedotov's main preoccupation, and it is to this problem that he dedicated his numerous contributions to the various periodicals of the emigration.[4] Thus, in 1935, Fedotov took another step in his research by moving from the study of exceptional individuals to the study of popular religion. He published a short critical essay on popular religious poetry,[5] which reflected the beliefs of simple Christians and, sometimes, the remains of paganism in ancient Russia. *The Russian Religious Mind* continues the same trend and is a masterly synthesis of Fedotov's life work. Even incomplete — it should, in fact, be extended up to our own time — it represents not only a specialized study of religion in Russia, but a highly original and provocative view of Russia's historical destiny in its entirety.

Fedotov himself liked to contrast his appreciation of Russia with that of the classical Russian historiographers, Soloviev and Klyuchevski. For the latter, the Muscovite tsardom, created in the fifteenth and sixteenth centuries after the downfall of Mongol domination, represents the peak of the original Russian civilization. In the view of the nineteenth-century Slavophiles, who influenced that historiography, the empire of Peter I is itself a betrayal of the original

---

[4] The reader will find a complete bibliography of the works of Fedotov at the back of this volume.

[5] *Stikhi dukhovnye: Russkaya narodnaya vera po dukhovnym stikham* (Spiritual Poems: The Russian People's Faith as Reflected in Spiritual Poems), Paris: YMCA Press, 1935.

Russian way and a surrender to the foreign West. Fedotov, on the contrary, admires Kiev and St. Petersburg, while condemning Moscow as the dark ages of Russian history that saw the triumph in Russia of a kind of nationalized, and thus corrupted, Byzantinism, partly reborn in the modern Soviet state. The main originality of his scheme is that it breaks resolutely with the Slavophile contempt for the West; both Kiev and St. Petersburg shared with Western Europe a common civilization and a common ideal of freedom and human dignity: Kiev by the organic assimilation of the Christian faith, St. Petersburg by the simple imitation and adoption of everything coming from the West.[6] This second volume of *The Russian Religious Mind* shows the growth of Muscovite ideology in Russia and presents the evidence of its gradual victory over the remains of Kievan culture, the Mongol domination, the imperial centralization of the state, the suppression of the Novgorod Republic, the triumph of the Josephite party over the nonpossessors, and the final tragedy of Russian spirituality.

Many will, of course, disagree with some of the author's schemes. I do not think, for example, that Fedotov's appreciation of Byzantium is quite correct; Kiev and not Moscow was in reality the true heir of Byzantinism, which cannot in any respect be equated with Oriental totalitarian despotism and which, in part, bequeathed to Russia many of the spiritual traditions that Fedotov rightly accuses Moscow of having forgotten. But the picture of the spiritual world of the Russian Middle Ages as given by the author is the most suggestive and successful of all similar attempts.

In recent years numerous scholarly publications in the Soviet Union have been devoted to the Russian past, and

---

[6] For a synthetic exposition of these views by Fedotov, see "Rossiya i svoboda" (Russia and Freedom), *Novy Zhurnal*, no. 10, New York, 1945, pp. 189–213; reprinted in *Novy Grad*, Yu. P. Ivask, ed., New York: Chekhov Publishing House, 1952, pp. 139–171.

most particularly to the social, political, and religious crisis of the late fifteenth and early sixteenth centuries. Important publications of original texts, monographs on key personalities, and specialized studies appear in numbers under the signatures of very qualified scholars like A. A. Zimin, Ya. S. Lur'e, A. I. Klibanov, N. A. Kazakova, and others. The critical analytical materials brought forward by these authors are undoubtedly of great value, but their conclusions are generally limited by the obligatory Marxist presuppositions that all social and religious developments are determined by economic factors. This means, in fact, that their inquiries stop at the very point where the religion of the Russian people starts. A new trend, however, seems to be developing in Soviet historiography recently. An example of this is the book by D. S. Likhachev that defines the problem of humanity — and therefore of humanism — in a manner that transcends the usual narrow Marxist problematics.[7] However, even there, the problem of religion, taken in its proper sense, remains out of the picture.

We refer the reader of this volume in a few short footnotes to the major achievements of recent Soviet scholarship in the fields touched by Fedotov when he wrote these chapters some years ago. Thus, the reader will be able to pursue by himself, if he so desires, the study of the problems involved. It is obvious, however, that Fedotov's approach is so much broader than that of modern Soviet historians, that his views generally remain original even when modern research is taken into account. And from the purely historical point of view, the scale of Fedotov's research covers much ground that remains otherwise practically untouched. His study of the *Izmaragd*, for example, is an entirely original endeavor. Therefore, the publication of this present book, even in a form less complete than its author had initially in-

---

[7] *Chelovek v literature drevnei Rusi* (Man in the Literature of Ancient Russia), Moscow and Leningrad, 1958.

tended, is a contribution to our contemporary knowledge of Russia, of the original traits of Russian Christianity, and of the Christian faith in general.

As we have mentioned, when Professor Fedotov died, the second volume of *The Russian Religious Mind* was not finished. A handwritten note found with the manuscript describes the author's complete project; the contents were to be as follows:

1. Historical Background
2. Popular Religion
3. *Izmaragd* (educated laity)
4. Strigolniks (the first heresy)
5. The Princes
6. Democratic Cities
7. Moscow
8. St. Sergius
9. St. Stephen of Perm
10. The Northern Thebaid
11. St. Nilus Sorski
12. St. Paphnutius of Borovsk
13. St. Joseph of Volok
14. The Fools for Christ's Sake
15. Religious Art
16. Conclusion

Three of these projected chapters, "Democratic Cities," "Moscow," and, most unfortunately, the "Conclusion" were never written. Chapters 2 and 3 have been here combined in a lengthy section entitled "Normal Christian Ethics"; the chapter on "The Princes," here entitled "The Feudal World," ends in the middle of a sentence.

It was obviously not within our competence to fill these gaps in Fedotov's masterly work. We dared to do so only by using Fedotov's own pen, by providing an English translation of some of his earlier Russian writings which correspond to the missing chapters. We are fully aware of the fact that the literary homogeneity of the book suffers from this method but our primary concern has been to show Fedotov's thought and general historical point of view. The latter, in fact, would not be apparent at all if, for example, there was not a chapter devoted to the "democratic cities" of Novgorod and Pskov, which the author rightly considered to be the last direct inheritors, in medieval Russia, of the ancient Kievan Christian civilization. Consequently, we have included as Chapter V of this book, a translation of an article on "The Republic of St. Sophia" published a few months before Fedotov's death.[8] The article is obviously written for the general public and does not correspond to the general scholarly level of the rest of the book, but it represents to some extent what Fedotov thought about Novgorod and gives an indication of what the finished chapter might have been like.

Chapters VIII to XIII, translations of the corresponding parts of his Russian work on the saints of Ancient Russia, are substantially as they were prepared for publication by Fedotov himself. Thus, since several chapters from the first volume of *The Russian Religious Mind* come from the same source, and since Fedotov's two English volumes are but an expanded and remodeled version of *Svyatye drevnei Rusi* — the general underlying thought being identical — it seemed to us justifiable to have two additional sections simply translated from the Russian, the chapter on "The Tragedy of Russian Spirituality" and the Conclusion. To a certain extent these sections make up for the absence of the projected chapter on Moscow and provide Fedotov's "last word." We are well aware that the book deserves a wider synthetic conclusion, but only the author could have provided this, and Divine Providence decided otherwise.

---

[8] "Respublika Svyatoi Sofii" (The Republic of St. Sophia), *Narodnaya Pravda* (The People's Truth), no. 11–12, New York, 1950, pp. 21–23.

Yet, as incomplete as this volume is — and presented more as a collection of rather independent studies on related subjects than as a work of synthesis — Fedotov's work will be welcomed, we feel sure, by all those who are interested in contemporary social and religious developments in Russia, or in Russia's past, or in Orthodox Christianity in general. The miraculous survival of the Orthodox Church in Russia, its attitude toward the state in the past and at present, its particular role in the ecumenical movement, its original spirituality, and the ethos of Russian Christians facing the contemporary world, can only be explained in the light of the past. No one, to my knowledge, except Professor Fedotov has ever attempted to study Russian history from original sources with all these questions in view.

The posthumous publication of this book has been made possible through the tireless concern of Mrs. Helen Fedotov. Translations from Fedotov's Russian works are due to the able competence of Mrs. Lydia Kesich. Mr. Thomas E. Bird, Mr. John B. Dunlop and Miss Ann Orlov greatly contributed to the task of the editing and the proofreading of the manuscript. To correct and edit a text written by an author whose native language was not English was far from being an easy task: if a few awkward phrasings remain, this is due to the editor's fear of tampering with the author's thought.

The complete bibliography of Fedotov's works which concludes this volume, and which suggests the wide scope of his understanding of Russia's destiny, has been prepared with extraordinary competence and accuracy by Mr. Bird.

John Meyendorff

June 7, 1965
St. Vladimir's Seminary
Tuckahoe, New York

THE RUSSIAN
RELIGIOUS MIND (II)
THE MIDDLE AGES
The 13th to the 15th Centuries

VOLUME FOUR
IN THE COLLECTED WORKS OF
GEORGE P. FEDOTOV

The following abbreviations are used throughout the notes:

OIDRMU   *Obshchestvo istorii i drevnostei Rossiiskikh pri Moskov-skom Universitete, Chteniya* (Readings of the Society of the History and Antiquities of Russia at Moscow University)

PDP   *Pamyatniki drevnei pismennosti* (Monuments of Ancient Literature)

PDPI   *Pamyatniki drevnei pismennosti i iskusstva* (Monuments of Ancient Literature and Art)

PG   *Patrologia Graeca,* ed. J. P. Migne, Paris, 1857–1912.

PL   *Patrologia Latina,* ed. J. P. Migne, Paris, 1844–1890.

PSRL   *Polnoe Sobranie russkikh letopisei* (Complete Collection of Russian Chronicles), St. Petersburg, 1841 ff.

RIB   *Russkaya Istorischeskaya biblioteka* (Russian Historical Library)

RRM   *Russian Religious Mind: Kievan Christianity*

SORYaS   *Sbornik otdeleniya russkago yazyka i slovesnosti Akademiya Nauk* (Academy of Sciences, Collection of the Section on Russian Language and Literature)

ZhMNP   *Zhurnal Ministerstva Narodnago Prosveshcheniya* (Journal of the Ministry of Popular Education)

ZNU   *Zapiski Novorossiiskago Universiteta* (Notes of Novorossiisk University)

I

HISTORICAL BACKGROUND

THE RUSSIAN MIDDLE AGES

*B*y the term "Russian Middle Ages" we understand the two and one-half centuries between the Mongol conquest of Russia (1237–1240) and the establishment of the Muscovite monarchy (ca. 1500). The period that preceded the Middle Ages is known as the era of Kievan or Ancient Russia and that which followed as the era of the Muscovite principality. Kiev and Muscovy each represents a separate cultural formation, complete in itself and very different from the other. The beginning of the Russian Middle Ages cannot be ignored even in the most schematic outline of world history. The Mongol conquest is the most fateful catastrophe suffered by Russia during her entire history. The whole character of her life — social, political, and cultural — changed during this period. Even the geographical focus of Russian history shifted from Kiev to the northeast. This part of the great plain, which had been on the periphery of the Kievan federation of principalities, was incorporated in the great principality of Vladimir, and later of Moscow. This was Great Russia — called such by the Byzantine Greeks as early as the fourteenth century — the Great Russia that succeeded in throwing off the Mongol yoke, in uniting all the branches of the Russian nation, and eventually in creating a multinational empire. The rest of southern and western Russia, once the most cultured and, politically, the most influential of the Russian lands, together with the city of Kiev itself, was conquered by the Lithuanians and the Poles. After being incorporated for three or four centuries in states where Roman Catholicism and Western civilization were predominant, these branches of the Russian nation grew into separate ethnographical units and, finally, separate nationalities: the Ukrainians (Little Russians, again following the Greek name) and the White Russians (etymology unknown).[1]

In modern times, moved by nationalistic feelings, Ukrainian historians, like Professor Michael Hrushevsky, claim that the whole Kievan period lies within the exclusive domain of Ukrainian history and thus deny any and every link between Kiev and Great Russia or Muscovy.[2]

This is an obvious exaggeration. Even if one recognizes in Kiev and Moscow two cultural formations one cannot deny that the name of the nation, the language, the political tradition, and the dynasty of ruling princes (Rurikides) remained unchanged after the Mongolian conquest. The bulk of Kievan literature was bequeathed to Great Russia. Every Northern historian began his annals by transcribing the ancient Kievan Chronicle, the so-called *Primary Chronicle* or Chronicle of Bygone Years.[3] The ecclesiastical organization remained the same; Russia was a metropolitan province of the patriarchate of Constantinople. The prelate who resided in Vladimir and, later, in Moscow received the title of metropolitan in direct succession from the see of Kiev. The continuity of tradition was even more marked in the religious and cultural domain with which we are dealing here than in the political and social spheres.

The end of the Russian Middle Ages cannot be specified as precisely as can its beginning. The Mongol yoke was thrown off in 1480, and the concentration of political power

---

[1] This question of etymology is discussed in N. P. Vakar, *Belorussia: The Making of a Nation — A Case Study,* Cambridge, Mass., 1956.

[2] M. Hrushevsky, *A History of the Ukraine,* New Haven, 1941. This is a shortened version, in English, of the original ten volumes, which have been published in a new edition by Knihospilka, *Istoria Ukraini-Rusi,* New York, 1954–1958.

[3] This is available in an English edition. See *The Russian Primary Chronicle,* S. H. Cross and O. P. Sherbowitz-Wetzor, eds., Cambridge, Mass., 1953.

in the hands of Ivan III in Moscow took place in approximately 1517 (Ryazan). This period, between the conquest and the consolidation of the Muscovite monarchy has sometimes been described by Russian historians as *udel'naya Rus* (Russia of the *udels*).[4] This can also be translated, with a permissible degree of inaccuracy, as "Feudal Russia." A. Eck, writing in French, coined the expression "Le Moyen-Age Russe,"[5] to distinguish the Russian Middle Ages from the Kievan or ancient period. We shall follow his fortunate *trouvaille*.

For many, if not for most scholars, the Russian Middle Ages lack any original character; they are considered as a transitional period between Kiev and Muscovy or, rather, as an obscure prelude to the latter. Those whose political interests are aroused by the growth of the Russian-Muscovite state see the gist of the medieval centuries in the "rise of Moscow" — that is, the continuous expansion of the principality of Moscow at the expense of the feudal princes until they were totally absorbed. Thus, the period is deemed nothing more than the prologue to Moscow's greatness. Original medieval literature is still more sparse than Kievan or Muscovite works, and so the apparent cultural poverty of the age also contributes to its general neglect by scholars. Yet such an impression is completely reversed when we turn from literature to art and to the spiritual life. Surprisingly the most obscure historical age of Russia is revealed as the golden age of Russian art and Russian sanctity. Never before or since has this climax of mystical life and religious art been surpassed or even paralleled in Russia. The Muscovite principality was to live on the remnants and, later, on the petrified byproducts of the creative medieval spirit. The Middle Ages lacks a literary expression of its creativity,

---

[4] An *udel* (share) was the territory inherited by a prince from his father.
[5] A. Eck, *Le Moyen-Age Russe*, Paris, 1933.

however, even more than Kievan Russia does, and it is this that conceals its light under a bushel. Medieval Russia seems like a young and mystical girl, rich with inner experience, beautiful of countenance, but silent, and, when she does speak, tongue-tied. To her we shall devote the major part of this book.

THE EFFECTS OF THE MONGOL CONQUEST

For generations it was fashionable for Russian historians of the juridical and sociological schools[6] to ignore the tremendous impact of the Tatar invasion and conquest upon the inner life and institutions of medieval Russia. To accept the impact of bare violence seemed to destroy the evolutionary logic of historical development; historical evolution had to be determined from within not from without. This kind of rigid adherence to doctrine (Hegelian in origin) has now been outgrown. The doctrine of immanent evolution is particularly inapplicable to Russia, which has always stood at the center of cultural crosscurrents — from Byzantium, Western Europe, and the Moslem East. With the Tatar conquest Russia was drawn not into the sphere of Eastern civilization but of barbarism, against which it had struggled so long in the days of Kiev.

Contemporary chronicles and legendary tales composed under the immediate shock of the invasion of Baty (1237–1240) do not spare the grim details of ruin and devastation. Flourishing cities, like Kiev, Vladimir, Ryazan were razed, their whole populations were massacred or carried off as slaves and most of their princes were slain in battle or in

---

[6] S. M. Soloviev, *Istoriya Rossii s drevneishikh vremen* (The History of Russia from the Earliest Times), 23 vols., Moscow, 1857–1871, new ed., Moscow, 1959–. V. O. Klyuchevsky, *Kurs russkoi istorii* (A Course of Russian History), 5 vols., Moscow and St. Petersburg, 1904–1922, 2 ed., Moscow, 1937; translated by C. G. Hogarth, *A History of Russia,* New York, 1911–1931.

captivity. The scope of the disaster can be gauged by the fact that such once great cities as Pereyaslavl and Ryazan, the capitals of their respective principalities, disappear from history from that date on; the later city of Ryazan was rebuilt on a different site. An Italian missionary and traveler, Plano Carpini, who passed through Kiev five years after the catastrophe, reports that only about 200 houses were left of the city; the majority of the inhabitants of the land were killed or enslaved; the environs of Kiev were strewn with human skulls and bones.[7] Even today the scarcity of manuscripts written in the Kievan period is eloquent evidence of the thorough destruction of the monastic libraries in southern Russia.

The worst feature of the Mongol conquest was that the Tatar inroads were repeated constantly, though on a diminishing scale. A local insurrection, a refusal to pay tribute, or a feud between princes, over and over again, saw the appearance of a Tatar army with an inevitable sequel of massacre and ravaging. Such pogroms recurred every decade until the second quarter of the fourteenth century. It was only after that time that Russia enjoyed even relative security. In fact Moscow was devastated again by the Tatars in 1408, and as late as 1455 the Great Prince Basil II of Moscow was defeated and taken prisoner by the Tatars of Kazan.

However, not all Russian cities were captured or destroyed by the Tatars. The cities of the north and the west, on the whole, were spared; neither Novgorod nor Rostov was ever sacked by the Khan Baty. And it is still more important that the victors did not settle down among the subject population; they did not even create their own administrative organization. Nomads by taste and conviction the Tatars remained on the steppes of southeastern Europe, outside of

---

[7] Quoted in Soloviev, *Istoriya,* vol. II, bk. III, ch. 3, pp. 319, 332, 333, 336, 337.

Russia proper. They were satisfied by the recognition of their
sovereignty and with regular tribute. For some thirty years
Tatar officials, the *baskaks,* were charged with the collection
of tribute in the Russian towns. Later (the exact date is
uncertain) the collection of tribute was assigned to the Russian princes themselves, especially to the one among them
upon whom the Khan had bestowed the title of Great Prince
(*Veliki Knyaz*) — a charter of primacy in the Russian lands.
Thus, Russia continued to be ruled by her native princes as
before, according to her own laws and traditional customs.
But, if her internal development was not interrupted, it was
certainly slowed down. The blow to national pride was deep
and ineradicable. The princes who were obliged to journey
to the Khan's capital on the Volga River (Sarai), or even to
the Great Khans in Mongolia in order to bring back charters
for their hereditary principalities or the title of Great Prince
quaffed a full cup of humiliation. And it was not long before
they tried to invoke the protection of the conquerors against
their own fellow princes in their unending struggle for territories and power.

In the Golden Horde, as the Tatar state was called,
causes were not won according to the patterns of justice of
Russia's traditional rights but were won through bribery or
through acts of political abjection. Thus, it is obvious that
Tatar rule brought about a demoralization in the domain of
political ethics. Every page of the chronicles written during
this period bears eloquent testimony to this fact.

THE CHURCH AND THE CONQUERORS

The immediate reaction of the religious conscience to the
catastrophe was twofold. On the one hand, the dominant
note was an acknowledgment of the judgment of God. The
unheard-of annihilation of the Russian armies, one after another, because of the rivalry and divisions among the princes,

was an obvious indication of the wrath of God, who was punishing Russia for her sins. Here is the appraisal of a contemporary chronicler:

It was no longer possible to withstand the wrath of God. In ancient times when the Lord led the Jews into the promised land he said to Joshua, the son of Nun: "I will send before you vacillation and terror, fear and trembling." In like manner the Lord today has taken away from us our strength, and for our sins has visited us with vacillation and terror, fear and trembling. And the wisdom of those capable of mastering the arts of war has been swallowed. And firmness of heart has been changed into feminine weakness, and, therefore, not one of the Russian princes has come to the aid of the others.[8]

On the other hand, to provide a soothing balm for the national wound, legendary stories were told about the exploits of a handful of heroes. The principality of Ryazan was particularly rich in such legends. The story was told there of a noble Princess Eupraxiya who killed herself and her infant son by leaping from a tower to avoid slavery and violence. And the chief hero of Ryazan was a certain Eupatius Kolovrat who, with a few companions, fought the immense army of Baty until, to the last man, all the heroes were slain. Baty himself is said to have admired Kolovrat's bravery and even to have uttered in regret: "If such a one had served me I should have held him close to my heart." [9] In the epic legends of Ryazan we have a survival of the chivalrous ideals of Kievan times, the same ideals that are reflected in the chronicles of the twelfth century and the famous *Tale of Prince Igor.*

---

[8] Laurentian Chronicle, *PSRL,* vol. I, no. 1, Moscow, 1862.

[9] "Povest o razorenii Ryazani Batyem" (Tale of the Sacking of Ryazan by Baty), in I. I. Sreznevski, ed., *Svedeniya i zametki o maloizvestnykh i neizvestnykh pamyatnikakh* (Information and Notes on Little-Known and Unknown Monuments), sec. 39, p. 88, in *SORYaS,* vol. I, St. Petersburg, 1867. See also A. S. Orlov, *Geroicheskie temy drevnerusskoi literatury* (Heroic Themes of Ancient Literature), Moscow and Leningrad, 1945, p. 107.

Some of the princes who were killed in battle against the Tatars or in captivity were later canonized as holy martyrs — among others, Yuri Vsevolodovich, the Great Prince of Vladimir; his nephew Basil; of special importance, Michael, the Prince of Chernigov and Kiev. Later we shall have an opportunity to study the evidence of their lives.

But, despite the blow inflicted by the Tatars, national pride also found some comfort in the memory of the former glory of the Russian land; this memory was faithfully preserved in the unbroken work of the chroniclers, as well as in an unusual literary fragment known as "The Tale of the Ruin of the Russian Land." [10]

Yet the theme of punishment and repentance also prevailed. The summons to repentance provides the content for five of the seven still extant sermons of Serapion, the Bishop of Vladimir, written about 1257. He is indefatigable and bitter, like the ancient prophets of Israel, in calling attention to the abyss of present woe:

The strength of our princes and our chieftains has disappeared. Our valiant warriors have fled overcome by fear; most of our brothers and children have been led away into captivity; our fields are overgrown with brush; our greatness is abased; our beauty is destroyed; our wealth turned to the profit of strangers; our work is bequeathed to the foreigners; we are scorned by our neighbors, laughed at by our foes.[11]

Despite the passage of many long years the acute pain inflicted by the barbarian conquest was not mitigated. "The time of our oppression and torments already approaches forty years and famine and plague do not cease; we cannot eat our fill . . . Who then has brought us to this plight?

[10] "Slovo o pogibeli Russkiya zemli" (Tale of the Ruin of the Russian Land), Kh. M. Loparev, ed., in *PDP*, vol. 84, St. Petersburg, 1892.

[11] Serapion, Sermon III, in Eugene V. Petukhov, ed., *Serapion Vladimirski: russkii provednik XIII veka* (Serapion of Vladimir: Russian Preacher of the 13th Century), St. Petersburg, 1888, pribavlenie, p. 8.

Our lawlessness and our sins, our disobedience, our unwillingness to repent." [12]

It is remarkable but in accordance with the spirit of the
ancient Russian Church that, in the catalogue of sins for
which God punishes the Russian nation, Serapion assigns
first place to social sins: "vile and cruel courts, bloody usury,
and all sorts of robbery, stealing, and brigandage" followed
by "unclean adultery . . . vile speech, lying, slander, perjury, and calumny, and other works of Satan." [13] The necessary corollary to the social indictment is the social character
of the penance the preacher calls for: "Let us offer our love
to God, shed tears, give alms to beggars according to our
means; when able to assist the poor, let us rescue them from
distress." [14] With these words Bishop Serapion thus proves
himself a true representative of ancient Kievan Christianity,
in its finest evangelical aspect. He belonged to the class of
enlightened prelates as we shall see later.

Between these two extremes of desperate resistance to
the savage conqueror and the humble acceptance of defeat
and slavery as the righteous punishment of God, Russia
lived for almost a century, until the Tatar raids ceased and
the country began to think of the possibility of liberation.

The different policies adopted by the Russian princes
found their religious parallels in the different trends of the
hagiographical documents. Among the canonized princes
some died as martyrs for the faith or as defenders of their
people. Besides St. Michael of Chernigov, the most famous
of the prince-martyrs, there was Michael of Tver who dared
to revolt against the Tatars, more than sixty years after the
conquest, and was executed at the Tatar capital in 1319.[15]
On the other hand, there are saints whose lives display pro-

---

[12] *Ibid.*, Sermon II, p. 5.

[13] *Ibid.*, Sermon I, p. 2.

[14] *Ibid.*, Sermon II, p. 6.

[15] *PSRL*, vol. XV, St. Petersburg, 1863, cols. 411–412.

Tatar tendencies. The greatest of these was the Prince Alexander Nevski, for whom the West was the most serious enemy. His victories over Swedish and German crusaders made him a national hero, but he had to pay for his Western activities with unconditional submission to the khans.[16] Another canonized prince, St. Theodore of Yaroslavl, was banished from his city and sought refuge in the Horde where he lived for years, marrying a Tatar princess and finally reconquering Yaroslavl with Tatar forces.[17] The third saint of this group was himself a Tatar prince, a baptized relative of Baty. After settling in Rostov he founded a monastery and insured its security with a donation of land and privileges of immunity. Many generations later, when Russian princes attempted to encroach upon these privileges a "Life of St. Peter, the Prince of the Horde" was composed in which the monastery's immunity was defended by appealing to the khan's charter.[18]

This latter incident is an example of a curious situation; the Tatars seen as protectors of the Church. Indeed, the case of Rostov was not an isolated instance, but an indication of the general trend of Tatar policy. Genghis Khan bequeathed to his successors a tolerance toward all the religions of the conquered nations. Moslems, Buddhists, and Christians enjoyed an equal protection of their faith from their heathen conquerors; the Tatars were converted to Islam only in the middle of the fourteenth century. The basic reason for this tolerance was the absolute confidence of the Tatars in the efficacy of the prayers offered by the priests

---

[16] V. Mansikka, "Zhitie Aleksandra Nevskago: razbor redaktsi i tekst" (The Life of Alexander Nevski: An Analysis of the Editions and the Text), in *PDPI,* vol. 180, St. Petersburg, 1913.

[17] N. I. Serebryanski, *Drevnerusskiya knyazheskiya zhitiya* (Ancient Russian Lives of Princes), in *OIDRMU,* no. 254, Moscow, 1915.

[18] "Povest o Petre tsareviche Ordynskom" (Tale of Tsarevitch Peter Ordynski), in *Pravoslavnyi Sobesednik* (Orthodox Converser), no. I, Kazan, 1859.

of all confessions for the welfare of the khans. In exchange for prayers the khans of the Golden Horde bestowed large economic and juridical privileges upon the Russian Church; they exempted the clergy as a whole from paying taxes; they gave the bishops extensive jurisdiction over all the population dependent on the Church. Never before or after the Mongol domination, did the Russian Church enjoy such privileges, and the metropolitans of Moscow carefully preserved in their archives the so-called *yarlyks* — the charters of the khans.[19]

Under these circumstances the Church was eliminated as a factor in the national resistance for a long time. Heavy taxation, which was the main cause of the popular uprisings, was not a problem for the Church. In certain places, as in Tver in 1339, some bishops, because of their close connection with the local princes and population, let themselves be drawn into an anti-Tatar movement.[20] On the whole, however, the bishops, particularly the metropolitans, behaved with great caution toward their conquerors; in their prayers for the "tsars" — they used this title to designate the khans — they affirmed the duty of all to obey the divinely established powers. This attitude changed only after the second half of the fourteenth century when Moscow felt sufficiently strong to initiate a policy of national resistance.

The impact of the Tatars upon social and moral life has been evaluated in various ways by Russian historians. Traditionally, the Tatars have been blamed for all the ills and vices of ancient Muscovite life: the cultural backwardness of medieval Russia, the crudity of morals, the low status of women, and so forth. In the religious sphere they have been

---

[19] M. D. Priselkov, "Khanskie yarlyki russkim mitropolitam" (Khans' Charters for Russian Metropolitans), in *Zapiski istorikofilologicheskago fakulteta* (Notes of the Historical Philological Faculty), vol. 33, St. Petersburg, 1916, pp. 1–115.

[20] *PSRL*, vol. XV, St. Petersburg, 1863, pp. 418–420.

held responsible for the ritualism and materialism that eclipsed the more spiritual and evangelical conception of Christianity; in the social and political sphere, the autocracy of the tsars and the general enslavement of all classes by the totalitarian state also have been often ascribed to the Tatar pattern. The antiliberal reaction among Russian émigré intellectuals has brought about a complete reversal of this appraisal. The so-called "Eurasian" school of the 1920's lauded the Muscovite state, which was based upon the principle of general "service," and its corresponding social ethics. Ritualism was declared a source of social energy and the most typical and precious feature of Russian religion. On the other hand, these historians emphasized the affinity of this type of society and religion with the Moslem world. According to this point of view, Genghis Khan was considered the real creator of the Russian state, the tsars of Moscow, the successors of the khans, and Russian Orthodoxy, a religious parallel to the Turanian (Turkic) type of Islam.

It is necessary that we refrain from taking sides in the controversy at this point. Only an analysis of religious and moral currents in the medieval period can provide a key to the problem. The answer cannot be formulated until we have concluded our investigation. At the outset, however, we must make two remarks, necessary for our general orientation.

The first is concerned with the immediate result of the Tatar conquest upon religious life. It was disastrous. One need not take at face value the denunciations of a Serapion who insists that the people show no improvement despite all the terrible manifestations of God's wrath. One fact speaks for itself. For approximately three quarters of a century after the conquest there is no record of an ascetic saint or of a founder of a monastery. No one, except for a few saintly princes, was canonized in this period. It would seem that not prayer but the sword was the refuge of these desperate generations. It was only in the second quarter of the fourteenth century that a new monastic movement came into being — on a scale unknown in ancient Kievan times.

Our second remark, which in part anticipates our conclusions, is that the full impact of Tatar rule was felt only in the later, Muscovite period, that is paradoxically enough, after the liberation from the yoke. As long as the Tatars were considered a national foe the moral reaction was strong enough to offset the temptation to imitate them. After the middle of the fifteenth century, however, the Tatars, baptized and nonbaptized, came in large numbers to serve the Great Prince of Moscow. They entered the ranks of the Russian gentry and even the nobility. A century later, Ivan the Terrible, the conqueror of Kazan and Astrakhan, two of the Tatar states, began the enduring offensive against Asia. And the deeper the Russians penetrated into the Eurasian continent the more strongly did they feel the fateful spell it exercised on the spirit of their civilization.

POLITICAL AND SOCIAL STRUCTURE

The influence of the Tatars was not felt in equal measure in the various political areas into which Russia was divided. The first, immediate, and irreparable split was that between eastern and western Russia, or, speaking in ethnological terms, between Great Russia in the east and Little Russia (or the Ukraine) and White Russia in the west. The Tatars were never able to conquer the western Russian principalities on the Dnieper River and beyond, although they ruthlessly devastated the southern lands. After the catastrophe of 1240, Galich, the most western Russian territory, experienced a short-lived yet brilliant revival; Prince Daniel was even crowned king. But the Russians of the west, separated as they were from their eastern brothers, finally

proved too weak to withstand the onslaught of their neighbors and gradually found themselves incorporated into the
states of Lithuania and Poland, united since 1386 under a
common dynasty of kings. The Poles, Roman Catholics, conquered Galich and Volyn in the first years of the fourteenth
century. The Lithuanians, who inhabited the forests and
swamps between Russia and Poland, were heathens and bar-
barians at the time of the Tatar invasion. In the course of a
century, or somewhat longer[21] they succeeded in subjugating
one by one, the Russian principalities of Polotsk, Smolensk,
Kiev, Chernigov, and others without any great military exploits or destruction on a large scale. The Lithuanian conquerors soon fell under the cultural sway of their more civil-
ized subjects. Russian became the official language of the
Lithuanian state, and Russian law and Russian institutions,
the main content of the "Lithuanian Statute." Part of the
Lithuanian aristocracy was completely Russified. In matters
of religion the Lithuanian princes oscillated, for a time, between Russian Orthodoxy and Western Catholicism but
when the Lithuanian Great Prince Jagiello was elected king
of Poland under condition that he adopt the Roman Catholic faith the wavering ceased. The Great Princes of Lithuania were Catholic, although a considerable portion of the
Lithuanian nobility, including some families of princely
origin — the Lithuanian (Gediminovichi) and the Russian
(Rurikovichi) — was Orthodox. No attempts at forced conversion were made during this period; neither were the
Orthodox Russians in Galich and Volyn molested. This was
a happy enclave of religious freedom in the medieval world.
Yet the difference between Poland and Lithuania, although
they were united by common dynasty, was very marked.
Poland was a Roman Catholic country with a Western, Latin

---

[21] Smolensk was conquered by the Lithuanian Prince Vitovt only as late as
1404.

culture; Lithuania was mainly Orthodox and Russian. The Russians who lived there felt a peculiar Russian-Lithuanian patriotism and were by no means attracted by the lot of the eastern Muscovite Russians. This suggested to the Lithuanian princes the possibility of extending their frontiers to the east with the final aim of uniting all Russian lands under their rule. Thus began the lasting strife between Lithuania and Moscow; in each country there was an attempt to gather the Russian principalities around one of two possible political centers, Vilno or Moscow. The connection with Poland in the first case, and with the Tatars in the second, the divergent forms of government — a Western feudalism, with a parliament and political freedom for the aristocracy, and a centralized Oriental despotism — made the opposition sharp. One circumstance weighed heavily in Moscow's favor. Orthodoxy was not even remotely threatened or endangered by the Asiatic world, but the Roman Catholic princes of Lithuania and the kings of Poland were heretics in the eyes of the Russian people; the Russians understandably could not overcome a distrust of the heterodox West.

In this volume we are concerned only with eastern or Great Russian society. For two centuries, the fifteenth and sixteenth, western Russia is almost silent. No literary documents have been preserved; legal documents and scant chronicles comprise almost all we have of the western Russian literature of the period. The western revival occurs in the sixteenth century and in the seventeenth begins to have a mighty influence upon Muscovite Russia.

When we turn to Great Russia, which developed its culture more or less freely under the Tatar domination, we must keep in mind the deep social and spiritual distinctions that prevailed among the three component parts of her territory: the part held by the feudal princes, the free cities of

Novgorod and Pskov, the part belonging to the Great Prince of Moscow.

The partition of the feudal territory continued and increased among the prolific descendants of the house of Rurik. All Russian princes were Rurikides, although this blood tie was watered down and became of less importance as a unifying element on the national scale. The princes ceased to migrate from town to town, they settled down in their respective udels and the family right of succession from father to sons completely replaced the clan principle, which implied the right of lateral succession: each udel became an independent state.

As no law of primogeniture existed, the parceling out of the udels reached a point in the fifteenth century where the udels sometimes differed very little in size from the private estates of the boyars. Much more than in Kievan Russia, agriculture dominated the economic life of the population and the political considerations of the princes. Colonization, the clearing of virgin forests, and the employment of free peasants as workers, comprised the chief basis of economic power. Commerce, certainly, was not extinct but became more restricted. The Byzantine trade lost its former importance not so much because of the Tatar peril as because of the shifting of the commercial routes in Eastern Europe at the time of the Crusades. Yet three main roads remained open to foreign trade: the eastern, through the Volga and the Golden Horde; the southern, through the Crimea, where the Genoese founded their colonies (Caffa); and the western, via the Baltic Sea, to the German Hanse. The latter route was used by the city of Novgorod, and this city was the only place where commercial activity deeply affected the social structure and life of the population. Everywhere else the agrarian pattern prevailed.

However, the complete partition of the princely udels

was offset in part by an opposite trend: the integration of small udels into great territories, each with its own Great Prince. Originally, there was but one Great Prince, in Vladimir; he had been appointed by the khan of the Golden Horde, but the city of Vladimir, and the other towns belonging to it, never had been able to recover completely from their destruction in 1237. The city of Vladimir had ceased to be merely a principality by itself and had been annexed under the title and rights of the Great Prince, whose seat and center of power remained within his own hereditary udel. The right to the title of "Great Prince of Vladimir and of All Russia" (*Veliki Knyaz vladimirski i vseya Rusi*) became the cause of contention among the most powerful feudal lines. These were the princes of the new cities which sprang up soon after the Tatar invasion; Tver, Moscow, and Nizhni Novgorod. Besides the Great Prince of Vladimir, other Great Princes began to appear as the heads of local princely houses in Tver, Ryazan, Nizhni Novgorod-Suzdal. Although Moscow was the most successful competitor in the struggle, Tver and Ryazan were still fairly independent in the fifteenth century. Each of these great principalities was a world of its own with its own historical traditions, reflected in local chronicles, local dynastic patriotism, and local sacred shrines. The princes were less warlike and foolhardy than they had been in the Kievan period. They cared more for the economic welfare of their lands, which were no longer exchangeable properties. However, the feudal spirit of honor and valor was not extinct.

Novgorod the Great (as distinguished from the many other Novgorods in Russia) was not just one city among others. It was the political center of an immense territory that surpassed in size all the other principalities of Great Russia put together. The whole north of Russia, from the Baltic Sea to the Urals and beyond, belonged to it. True, this huge territory was sparsely populated, and consisted for the most part of forests and swamps, but the forests yielded the precious furs which were the chief article of export from Novgorod. Through this commerce with the German Hanse great wealth was accumulated in Novgorod, which contrasted sharply with the general poverty of Russia. A powerful aristocracy, in a continuous struggle for power among the noble families, ruled the city, and yet the constitution of Novgorod was democratic and republican. Thus Novgorod was similar in certain ways to the Italian communes of the Middle Ages. There was a prince in Novgorod, but he was not the ruler; he was a military chief who played only a limited role in the administration of justice and was elected from among numerous Russian Rurikides. His power was not hereditary or even life-long. At the time of his first quarrel with the citizens they "showed him the way out." Before accepting his position, he "kissed the cross," that is, took an oath, promising to observe all the rights and privileges of Novgorod. The center of power, legislative, administrative, and judicial, was the general assembly (*veche*) which elected all the officials of the state. Novgorod was a "direct" democracy with no representative system. This was its main weakness because, in the tumultuous setting of the *veche*, a normal deliberation of state affairs was difficult and arguments often ended in violence and bloodshed.

Another handicap for Novgorod was its dependence upon imported grain from the "lower," that is, southeastern Russian territories. This is why Novgorod could not break relations, for any length of time, with the Great Prince of Russia; famine would be the certain result of such conflicts. The free city was, in practice, obliged to call the sons or relatives of the Great Prince to serve as its princes, and in the fifteenth century they even summoned the Great Prince himself, who, in turn, sent his deputy. Nevertheless, in spite of such handicaps, Novgorod stayed a free city until 1478. With all the shortcomings of a direct democracy Novgorod remained for more than 200 years the freest, the wealthiest, and the most cultured territory of Russia. As an Orthodox republic it was a unique political institution in the Eastern world.

The city of Pskov, which was one of Novgorod's "suburbs," that is, subject towns, became independent in the fourteenth century and was called the "younger brother" of Novgorod. It had its own princes, elected and not hereditary, and a democratic constitution similar to that of Novgorod. As its territory bordered on the domains of the "Teutonic Order," Pskov was a Russian outpost involved in a constant defensive war against the German "drive to the East." This imprinted a warlike and adventurous character upon this merchant republic which is clearly reflected in the local chronicles and the few remnants of Pskov literature.

The principality of Moscow was the last to emerge in the feudal world of Great Russia. Moscow was a village in the twelfth century, a frontier fortress for Vladimir in the thirteenth. That it fell to the lot of the youngest son of Alexander Nevski, Daniel, was an indication of its unimportance. Yet Daniel's sons, Yuri and Ivan Kalita ($+$ 1341) succeeded in defeating Tver in a struggle for the title of the Great Prince, and from that time on, except for a few setbacks, Moscow held a position of prominence over "all Russia" (which meant Great Russia only). This astounding success was due, in the first place, to a shrewd policy toward the Tatar overlords. For three generations the Moscow princes had been loyal subjects of the khans. They never participated in revolts, and assisted willingly in suppressing them. This was the reason for the relative quiet and order that the territory of Moscow enjoyed and it was what attracted many new colonists from other, more harassed lands. Certainly, it was the only reason why the Metropolitan Peter, a native of the Ukrainian Galich, preferred Moscow as his residence to the venerable but ruined Vladimir. His successor, a Greek, Theognostos, confirmed this transfer of the see (nominally, still that of Kiev). From that time the heads of the Russian Church gave whole-hearted support to the political claims of Kalita's successors. Metropolitan Alexis, a Russian by birth, even acted as regent during the minority of Prince Dimitri (Donskoi). Since that time the interests of the Church were virtually identified with those of the Moscow dynasty, despite incidental protests from the patriarchs of Constantinople and some bishops. Strengthened by the assistance of the Tatars and the Church the Moscow princes inaugurated a policy of the continuous expansion of their udel. Any means were acceptable to them — from purchase or bequest to direct or indirect violence including pressure, conquest, perjury, or treason. With such a policy, in the course of the fourteenth century, they built (after Novgorod) the largest, the most powerful, and the best organized principality in Russia. Many administrative practices borrowed from the Tatars were employed in the government of the state. Moscow's influence was felt throughout all Russian territories. Thus, a Moscow prince, Dimitri, dared in 1380 to challenge the khan and to emerge victorious from the battle of Kulikovo. This was a premature success, which was followed by a long eclipse of Moscow's progress. Dimitri's son Basil, who married a Lithuanian princess, lived under the protection of Vitovt, his powerful father-in-law. His grandson, Basil II, "the Blind," had to endure a long and difficult feud against his cousins of the same dynasty. And the Church, in the person of the non-Russian metropolitans, the Bulgarian Cyprian and the Greek Photius, was emancipated temporarily from Moscow and its dynastic interests. The all-Russian and even ecumenical character of the Church was emphasized once again. Yet, it was but a temporary respite. In the last half of the fifteenth century Ivan III, in a strikingly precipitous sequence of events, conquered or peacefully annexed several remaining feudal principalities (Tver, Rostov, and Novgorod). He was the first autocratic ruler of Great Russia, although he did not assume the title of tsar. His ambition, however, went even further. He married a Byzantine princess, Sophia Paleologue, a niece of the last Byzantine emperor, and with a minimum of effort abolished the last vestiges of Muscovite dependence on the weak khans of the Golden Horde (1480).

After that Russia or Muscovy, as a united, independent, and powerful state, began to advance a claim to the spiritual and political legacy of Byzantium. The Byzantine Empire no longer existed; in 1453 Hagia Sophia had become a mosque. Somewhat earlier an ecclesiastical split had occurred between Byzantium and Russia on the issue of the union with Rome. Threatened by the Turks, Emperor John asked assistance from the Pope and, at the Council of Florence, together with the Patriarch of Constantinople and other Church dignitaries, acknowledged papal primacy and other Roman dogmas. Isidore, the last Russian metropolitan of Greek origin, was one of the initiators of this union (1438). But Russia did not follow him. Upon his return to Moscow he was arrested as an apostate from Orthodoxy; the Council of Russian Bishops elected his successor, Jonas, without either the consent or confirmation of Constantinople (1448). This began the de facto autocephaly of the Russian Church. It did not develop into an open schism with Greece although the Eastern patriarchs were not to recognize the new status of the Russian Church until a century later (1589), when the Metropolitan of Moscow received the title of Patriarch.

However, one of the consequences of this ecclesiastical autocephaly was a division within the former all-Russian, still nominally Kievan, province. The Western or Lithuanian Church received its own head, with the title of Metropolitan of Kiev and Russia, directly from the Patriarch of Constantinople, who was now living under Moslem rule and had long since forgotten the unfortunate union with Rome. After the fall of Constantinople the Great Prince of Moscow considered himself the only Orthodox monarch in the world and the ideologists of Muscovite nationalism made great capital of his unique position.

This was the end of a long process. For two centuries there had been a constant struggle between the growing power of Moscow and the rest of the Russian world, feudal and republican. Moscow's victory was possible because its adversaries were divided. And, in addition, there can be no doubt that large masses of the population, the lower classes in particular, welcomed the Muscovite monarchy. It meant an end to the feudal wars and the establishment of a permanent, if despotic, order. This law and order was purchased, however, at a high price, paid for, largely, by the upper classes. The new order was imposed through severe and sometimes revolutionary means. The feudal princes often ended their lives in Moscow prisons; the free institutions in the various cities were abolished; the property of the local boyars, even of the Church in Novgorod, was confiscated; and many noble and rich families were transplanted to other provinces to make room for newcomers from Moscow. The new territories were deliberately subjected to the lawless exploitation of the Moscow *voevods* (governors) and *dyaks* (officials). Justice was never a strong point of the Moscow administration. Despite later revisions in the original local chronicles the bitter laments of the enslaved populations in Novgorod, Pskov, Rostov, and Yaroslavl can still be heard.

In the fifteenth and sixteenth centuries Lithuania became the last hope of all the enemies of Moscow. Indeed,

Great Russia was torn in two directions — west and east. Politically, the west was Lithuania, where the Kievan heritage and the spiritual influence of Byzantium were, through Polish influence, counterbalanced by weak (at this period) radiations of Latin European culture. The east was Moscow, where Byzantine culture was already mixed with a small, but ever-growing, current of Turanian and Moslem civilization.

THE CULTURAL DEVELOPMENT

Unlike Kievan Russia, in its cultural and spiritual evolution, medieval Russia proceeds very definitely in a single direction. It maintains the earlier direction of its political and social development, although with a lag of approximately one generation. At the end of the thirteenth century, the time of the Mongol catastrophe and its aftermath, there are still survivals of an ecclesiastical and literary elite brought up in Kievan schools. To this period belong the heroic legends of the Tatar invasions, the "Tale of the Ruin of the Russian Land," the life of St. Alexander Nevski, all in an epic-heroic style, and the impressive sermons of Serapion. The thirteenth century, whether before or after the Tatar conquest is unclear, also produced a Russian version of the Greek *Palaia*, the short paraphrase of the Old Testament with sharp anti-Jewish polemics, the so-called "*Palaia* Interpreted."

Following this period, however, the cultivated generation died out. The fourteenth century is almost a blank page in the history of Russian literature. Of course, the annalistic chronicles were never abandoned, and were particularly rich in Novgorod. Yet, apart from them and some official episcopal letters, we have only the notebooks of two traveler-pilgrims to Constantinople. Nonetheless, a growing progressive trend after 1300 is unmistakable. Despite a profound bar-

barization as compared with Kiev, the two medieval centuries are a period of uninterrupted growth. This imparts vigor and significance even to the most modest literary documents.

At the end of the fourteenth century a mighty cultural stream from outside brought forth a new literary revival in Russia. It came from the same Balkan Slavs who, in the tenth and eleventh centuries, had supplied Russia with all of its literature in the Slavonic (Old Bulgarian) language. The Balkan Slavs, this time not only Bulgarians but also and in a very particular way Serbs, experienced a renaissance in the fourteenth century, which was marked not so much by original production as by a new wave of translations from the Greek and the elaboration of a new ornate style. From the monasteries of Constantinople and Mount Athos, where Russian monks lived side by side with Serbs and Bulgarians, new writings penetrated into Russia. We know the names of some of the Russians in Greece who were active as copyists and even as translators; we still possess some of their manuscripts.[22] Many ties bound these Russian monks abroad with the Russian monastery of the Holy Trinity founded by St. Sergius. Some outstanding Slavs also came to Russia and deeply influenced its ecclesiastical and literary life. Cyprian was one of these. He was a Greek-educated Bulgarian, who was sent from Constantinople to both Lithuania and Moscow as metropolitan; he is well known for his activities in liturgical reform; he introduced a new ritual (that of Jerusalem) into Russia as well as a new version of the liturgical books, thus bringing Russia up-to-date with the contemporary Byzantine liturgical development.[23] Another, the Serb Pachomius, a monk from Athos, began his Russian career as

---

[22] A. I. Sobolevski, *Perevodnaya literatura Moskovskoi Rusi XIV–XVII vekov* (Literature in Translation in Moscow Russia in the 14th–17th Centuries), St. Petersburg, 1903, pp. 24–26.

[23] I. D. Mansvetvov, *Mitropolit Kiprian v ego liturgicheskoi deyatelnosti* (The Metropolitan Cyprian and His Liturgical Activities), Moscow, 1882.

a scribe in the Holy Trinity Monastery and became famous in Moscow and Novgorod for his hagiographical works. He revised and wrote anew about a dozen of the lives of Russian saints in a highly elaborate Serbian style, that established a hagiographical canon in Russia for almost three centuries.[24] A third of these southern Slavs, Gregory Tsamblak, a metropolitan of western Russia, left a collection of solemn sermons for Church festivals, which enjoyed great popularity even in Muscovy.[25]

Between the Serbs (or Bulgarians) and the Russians there was hardly any language barrier. Although popular spoken idioms went separate ways, the literary language remained the same, Old Slavonic with slight differences in pronunciation and spelling. Greek, on the contrary, was inaccessible to the majority of the literate people in Russia. This is the opinion of A. L. Sobolevski, one of the finest scholars of Ancient Russian literature: "The reader in Ancient Russia, with a few rare exceptions of no great importance, did not know a single foreign language." [26] As the problem of the knowledge of Greek is of paramount significance for the appreciation of Ancient Russian culture we must consider it in some detail.

Strangely enough, we possess more evidence about the Greek language in Russia for the Middle Ages than for the Kievan period. This is because the libraries of this period were better preserved than those of the earlier. A priori one ought to presume that there were closer relations between Byzantium and Kiev than between Byzantium and Moscow or between Byzantium and Novgorod. However, the rela-

---

[24] V. Yablonski, ed., *Pakhomi Serb i ego agiograficheskie pisaniya* (Pachomius the Serb and His Hagiographical Writings), St. Petersburg, 1908.

[25] A. I. Yatsimirski, *Grigori Tsamblak: ocherk ego zhizni, administrativnoi i knizhnoi deyatelnosti* (Gregory Tsamblak: A Sketch of His Life, His Administrative and Literary Activities), St. Petersburg, 1904.

[26] Sobolevski, p. VI.

tions between Russia and Constantinople were not completely
severed after the Mongol conquest despite the increased difficulties in travel. Greek metropolitans arrived in Russia
with their clergy as before. Russian candidates for the metropolitan see had to go to Greece themselves and to spend
months or even years there. They had to keep busy, soliciting
and bribing, in order to overcome the Greek unwillingness to
consecrate native bishops for the highest post in a dependent
Church. St. Alexis went to Constantinople twice and spent a
whole year there before he obtained his consecration. After
his death no less than three Russian bishops, sometimes one
after another, sometimes simultaneously, went to the capital
of the empire to strive for the highest see, but in vain. Russian clergy, therefore, must have returned from Greece with
some knowledge of spoken, medieval Greek (or perhaps
even gone with this knowledge) which, in ecclesiastical vocabulary, was not very remote from patristic Greek.

The patriarchs of Constantinople did not limit their
interest in Russian affairs to appointing the head of the national Church. We possess scores of letters from the patriarchs to Russian princes and bishops both in the Greek
original and in Russian translation. They concern various
matters: the complaints of some princes on the unjust administration of the metropolitan, the canonization of a saint,
the relations between the metropolitan and the bishop of
Novgorod, the suppression of a new heresy, and so on. From
time to time some bishops of Greek origin appear in Russian
cities. They are probably responsible for a local custom in
the cathedral of Rostov where one of the two choirs sang in
Greek, the other in Slavonic. There was a monastery in the
same city which owned a library of Greek books, which attracted a young man, eager to learn, the future St. Stephen,
Bishop of Perm. St. Stephen was one of the few Russians,

whom we know by name, about whose knowledge of Greek there can be no question. We cannot be so certain about the Greek of Stephen's biographer and fellow student at Rostov, Epiphanius, known as "the Wise." He likes to display Greek words in his writings, but his very choice indicates the scantiness of his vocabulary and the exclusively oral origins of his knowledge. Instead of using Greek words to convey abstract and theological notions, where Greek words would be more necessary, he writes, for example: "*Arkuda*, that is, the bear," using a popular word and not a classical term at that.[27]

Spoken or medieval Greek was better known in Russia than the classical language of the Church Fathers.[28] It is clear that some people did have a command of the latter, however, because two fourteenth-century manuscripts contain new translations, or rather, new versions of the Slavonic Gospels, undoubtedly written by Russians. One is dated 1383 and was written in Constantinople; the other is traditionally ascribed to the Metropolitan Alexis, although this attribution is doubtful.[29] The quality of these works shows more than an ordinary mastery of the language.

An interesting manuscript has been preserved from the end of the fourteenth century with the pretentious title "Finely Worded Greek Speech." In content it is nothing more than a short Greek-Russian dictionary intended for the use of Russian pilgrims or monks in Greece. It is not unlike the pocket dictionaries of modern travelers. The Greek words are transliterated into the Russian alphabet.[30] After

[27] *Zhitie sv. Stefana, episkopa permskogo* (Life of St. Stephen, Bishop of Perm), V. G. Druzhinin, ed., The Hague, 1959. Introduction by D. Čiževski.

[28] Sobolevski, pp. 283–289.

[29] Sobolevski, pp. 24, 26–31.

[30] Sobolevski mentions the presence of several such "dictionaries" in fourteenth- and fifteenth-century manuscripts, p. 288.

the Union of Florence (1443), however, Russia's ties with Greece were weakened and, as a consequence, the knowledge of Greek decreased too.

In the late fifteenth century an energetic Bishop of Novgorod, Gennadius, undertook the first complete edition (in manuscript) of the Slavonic Bible. Twelve books of the Old Testament were translated from Latin instead of Greek. The difficulty of finding either the Greek text or a man capable of reading it was the obvious reason. The same situation also prevailed in Moscow at the beginning of the next century. The Great Prince Basil III could find no one to translate the Greek commentary on the Psalter which was discovered in the palace library. The prince had to write to Mount Athos to ask for a monk who could at least translate it into Latin.[31] Latin was better known because it was used in the diplomatic relations with the Western states.

In the present state of scholarly research it is still impossible to single out from the enormous quantity of books translated during the Mongol period those texts which are the work of Russian translators. They were few, of course, in comparison with those imported from the Balkans. The extent of this literature defies any exact chronological classification. Many works could have been translated during the previous Kievan period. However, the extreme rarity of ancient manuscripts prevents one from making any final judgment. Sobolevski ventures the view that with the new translations "Russian literature almost doubled."[32] Even if this estimate is exaggerated, Sobolevski is undoubtedly right in stating that "the translations were more widely read than the original works and affected the people's imagination more strongly . . . New epochs in the history of Russian culture were also inaugurated with new translations . . .

---

[31] Sobolevski, p. 285.
[32] Sobolevski, p. 14.

Cultural movements in Muscovite Russia found their expression not in original works but in the selection of translations." [33] Unfortunately, a study of the influence of individual Greek authors and their works upon original Russian literature is still to be made.

As was true in Kiev, most of the translated works served a practical religious use; that is, they were used for edification and training in the spiritual life. Exegetical works, used to comprehend the Holy Scriptures, were highly supplemented and may be considered sufficient for their purpose; of particular value was the commentary on the four Gospels by Theophilactus of Bulgaria (eleventh or twelfth century), based on Chrysostom and other ancient Fathers. This author remained the classical expositor for the Church even in the nineteenth century. Some other commentaries (on Acts and the Epistles) had the character of collections or *catenae* and thereby preserved the valuable contributions of ancient scholars who were otherwise ill-famed for their heterodoxy: Origen, Theodore of Mopsuestia, Apollinarius, and Severus of Antioch.

As regards the dogmatic legacy of the ancient Church, medieval Russia did little to remedy the poor and inadequate selection of the earlier period: Cyril of Jerusalem and John of Damascus (as general textbooks), Gregory Nazianzen, and (probably the result of Bulgarian taste), St. Athanasius' *Contra Arianos*. The last work remained probably inaccessible to average Russian readers — but serious efforts were made to elucidate the lofty and abstract thought of St. Gregory rendered almost unintelligible by awkward and literal translation; the commentary by Nicetas of Heracleia was a helpful guide.

A new and very important event was the translation of the entire *Corpus Areopagiticum*, the four treatises and let-

[33] Sobolevski, p. VI.

ters of an unknown Christian neo-Platonist of about A.D. 500.
The translation was made in 1371 by a Serbian monk, Isaiah,
and by the fourteenth century was already known in Russia.
The *Corpus* is very difficult theology, not only for the
medieval Russian mind. The thought of Pseudo-Dionysius
is philosophically overladen, deliberately obscure, sometimes
abstruse. The translation was literal and not overly intelligi-
ble.[34] Yet, the five preserved manuscripts of the fourteenth
and fifteenth centuries, mentioned by Sobolevski, provide
evidence that Pseudo-Dionysius was read in Russia. The
vogue for his work was, doubtless, connected with the new
mystical trend of that time. Despite prevalent opinion, however, the impact of Dionysian theology was much stronger
in the Christian West than in Russia.

Among the ancient Fathers, John Chrysostom and
Ephrem the Syrian remained the most read and the most
loved authors — evidence of the practical and ethical orientation of the Russian mind. A new collection of Chrysostom's
homilies was added to those known in Kiev, *Andriadis*,
Zlatostrui, and *Zlatoust*. In the middle of the fourteenth
century a Bulgarian monk, Dionysius, translated a volume of
Chrysostom's sermons from the Greek which was known
under the title of *Margarit* (the Pearl). In Russia it soon
became the most popular of all collections of Chrysostom.   ·

There were innumerable translations of the Greek lives
of saints and *Paterika*, which almost exhausted the entire
store of originals, and a very rich selection of Greek sermons
and ascetic treatises. Together, works of this type consti-
tuted the core of Russian libraries. It was in the ascetical
works that the most valuable accretions were made at this
period. Kiev had had to content itself with the classical *Lad-*

---

[34] A. V. Gorski and K. I. Nevostruev, *Opisanie slavyanskikh rukopisei
moskovskoi sinodalnoi biblioteki* (Description of the Slavonic Manuscripts of
the Moscow Synodal Library), Moscow, 1855, II, 2.

der of John Climacus, but now the list of spiritual teachers read in Russia was increased to include thirty names, almost completely covering the Greek branch of the Christian spiritual tradition. Nilus of Sinai (fifth century) and Abbot Dorotheus (sixth century) were among the most popular. Most significant, however, is the fact that after the fourteenth century the exponents of Greek and Oriental mysticism, which had heretofore been ignored, began to appear in Russia. Among them we find Isaac the Syrian (seventh century) and Simeon the New Theologian (tenth-eleventh century), and most of the spokesmen for the contemporary Hesychast movement in Greece: Gregory the Sinaite, Callistus, Ignatius Xanthopoulos, and others.

They at once became the guides of Russian monasticism. Characteristically, the dogmatic movement in Byzantium, which was linked with Hesychasm and culminated in the great figure of Gregory Palamas (1296–1359), remained quite unfamiliar in Russia. Despite the veneration of St. Gregory Palamas, introduced in Russia by the Metropolitan Cyprian, his treatise against the "Latins" (Roman Catholics) was the only one of his works that was translated and found a place among the many other polemical productions of this kind.

The prevailing type of Russian book was, as before, not the work or the works of a given author but a collection of fragments of different content, belonging or attributed to different Church Fathers. Because of the high cost of books, a single book had to serve as a library and, therefore, had to be as encyclopedic as possible. The moral influence predominated; dogmatic fragments were engulfed in a sea of edifying material. Among the translated, ready-made encyclopedias of ethical extracts, which were already popular in Kiev, were those of Anastasius the Sinaite and Nicon of the Black Mountain. The latter enjoyed particular esteem with his two collections entitled the *Pandectae* and the *Taktikon*.

In conclusion, we may be able to derive a general notion of the character and extent of Russian erudition at the end of the fifteenth century by examining the only catalogue of a Russian monastic library which the ravages of time have spared for us.[35] The monastery of St. Cyril was second only to the Holy Trinity of St. Sergius in both its secular wealth and its spiritual influence on Russian monasticism. In 1489 Gennadius, Archbishop of Novgorod, was searching for the necessary books to combat the new heresy of the Judaizers; he wrote his request to the three richest monasteries in his diocese, of which St. Cyril was one.

According to the catalogue of St. Cyril, a real cultural achievement for the time, its library consisted of 212 books;[36] we know that Holy Trinity, probably the richest monastery, had about 300 volumes at this time.[37] The distribution of the books by content is of paramount interest. More than half of the library consisted of liturgical books and of those biblical writings that are used in the liturgy of the Orthodox Church. This group includes 110 items.[38] The Holy Scriptures — for private, not liturgical, use — are represented by 11 volumes, only one of which is a book of the Old Testament (Jeremiah). However, two Apocryphal writings supplement this lack: the "Vision of Isaiah" and the "Wanderings of John"; the latter appears with the Book of Revelation. In this connection it is interesting to

---

[35] N. K. Nikolski, "Opisanie rukopisei Kirillo-Belozerskago Monastyrya sostavlennoe v kontse XV veka" (Description of the Manuscripts of the St. Cyril Monastery Compiled at the End of the 15th Century), in *Izdaniya obshchestva lyubitelei drevnei pismennosti* (Publications of the Society of Lovers of Ancient Letters), vol. 113, St. Petersburg, 1897.

[36] The catalogue is not quite complete. See Nikolski, p. XVI.

[37] Nikolski, p. XLVI.

[38] To this must be added that most of the Collections in the library belong to the type of "panegyricons," that is, anthologies of sermons used at church festivals.

note that in Archbishop Gennadius' inquiry the didactic book of Menander (Byzantine excerpts from the Athenian comedian of the fourth century B.C.) was mentioned among the Wisdom books of the Bible.

The three following categories find almost equal representation (from 22 to 26 volumes): Lives of the saints, ascetical treatises, and collections of various content. The writings of the Church Fathers, for the most part moralists and ascetics, take up 14 volumes. Only four items by three authors treat dogmatic issues; they are Cyril of Jerusalem, Gregory Nazianzen, and Pseudo-Dionysius. Only one Russian, or rather Slavic author is mentioned in the catalogue, Gregory Tsamblak, the Metropolitan of Kiev, whose feast-day sermons are primarily of liturgical interest. Some Russian authors found a place in the numerous collections, which are described in detail by the librarian of St. Cyril's monastery.

If one takes the number of items as an indication of popularity, the most widely read authors were: Gregory Nazianzen (2 volumes), Simeon the New Theologian (2 volumes), Nicon (3 volumes), Dorotheus (3 volumes), John Chrysostom (3 volumes), Isaac the Syrian (5 volumes), and John Climacus (7 volumes). No book of secular, historical, or scientific content found its way into the library of St. Cyril.

However scant original Russian works are, in comparison with the translated literature, they provide the main sources for our investigation. With regard to the Greek theological works one cannot be certain of the degree of their assimilation by the Russian reader. Generally speaking, this depended on the simplicity and popular character of their exposition, a criterion hardly favorable to authors like Gregory Nazianzen or Pseudo-Dionysius. But the popular theological encyclopedias of Anastasius the Sinaite and Nicon of Black Mountain, the sermons of Chrysostom and Ephrem the Syrian, deeply imprinted themselves upon the Russian mind. Their basic ideas, even their phraseology, are constantly found in original Russian writings. We shall limit ourselves here, however, to a very brief survey of these works, since the analysis of original Russian literature is the main subject of this book.

Russian chronicles in the form of annals remain the richest literary genre of the period, particularly in Novgorod. From the fifteenth century on, hagiographical literature became widespread as a result of the pioneer work of the two great stylists, the Serb Pachomius and the Russian Epiphanius the Wise. At the end of the fifteenth century we meet at last two great authors and great personalities; St. Joseph of Volok and St. Nilus Sorski, who represent the two different monastic and religious outlooks of their age. Both of them composed something more than occasional letters or sermons; each has left one real book, the first theological works to appear on Russian soil. These are Nilus' *Ustav* (Statute) and Joseph's *Prosvetitel* (Enlightener). It goes without saying that the plethora of edifying and canonical letters by bishops and metropolitans continues through all this period. On the other hand, the sermons which have been preserved are rare. After Serapion in the thirteenth century, who was a survivor of Kievan culture, the only known homilist is Gregory Tsamblak, who stands in the Byzantine tradition of rhetoric.

It is very characteristic of the Russian mind that despite the poverty of literary documents, the Middle Ages left a comparatively abundant literature of memoirs on historical and geographical subjects. There are extant descriptions of pilgrimages to Constantinople and Jerusalem, two travel accounts by Russian clerics sent to the Council of Florence (1438), and a highly interesting account by the Russian merchant Nikitin, who traveled to India. Among the historical tales or stories, which were mostly incorporated into the annalistic collections, many are centered around the Mongol conquest, and the glorious battle of Kulikovo (1380). To the group of Kulikovo tales belongs the series of epic works (in prose) of which the main one is called *Zadonshchina* (the Trans-Doniad). And, finally, the great historical tragedy of the fall of Constantinople found a contemporary memoirist, a Russian living in Constantinople, who described the terrific events under the pen name of Nestor Iskander (Turkish for Alexander). The juridical literature of laws and charters, particularly the testaments of Russian princes, also contains many valuable features which can contribute to the understanding of the religious mind.

The source material is not so sparse as it would appear if judged by purely literary standards. And, what is very important, all the Russian literature of the medieval period stems from the needs and problems of the time. It is no longer a reflection of Greek or South Slavic ideas, as it was sometimes in Kiev. The period of inspired discipleship was over. Impoverished as Russian culture was, it gained in original power and a sense of responsibility. Russian thought from now on is involved in a struggle with its own vital problems, social, moral, and religious. This is what imparts freshness and vigor to all its expressions.

II

NORMAL CHRISTIAN ETHICS

*T*HE Russian Middle Ages were not rich in literary figures; there does not even seem to have been much ecclesiastical preaching. If some bishops or priests continued to teach the rudiments of the Christian faith and morals, their modest exercises were not deemed worthy of being given permanence in writing. The need for liturgical sermons was satisfied by the ready-made anthologies of the classical preachers, mostly Greek, John Chrysostom being the favorite. Only a few canonical epistles by bishops have survived and they lack a readily distinguishable religious note. Literary and educated laymen, like those of the Kievan period, have not left any writings that have been preserved.

In compensation, however, the fourteenth and fifteenth centuries have left us an abundant and anonymous literature of "articles," short chapters of varied content compiled in so-called "Collections" (*Izborniki*). The contents of most of these anthologies were fluid and easily interchangeable, but some Collections assumed a more or less fixed form, being copied traditionally for generations. According to their content they fall naturally into three types — liturgical, ascetic, and moral. The first type consists of the lives of saints and of sermons for the yearly feast and fast days.[1] The second, or ascetic type, is intended for monks and is composed of classical Greek treatises on the spiritual life, a category we treat more in detail later in this chapter. The third type, moral Collections, is designed for general use, that is, mainly for use by the laity and by married clergy. Among these Collections some are the result of individual choice and re-

---

[1] The Slavonic names of the liturgical books of this kind are *sbornik* and *torzhestvennik*. In their definitely fixed form they were first printed in the seventeenth century and reprinted in this way ever since. They no longer form part of liturgical usage except in some monasteries.

flect particular tastes or simply the casual composition of a private library, but most of the moral encyclopedias fit into the category of the fixed compositions that are designated by a common title. However, there is still a great variety of versions within each category.

After we note the Collections that are composed exclusively of the sermons of Chrysostom, whether genuine or spurious, which are entitled *Zlatostrui* (the Golden Stream) and *Margarit* (the Pearl), only two anthologies are left for analysis, and these are entitled *Zlataya Tsep* (the Golden Chain) and *Izmaragd* (Emerald). Both originated in the fourteenth century and the source of their flowery titles is to be found in the Byzantine tradition of the *Catenae Patrum* (Collections of Excerpts from the Fathers). In the preface to one of the Greek anthologies of the eleventh century, which, incidentally, was very popular in Russia, one reads: "One chapter is linked to the other as in a golden chain, intertwined with precious stones and pearls, that is to adorn the throat of a Christian." [2] The Russian anthology, entitled "The Golden Chain," is represented by a very limited number of manuscripts. On the other hand there are approximately 200 copies of the *Izmaragd* manuscripts.[3] It was undoubtedly the favorite book of devotional readings for the Russian laity for approximately four centuries. These books, if any, can safely be used as a guide for the study of lay ethics in medieval Russia. Although nothing is known of their author, it is the common opinion of scholars that he

[2] From the *Pandectae* by Nicon of the Black Mountain, ch. I. The Greek original has never been published. The quotation is taken from I. I. Sreznevski, ed., *Svedeniya i zametki o maloizvestnykh i neizvestnykh pamyatnikakh* (Information and Notes on Little-Known and Unknown Monuments), sec. 55, p. 224, in *SORYaS*, vol. XII, St. Petersburg, 1875.

[3] A. D. Sedelnikov, "Sledy strigolnicheskoi knizhnosti" (The Traces of Strigolnik Literature), in *Trudy Otdela drevne-russkoi literatury, Akademiya Nauk SSSR* (Academy of Sciences, USSR, Works of the Section on Ancient-Russian Literature), Leningrad, 1934, I, 28.

must have been a Russian, who lived in the fourteenth century, the date ascribed to the oldest of the manuscripts.

Most of the chapters of the *Izmaragd* are inscribed with the names of Greek Fathers and, if these attributions are not always correct, their Greek provenance, and in many cases, their original sources have been ascertained. Russian items are interspersed very sparsely in these Greek materials, but the essentially Greek origins of the *Izmaragd* must not delude us as to its national character. The selection itself was Russian, not Bulgarian as in the case of earlier literature. Age-long and intimate acquaintance with these Greek extracts, in many cases adopted and altered by translators and copyists, made them a vital element in Russian religious and moral life. Though not an immediate expression of this life the Greek extracts molded and transformed it for centuries; their influence certainly surpassed that of the few Russian preachers and moralists in their vigor and sometimes wit of expression as well as in the authority of great and saintly names. In this respect the influence of the Greek Fathers, as selected and simplified by Russian readers, may have not only rivaled but even surpassed that of the Holy Scriptures. It has been noted that Russian folk songs of religious content take their subjects not from the Bible directly but from the Apocrypha or Greek sermons included in the popular Collections.

Thus, the distinction between Greek and Russian literary documents, which was so essential in the Kievan period where it corresponded to different types or strata of Russian Christianity, loses its importance after the Mongol conquest. But this does not mean that Byzantinism in Russia had scored a definite victory by this time. Quite the contrary is true. By far the majority of Fathers cited belong to the ancient Church. Purely Byzantine features were subdued and counterbalanced by Russian evangelism, which was enkindled by teachers like John Chrysostom or Ephrem the Syrian. As a result a certain religious balance was formed, which remains a classical model for Russian Orthodox piety. The *Izmaragd* is the best key to the comprehension of this piety. Unfortunately, despite all the critical studies, the *Izmaragd* remains unpublished. The only existing edition, which pursues practical devotional purposes, is little known and unavailable outside Russia.[4] A Russian literary historian, V. A. Yakovlev, did some preparation for a critical edition of this important work, but his plan, as is true of many Russian literary and scientific projects, has never been completed. Yakovlev published, instead, a critical study of the *Izmaragd* manuscripts; he divided them into five classes and printed long excerpts from each chapter of the two main versions.[5] Most of the articles in the *Izmaragd* have been printed elsewhere, in historical reviews and in anthologies of ancient Russian literature.[6] The available printed material, which certainly cannot substitute for the stores of manuscripts unavailable in the United States, provides the basis for the following analysis. Some isolated "articles,"

---

[4] This edition of the *Izmaragd* appeared in an Old-Believer journal *Zlatostrui* (Golden Stream), published in Moscow in 1911.

[5] V. A. Yakovlev, "K literaturnoi istorii drevne-russkikh 'Sbornikov' — opyt issledovaniya 'Izmaragda'" (The Literary History of the Ancient Russian 'Collections — A Research Essay on the 'Izmaragd'), *ZNU*, vol. 60, Odessa, 1893. Hereafter we will distinguish between the two main versions by citing *Izmaragd* I or *Izmaragd* II.

[6] Especially in A. S. Arkhangelski, *Tvoreniya ottsov tserkvi v drevne-russkoi pismennosti: Izvlecheniya iz rukopisei i opyty istoriko-literaturnykh izucheni* (The Works of the Church Fathers in Ancient Russian Writing: Extracts from Manuscripts and Essays in Historical-Literary Studies), 4 vols., Kazan, 1889–1890. Also in A. I. Ponomarev, ed., *Pamyatniki drevne-russkoi tserkovnouchitelnoi literatury* (Monuments of Ancient Russian Ecclesiastical Educational Literature), 4 vols., St. Petersburg, 1894–1898; N. K. Nikolski, "Materialy dlya istorii drevne-russkoi dukhovnoi pismennosti" (Materials for the History of Ancient Russian Spiritual Letters), in *SORYaS*, vol. 82, St. Petersburg, 1907, no. 4, pp. 1–168; and Sreznevski, ed., *Svedeniya*, in *SORYaS*, passim.

sermons, or admonitions are cited inasmuch as they are capable of illuminating the points of doctrine treated in the *Izmaragd*.

Among the versions of the *Izmaragd*, as classified by Yakovlev, the distinction between the first version and the second is very relevant for our purpose. Not only is the second one, that of the fifteenth or end of the fourteenth century, twice as long as the primitive version of the early fourteenth, but by suppressing some articles of the first it betrays a religious tendency which is of paramount significance in the evolution of Russian thought. The second version, preserved in approximately 200 manuscripts, has remained the guide for posterity; the first, surviving in only three manuscripts, reflects the spirit of the fourteenth century, or one of its trends.

The order of the chapters in the *Izmaragd*, as in all Russian Collections, betrays a very slight concern with and talent for systematization. It prefers to follow a psychological association or chain of ideas. From within a generally unified religious and ethical outlook the compilers of the anthologies are eager to show different aspects of patristic doctrine, so as to offer their readers, side by side, the opposing views of the Church Fathers. There are no direct contradictions — like the *sic et non* of Abelard — but different tendencies are not concealed. The editors were thoroughly aware of the complexities of the moral life, of the difficulty of discovering the safe way to salvation. One can discern in them, after a fashion, the dialectic of practical reason, which can lead sometimes to paradoxes without abandoning the practical soil of experience; their axiological aim is to be a guide and not an ideological mirror.

Thus, the *Izmaragd* is far from a collection of commonplaces on medieval morals. Commonplaces are present in abundance, but their juxtaposition, and often their sharp and witty expression possess an undeniable attraction even for the modern reader. With a minimum of abstractions he will find reflected in them the same eternal ethical problems that face modern man.

All the versions of the *Izmaragd*, as in practically all Russian Collections, begin with a group of articles on "books" and "book reading." This is not only a practical introduction to religious studies but, at the same time, a doctrinal indication of the sources of Christian faith and morals. Just as at the very threshold of modern catechetics we find the doctrines about the Holy Scriptures and — in the Catholic as well as in the Orthodox Church — those about sacred tradition, so in ancient Russian Collections we are met at the start with teachings about "books."

The Russian idea of "books," or even "sacred" or "divine" books does not correspond to the theological idea of the "Holy Scriptures" as a God-inspired, infallible set of writings, commonly known as *the Books* (Bible). There was no attempt in Russia to distinguish divine revelation from theology, as represented in the writings of the Church Fathers. All religious literature is "sacred" and "divine," and tradition is included in the Scriptures and participates in the charisma of divine inspiration. Of course, the Russian scribe does not reflect on these theological concepts; he hardly knows them, and the oral tradition or the independent authority of the Church has no place in his sphere of ideas. Going still further he is prone to include all his books in the sacred sphere since his library contains practically no other literature except "divine." Hence, his extreme veneration of all books and their wisdom.

"Books are similar to the depths of the sea, whence the divers bring forth precious pearls." [7] "Know, o man, that books are the mother of all good, who feeds her children

---

[7] *Izmaragd* I, ch. 3. Printed in Arkhangelski, III, 114.

. . . Sell what you possess and buy sacred books . . ."[8] "Spiritual nourishment is concealed in the vessels of books, brought down from heaven." Of this nourishment it was said: "It is the bread of angels which man consumes."[9]

Book reading in Ancient Russia was, certainly, not contemplated from the point of view of theoretical knowledge; it was the school of practical conduct. An instruction of "how it is becoming for a Christian to live" suggests: "Always read sacred books and heed them, doing what is written in them."[10] "Many have deviated from the right way by not reading divine scriptures and perished . . . for God has revealed to men through sacred books how to discover all the snares of the devil."[11] The editor of the second version of the *Izmaragd* repudiates energetically the erroneous view, probably widespread at his time, that book reading is not our business, but that of the monks: "O man, what do you say, being yourself in such a tumult and power of this world! Why do you not reject your sorrows reading books?"[12]

It is very impressive that books are mentioned not only in introductory chapters but on every occasion that the subject touches on the essentials of faith. This is natural for the medieval mind which understands Christianity primarily as the religion of law. "God said: 'He who is loving will study my law day and night,' which means books. Books are created by the Holy Spirit. He who holds them in his hand cannot forget those terrible books of the age to come of which it is written: 'The books of the Judge will be opened.'"[13] And, vice versa, concern for the sacred books

---

[8] *Izmaragd* I, ch. 71. Printed in Arkhangelski, IV, 228.

[9] *Izmaragd* I, ch. 24.

[10] *Izmaragd* I, ch. 27. Printed in another version in *Pravoslavnyi Sobesednik* (Orthodox Converser), Kazan, 1858, p. 512.

[11] *Izmaragd* I, ch. 4.

[12] *Izmaragd* II, ch. 3.

[13] *Izmaragd* I, ch. 7.

enters into the picture of the Last Judgment: "Woe to those who blaspheme sacred books and do not heed them . . . It will be said to them at that time: 'The market is already dissolved and there is no time left for repentance; those who rail here at the sacred books and have no faith [in them] will be tortured there.' " [14]

The emphasis on learning imposed by Christian ethics imprints a rationalistic character. Hence, the appalling maxim often found in Ancient Russian literature: "Ignorance is worse than sin," with the following justification: "He who knows, if he sins in something, knows of what to repent, but the ignorant one, if he sins, thinks not to have sinned and is not aware of having done any evil." [15] The way from doctrine to conduct is not held very arduous and the tragic experience of St. Paul (Rom. 7:19) is strange to the naïve optimism of the Russian medieval mind. The impact of the "sacred books" upon the human spirit is described without any reference to the action of Grace. Sometimes it is explained as the effect of exercise or habit: "Water dripping repeatedly penetrates even stone; likewise reading books leads to the true way and loosens the bonds of sin." [16]

In a practical instruction on how to read with spiritual benefit prayer is suggested, together with intense attention to the meaning of the text:

When you sit down to read or to listen to divine words, first of all pray to God that he may open the eyes of your heart [to enable

---

[14] *Izmaragd* I, ch. 36 (from Ephrem the Syrian). Printed in Arkhangelski, III, 18.

[15] *Izmaragd* I, ch. 3. Printed in Arkhangelski, III, 114. Compare "The Preface to Repentance" in A. S. Pavlov, ed., "Pamyatniki drevne-russkago kanonicheskago prava" (Monuments of Ancient Russian Canon Law), in *RIB,* vol. VI, St. Petersburg, 1880. Also G. P. Fedotov, *RRM,* I, 241.

[16] *Izmaragd* II, ch. 3. Printed in the works of St. Cyril of Turov to be found in M. I. Sukhomlinov, ed., *Rukopisi grafa A. S. Uvarova* (Manuscripts of Count A. S. Uvarov), in *PDP,* vol. II, St. Petersburg, 1858. See also Arkhangelski, IV, 94.

you] not only to read what is written but also to fulfill it; lest reading the doctrine of the saints may bring a sin to you if not fulfilled. When you read books do it attentively and heed with all your heart, read the words twice, not only turning over the pages; read without sloth in order to acquire the fruit of salvation, and the fear of God will dwell in you. [17]

Prayer and attention are not sufficient. For understanding, man needs reason, a natural gift of God. "It is fitting to read sacred books with understanding; without understanding, it is the same as with medicine. If one drinks it without knowing what harm it can do he dies." [18] And, generalizing from this precept: "All the holy Fathers have said that it is proper to search for salvation with understanding [reason] and not to toil without understanding. Every Christian ought to live in purity and do all according to reason and not to drift on unaware." [19]

This reference to reason is justified in the truly Hellenic conception of the kingly and dominant position of reason among the faculties of the soul. "Reason in man is located in the top of his body, between the brain and the sinciput, because it is the king of the whole body and of the very soul." [20] In a fragment attributed to St. Basil, which reflects the anthropology of classical patristics, man is addressed in the following way: "O man, thou hast received from God reason and understanding, skill and intelligence; all is subject to thee in mountains and deserts, in water and air, all is given

[17] *Izmaragd* I, ch. 2 (from the Greek). Printed in *Prasoslavnyi Sobesednik,* Kazan, 1858, p. 179; and in V. Shimanovski, ed., *Sbornik Svyatoslava 1076* (Collection of Svyatoslav of 1076), 2 ed., Warsaw, 1894, pp. 01–02.
[18] *Izmaragd* I, ch. 62 (from St. John Chrysostom). Printed in I. I. Sreznevski, ed., *Drevnie pamyatniki russkago pisma i yazyka X–XIV vekov: obshchee povremennoe obozrenie* (Ancient Monuments of Russian Writing and Language from the 10th to the 14th Centuries: A General Periodical Survey), 2 ed., St. Petersburg, 1882, p. 195; and in Arkhangelski, IV, 120.
[19] *Izmaragd* I, ch. 31. Compare ch. 42.
[20] *Izmaragd* II, ch. 67.

to thee for thy needs and good . . ." And as corollary to this: "O man, let reason dwell in thy head and the understanding of the kingdom of heaven . . ." There follows a long enumeration of the necessary moral virtues, but, significantly enough, reason stands above and before all.[21]

Nothing in either version of the *Izmaragd* betrays any apprehension of the harm that can come from bad or heretical books. All books are tacitly assumed to be sacred or divine. And yet ancient Russia possessed Indexes of the apocryphal and prohibited books bequeathed by the Greek Church. One of these Indexes was inserted into the *Nomocanon,* the book of canon law in the version received from Serbia in the thirteenth century. Cyprian, Metropolitan of Moscow, published his own edition of this Index.[22] Russia seems to have paid little attention to it, judging from the great popularity and the growing dissemination of apocryphal literature. Still, we do possess from the medieval period an article or sermon which reveals a genuine fear of heretical books. This fragment, of undoubted Russian origin, is entitled: "On Reading and Studying Books" and is attributed in manuscripts either to St. Ephrem or St. Cyril.[23]

At the beginning the author advises the reading of sacred books and gives a brief enumeration of them: "The Gospels, the Epistles, the Paroemiai, the Psalter and other sacred books." The intention of defining the canon of the Holy Scriptures is undeniable. But in naming the Paroemiai, that is, excerpts of the Old Testament for liturgical reading, the author makes a jump from the biblical into the liturgical sphere; either he is himself unacquainted with the full content of the Bible or he does not presuppose such an acquaint-

---

[21] *Izmaragd* I, ch. 42.

[22] N. S. Tikhonravov, "Otrechennye knigi drevnei Rusi" (Apocryphal Books of Ancient Russia), in *Sochineniya* (Works), Moscow, 1898, I, 144–146.

[23] This article is published by Nikolski, "Materialy," pp. 81–82.

ance on the part of his readers.[24] He continues his suggestions: "By all means do not look into prohibited books." And these are the prohibited books: "astronomy, astrology, interpretation of dreams, divination of signs, of birds, of thunder," and so on. Then follows a list of books on divination, which were widespread in ancient Russia. They belong, at the worst, to the realm of magic or occultism; one cannot speak either of apocryphal or heretical books in this list. We are unable to determine whether the author knew of the Apocrypha as prohibited literature and whether he was able to furnish a list of that literature. At any rate he knew of the existence of a class of dangerous books. What is more, he knew (following the ecclesiastical tradition) that heretics "wrote false words in the sacred books for the delusion of the ignorant." The falsification of Holy Scripture seems to create a much more dangerous situation than the existence of heretical literature. What then is the means of discerning the true sense of the sacred words? The author gives his criterion: "The holy men had a spirit that was right and not perverted, and reason, given by God; having books, they did not pervert them and followed their doctrine . . ." The heretics also possessed sacred books but they did not have the right reason given by God. In determining the source of their intellectual defectiveness the author offers his own naïve explanation: "For their soul was stinking because of . . . wine." (Judges 13:7)[25]

As we see, the anonymous author does not refer either to grace or the authority of the Church as a supreme authority for doctrine. He retains the same approach of moralism and rationalism as the compilers of the *Izmaragd*. The no-

---

[24] Compare the similar enumeration in a contemporary manuscript "The Paroemiai, the Psalter, the Gospel, and Collections of the Books of Holy Fathers and the Apostles," quoted by Nikolski, "Materialy," p. 134.

[25] Nikolski, "Materialy," p. 82.

tion of the Church as the universal institution or the Mystical Body of Christ was too abstract and difficult for the Ancient Russian mind. The word "Church" was almost exclusively used in the designation of the temple. The authority of the Church must then be sought in the authority of the clergy.

Some chapters of the *Izmaragd* are concerned with the duties of priests as well as the duties of laymen toward priests. Only the second version has a special article on "how to honor priests," and in it "priestly authority and honor" is based not upon the sacramental power and grace of priests but upon their care of souls: "You [laymen] are anxious about your own salvation and theirs is the great care of how to order the lives of those entrusted to them, knowing that, if they do not teach, they have to face a merciless judgment." The unworthy behavior of a priest does not dispense the faithful from the obligation to respect him. "Listen to his instruction if he teaches what is right, do not examine his life nor blame him." [26] The last condition — "if he teaches what is right" — makes the layman the arbiter of sound teaching, and that is fair because both he and the priest have the same source of truth — books. In an exhortation addressed by an unknown [Russian?] author to his fellow priests this is said explicitly: "If we stop reading books what is our advantage before simple folk [laymen]?" [27] The other side of this same rationalistic outlook is the right and duty of laymen to teach. "Do not speak [laymen]; if I had the right of teaching I would instruct many . . . 'Perhaps you have children, friends, and relations . . . you can instruct them perfectly and be granted a greater reward.'

[26] *Izmaragd* II, ch. 56. Printed in Arkhangelski, IV, 195 and Shimanovski, ed., *Sbornik Svyatoslava 1076,* p. 015.

[27] *Izmaragd* I, ch. 72. Printed in part by Arkhangelski, IV, 67; Pavlov, ed., *RIB,* vol. VI, no. 7.

For it is said: 'if even any one of the simple folk possesses the word of wisdom he must not hide it.' " [28] What then if bishops and priests do not teach at all or even teach falsehood through ignorance or contempt of books? This situation is boldly faced by the author of the article on "false teachers," who does not stint in fulminating against the unworthy clergy:

> Woe to you, blind preceptors, who did not study well and are not strengthened with the wisdom of books, you who adorn vestments and not books, who have abandoned the word of God and serve your belly, whose God is the belly! . . . They are filled with the wealth of possessions and are blinded, neither teach themselves nor allow others to. Of such the prophet said: "There will be in the last days revilers of books, walking after their lusts, and false teachers, who will induce many into damnation and many will follow their teaching not salutary but wrong and weak" . . . When pastors become wolves then sheep have to tend sheep; in the day of famine that is of death, in the absence of the bishop and teacher, if a simple man will teach right, this is right . . . Accept good teaching if you hear it from a simple man, and do not accept bad, even if a bishop teaches it; remember that the Scripture also says: "you will know them from their fruits." [29]

The fact that "books" and human reason are a sufficient source of truth and guide in life is a possible conclusion from the premise that the books contain everything necessary for salvation. And this is indeed the conviction of Russian authors: "Nothing is omitted by the sacred books which serves our edification. Tears come to my eyes when I hear some of the clergy saying: 'this is not written in books.' " [30]

Upon this solid base of sacred books, that is, upon the revelation of God and the experience of saints — which are

---

[28] *Izmaragd* I, ch. 16.

[29] *Izmaragd* I, ch. 71 (from St. John Chrysostom). Printed in Arkhangelski, IV, 228.

[30] *Ibid.* (from the *Blasphemia,* a Greek work translated in the fourteenth century). Compare Sedelnikov, I, 134.

not distinguished in principle — Christian ethics is constructed. The layman, as he is not at a disadvantage before
the priest in the knowledge of the way to salvation, also does
not lag behind the monk in his chances of attaining it.
Although in all Catholic systems of ethics, monasticism, or
virginity, occupies a higher rank, the *Izmaragd* is a book
for the laity and its compilers are eager to encourage their
readers, even at the expense of that counselled path to
perfection. They struggle against the prejudice that salvation is impossible or particularly difficult in the world[31] and
emphasize the dangers which await man in a monastery or
in the desert.

The pseudo-Athanasian sermon on various forms of
salvation insists that "God has granted us many and various
ways to salvation . . . God does not require the same life,
fasting and purity, from men in the world as from those
living on mountains and in deserts . . . Many living in the
world have attained the degree of those who became famous
in asceticism."[32] The answer of St. Niphon silenced those who
disparaged the status of laymen, as they enticed them with
monastic ideal: "My son, nobody is saved by pleas, men are
saved or condemned by deeds."[33]

The classical hierarchy of values is preserved in a short
article attributed to Chrysostom: "If you desire to live
without sorrows, o man, avoid the tumult of the world; but
if it is impossible for you to do so, even living in the world
you will not be deprived of the kingdom of God, provided
you are generous and merciful and shun all kind of evil."[34]

---

[31] Compare the views of Cyril of Turov in Fedotov, *RRM,* I, 138.

[32] *Izmaragd* I, ch. 46. Printed in Arkhangelski, IV, 52. Compare *Izmaragd*
I, ch. 43.

[33] *Izmaragd* II, ch. 32. See also *Vita Nephontis,* ch. 64, in A. V. Rystenko,
ed., *Materialen zur Geschichte des Byzantinisch-Slavischen Literatur und
Sprache,* Odessa, 1928, p. 36.

[34] *Izmaragd* II, ch. 69. Compare chs. 71 and 138.

However, the compiler of the *Izmaragd* is not content with this modest statement. He passes from the defensive to an attack against the abuses of monastic life. For many the renunciation of the world results in idleness and parasitism. "Many, having come to a monastery and there being unable to endure prayers and labors flee away and return like dogs to their vomit; others falling in despair commit graver sins than before; some ramble through towns, eating gratuitously other people's bread . . . passing their day in anticipation of where some banquet may be prepared." [35]

Still more severely treated are those who are driven to a monastery in the hope of shunning the burden of their social duties:

> If some one retires to a monastery because of poverty or, being unable to take care of his children, abandons them, he seeks there not the love of God; he does not wish to labor, but is anxious to repose and to serve his belly; such a one denies the faith and is worse than a pagan . . . For the children, abandoned by him are starving and suffering from cold, and with tears and pain they curse him, saying: "For what did our father beget us?" . . . O brethren, if we are ordered to nurture strange orphans and not to dispose of them, how much more not to abandon our own children! . . . Not to the monks was it said: "I was naked and you have clothed me . . ." [36]

And yet, a monastic outlook casts its shadow upon the lay ethics of the *Izmaragd*. We can detect it in ascetic rules of life, in the menacing reminders of death and the Last Judgment, and in the general depreciation of life — in making life seem senseless and hopeless. The "Sermon of the holy fathers on the delusion of this world" proclaims that "in the world all is in disorder and full of untruth . . . truth has perished and untruth has covered the earth . . . our real native land is heaven but we know it only by

---

[35] *Izmaragd* I, ch. 26.
[36] *Izmaragd* I, ch. 27. Printed in *Pravoslavnyi Sobesednik,* 1858, p. 512.

hearsay, having no idea of it." To demonstrate this a parable
of purely Platonic inspiration is told. A pregnant woman
was thrown into prison where her son was born and grew up
with no experience of the visible world and its beauty. The
mother "often told him about the sun and moon and stars,
about mountains, hills, and woods; how birds soar and
horses run and the earth yields grain and the vine and
vegetables." But the son who had seen nothing but darkness
does not believe in these tales. "Likewise, we who are born
in this life of exile have no belief in the heavenly life but
know only this short-lived existence, in which we are born,
with its poor and miserable pleasures." [37]

This Platonic mood, the longing for the celestial homeland, is rarely expressed by Russian authors. Somewhat
nearer to the Russian mind is the Oriental Buddhist parable
which also found its way into the *Izmaragd*. It is the parable
of the Wanderer and Unicorn, well known in medieval
literature. Fleeing from the pursuing unicorn [in the *Izmaragd*, a lion and a camel] the wanderer fell into a prec-
ipice and hung upon a bush. Its root is perpetually gnawed
at by a dragon but, even though surrounded by death on all
sides, the man is in a hurry to gratify his greed by picking
golden and silver leaves [Russian version].[38] The idea that
truth and justice have hopelessly perished in this world,
which was found in the first Platonic parable, took strong
roots in Russian soil or perhaps even sprang from it. "Truth
and untruth" or "justice and injustice"[39] is the title of

[37] *Izmaragd* II, ch. 76. Compare the similar idea, although not the symbolic
form, in the sermon "On the Glory of this World" in Ponomarev, ed.,
Pamyatniki, vol. I, no. 39, St. Petersburg, 1894.
[38] *Izmaragd* I, ch. 10. This parable is taken from the legendary life of St.
Barlaam and Joasaph but attributed by the compiler of the *Izmaragd* to
"Bulgarian books," perhaps a faint recollection of Bogomil literature without
any suggestion of heresy.
[39] On the double meaning of the Russian word *pravda*, see Fedotov,
RRM, I, 220.

another chapter of the *Izmaragd*, of great moment for the history of Russian ethics. "In the beginning, God created justice in men, but later, through the devil's action, injustice rose up and men accepted and loved injustice, abandoned and repudiated justice, and justice let them walk after their heart's desire." [40] For the first time this theme makes its appearance [in the fifteenth century] in written literature. In Russian folklore it is developed in songs and tales and, in fact, became one of the deepest convictions of the Russian people: "Justice lives in heaven, injustice on earth." [41] Yet, in the *Izmaragd*, this concept is still free from dangerous social quietism and resignation. At first the triumph of evil is ascribed to man's free will — free even now as it was in the beginning of time: "we have free will and by our free will we perish in abandoning justice and we do evil, knowing the truth . . ." Even then the victory of evil is not definite. Life is represented in a true Christian sense as a struggle between the powers of Good and Evil, and man has his part in it. The *psychomachia* of Prudentius, so popular in the Western Middle Ages, has its Russian counterpart: "Lust rose against virginity and virginity perished; pride against humility, and hatred against love . . . Be aware, o men, be aware henceforth who is stronger, God or the devil, the enemy of all, and examine what is better, sin that ruins or *Law that saves*." [42]

Placed in the struggle of this life, which has no meaning other than as preparation for the future life in heaven, man must be guided by two moral principles. One is positive,

---

[40] *Izmaragd* II, ch. 135. Printed in Ponomarev, ed., *Pamyatniki,* vol. I, no. 40.

[41] Compare "The Song of the Dove Book," reprinted in G. P. Fedotov, *Stikhi dukhovnye* (Spiritual Poems), Paris, 1935, pp. 142–144, from P. A. Bezsonov, *Kaleki perekhozhie* (Wandering Cripples), Moscow, 1861–1864, no. 77.

[42] *Izmaragd* II, ch. 135.

the law of charity; the other negative, the fear of God. The old Jewish-Christian ethical dualism (*phobos* and *agape*), which can be observed in documents of Kievan Russia,[43] runs through all the medieval period as well. Practically all the chapters of the *Izmaragd* can be classified under these two headings, with some "articles" on humility interspersed.[44] Purely religious duties, irreducible to ethical norms, occupy a very restricted place.

It is not easy to say whether *agape* or *phobos* dominates in the *Izmaragd*. The compiler obviously tried to preserve a fair balance between them. Numerically, charity is treated more widely and in more detail, but fear is also emphasized very strongly. The first version of the *Izmaragd* begins with the so-called "Hundred Chapters" of Pseudo-Gennadius, in the Greek pattern of a moral catechism, based on a balanced synthesis of fear and love with the predominance of the former.[45] In the order of the following chapters, far from systematic though they are, fear appears before love, immediately after the introductory articles on books. Chapter 8 of the first version gives an enumeration of virtues based exclusively upon the *phobos* principle: "first, that fear which the angels have, humility and submission, meekness, mildness, soberness, obedience, attention and other virtues." The following chapter, rather abruptly and unexpectedly, fulminates against those who deny the pains of hell. The compiler must have been fully aware of a tension between the two ethical trends. Not daring to affirm his own opinion he cites the contradictory answers to the question of what the highest virtue is. In the group of chapters treating of love two are

---

[43] Fedotov, *RRM*, I, 206 ff., 218 ff.

[44] About the central position of humility in the scale of Christian virtues, see Fedotov, *RRM*, I, 210–211.

[45] Compare the analysis in Fedotov, *RRM*, I, 205. In the manuscripts of the *Izmaragd* the name of Pseudo-Gennadius appears for the first time in the title of this work.

dedicated to the glorification of love and two to its limitations. "On love and envy" by John Chrysostom and "on
love" by Ephrem are really based on the words of these
Fathers. Chrysostom, with his usual eloquence, ranks love
first: "Love is greater than continence; love has a great daring and elevates from earth to heaven . . . If someone
works wondrous miracles or is devoted to labors and fasting,
sleeps on the ground, preserves purity and virginity, gives
alms, prays much and so on, but is envious, hateful, and
irascible, such a one is more damned and cursed than a forni-
cator and adulterer, thief and robber." [46]

St. Ephrem is still more emphatic: "What is the use if
somebody prepares a sumptuous dinner, invites the king and
arranges everything in kingly fashion but has no salt — how
can that dinner be enjoyed? . . . Love is the salt of the
virtues . . . There is nothing more sublime than love either
in heaven or on earth . . . This love brought the Son of
God down from heaven to us . . ." [47]

Two chapters on "discretion" in love try to discriminate
between godly and sinful love. In the first, obviously of
Russian origin, three facets or kinds of love are distinguished.
The first is a divine gift from the Father and Son and Holy
Ghost. The second is "human love, love of the body, of
cups and of the belly . . ." The third, and positively
"cursed" love is described as the "love of tsars and princes,
which is sought by men who resort to the charms of magicians
in order to obtain the favor of the great . . ." So far this
moral casuistry is blameless. Not so the peremptory conclusion: "He who wishes to be kind to everyone without discretion is detested by God." [48]

The last idea is developed in the subsequent chapter

---

[46] *Izmaragd* I, ch. 16.
[47] *Izmaragd* I, ch. 19.
[48] *Izmaragd* I, ch. 20.

which begins with a reference to "many holy fathers." Its monastic provenance is beyond doubt, and it represents the most drastic and dangerous encroachment of asceticism into the sphere of general Christian ethics. "The holy fathers say that it is becoming to rescind many kinds of love and act with discretion; some people[49] desire to be kind to everyone but they do not know the truth." The truth is that the Lord commanded us to love our enemies but not His. "And these are God's enemies: The Jews and all who transgress God's commandments and pretend to be Christian while they have little faith and do their own will."[50] Literally taken this judgment would put into the category of God's foes practically the whole of mankind and leave no place for love at all. We are far from the relative tolerance of the Kievan clergy, even of the Greek metropolitans, toward the heterodox. In earlier days no one was excluded from the general duty of Christian charity.[51] The ascetic motive of this anti-caritative attitude betrays itself in the next sentence: "If you speak to them of the vanity of the world . . . they reply referring to love." The conclusion is: "There is a pernicious and a salutary love as there is pernicious and salutary justice, pernicious and salutary untruth." Love is thus put on the same level with falsehood.

In the second part of the chapter the compiler goes over to the positive scheme of the ethical hierarchy of values to give first place — in a deliberate contradiction of the classical authorities — to obedience. Obedience "is king over

[49] In the text printed by V. A. Yakovlev the word is "heretics." We give the reading that appears in Nikolski, "Materialy," no. 14, p. 110, which suggests a corruption in a Greek original: *hairetikoi* instead of *heteroi*.

[50] A less extended list of God's enemies is offered in chapter 24 of the same *Izmaragd* I: "The Jews and the heretics and all who keep a wrong faith pervert themselves to heterodoxy and argue about a strange faith and praise a strange faith and love the double faith — with them it is not becoming to keep peace."

[51] Compare Fedotov, *RRM*, I, 390.

all good works and all virtues. Fasting leads up to the doors:
alms, to heaven; charity and peace, to the throne of God,
but obedience will put you at the right hand of God." This
remarkable article is not quoted in its entirety by the compiler of the *Izmaragd*. There is an extant manuscript that
contains the beginning which has been omitted in the *Izmaragd*. Here the "spiritual father" gives the layman proof
of his anti-evangelical postponement of love. In answer to
well-known New Testament quotations the father teaches
how to interpret with "discretion": "First have faith; second,
hope; third, love, of which you are speaking. Confront them
with the fear of God, and you will begin to understand which
is higher. Tell me, whether obedience is generated by love,
or love by obedience." The father is convinced of the latter.
In an obvious polemic against the opinion of Ephrem, cited
above, he ascribes to obedience the incarnation of Christ:
"First, Jesus Christ obeyed God the Father and descended
to earth and was incarnate for the love of man . . . See,
my son, obedience is the beginning of love, and from obedience and submission spring love, first faith, then hope, at
last love." [52] The father tries thus to relegate love not
merely to the second place, but to the fourth. The purpose
of this development in the *Izmaragd* is hardly due to chance.
We can speculate that the compiler, by suppressing it, tried
to avoid an open clash with his authorities although the essential disagreement could not be concealed.

On the basis of these general ethical principles we can
see the way in which the concrete pattern of Christian life
emerges — through the maze of piecemeal fragments. All
of them can be treated under the rubrics of love and fear
with humility as a connecting link.

Love must be considered from its psychological, subjective side as a state of mind. It is treated in this way in

---

[52] N. K. Nikolski, "Materialy," no. 14, pp. 109–110.

ascetic literature; and objectively, that is, from its social side, in human relations. *Izmaragd*, as a book for the laity, has primarily in view the social aspect of love, though the subjective aspect is by no means neglected. It seems to be an axiom that a layman can be saved only by love. Pseudo-Athanasius, after pointing to the variety of the ways to salvation, continues immediately: "For to love one's neighbor is an activity of the soul that does not require bodily fasting."[53]

"Activity of the soul" is an exact term for the core of the Russian conception of love as laying somewhere between a state of the soul and action of the hands. As a state of the soul meekness is praised in a Russian sermon attributed (wrongly) by modern editors to Cyril of Turov. Here meekness is valued more than wisdom and is called the "mother of all virtues."[54] From the Byzantine code of conduct a practical suggestion is borrowed: "If someone vexes you, keep still and turn his heart to loving you; do not mock any man."[55] "In a peaceful mind the Holy Trinity has its dwelling. But even if an irascible man resuscitates a corpse, God will not accept him."[56] "Angels never have wrath . . . and demons never have mercy nor peace . . . Therefore an irascible man is called a house of demons."[57] It is especially abominable to enter a church in a state of anger.[58] On this point the precept of the *Izmaragd* is confirmed by another admonition widespread in Russian manuscripts.

---

[53] *Izmaragd* I, ch. 46. Compare above p. 54.

[54] *Izmaragd* I, ch. 33 (and II, ch. 37). Printed among the works of St. Cyril of Turov in Ponomarev, ed., *Pamyatniki*, vol. I, no. 33.

[55] *Izmaragd* I, ch. 63.

[56] *Izmaragd* I, ch. 15.

[57] *Izmaragd* I, ch. 72. This chapter is the Instruction of the Bishop of Novgorod John Elias (12th century). Printed in Pavlov, ed., *RIB*, vol. VI, supplements, p. 347. Translated in L. K. Goetz, *Kirchenliche und kulturgeschichtliche Denkmäler Altrusslands nebst Geschichte des russischen Kirchenrechts*, Stuttgart, 1905, pp. 343 ff.

[58] *Izmaragd* I, chs. 7 and 47.

It is a great evil to enter a church feeling hatred against anyone . . . Man, have you come to pray or to lie? Have you not
heard what the priest proclaims during the divine service: "Let us
love one another!" . . . What are you doing, man, at the time
when six-winged angels concelebrate, covering the body of Christ
on the sacred altar, when cherubs sing the thrice-holy song, seraphs
stand trembling, the priest prays for all people, the Holy Spirit
descends, and angels write the names of the peaceful men entering
the church? How is it that you are not afraid, my friend, and how
do you ask forgiveness without yourself forgiving? [59]

If an angry man dares to approach the Communion chalice
the cosmic effects of this sacrilege are terrific: "The nether
world will be shaken and the highest celestial powers will
tremble." [60]

It is noteworthy that this condemnation of wrath is not
mitigated by a distinction between righteous and unrighteous
wrath so common in ascetic literature; [61] although "discretion in love," which excludes the enemies of God, seems
to justify a "righteous" wrath against them. However, the
evangelical virtue of "non-judging" was much more strongly
impressed upon Russian hearts. In the *Izmaragd* it is enjoined by the (genuine) article of Anastasius the Sinaite:
"There is another way to salvation, without fasting or
waking, without bodily labors; judge no one, even if you
see one sinning with your own eyes." [62] In a group of manuscripts this spiritual advice is confirmed by a story taken
from the patericons (ancient collections of Lives of holy
monks). "A man living in the monastic habit . . . fell ill
unto death . . . He was not in the least afraid of death

---

[59] Ponomarev, ed., *Pamyatniki*, vol. I, no. 35.

[60] *Izmaragd* I, ch. 7.

[61] Compare Johannes Cassianus, "De coenobitorum institutionibus," lib.
VIII, cap. 6, 7, 8 in *PL*, vol. 49, cols. 333–339, and index 3, cols. 825–827.
See also *Dictionnaire de Théologie catholique*, Paris, 1930, *s.v.* Colère, vol.
III, cols. 357–358.

[62] *Izmaragd* I, ch. 48. Compare Anastasius the Sinaite in *PG*, vol. 89, col.
845A.

but thanked God from all his heart." One of the brothers asked him the reason for his confidence, which was especially amazing because "since you became monk we have seen you spending your life in sloth and neglect." "Truly, venerable father," was the answer, "I have been spending my life in sloth, but since I renounced the world and became a monk I have not condemned anyone." In his death vision he saw an angel tearing up the list of his sins.

This virtue of non-judging stands in conflict with the universal duty of teaching enjoined in other chapters of the *Izmaragd*.[63] Here, certainly, the two ethical schools were, and still are, in strife. But the evangelical precept of non-judging, through all the age of Russian Christianity, remained, if not the prevalent, the most characteristic feature of the national mind.

"The activity of the soul" on which Pseudo-Athanasius insists necessarily leads to relations with fellow-men and not always in the simplest form of alms-giving.

> If you have no property, if you are a widow or orphan, and see someone naked or hungry or shivering from frost, bring him into your home, warm him and give him of what you have; this gift of yours will be credited to you by God more than thousands of talents given by the rich. If you have not even this, sigh with the sorrowful, grieve about the poverty of the destitute, calm them, and this will be credited to you by God as alms-giving.

On the other hand, no moral perfection, even in the virtues of love, will help man if not transferred into charitable action. "Judgment should be without mercy to him who did not show mercy. What good will it do the rich man who has no anger but has no mercy for the poor either . . . even if he is deemed to be humble and non-judging . . ."[64]

---

[63] *Izmaragd* I, chs. 16 and 71.

[64] *Izmaragd* I, ch. 46. Printed in Ponomarev, ed., *Pamyatniki*, vol. I, no. 13 and in Arkhangelski, IV, 52.

Among the numerous chapters in the *Izmaragd* on charity, all in the spirit of the Gospel and some of them sublime, there is one which strikes the opposite note, that of egotistic practicality, although one might use a stronger expression. This is a sermon on pledges and lending. The author suggests:

> Do not lend money to a man more powerful than you; that will mean losing it; do not pledge beyond your strength . . . If you see someone who has fallen in the water and you can help him, extend to him your cane and drag him out; but if you stretch out your hand to him and are not able to draw him out he will draw you to the bottom and both of you will die . . . Let everybody help his friend and brother according to the measure of his strength; and God will not exact his command from man beyond his power.[65]

Looking for the source of this chapter we find it in the so-called *Pandectae* of Antioch, a Byzantine monastic compilation of the eleventh century. It is still foreign to the general trend of the Russian mind in the fourteenth century but, nonetheless, it did not remain without influence. The full fruit of ethical Byzantinism in Russia ripened in the sixteenth century, but the beginnings of the demoralization were in much earlier times.

Without any doubt, with all qualifications, alms-giving stands at the center of practical charity but it would not serve any useful purpose to review all the precepts and parables of the *Izmaragd* concerning this form of charity. In ancient Russia it was at all times considered as the virtue *par excellence* since it was based upon the Old Testament as much as upon the Gospels. A classical maxim (Prov. 19:17) is "He that hath pity upon the poor lendeth to God." [66] The *Izmaragd* comments: "Give alms; it is your true friend who delivers you from eternal torment." Taken too literally,

[65] *Izmaragd* I, ch. 66. Printed in part in Arkhangelski, IV, 11.
[66] *Izmaragd* I, ch. 47. Printed in part in Arkhangelski, IV, 59.

this maxim runs a risk of which the history of medieval ethics
gives abundant evidence. The way of salvation can become
a damning affair in the proper sense, if considered a mere in-
vesting of money toward a reward in heaven. Particularly
misleading was the use of the Gospel parable on the unrighteous steward, which is quoted together with Daniel on alms-
giving: "Make friends for yourselves with unrighteous mam-
mon" (Luke 16:9). The compilers of the *Izmaragd* were
fully aware of this danger, and most of their injunctions on
alms-giving were intended to parry it.

First, the act of alms-giving must not be separate from
the loving communion of souls.

> What is the use, if a poor man comes to you, and you some-
> times give him a crust of a loaf, not condescending to share with
> him your repast? And even that you give only once in a while but
> more often you insult him. Such alms are not perfect . . . The
> Scripture says: "He who annoys the poor irritates the Creator." [67]

The person of the poor is sacred. He is the living image
of the humiliated Christ. This evangelistic idea, expressed
most drastically in the Greek life of St. John the Merciful,
found its place in the *Izmaragd* in the form of a story of an
abbot told according to some ancient patericon. This abbot
liked to cultivate friendship with boyars and rich people.
One day when he banqueted with his distinguished guests
a beggar remained the whole day at the gate of the monastery
waiting for admission. The abbot did not let him in "not
knowing that this was Christ, the Savior of humble toiling,"
"the Lord, rich with mercy." When at last the abbot admitted Christ he heard his just condemnation: "Because thou
lookest for glory and honor from men for riches' sake thou
art deprived of my kingdom and will be foreign to the
saints." [68]

---

[67] *Izmaragd* II, ch. 132.
[68] *Izmaragd* II, ch. 158.

The second qualification of social charity is "not to give alms out of iniquitous acquisitions." [69] Considered iniquitous are not only possessions acquired by crime or sin (like usury) but even ordinary property administered with the callous selfishness of private interest.

> You gave alms to the poor, you, a rich man, and well you did, but somewhere your servants, tending your oxen, damaged the field of your poor neighbors whom besides, you yourself had forced into serfdom with malicious oppression and iniquitous punishment. Better, o foolish man, that you have mercy on your household, lest they go in sorrow, and abstain from violence and oppression than present God foolishly with possessions gathered by iniquity.[70]

This picture can be located as well in medieval Russia as in the later Roman empire. But the following invective betrays typically Russian features: "What profit is it to despoil someone, a poor man or an orphan, and to give to another . . . It is better not to plunder than to give alms to strangers. The gifts of those who offend widows and do violence to orphans, as well as those of plunderers and fornicators and pot-house keepers are not acceptable [to God]." [71] The same rule is applied to gifts for the Church. In this case the temptation was still stronger for the medieval man, who saw in the posthumous prayers of the Church his main chance for salvation. Yet, often found in Russian manuscripts is the epistle of Isidore of Pelusium to the Bishop Eusebius:

> You are building a church in Pelusium, which is adorned, it is said, with a great art, but you build it by iniquities, by oppressing orphans and violating the poor. It is abominable to build Zion upon blood, Jerusalem upon iniquity. God does not ask an offering from iniquity . . . but abhors it as a stinking dog. Stop building by iniqui-

---

[69] *Izmaragd* I, ch. 72.

[70] *Izmaragd* I, ch. 39. Printed in Arkhangelski, IV, 109 and taken in part from genuine St. John Chrysostom.

[71] *Izmaragd* II, ch. 34 (taken from Nicon's *Pandectae*).

ties lest that church would be raised to the height for convicting you before God and crying against you ceaselessly high in the air forever.[72]

The principle set by St. Isidore was, obviously, too severe; hardly any church could be built under the strict condition of employing exclusively untainted money. The necessity of finding a compromise explains a curious legend created in Novgorod and preserved in manuscripts of the fifteenth century. It is a legend of *Posadnik* Shchilo. This legend is concerned with the circumstances of the building of a church and monastery, dedicated to "Our Lady of the Veil" (*Pokrov*) in the province of Novgorod. According to the chronicles the church was built in 1309 by the monk Olonius nicknamed "Shchilo." Popular tradition made of him a *posadnik*, the supreme officer of the Novgorod republic. The legend tells that he was very rich, but his wealth was earned from lending money, that is, from usury. In a commercial city like Novgorod this procedure was certainly not uncommon, and the legend emphasizes, deliberately, the modesty of Shchilo's rate of profit. In fact it is specified by the legend that it was ridiculously low (one-half of one percent). On the day of the consecration of the new church the archbishop asked the builder about the origin of his money . . . Learning the truth he treated Shchilo with extreme severity: "You are similar to Esau (confusion with Jacob) having obtained my blessing with a lie." Thereupon he orders the guilty one to confess his sins, to put on a shroud, and to lie down in a coffin while funeral prayers are sung over him. After this was done the floor of the church caved in and the coffin disappeared in an abyss. On the wall next to the place where the coffin stood the archbishop ordered them to paint a picture representing Shchilo in hell and the

---

[72] *Izmaragd* II, ch. 40 (taken from Isidore of Pelusium). Printed in part by Arkhangelski, IV, 57.

nonconsecrated church was sealed up. The grieving son of
the departed asked the prelate what he could do for the
soul of his unfortunate father. On the archbishop's order he
had a requiem service celebrated for forty days in forty
churches and distributed alms; in particular, he was to "give
enough to priests and psalmists." A forty-day requiem,
sorokoust, was the usual Russian form of the commemoration
of the dead. Here it is multiplied forty times. After the
sorokoust the head of Shchilo appeared on the picture above
the fires of hell. On the repetition of these propitiatory
prayers, Shchilo's image was seen up to the waist. After the
third sorokoust Shchilo was out of the fire, and his coffin
reappeared on the floor of the church. Shchilo was thus
pardoned, but not returned to life; this time he was buried
with ordinary prayers and the church reconsecrated.

In this variant of the legend (probably not the primitive one) two tendencies are reconciled; the radical one,
prohibiting interest at its smallest rate and, so to say — the
most generous form, especially in gifts to the church, and
the moderate clerical one showing the way that both the sinner and the Church (or the clergy) could enjoy, respectively,
pardon and benefit. That the way of reconciliation leads
not through ethical atonement but through ritual and the
payment of money (analogous to indulgences in the West)
shows the lowering of religious standards. The financial
interest of the clergy (every requiem service was to be paid
for) is obvious. But even in this clerical version the poor are
not forgotten and the alms, together with requiems, are
instrumental in saving Shchilo's soul.[73]

---

[73] The legend of Shchilo was published by N. Kostomarov, ed., *Pamyatniki
starinnoi russkoi literatury* (Monuments of Ancient Russian Literature),
4 vols., St. Petersburg, 1860–1862. It has also been the object of an interesting study by I. P. Eremin, "Iz istorii russkoi povesti: Povest o posadnike
Shchile" (From the History of the Russian Tale: The Tale of the Posadnik
Shchilo), in *Trudy komissii po drevne-russkoi literatury, Akademiya Nauk*

The theme of alms is closely tied up with that of wealth and of its perils and of the right manner in which it is to be used. Here also the Russian *Izmaragd* follows in the steps of the classical Greek Fathers. We find a justification of the right use of wealth, in the tradition of Clement of Alexandria: "I do not speak against those rich who live righteously with their riches but I accuse those possessing riches who live in greed. As wine is created for a double effect — for the wise unto joy, for the foolish unto sin and damnation — likewise wealth is given to one for salvation, but to the greedy for greater sin, damnation, and eternal torments . . ."[74] The comparison with wine is not very promising for the rich; besides, this relative justification is found only in one chapter of *Izmaragd* which overflows with invective against the rich.

A classical standard of possession is given in the idea of stewardship: "Fortune is not born with you but is entrusted to you by God for a few days: therefore, distribute, as a steward, what is entrusted to you anywhere the entruster orders."[75]

The flaming philippics against the rich breathe a biblical prophetic spirit shaped in the Hellenistic rhetoric of the Fathers of the fourth century; they often are literal excerpts from St. John Chrysostom and St. Basil. They attack wealth from either an ascetic or a social point of view; mostly from both at once. As usual, social interests prevail. From the ascetic or personal point of view the craving for goods is perilous and even fatal in its insatiability. The ascetic Fathers, following the Stoic pattern, found greed (or more exactly

SSSR (USSR Academy of Sciences, Works of the Commission on Ancient Russian Literature), Leningrad, 1932, I, 59–151.

[74] *Izmaragd* I, ch. 38 (taken from St. John Chrysostom). Printed in Arkhangelski, IV, 199.

[75] *Izmaragd* I, ch. 64. Printed in Ponomarev, ed., *Pamyatniki,* vol. I, no. 29.

argyrophilia) a vice against nature, and in this sense the worst of the seven capital sins. The *Izmaragd* quotes: "Waters grow troubled and afterwards subside; winds blow and are calmed again, but a man who is troubled about his possessions never stops hoarding."[76] And yet the object of this passion is quite futile and, in this sense, again unnatural. "A man possessed by greed is similar to one who is ill with fever and thirsty after water; he then believes that he is able to drink up all rivers, but when water is brought to him one dipperful is enough."[77] The impossibility of enjoying one's possessions beyond the short limits of one's life renders their accumulation pointless. For the Russian compiler, greed is not merely one sin among many, but the sin *par excellence* as is lust or pride for the ascetic mind. Considering the perverted state of the sinful world, its "tumult," he finds the struggle for wealth at the root of all evil.

> Every man living without reason perturbs himself and hoards, and he does not know for whom he is hoarding . . . See, my brothers, we walk to and fro, as in the dark, for everything is now in disorder. This one robs a fortune from another and that one takes lands . . . He who does not possess is in distress and he who does, thinks of spoliations, boasts and prides himself, gets drunk and quarrels with many, elates himself with lies, detests truth; the earth cannot bear all the evil, the wind raises the stench and wickedness of mankind to the very ether; for the sake of riches life is being overthrown by riots.[78]

The preacher here goes from the particular to the universal and extends his arguments against the rich into a picture of cosmic decadence. The physical infection of nature by human sins and the suffering of the earth are features especially painful to the Russian conscience. The sufferings

---

[76] *Izmaragd* II, ch. 35. Printed in Arkhangelski, IV, 149.

[77] *Izmaragd* I, ch. 65.

[78] *Izmaragd* I, ch. 44. Printed in part in Arkhangelski, IV, 149.

of Mother Earth under the burden of iniquity occur in Russian folk songs and must be taken in a mythological sense; at least it has a mythological aftertaste for Russian lips.[79] Purely metaphorical, though, are the complaints of personified gold:

All gold which is fettered and confined by the rich, methinks, exclaims: "O wealthy gold-lovers, for what do you wrong me? Why do you receive me as an honorable friend but afterwards dishonor me like a criminal, bind me with irons, bury me in the earth, send me, from darkness to darkness, into your hands? If you wish to let me look at the light let me pass into the hands of the poor, I pray you." [80]

For personal salvation it is better to get rid of wealth as a wanderer prefers to give robbers his money and save his life; or as sailors, during a storm, throw their freight overboard.[81] The connection of wealth with sin seems inseparable in spite of theoretical distinctions.

All the ascetic condemnations of wealth cited above imply social sins: cruelty and spoliation besides purely personal greed. We have little to add in the matter of social invective. "For possessions' sake a free man is enslaved and sold . . . Gold-lovers like to frequent tribunals . . . tell lies and commit perjury against one another." [82] The invective is composed in various styles. Some are tuned to the solemn rhetorical pitch of Chrysostom, like one attributed to St. Basil:

Wherever thou turnest thine eyes, o rich man, thou wilt see evils: here an orphan is crying because of thee, there the poor whom you

---

[79] Fedotov, *Stikhi dukhovnye,* p. 79. The influence of the apocryphal vision of St. Paul is very probable. Compare N. S. Tikhonravov, *Pamyatniki otrechennoi russkoi literatury* (Monuments of Apocryphal Russian Literature), 2 vols., Moscow, 1863, II, 40–41.

[80] *Izmaragd* I, ch. 44. Printed in part in Arkhangelski, IV, 149.

[81] *Izmaragd* II, ch. 157.

[82] *Izmaragd* II, ch. 35. Printed in Arkhangelski, IV, 149.

wronged by not showing mercy to them are proclaiming to God against thee. Here slaves are walking naked and beaten, somewhere else I see other people tormented by thy usury; they throw themselves into the water and will rise against thee in the day of the departure of the soul.[83]

Sometimes the image is chosen more discreetly and more effectively like a very popular saying attributed to St. Maximus:

O rich man, you have lighted your candles in the church on candelabra; well have you done so; but once a poor man whom you have wronged will come in the church; he will sigh and shed tears because of you and he will quench the light of your candle with his tears.[84]

We find sentences which breathe a folk humor in the style of popular adages, probably of Russian coinage:

The poor can as little remain friends with the rich as a wolf with a lamb . . . What is there in common between a pot and a kettle? That is how can the poor argue with the rich; the wretched pot will be broken and the rich continue to add reproaches.

Invective against the rich is interspersed with positive suggestions as to the right use of wealth. Here the disagreement begins. The medieval reader who wished to find in the *Izmaragd* a straightforward guide in these questions of conscience must have been disappointed. The contradictory answers, all in the most peremptory style, reflect the weakness of a positive appreciation of wealth in the Christian tradition. As one of the authors of the *Izmaragd* affirms, wealth is given to man "for temptation"[86] and not as a positive gift of God.

That wealth must be distributed and not accumulated,

---

[83] *Izmaragd* I, ch. 39.
[84] *Izmaragd* I, ch. 38.
[85] *Izmaragd* I, ch. 65. Taken from Ecclesiasticus, ch. 13.
[86] *Izmaragd* II, ch. 44.

or hoarded — a common trend in a natural economic system, a "virtue" in capitalism — has already been observed. The question is to whom is it to be distributed? There are three claimants to the possessions of the rich: the poor, "one's own people," and the Church. Among these three conflict is permanent. The rights of the poor are best justified as being based on the Gospel and patristic doctrine. But "one's own people" are serious competitors. This notion covers two, or even three social groups: the family in a narrow sense, the family in the ancient sense, including servants and slaves, and the clan, or the group of all blood relatives. In all probability the vagueness of the general notion of "one's own people" is intentional and conceals the tendency to save the interests of the less defensible groups: the family and relatives.

Indeed, in a sermon attributed to Chrysostom and conceived in a severe patristic spirit, after having enjoined the principle of the stewardship of wealth and the duty of giving it away, the author continues:

Do not say, "I gather wealth for my children," but entrust your wealth to God . . . To Him commit also your children and your wife; and do not say, "My children will commemorate me in their prayers." Every one of you must take care of your own soul and not hope to be saved by other people's offerings. Even if they will commemorate you, it will not be in the same way as you would have it. And if your children be fools or drunkards or thieves or fornicators all that is left to them will be to no good purpose. Intend rather to leave your children well-bred than rich.[87]

But this sermon is isolated in Russian homiletic literature, more prevalent is the maxim equivalent to the English "charity begins at home." "This is a true and goodly love — to destroy poverty, that is, not to despise those of your

---

[87] *Izmaragd* II, ch. 64. Printed in Ponomarev, ed., *Pamyatniki*, vol. I, no. 29.

family (*rod*) who are indigent . . . If you distribute five times more to strangers and despise your rod in poverty, this will be of no avail."[88] And conversely: "This is hypocrisy and not love — to be ashamed of the rich and to offend the poor, to benefit orphans and to leave one's own in sorrow and all one's family [or clan][89] in distress, starving and naked."[90] Here children and servants are taken together as belonging to the rod. Again, the same idea is used in reference to the Old Testament: "O you foolish and merciless ones, do you not hear the Scripture which says: 'Blessed is the man who has mercy upon his servants and does not leave his family [*rod*] in sorrow.' "[91] By rod is probably meant this sentence: "This is called love, not to despise the poverty of one's rod."[92] But in the following article entitled "It is becoming to give alms first to one's household (or domestics)," the author has in mind servants.[93]

Further on we shall return to the moral doctrine concerning children and servants. It suffices now to note that servants, and not children, have a privileged place in these teachings because they stand nearer the category of the poor, sanctified by tradition, and also because they are the least protected class in society.

Gifts to the Church, considered so effective, through liturgical commemoration, for personal salvation are already limited by the demand that the gifts offered to God be pure. The care of one's family is another limit. But clerical interest [in gifts], generally alien to the *Izmaragd*, found expression, at least in some manuscripts, and reveals a pic-

---

[88] *Izmaragd* I, ch. 16.
[89] On the meaning of *rod* see Fedotov, *RRM,* I, 15.
[90] *Izmaragd* II, ch. 126. Printed in *Pravoslavnyi Sobesednik,* 1859, 132.
[91] Yakovlev, *ZNU,* vol. 60, p. 218.
[92] *Izmaragd* II, ch. 44.
[93] Yakovlev, *ZNU,* vol. 60, pp. 217–218.

turesque though satirical glimpse of Russian family life. These are clearly Russian interpolations.

Arrange your life well, allot a part of your possessions to God and all the rest declare to your children before witnesses during your life; and do not believe your wife's lies: many wives are perfidious, and for their sake this is written. If you do not declare your possessions to your children before witnesses your wife, concealing your possessions will remarry like a harlot; and thus you will not have commemorations (prayers) nor will your children receive their just possessions.

The following scene gives evidence that the author is more interested in "commemorations," that is, in donations to the Church than in the well-being of children.

Very often, if the husband beset by illness wishes to distribute his possessions for his soul's sake, his wife will say weeping: "And what will I have to eat, my lord, when I take the veil after your death." [94] And he thinks: "This is the proper posthumous prayer for me; my wife will take the veil after my death." But she, cunning woman, getting hold of her husband's possessions, like a whore, remarries . . . Yet a good wife will save her husband even after his death.[95]

The cynicism of this practical advice stands out in sharp relief amid the serious and often sublime rules of the *Izmaragd*. This article does not belong to either of the two first versions of the *Izmaragd*. It is a later addition reflecting rather the conditions of everyday life than moral principles. Life has begun to dictate to ethics, lowering their level.

A low estimate of woman's character remains, however, a constant feature in all Russian literature. This will be clear

---

[94] Russian medieval convents were a kind of hospice for widows and unmarried women who were received there on the condition that a certain endowment be paid.

[95] Yakovlev, *ZNU*, vol. 60, pp. 225–226. Printed in *Pravoslavnyi Sobesednik*, 1858, p. 509.

as we approach the circle of family life and become acquainted
with the duties of the paterfamilias toward the individual
members of his household. This inner circle consists of the
wife, children, and servants. The relations of the head of
the family to all dependent members are not regulated by
love or charity alone. Here the element of fear as a method
of education exerts its influence. One would even say that this
influence is more prominent than that of charity.

Best of all, in doctrine not in life, is the moral attitude
toward servants. Precisely because of their humiliated and
oppressed social standing they require the protection and
particular care of the moralists. On the other hand, their
moral life is the responsibility of their master; hence the
severe and yet moderate rules for their education. Here,
also, two schools can be observed and distinguished according to the role ascribed to charity. The more severe school is
represented by an instruction of Byzantine provenance which
was widespread in medieval Russian literature.

He of you who has slaves and maidservants must teach them and
urge them toward baptism, repentance, and God's law. You are an
abbot in your home and if you do not teach through fear and kindness you will be responsible for them before God. Feed them sufficiently, give them clothing and drink, and do not insult them, because they are of the same nature as you, and only entrusted by God
under obedience to you. If you do not give them sufficient food and
clothing and they, being unable to bear nakedness and hunger, go to
steal and to rob, you will answer before God for their blood, if your
slave be killed or tortured.

Order your servant or maid to work that you may repose. If the
slave is slack in work he begins to seek freedom; for idleness teaches
many evils.[96] But do not burden your slave beyond his strength lest
his soul sigh toward God in sorrow against you, and God, hearing
him, pour his wrath upon you . . . If he does not obey you . . .
do not spare him, not beyond his strength, but in discretion, as the

---

[96] Compare Ecclesiasticus 33:26–28.

Wisdom of God [97] tells us, up to six or nine strokes, or if the guilt is very great, thirty strokes; more *we* do not allow. If you teach him in this way, you will save his soul and preserve his body from being beaten by people. Be not excessive in treating any flesh. If you have a slave whose goodness was tested, treat him as your brother . . . Do everything with consideration, not in anger but in zeal.[98]

We see here that various moral motives combine with purely practical considerations of personal interest. In one of the later manuscripts of the *Izmaragd*, undoubtedly the work of a Russian author, we find that quite a different treatment of servants is suggested. Nothing is said about punishment; the author believes more in the efficacy of kindness. Among other counsels of charity we read here:

> If you return from the prince in a cheerful mood, act so that in your home people also walk without sorrow; for this is no small good deed to rid your household of sorrow, sighs and tears. If they deserve punishment let them rather be pardoned; for mercy more than lashes will make them tremble and edify them. If you act in this way you will also find mercy instead of punishment on the departure of your soul.[99]

Unfortunately, this article was transcribed, read, and heeded much less than the classical one cited above.

As compared with servants the *Izmaragd* pays less attention to children, relying obviously upon natural paternal affection. On the contrary, it tries to restrain this natural affection where it interferes with personal salvation. It warns against hoping for posthumous love by wife and children and against relying on their prayers: "There is no help from them before God; they will follow you to the grave and

---

[97] The author has in mind the book of the Wisdom of Joshua, son of Sirach, or Ecclesiasticus.

[98] *Izmaragd* I, ch. 58. Printed in Ponomarev, ed., *Pamyatniki,* vol. I, no. 65, and Arkhangelski, IV, 18.

[99] Yakovlev, *ZNU,* vol. 66, pp. 217–218.

return home thinking only of themselves and quarrelling about their inheritance." [100]

The educational system, unlike the treatment of servants, has a one-sided character; it is based on fear alone without the admission of love or tenderness. The only chapter of the *Izmaragd* I that treats the subject enjoins:

Chrysostom says that he who does not teach his children the will of God, will be condemned worse than a brigand; for the brigand kills the body but the parents who do not teach their children, will destroy their souls . . . O men, listen well to these counsels and teach your children from an early age. The Wisdom of God says: "He who loves his son must not spare his admonitions against him." Teach him in youth and he will tend your old age. But if you do not teach him early, he, in obdurate will, will not obey you . . . If your son or daughter will not obey you do not spare him. The Wisdom of God says: "Give him six or twelve lashes." If you teach him with care he will not die but will be more healthy, and you will save his soul . . . [101]

A daughter is a matter of particular concern: "If some of you have a daughter instill fear within her that she should walk in obedience, lest in foolishness, having her own will, she ruin her virginity and cause your acquaintances to laugh at you." [102] This is illustrated by the story of the priest Eli from the book of Samuel (or Kings), who brought the wrath of God upon himself and all his house through his soft treatment of his sons. The story was not taken from the Bible but from Chrysostom's "Education of Children," which was well known in Russia. The Church Father himself is quoted together with a biblical reference: "Chrysostom says that he who does not teach his children the will of God will be

---

[100] *Izmaragd* II, ch. 47 (from the Life of Barlaam and Joasaph).

[101] *Izmaragd* I, ch. 55. Printed in Ponomarev, ed., *Pamyatniki*, vol. I, no. 63. See also N. Lavrovski, "Pamyatniki starinnago russkago vospitaniya" (Monuments of Old Russian Upbringing) in *OIDRMU*, vol. III, Moscow, 1861, p. 3.

[102] *Izmaragd* II, ch. 51. Arkhangelski, IV, 179.

condemned worse than a brigand; for the brigand kills the body but the parents who do not teach their children, will destroy their souls."

The main source of these instructions is to be found in the book of the "Wisdom of Joshua, son of Sirach" (uncanonical), undoubtedly the favorite book of the Old Testament in ancient Russia. It was transcribed in the first known Russian Collection of 1076 and also in the *Izmaragd*, and is used together with the Proverbs of Solomon under the name of "Wisdom of God." [103]

There is a reverse aspect to the duty of parents — the duty of children toward their parents. Fear dominates, if that is possible, to a still higher degree. Love is hardly mentioned. The proper attitude toward parents is defined thus: "Serve them with fear as a slave." To honor one's parents, to tend one's mother in her old age, to gratify one's father — this is the positive content of the fifth commandment which is here called "the main one." The negative features are a host of terrifying threats and curses upon the head of the sinner.

He who insults his parents sins before God and is cursed by men. And he who beats his father or mother must be excommunicated from the Church and must die a terrible death. For it is written that the father's curse will wither, and the mother's curse will uproot. "Let the eye be plucked out of him who mocks his father and annoys his mother, let the ravens of the valley pick it up and eagles eat it . . ." (Proverbs 30:17) [104]

Yet, the same mother who must stand so high in the eyes of her sons is deeply humiliated as wife and woman. Ancient Russian literature from Kievan times abounds in satires against women, mostly entitled "On Good and Bad Women"

---

[103] Compare Fedotov, *RRM*, I, 225–226.

[104] *Izmaragd* II, ch. 55. Printed in Ponomarev, ed., *Pamyatniki*, vol. I, no. 64 and Lavrovski, "Pamyatniki," pp. 5–6.

or simply "On Bad Women." Their main source was found
in (spurious) sermons of John Chrysostom, Ephrem of
Syria, and Herodias. But where the ancient Fathers give two
opposed portraits, Russian compilers abbreviate or content
themselves with only the negative features. Since pre-
Mongol times Daniel the Exile was famous for his anti-
feminine invectives.[105] The *Izmaragd* in both versions gives
two examples of differing tendencies — a caustic satire and a
positive instruction.

> No wild beast can equal a malicious and bitter-tongued woman.
> The lions venerated the prophet Daniel in their den, but Jezebel
> murdered Naboth. The whale preserved Jonah intact in its belly, but
> Delila having shorn Samson, her husband, betrayed him to his ene-
> mies . . .

And so it proceeds through the Old and New Testaments.

> Elijah feared Jezebel and fled to the desert. Alas, a prophet was
> afraid of a woman! . . . Worse than any evil is a malicious woman.
> If she is poor, she is rich with hatred. If she is rich, double is the
> evil, incurable the disease, untamable the beast. I have seen lions
> and bears tamed by kind treatment, but a bad woman elates herself
> while being tamed and rages while blamed. If she has married a
> boyar she always spurs him to perfidy [the Russian text says: "to
> robbing and spoliation"]; if she is the wife of a poor man she
> teaches him anger and quarreling . . .[106]

But the Russian compiler outdoes his model with apho-
ristic barbs in the style of Daniel the Exile, borrowed in
part from another ancient Russian Collection of holy writings known as *Melissa* (the Bee)[107]: "It is better to suffer

---

[105] Fedotov, *RRM,* I, 260.

[106] *Izmaragd* I, ch. 53 and II, ch. 52. This article is a textual translation
from a Greek sermon attributed either to St. John Chrysostom or Ephrem
the Syrian and printed with Chrysostom's *Spuria* in *PG,* vol. 59, cols. 485–
490.

[107] On *Melissa* compare M. N. Speranski, "Perevodny sbornik izrecheni
v slavyano-russkoi pismennosti" (Translated Collections of Short Sayings
in Slavo-Russian Writing), in *OIDRMU,* volumes for the years 1901–1905.

from fever than to be mastered by a bad wife. A malicious wife is like a storm in the house. Better to boil iron than to teach a bad wife . . . Do not entrust your secrets to a bad wife lest you perish. Rare is the wife who would not tell your secret to others." Such wives give birth to evil children, like Cain, the first born after the sin was committed. "If a child is conceived after a transgression of the law, there can be no good in him." Some concluding lines which mention good women like Rebecca and Sarah and Hannah and Elizabeth soften but little the bitterness of the preceding invective.

The positive ideal is described according to St. Paul. Obedience and silence are the chief virtues of a wife. "Listen, o wives, to the precept of God and learn to obey your husbands in silence." A good submissive wife enjoys the trust of her husband who, according to the apostle, has to take advice from her, as in the case of common fasting or abstinence. Such a wife always does something good: "Having found linen and wool she makes various and fair cloths and sells them to merchants, and she herself is clothed in fair garments, red and purple . . . she gets up by night and distributes sufficient food to the servants . . . all the night her lamp is not quenched. And she gives to the poor the fruits of her toil."

The good wife is a treasure for her husband. She "cheers her husband and fills his years with content and peace . . . A good wife is more valuable to you than precious gems. Having found her the husband rejoices in her as having found honor and glory." [108]

The endeavor of the *Izmaragd* to preserve a just balance

---

[108] *Izmaragd* I, ch. 52. Printed in Arkhangelski, IV, 175 and I. S. Nekrasov, "Opyt istoriko-literaturnago issledovaniya o proiskhozhdenii drevne-russkago Domostroya," (Essay on the historical and literary investigation of the origins of the Ancient Russian *Domostroi*), in *OIDRMU,* vol. III, Moscow, 1872, p. 110.

in portraying the good and bad wife is evident. Unfortunately
the negative features show a richer and more striking development and thus the general picture of a wife coming from
the pen of either Greek or Russian authors turns out to be a
rather gloomy one.

It is a sad ideal of family life which is offered by the
Izmaragd. Despite all the injunctions to charity toward
one's "own folk" only the less privileged, the servants and
poor relatives seem to benefit from them. Wife and children
live under the law of fear, not that of love.

The home with which the *Izmaragd* deals is that of a rich
or well-to-do man. It is in this social class that the *Izmaragd*
expects to find its readers. This explains adequately the over-
emphasis of the dangers of wealth. But the same warnings, in
their radicalism, give evidence that the *Izmaragd* is free
from the temptations of upper-class ethics, either aristocratic
or bourgeois. A certain idealization of poverty can be seen in
the image of Christ as beggar.[109] On the other hand, beggar-
liness or pious idleness is not the ideal. In the second version
of *Izmaragd* very strong warnings are directed against idleness and laziness. Here labor, especially manual labor, is
invested with a religious value and is even set on the same
level as monastic renunciation.

God promised workers health from their working, salvation from
their toiling . . . If you shun earthly toiling you will not find
celestial goods. The earthly worker resembles the monks of the
desert in their life and work. For he goes out early for the work in
the fields, shaking off his sleep; he likes deserts [fields] more than
his home and resists heat and cold with his hard labors . . . Feeding the poor and giving alms to the needy from the fruits of his
labors he gives to Christ himself. Laziness is the mother of all ill
deeds . . . If God cared for the lazy he would make the untilled

---

[109] *Izmaragd* II, ch. 158 (cf. note 68). Compare ch. 43 of the "Life of
St. Niphon," one of the sources of Izmaragd.

fields grow the wheat and the forest bring forth all kinds of vegetables . . . But every lazy man will wear poor and ragged garb.

Then follow the enumeration of the callings, which are pure
and pleasing to God:

> Some people apply themselves to agriculture, others tend cattle
> in fields and, giving money to God therefrom, are saved. Others cut
> hay and breed lambs, feed and clothe the poor and infirm. Still others
> navigate by sea and ride by land, engaging in commerce . . . And
> you, women, set your elbows to work and your hands to the spindle,
> and give alms therefrom.[110]

It is easy to observe from this selection, that, of all callings, manual work and particularly that of the peasant is the
most pleasing to God. This is also proved by a legend which
comes from the Russian city of Murom.[111] Once upon a time
there was a terrible drought in Murom. As the prayers of
the clergy and citizens were of no avail the bishop heard
at last a revelation from heaven telling him that prayers
would be accepted from the first stranger to enter the city.
This person turned out to be an old woodcutter with a fagot
on his shoulders. A heavy downpour immediately followed
his prayers. To the inquiries of the bishop into his private
life the old man explained: "I am a sinner, and I have never
had any quiet in my life with which to comfort my soul."
Every day he cut and sold wood; he often starved but did
not ask for alms; instead he gave them. "I did not eat at
the expense of the others." [112]

We should note that in all these instances alms are men-

---

[110] *Izmaragd* II, ch. 48. Printed in Arkhangelski, IV, 44.

[111] This legend is taken from the "Life of St. Niphon," ch. 76. The Slavonic
word "Murin" (Moor or Ethiopian) designating the hero's nationality became the name of a Russian city in the *Izmaragd*. As cited in our note 33
the *Vita Nephontis* was published by Rystenko in 1928. In the version printed
by Kostomarov we still read the correct meaning: "In the Moorish province."

[112] *Izmaragd* II, ch. 102. Printed in Kostomarov, ed., *Pamyatniki*, I, 78.

tioned as an inevitable or, at least, as a normally prescribed means of salvation. There is no degree of destitution which dispenses one from active charity. To live as a beggar is not considered as a religious ideal as it is in a purely kenotic ethical outlook. Nevertheless, poverty, in a working state, is regarded as a more blessed social standing than wealth. Commerce is not excluded from the works of salvation under its aspect of toil. Among the positively prohibited professions are listed those of tavern-keepers and usurers. Later we shall find musicians and jugglers in the same proscribed company. The closing of taverns was considered in a program of social reforms drafted by a saint, Cyril of Belozersk, for his prince. As for usury it was not easy to condemn it flatly because interest was inherent in the commercial exchange. The prohibition of interest is found in many canonical and literary documents, as in the Shchilo legend. But sometimes it is modified by permitting the fixing of a moderate interest. Thus, in an article of the *Izmaragd,* one reads: "Let us get rid of usury . . . But take six rezons for one grivna lest you may not be condemned." [113] Considering the value of money at that time[114] the above prescription fixes six percent as normal interest on a loan.[115]

With a slight secondary emphasis on active work the whole social ethics of the *Izmaragd* is reduced to charity while the second and the dark hemisphere of Russian religion is determined by fear. In the border region between charity and fear, the field of humility, the central Russian virtue is liable to various interpretations. The religious mean-

---

[113] *Izmaragd* II, ch. 127. Printed in *Pravoslavnyi Sobesednik,* 1859, p. 132.

[114] Compare Sreznevski, ed., *Svedeniya,* in *SORYaS,* vol. XII, St. Petersburg, 1875, sec. 57, pp. 307–308, where 7 rezons (7 percent) is held to be the norm.

[115] In a prologue of the thirteenth century there is a sermon against usury. *Ibid.,* sec. 41, pp. 25–26.

ing of humility is ambiguous, since it can represent an expression of the kenotic following of Christ as well as a fear of God.[116] It is significant that the chapters of the *Izmaragd* dealing with humility are pervaded with an unequivocal kenotic spirit.

The Lenten period, the most significant part of the Orthodox calendar, opens with the Sunday of the Publican and the Pharisee. A sermon recommended for reading on this day was taken from Chrysostom and, because of its position in the Church year, was, perhaps, the best known sermon in ancient Russia. The Collection known as *Zlatoust* begins with it. The author uses the following allegory:

There were two charioteers, the publican and the pharisee. The pharisee had harnessed two horses in order to reach eternal life, one horse of virtue and prayer, fasting, alms-giving, the other horse of pride, boasting, damning. And pride knocked against the virtues and the chariot of law was broken and the vain driver was killed.[117]

Another chapter of *Izmaragd* offers a whole series of images taken from horticulture. Proud virtue is "a garden spoiled by dry branches . . . As the weight of fruit breaks branches pride destroys a virtuous soul . . . A proud man is like a tree which has no roots and soon falls." The implication is purely caritative:

Thou art a creature of God, do not deny thy Creator; consider thy nature and look at thy kindred, who are of the same nature, and do not repudiate thy race for pride . . . If thou art rich and he is poor, he is higher before God.[118]

Here God in his greatness does not shrink man into

---

[116] Fedotov, *RRM,* I, 210.

[117] *Izmaragd* I, ch. 17. Printed by D. V. Petukhov, "Drevniya poucheniya na voskresnye dni velikago posta" (Ancient Instructions for the Sundays of Great Lent), in *SORYaS,* vol. XL, St. Petersburg, 1886.

[118] *Izmaragd* I, ch. 14. Printed in Ponomarev, ed., *Pamyatniki,* vol. I, no. 34.

nothingness — the *phobos* motive of humility. But, elsewhere, another image of God, as a terrible judge before
whom man leads his miserable existence in fear and trembling, is not lacking. The fear of God, as it is reflected in
moral medieval codes, did not originate in love or in a vision
of God's purity and perfection as contrasted with man's unworthiness. The medieval fear is of a simpler, more egotistic
kind; it is a fear of punishment — unspeakably horrid and
eternal punishment. This explains why one of the first
chapters of the *Izmaragd,* which sets fear as the basis of all
virtue, is followed by one that castigates, with extreme
severity, those who doubt the tortures of hell.

> What pains are not worthy of those who say there are no tor-
> ments for sinners . . . Some ignorant people tell us that God is lov-
> ing of mankind and will not torture sinners . . . If the wicked are
> not tormented this means that the good are not crowned.[119]

We are eager to know whether these doubters who trusted
overmuch in God's mercy were to be found in Russia or in
Greece, whence the sermon originates. The fragment is borrowed, indeed, from Nicon's *Pandectae* (ch. 32) and in
Slavonic translation we find the incriminating ideas: "I have
heard lovers of sin who say that Christ threatens with pains
only to intimidate." The absence of these words in the Greek
original is tempting; but the compiler may have drawn them
from another source or from another version of the same
Nicon.[120] Our question is still not answered.

What we see clearly is that hell is presented as a moral
postulate, as justice epitomized, without which paradise
would be impossible because it would be unjust. The second
version of *Izmaragd* develops the thought of the imaginary
injustice done to the saints: "Tell me, why have they toiled

---

[119] *Izmaragd* I, ch. 9 (from St. John Chrysostom). Printed in Arkhangelski, IV, 134.

[120] The Greek text of Nicon is not yet published.

in this world; some being tortured and murdered and variously oppressed, others having mortified themselves, their bodies with fasting, vigils and a hard life?"

The author does not desire God's mercy for sinners because he does not believe in gratuitous salvation. Everything happens according to moral law. In what then does the redemptive work of Christ consist? Is he our real Savior? The fact that the author poses this question in connection with the torments of hell is evidence of the sharpness of his mind. Yet, the answer he gives seems to destroy the very basis of Christian faith: "Our Lord Jesus Christ, seeing us perishing in evil, descended from heaven to earth for this reason: 'If I,' he said, 'did not come and tell them so, they would not have had sin, and now they have no excuse for their sin.' For all is known to us, and if we fulfill God's precept we shall be saved; if not, condemned." [121] If this statement is to be taken literally, Christ is not the Savior but the lawgiver and judge, and his law is more severe and harder to fulfill than the law of the Old Testament. It is in its perfection that the ambiguous advantage of the New Testament lies. Here we are far from the "merciful Lord" of kenotic Christianity. But both are broken fragments from the same mosaic.

The fear of God, or Christ, manifests itself in eschatological visions which give a deep perspective to human life. Beginning with the most removed and terrifying horizon they range as follows: hell, the Last Judgment, the horrors of the last day, individual death and its afterpains, the precursors of death in human life.

The torments of hell are not depicted in detail with specifications for singular sins as they are on the walls of medieval churches. But their terror and even practical universality are reflected in this report to lighthearted optimists: "There are many 'self-judgers' [presuming the judgment

---

[121] *Izmaragd* II, ch. 27.

of God] who deceive themselves; when they hear of the Judgment and torments they laugh and say: 'Am I worse than everyone else? Let me only enjoy the pleasures of this life; as all people do so do I.'" When the Judgment comes "this self-judger will be dragged by cruel angels to the place of torment and, seeing it, will shudder and beat his face with his hands; looking here and there, he will think of fleeing, but have nowhere to flee being held strongly by the angels. And the angels holding him will say unto him: 'Why dost thou thrash about, why fear, o miserable one, why tremble, strange man? thou hast thyself prepared this place for thee; reap what thou hast sown . . . Thou are not alone but *where all people are*.'" [122] The idea underlying this cruel irony is that hell is not an unusual place for grievous sinners but the lot of the common man.

For the Last Judgment it was Ephrem the Syrian, the preacher of repentance, who contributed most of its gloomy colors. It belongs to the common fund of Christian myth: the cosmic cataclysm, the trumpets, the throne of the Judge, the river of fire before it, and the opened books. One feature must have seemed particularly bitter given the Russian feeling of blood kinship: "Nobody will help there; neither father his son, nor mother her daughter, nor one brother another, but every one will bear his own burden waiting for condemnation." [123]

The end of the world is to be preceded by times of utmost social and cosmic corruption. In a sermon of Pseudo-Ephrem the stress is placed on ecclesiastical decadence. He predicts "invasions of the heathen, the turmoil of the people, disorder in churches, misconduct of priests; they will serve only their flesh and not take care of things spiritual; the abbots likewise; the monks will be covetous of banquets and lawsuits,

---

[122] *Izmaragd* I, ch. 36. Printed in Arkhangelski, II, 107.
[123] *Izmaragd* I, ch. 28. Printed in Arkhangelski, III, 89.

irritable and living far from their holy father's rule; the prelates will fear the persons of the great, take bribes in courts, do wrong to orphans, fail to protect widows and the poor. Unbelief and fornication will dwell among men . . ." and so forth. If this piece of prophecy is the work of a Russian author we are entitled to see in it a kind of satire against ecclesiastics.

However, the "last times" is not an image but a terrible reality for the author who is serious in his warning: "O brothers, let us fear for all that is written is being fulfilled and all predicted signs are coming true; little remains yet of our life and age." [124] Still more gloomy and terrifying is the prospect offered by the apocryphal "Prophecy of Isaiah on the Last Days." Here social perversion is depicted on a larger scale, and laymen come into their own right:

Truth has perished and lies covered by the earth . . . Children insult their parents, fathers begin to abominate their children, brother will hate his brother . . . and mother will give away her daughter to fornication . . . their teachers will be hypocritical drunkards and monks possessed by the devil and foul-mouthed, their princes pitiless and their judges uprighteous . . . orphans and widows will cry having no protector . . . the woman will pursue the man for marriage and not the man the woman.

This is the limit of moral perversion. Thus far men have been agents of their own calamities. But here is introduced an offended God, who punishes social disasters with cosmic ones. Mother Earth will now suffer together with her children. It is God Himself who speaks:

For I will make the sky as of brass and the earth as of iron. And the sky will not give its dew nor the earth its fruits . . . and your plowers will not sing in the fields nor will the ox bear the yoke on its neck, and you will not find grain in your fields . . . And I will send upon you swarms of flies; they will eat your flesh

---

[124] *Izmaragd* II, ch. 142. Printed in *Pravoslavnyi Sobesednik*, 1858, p. 475 and Arkhangelski, III, 116.

and drink the blood of your children and lacerate the eyes of your
infants . . . And then there will be no laughter nor tale-telling
among you nor any devilish amusements, there will be no swift
steeds, nor fine garments, and you will fall down in death-throes, a
brother embracing his brother, and the child will die on the knees
of its mother . . . and from the sound of your cries the earth will
shake, the sun be darkened, and the moon change in blood . . .
Earth will cry as a beautiful maid . . . and then the Antichrist
will come.[125]

The prophesy of Pseudo-Isaiah belongs to the group of
Apocrypha which are better known in the Christian West as
well as in the East as the "Epistle on Sunday." In this
Epistle, fallen from heaven, Christ writes in his own hand all
the terrible threats for man's sins together with some particular injunctions as a means of averting God's wrath. The
veneration of the Sabbath Day (Sunday) is the most common of these precepts. In the Isaiah version there is no question of averting the unavoidable. The last day is coming.

Apocalyptic expectations, common to the Middle Ages
were especially vivid in Russia immediately after the Tatar
invasion (1240), and at the end of the fifteenth century. At
the later date there were no social or political reasons for
pessimism, but the approach of the seven thousandth year
of creation (1492) produced an effect similar to that of the
year 1000 in the West.

Individual death with all its horrors, among which the
posthumous trials of the soul and the strife between angels
and demons are the most terrifying, is the main object of
the long apocryphal "Sermon on the Heavenly Powers,"
or, as it is titled in the *Izmaragd*, "On the Departure of the
Soul." It was composed in the Kievan period by a Russian

---

[125] *Izmaragd* II, ch. 162. Printed in I. Porfiriev, "Apokrificheskie skazaniya
o novozavetnykh litsakh i sobytiyakh po rukopisi solovetskoi biblioteki"
(Apocryphal Legends about New Testament People and Events According
to a Manuscript of the Solovetski Library), in *SORYaS*, vol. XLVIII, St.
Petersburg, 1890, sec. 2, p. 4.

author, inspired by the Greek Life of St. Basil the Younger
and by Ephrem the Syrian.[126] Some elements of this picture
occur in an excerpt of the popular "Life of St. John the
Merciful"; here demons detain in the air a soul trying to
rise to heaven, and, "if they make certain that it performs
their will they do not allow this poor soul to go further." [127]
In another excerpt of Greek provenance we find an interesting and rather rationalistic idea that "the very passions and
desires which a man indulged in during his life transform
themselves into evil demons and, having cruelly fettered
the poor soul of a sinner, will lead it, crying and sobbing
bitterly, to a dark and fetid place where sinners are kept in
expectation of the Day of Judgment." [128]

The painful crisis of the parting of soul and body is
described allegorically in a parable or a riddle of Oriental
savor:

What does it mean: When the land will be devastated and the
king succumb? . . . The land devastated signifies the infirm body;
the king succumbing signifies reason taken away; the strong ones will
disperse — thoughts will perish; then the city of stone will be destroyed, that is, the bones of man; the wells will be dried up, that is,
tears will not flow from the eyes . . . Then the queen will leave
her throne as a dove its nest; that means, the soul will leave the
body of man.[129]

It may seem that the dramatizing of death and the
emphasis on the prospect of future pain would justify the
most wild lamentations over the dead. Yet, on this point, the
ecclesiastical ban is absolute. Revulsion at popular heathen
rites of violent lamentation over the dead played, perhaps,
the main part in Russian prohibitions. This indigenous

---

[126] *Izmaragd* I, ch. 12. Printed among the works of St. Cyril of Turov.
For a detailed analysis see Fedotov, *RRM*, I, 169 ff.

[127] *Izmaragd* I, ch. 58 (and II, ch. 11). Printed in Arkhangelski, IV, 111.

[128] *Izmaragd* II, ch. 96. Printed in Arkhangelski, IV, 50.

[129] *Izmaragd* II, ch. 99. This excerpt recalls Ecclesiasticus 12.

motive was strengthened by the injunctions of the early
Church Fathers, who were motivated, however, by Christian
hope and the longing for reunion with Christ. These motives
were completely foreign to the medieval mind. "We faithful must not imitate the infidel, tear our garments — beat
our breasts as the heathen does." [130] In another fragment the
heathens are replaced by the Sadducees, probably because of
the latter's disbelief in resurrection: "You, brothers and
sisters, do not imitate the customs of the Sadducees who are
taught these lamentations by the devil. He teaches some to
stab themselves, others to strangle or drown themselves in
water. Not only the heathen but many Christians do likewise. Some perish in despair, others become possessed by the
devil amid laments, others fall into heresies." [131] A third
author limits and humanizes, with good common sense, the
absolute ban on lamentations: "I do not teach you, man, not
to weep over the departed. But I prohibit you from weeping
and lamenting for many days, as do the infidels, lacerating
their faces and tearing their hair." [132] On this point all the
efforts of medieval preachers were to no avail. Ritual lament
remained forever a necessary element in the Russian peasant
funeral, with artistic improvisations which represent by no
means the least valuable branch of Russian folklore. [133]
Success was obtained with regard to laments over infants.
The reason is obvious: "For us death is a woe; for the infant,
repose and salvation. For what must they answer having par-
taken of no sin." [134]

The belief in the sinlessness of infants (up to seven years)

---

[130] *Izmaragd* II, ch. 83.

[131] *Izmaragd* I, ch. 13.

[132] *Izmaragd* II, ch. 70.

[133] Compare E. V. Barsov, ed., *Prichitaniya severnago kraya* (Lamentations of the Northern Region), vol. I, Moscow, 1872; and Elsa Mahler, *Die
russische Totenklage, ihre Rituelle und dichterische Deutung* (*mit besonderer
Berücksichtigung des grossrussischen Nordens*), Leipzig, 1935.

[134] *Izmaragd* I, ch. 13 (and II, ch. 83).

was always shared by the Russian people. After premature death infants become angels, and the only thing which can trouble their bliss are the tears that their mothers shed on earth.

While restraining exaggerated expressions of grief on the occasion of death, the Church insisted upon constant meditation on death as a means of moral education through fear. We find a very witty saying in the *Izmaragd* in this connection: "If there were no death we should eat one another; if we did not expect the Judge we should not hope for salvation." [135] If one of the lessons of death was the fear of retribution after earthly life the other was the deprecation of earthly goods which obstruct salvation. Some of these macabre meditations, which lack any Christian connotation, remind one of the Greek pagan moralists, who reached the Russian reader through the medium of the Church Fathers.

Examine, lords and judges, and dread God, you merciless and hardhearted. Come and see how we are being disintegrated, look into coffins and see one who was once a king or a prince . . . guess who was king or prince, who a general or soldier, who rich or poor . . . who a Jew or an Ethiopian. How can you recognize anyone or his bones; is not all dust and ashes and earth?

The nihilistic savor of this piece of rhetoric is, certainly, illusory. There is a terrible discrimination after death, not in bones but in souls. A thin line, a balance of the moral accent, divides posthumous bliss from damnation. Sacramental penance, with the absolution of sins on the deathbed, can shift this balance to the active side. On the contrary, death without penance, an unexpected or violent death implies an increased chance of damnation. This explains the popular belief of the Russian people in the damnation or, at least, a dangerous posthumous state for the drowned, or, in general, of the unknown whose corpses are found on highways. At one

---
[135] *Ibid.*

time all such corpses were held unworthy of a common
Christian burial but were laid at certain places in large open
pits until, once a year, a priest said funeral prayers over them
and the common grave was shut. These common graves,
located near a chapel, were called "God's houses" in old
Russia. The Church thus made a concession to the popular
prejudice which was in agreement with its own emphasis on
sacramental death rites.[136]

In the face of these facts one is able to appreciate at its
real value the attitude of the *Izmaragd* that dedicates three
chapters in the second version to the problem of sudden
death. At first it protests against the opinion that such an end
is in itself a sign of sin. To those who declare that the dead
man "received according to his deeds," it is retorted: "If
everybody received according to his deeds all the world
would perish miserably."[137]

Other people, more humane but skeptical, refuse to see
an act of Providence (God's judgment) in tragic death, for
example, in the death of a hundred-thousand warriors on a
battle field. They are admonished that "nobody can see by
what judgment God does such things, because even a righteous man sometimes ends in violent death for certain little
transgressions in order that he may, purified, enter into joy;
and the sinners receive relief from pain through violent
death."[138]

If violent death has a purifying, sacrificial meaning, it
can be a way to holiness. We know, indeed, that violent
death, after the pattern of St. Boris and St. Gleb, was the
reason for the canonization of many Russian saints.[139] On
the other hand, death without sacramental penitence remained

---

[136] E. E. Golubinski, *Istoriya russkoi tserkvi* (History of the Russian
Church), 4 vols., Moscow, 1880–1917, I, 459.

[137] *Izmaragd* II, ch. 82. Compare *PG,* vol. 86, col. 349.

[138] *Izmaragd* II, ch. 113

[139] Fedotov, *RRM,* I, 104–110.

an object of horror. Thus, people remained in a state of
uncertainty before these riddles of Providence. In the sixteenth century a peasant boy, killed by lightning, was canonized as a saint. However, before this his body was laid in
the forest, outside the churchyard, as a supposed victim of
God's wrath. Only miracles performed at his grave decided
his destiny.[140] Saint or damned, it can hardly be a common
man whom God's arrows strike.

The fear of thunderstorm is supposed to be natural and is
justified in the *Izmaragd,* which makes it the paradigm of
death or the Last Judgment. "Even now many times when
lightning and great thunder come are we all not frightened
and do we not fall down cowering; how then, brothers, shall
we endure it when we hear the sound of the trumpet?"[141]

The fear of other natural dangers is inculcated as pious
cautiousness which alone discriminates a martyr from the
suicide in the case of violent death. Here *Izmaragd,* or its
source, reasons in the fashion of moral casuistry: "If a man
leaves his house in winter in bitter cold and is frozen on the
way, he dies a suicide's death; but if somebody goes out in
a mild weather and on the way is overtaken by a disaster and
has nowhere to find shelter, he dies a martyr's death." The
same rule is to be observed in crossing a river. "If someone,
confident in crossing it by his own daring falls into trouble
and dies, do not bring such a one into the church, he is not
worthy, because he is a 'suicide.' Even so he who goes along
a dangerous road and is killed by brigands."[142]

It is easy to see that here the doctrine of fear goes so far
that it substitutes for the fear of God quite different kinds of

---

[140] St. Artemi Verkolski. Compare Fedotov, *Svyatye drevnei Rusi: X–XVII
st.,* Paris: YMCA Press, 1931, p. 221, and E. E. Golubinski, *Istoriya kanonizatsii svyatykh v russkoi tserkvi* (The History of the Canonization of
Saints in the Russian Church), Moscow, 1894.

[141] *Izmaragd* I, ch. 30 (from Ephrem the Syrian).

[142] *Izmaragd* II, ch. 82.

fear. In the Byzantine Pseudo-Gennadius "Hundred Chapters" the fear of God degenerates into the fear of men.[143] In the Russian *Izmaragd* it becomes the fear of nature. Even the abjectness of the physical posture pictured in connection with a thunderstorm does not repel. Cowardice becomes a Christian virtue; audacity is a grievous sin. Let us consider that, among all professional types of conduct, the *Izmaragd* passes over in silence the calling of warrior. The omission cannot be accidental. Neither the ethics of fear nor that of charity provides a basis for military virtues. This is a Byzantine system of values which gradually undermined the morale of Russian society and was to yield its full fruits in the age of Muscovy.

If a sudden death deprives man of the means of repentance, a long illness, on the contrary, can be an excellent preparation for a pious death. "Who endures illnesses here . . . will not be condemned in the next world . . . The Lord chastises whomever he loves." Illness, then, may be a sign of a particular grace of God and of personal righteousness.

When a man falls into a grave disease that tears the corpulence of flesh and destroys its beauty he does not care for anything except death; remembers his evil sins continuously, sighing and repenting; distributes his possessions to churches and the poor; gives freedom to his slaves; confesses everything from all his heart and becomes worthy of the Holy Communion; destroys sin and dies in righteousness. And he who is not ailing remembers none of these things . . . death will seize him unprepared and he will be dragged away with violence.[144]

From this ascetic point of view, which sees in illness a positive value, to seek help in medicine is a sin. "The men of our time, when in illness, abandon God and invite magi-

---

[143] Fedotov, *RRM*, I, 207–208.
[144] *Izmaragd* I, ch. 2 (and II, ch. 28). Compare *PG*, vol. 86, col. 332.

cians (*volkhvy*), physicians and wizards." The preacher makes no distinction between wizard and physician. "What are you doing, o man, resorting to men who cannot help themselves!" [145]

Of equal value with illness are all kinds of misfortunes that God may send to try, to purify, and to teach humility. But that is a commonplace among moralists. "Sorrows and pains make the sufferers glorious, as gold in fire becomes still brighter." [146] Another theory ascribes the origin of sorrows to the devil, rather than to God. The meaning of trial and the moral lesson remain the same. "Upon those who fear God the devil sends many sorrows. So thieves steal not where sticks and straws lie but they watch the whole night without sleep where a treasure is hidden . . . Defeat the devil by thanking God in distress." [147]

Distress and illness, ceaseless meditations on death, sustain man in a state of contrition favorable to repentance. Repentance is, indeed, the main fruit of this training in fear. Most of the fragments on the Last Judgment, attributed to St. Ephrem are entitled "On Repentance." Under this notion both the individual act of conscience and the sacrament of penance are understood. The lack of a dividing line between the personal and the sacramental is, perhaps, the most interesting feature of the *Izmaragd*. The moral preoccupation is obvious. The real aim of repentance is the change of life. "If you were a drunkard yesterday, be now a faster; did you yesterday fornicate with other people's wives, abstain now from your own; did you yesterday rob others' goods, distribute now your own in alms . . . this is true repentance which pleases God." The failure to change one's life must not, however, discourage: "Some people who often repent

[145] *Ibid.*
[146] *Izmaragd* II, ch. 74. Compare chs. 73 and 75.
[147] *Izmaragd* II, ch. 75.

their sins and commit them again fall into despair believing
that they have lost the fruit of all their labor . . ." [148]

They must repent again and again. But the vow to reform one's life is essential. That is why the problem arises as
to whether deathbed repentance is effectual. The *Izmaragd*
assures us that the negative opinion was not uncommon.
"Many say by the instigation of the devil that if one repents
before death, like an ox standing before the ax it is unworthy
to accept his repentance" (obviously, in the sacramental
way, that is, to give him absolution). The author finds this
reasoning "heretical." A priest acting on this premise "will be
anathematized by Jesus Christ himself." [149] This answer as
well as the "heretical" opinion are Russian. A translated
chapter concerning the same situation makes a distinction. If
one takes a vow not to sin and dies before reforming his life,
he is saved. But the same author is not so sure of the salvation
of a robber who is executed after his repentance. The author
is certain only that that sin is pardoned for which the robber
is punished; this solution contradicts both the Gospel and
Russian ethical sentiments. [150]

A transitional form from personal repentance to ecclesiastical penance is represented by several stories from the
ancient patericons which deal with monastic confession before
an elder or a congregation with these lessons: "Do not be
ashamed, o man, to confess thy sins"; or "we conceal our
sins to the joy of Satan." [151]

In the case of sacramental confession the *epitimia*, that is,
a penance imposed by the priest, is the necessary condition of
absolution. This is not meant in the sense of moral guidance

---

[148] *Izmaragd* II, ch. 77 (from Pseudo-Athanasius). Printed in Arkhangelski, IV, 71.

[149] *Izmaragd* I, ch. 73.

[150] *Izmaragd* II, ch. 78 (from Pseudo-Athanasius). Printed in Arkhangelski, IV, 71.

[151] *Izmaragd* II, ch. 136.

or of an additional exercise. No repentance without penance is the rule. The omission brings both the priest and the penitent to the very edge of perdition. "If one confesses his sins to his spiritual father, and the latter gives him no *epitimia* . . . he commits his soul to cruel torments and the insoluble bonds await both of them on the day of the terrible Judgment." The same article enjoins priests to conform in the imposition of penance with the "penitential" contained in the *Nomocanons* (books of canon law), and "not to act after your own sense lest you may destroy many souls through your ignorance." Undoubtedly this was the rule in the Russian Middle Ages although we know of an ancient penitential instruction under the title "Preface to Repentance" which is based on the complete discretion of the spiritual father.[152]

The Church has established fast days as special periods for exterior forms of repentance. Fasting is considered in the *Izmaragd* in connection with repentance. There is no attempt to discover its cathartic meaning as the purification of the sensual nature for the development of the spiritual. Fasting is penance, self-oppression, voluntary suffering. While insisting on this meaning the *Izmaragd* is eager to enlarge its moral content, to warn against a narrow and exterior conception of fasting as abstinence from food. As most instructions of the *Izmaragd*, those on fasting are dialectical. They begin, in the first version, with prophetic warnings following Isaiah and Chrysostom: "What profit is it for man to hunger with the flesh and die by his deeds? . . . What use is it not to wash oneself and then not to clothe the naked . . . what virtue is it to pray through the whole night in a warm house and let the poor die on the streets of starvation, barefoot and naked?" . . . Here it is charity which counterbalances fasting or, rather, makes fasting perfect. But "reasonable" fasting is also enlarged in an ascetic sense: "Fasting is not

---

[152] Fedotov, *RRM,* I, 241–244.

the abstinence from food but from the passions of flesh." A series of witty comparisons drives home the preacher's thought: "If you abstain from bread, but not from anger, you are not a man but a beast, for the beast does not eat bread but eats flesh and is full of malice . . . If you sleep on bare earth but nourish evil thoughts against your friend, you are not better than cattle; for cattle have no need of beds." [153]

On the other hand, the *Izmaragd* repudiates the objections of the adversaries of fasting who say: "Why hunger for those who live in purity?" The answer is also given in a comparison: "If medicaments are necessary for a physical wound, how much more for a spiritual one." It is true that the pharisee fasted in vain and the publican without fasting "received the fruit of virtue." But this is not the rule. "The Ninevites fasted and received grace from God . . ." We must "be accustomed to the laws of fasting." "Let not only your mouth fast but also your eyes, ears, and tongue, hands and feet and all your limbs; that is a fast pleasing to God." [154]

A positive justification for fasting is given, which is very sober and reasonable. According to St. Basil: "A good man with a little food will get rid of his illness as of a cruel cold . . . Fasting is the mother of health, the instructor of youth, the decorum of old age . . . Nobody's head aches· who drinks water." [155] In spite of the soundness of these counsels, the physical effect alone is considered here.

In many chapters practical issues are discussed in connection with the ecclesiastical periods of fasting. Besides Lent, two great fasts are mentioned, St. Peter's, before his and St. Paul's day, the 29th of June, and St. Philip's, before Christmas. They are called together "three luminaries created by

---

[153] *Izmaragd* I, ch. 31 (and II, chs. 6 and 117).
[154] *Izmaragd* I, ch. 32 (and II, chs. 115 and 116).
[155] *Izmaragd* II, ch. 107.

God for the enlightenment of infidel souls and the remission of sins." [156] We are told that "many people in Lent observe only the first, or St. Theodore's week, and neglect the others by reasons of sloth." [157] There are no detailed regulations on food, but the rule is mentioned that one should eat only once a day during Lent (except on Saturdays and Sundays). Three-hundred daily prostrations are also required.[158]

The Eastern Church observes two weekly fast days, Wednesday and Friday. With regard to these sacred days some legends sprang up early in the Greek Church, which belong to the realm of popular mythology. The Russian people, craving for mythological Apocryphas, eagerly adopted them. The *Izmaragd*, which in general does not favor apocryphal stories, meets this popular need in the interest of the rules of fasting. The three anecdotes, or rather, two with one variant, are sanctified by the great name of St. Pachomius. An angel appears to the saint, slays a lamb before him, and sheds its blood, which turns into milk. "Tell the people," says the angel, "what thou hast seen; they partake of milk and eggs on Wednesday and Friday, but in truth it is curdled blood." The second story tells that Pachomius encountered a funeral procession and saw two angels following the coffin. Answering his silent amazement the angels explained: "One of us is Wednesday and the other Friday. Because this man, up to the day of his death,

---

[156] *Izmaragd* II, ch. 124. The failure to mention the fourth great period of fasting in the Orthodox Church, which precedes the Feast of the Dormition of Our Lady (usually called the Feast of the Assumption in the West) from August 1–15 is helpful in dating the second version of the *Izmaragd*. The introduction of this fourth period of fasting coincided with the reception of the new Church "order" of Jerusalem by the Metropolitan Cyprian (1390–1406). This fixes the date of *Izmaragd* II at about 1400 contrary to the estimate of Yakovlev and others who date it at the end of the fifteenth century. J. M.

[157] *Izmaragd* II, ch. 154.

[158] *Izmaragd* I, ch. 77 (and II, ch. 154). Printed in *Pravoslavnyi Sobesednik*, 1859, p. 141.

honored us with fasting, abstinence, and alms, we now are accompanying him . . ."[159] A voice from heaven to St. James confirms fasting: "Blessed is the man who keeps it and when he departs from this temporary life, two angels, Wednesday and Friday, meet him and greet him with joy."[160] In the third version it is said: "If a man does not eat either cheese or milk or eggs on Wednesday and Friday, but only vegetables of the earth, when an angel comes to take his soul he leads it to the third heaven; the angel of Wednesday (the third day) meets him and says: 'Rejoice, soul, thou hast suffered much on earth for my sake,'" and they lead it to the fifth heaven where the angel Friday meets it with the same greeting. Those who neglected strict fasting on these days are punished terribly; they are crucified.[161]

One has the impression that these stories included in the *Izmaragd* do not fit in well with its moralizing doctrine on fasting.[162] However, they were accepted warmly by the Russian people who repeated them in folk-tales and songs in many variants.[163]

The mythology of the weekdays diverted attention from the main subject of fasting, repentance, and fear. Abstinence

---

[159] The first known version of this legend is the story in the Patericon of Mount Sinai. Chapter 303 of the ancient Slavic translation is missing in the printed Greek original. The Slavonic text is printed in Sreznevski, ed., *Svedeniya*, in *SORYaS*, vol. XX, St. Petersburg, 1800, no. 4, p. 81. Compare A. D. Karneev, "Veroyatny Istochnik 'Slova o Srede i Pyatke'" (The Probable Source of the 'Sermon about Wednesday and Friday'), *ZhMNP*, September 1891, pp. 160–175.

[160] *Izmaragd* II, ch. 120. Printed in *Pravoslavnyi Sobesednik*, 1859, p. 183.

[161] *Izmaragd* I, ch. 70.

[162] Yakovlev, *ZNU*, vol. 60, pp. 124–125; Karneev, pp. 160 ff. Compare I. Porfiriev, "Pochitanie sredy i pyatnitsy v drevnem russkom narode" (The Veneration of Wednesday and Friday by the Ancient Russian People), *Pravoslavnyi Sobesednik*, February 1855, p. 183.

[163] Porfiriev, pp. 181–198, and A. N. Veselovski, "Opyty po istorii razvitiya khristianskoi legendy" (Essays on the History of the Development of the Christian Legend), in *ZhMNP*, February 1877, pp. 186–252.

and a certain degree of asceticism are not limited to definite days on the calendar. A group of moral precepts in the *Izmaragd* is inspired by an ascetic spirit, of a rather negative character, which seems to proceed from fear. It is the ethic of self-restraint, directed primarily against the expression of the sensual instincts. One should expect to find, in this category, prohibitions against gluttony, drunkenness, and lust. To our amazement we find no mention of gluttony in either version and no chapter on sexual sins in the first version of the *Izmaragd*. In the second version fornication is mentioned occasionally as a sin while virginity is the highest moral state, but the whole weight of condemnation is aimed at adultery. Yet, adultery is not merely a sensual, but also a social sin, and its censure does not imply any ascetic tendency.

The following statement is but a commonplace: "Marriage is the law of God and fornication a cursed iniquity. These are the three states of human life: virginity, marriage, fornication. Virginity is glorious and angellike and Christ himself is the praise of virginity; marriage is less high, though without sin; . . . but fornication ruins many souls and leads to eternal torments." The attitude toward virginity is rather cautious, as is natural in a book destined for laymen: "Those who wish to keep virginity have to restrain from sin not only their body but also their thoughts; if someone burns in his imagination it is better for him to marry according to the law . . . And to the married it is forbidden, not by me but by God to separate themselves, wives from husbands or husbands from wives." [164] This practical Pauline injunction is very relevant in the light of much contrary advice in the Lives of ascetic saints (for example, St. Alexis). "If a terrible judgment awaits those

---

[164] *Izmaragd* II, ch. 151 (taken from I Cor. 7, 10). Printed in *Pravoslavnyi Sobesednik*, 1859, p. 453.

fornicating before marriage how much more those who, abandoning their wives, sin with others' wives; these are considered as pagans." The examples of sinners from the Old Testament, among whom the great names of David and Solomon are cited, are not very terrifying. More efficacious, however, and indicative of the preacher's social preoccupation is the warning directed to princes. "This is what we say to princes and lords: 'Do not take wives away from their husbands . . . for they were united by the same law and on the day of Judgment we all shall stand equally before God; do not ravish virgins either, do not insult the poor nor dishonor virgins: For they will cry against you to God.' "[165] Some stories from ancient patericons give examples of marital fidelity rewarded and adultery punished in hell.

The *Izmaragd* is extremely severe in its treatment of widows. As we have seen above, it considers it a matter of duty or decency that the surviving wife take the veil. Even if she remains in the world she is supposed to live a half-monastic life. For both widowers and widows "it is more blessed, after parting, to remain without copulation . . . If a widow is addicted to food and drink she is dead while living . . . If a widow wishes to extol herself and to wear the same garments and ornaments which she wore during her husband's life she should better remarry than fornicate." [166]

Drunkenness remains the main target of ascetic denunciations. They often accompany admonitions concerning quite different subjects, particularly attendance at church services and the observance of Sunday. Never is total ab-

---

[165] *Izmaragd* II, ch. 7. Printed in part in D. N. Dubakin, "Vliyanie Khristianstva na semeinyi byt russkago obshchestva v period do vremeni poyavleniya 'Domostroya' " (The Influence of Christianity upon Family Life in Russian Society prior to the Appearance of the 'Domstroi'), *Khristianskoe Chtenie* (Christian Reading), 1880, I, 311–361, 627–676.

[166] *Izmaragd* II, ch. 87.

stinence recommended. It could not be otherwise in a Catholic Church whose roots are fixed in the Mediterranean world where wine is considered not only a necessary strengthening nourishment but a religious symbol as well. The norm was found in the *Pandectae* of Antiochus: "Blessed are those who drink wisely as though not drinking, that is not up to inebriation. Hesychius said that it becomes him to drink who can hide drunkenness in his belly and retain foul words on his tongue. But if a fool is drunk and does not fornicate even the dead must be amazed . . . Blessed is water, which does not trouble the mind and blessed are the men who drink it." [167] The similarity of wine to wealth and marriage as tolerated goods is tempting for the modern reader. But wine is not cursed directly as wealth often is, and in this respect it is nearer marriage; although in marriage more often not abuse but transgression, that is, the deviation to the other "state," is condemned. The Russian preacher is very eloquent when he comes to speak on this truly national subject. Sometimes he is solemn and strikes a prophetic tone as in this piece:

How could I be indifferent when I see not only one house but the whole city on fire — not only within the city but even outside men are perishing . . . What is this fire? Tell me, when you are surfeited with wine or mead how do you feel inside? Is it not as if you were burned by fire? . . . I tremble to think how demons exult in you and Satan rejoices and dances . . . Even your children are forced by you into drunkenness . . . If you go to church how can you praise God? A drunken man, belching with stench, is abhorred by God as we abhor a dead and fetid dog. [168]

The few realistic details in this high-pitched oratory give the keynote of other Russian sermons which are very picturesque and sometimes disgusting in their description of

---

[167] *Izmaragd* II, ch. 64.
[168] *Izmaragd* I, ch. 60.

the social effects of drunkenness. The second version of the *Izmaragd* contains one under the title "Of These Who Do Not Get Up for Matins" where drunkenness is considered a main reason for nonattendance.

What do you do in missing, because of drink, the hour of prayer? . . . The Christian custom is first to dine, then to drink, and you, a man sir, spoil the whole day with drinking . . . Even cattle and dumb beasts laugh at us saying "We are without reason but do not act so, and these insatiable men . . . when drinking, pour into their bellies as into a vessel full of holes until they get into a rage from drinking." There are two kinds of drunkenness. The one is praised by many who say: "He is not a drunkard if he, being drunken, falls asleep." But I say: "Even a meek drunkard does evil; when he is drunk he sleeps like a corpse, wallows like a log, is smeared and stinking, and at the hour of Matins lies unable to raise his head . . . As to the pugnacious drunkard he fights and quarrels, insults the godly, still worse, if he has power, he wishes that all should be submitted to his vice; fearing blame, he detests the temperate, loves his like, those who indulge him, seducing him." [169]

Among the sermons against drunkenness there is one, borrowed from Chrysostom, which has a high doctrinal interest. It is a sermon on "avarice and drunkenness" where these two sins are set in opposition:

Many a slave of drunkenness blames the rich and the spoliator . . . But as he serves drunkenness and not God, so too the greedy man can not satiate himself with iniquitous possessions. The greedy man likes much riches and the drunkard much drinking. Greedy eyes are blinded with bribes, a drunkard's eyes are blinded with intoxication. One is deaf and does not hear the cries of the beggars through his avarice, the other's soul is deaf and does not hear the reading of sacred words; both serve the devil and not God. The avaricious man and the drunkard are brother. [170]

Behind the two condemned vices stand two moral principles. Here the ethics of love and that of fear are repre-

---

[169] *Izmaragd* II, ch. 71.
[170] *Izmaragd* I, ch. 34 (and II, ch. 109).

sented in conflict. The compiler is eager not to give either an advantage over the other. If we replace the two rival vices with the modern social categories of bourgeois and Bohemian the lesson will still retain its savor.

The complete absence of sermons on gluttony as contrasted with the abundance of those against drunkenness is a sign that it was not sensuality which was considered the core of sin. In other words purity was not the queen of Russian virtues. Virginity was not esteemed particularly on Russian soil, and even Our Lady was venerated in the aspect of Mother rather than Virgin.[171] As to gluttony, together with drunkenness it became a positively national vice in Muscovy (for the Middle Ages our sources are too few). Gluttony even entered into the complex of national piety, having created a particular threat for the outstanding days in the Church calendar.[172] Fasting had lost its quantitative side as far as the limitation of the amount of food was concerned and only the discrimination of kinds of food remained. One cannot maintain that the rank growth of this vice was the result of an age-long silence on the part of preachers; their fulminations against drunkenness had at all times but slight effect. But the silence itself is highly significant.

Rather than gluttony, the particular target of the preachers was found in all kinds of popular diversions, including music, singing, and dancing. In this regard the Kievan tradition prevailed inexorably.[173] The *Izmaragd* censures these diversions only in connection with Church feasts as a hindrance to their proper Christian observance, but this does not mean that they are tolerated on other days. Here is a picture taken from Russian life:

---

[171] Fedotov, *RRM*, I, 376.

[172] *Izmaragd* I, ch. 49 (and II, ch. 139). Printed in *Pravoslavnyi Sobesednik*, 1859, p. 465.

[173] Fedotov, *RRM*, I, 124, 234–235.

Go on any other days to the places of games and you will find them empty, go on Sunday to the same place and you will find people playing instruments, others dancing, still others clapping their hands, wrestling or provoking one another to evil [probably fist-fighting] . . . Woe to them, they will be condemned to outer darkness together with the devil.[174]

A very popular fragment from the "Life of St. Niphon" is directed against the music of the jongleurs.[175] It begins with a maxim of the saint: "As the sound of a bugle assembles soldiers, thus prayer assembles the angels of God, and flutes, lutes and devilish songs, dancing and hand clapping assemble about them shameless demons." To prove this statement, which is to be taken literally, Niphon recounts the following vision. Once, on the way to church, he met a crowd of demons, led by their prince, Lasion by name,[176] who explained to his satellites the strength and the weakness of the "Nazarenes." Their weakness is precisely the taste for "secular songs." As if to confirm his words there enters "a man, dancing and playing flutes, and after him a crowd of people . . . tied up together with a rope by an Ethiopian [demon] . . . A rich man gave a silver coin to the musician; the latter put it into his purse but the demons taking the coin from the flutist's purse sent it into the abyss to their father, Satan." [177] Thus, even the money paid to musicians goes to the devil.

As for dancing "it is the worst of all evils and especially dear to the devil."

---

[174] *Izmaragd* I, ch. 49.

[175] Cap. 127–128.

[176] The name is spelled differently in Greek and Slavonic manuscripts: Lasion, Alasion, Laxion, Lazarion. Lasios is a conjectural epithet of Dionysius. Compare W. H. Roscher, *Ausführliches Lexicon der Griechischen und Römischen Mythologie,* 6 vols. in 9, Leipzig, 1884–1937, and A. Pauly and G. Wissowa, eds., *Real-Encyclopädie der Klassischen Altertumswissenschaft,* 24 vols., Stuttgart, 1894–1963, *s.v.* Lasios.

[177] *Izmaragd* I, ch. 23. Printed in Kostomarov, ed., *Pamyatniki,* I, 207.

A dancing woman is called the bride of Satan, the devil's mistress, the demon's spouse. Not only she herself will be cast to the bottom of hell but also those who look at her with love and burn with lustful desires for her . . . a dancing woman is the wife of many husbands, through her the devil has seduced many both in dream and in life. It is a sin and a shame even for her husband to copulate with her.[178]

The intransigence of these inhibiting admonitions, which extend through the whole sphere of popular art and folklore, is amazing in view of the mildness of the Russian Church toward the sensual vices. Attempts have been made to explain this ambiguous attitude by pointing to the remnants of paganism reflected in the folklore ritual. Yet the condemners of music make no distinctions.[179] One of the possible explanations is found in the connotations of *phobos* religion. Everything that elates man or fills him with a sense of overwhelming joy removes him from the state of fear. Laughter in general is condemned as sinful, together with singing and all types of diversions. The spirit of Dionysius is cursed in music (spiritual) much more strongly than in wine (sensual) where the Bible and Christian symbolism militated against a Puritan attitude.

We conclude herewith the analysis of the ethical content of the *Izmaragd*. What we have seen is by far its larger portion. Purely religious instruction adds but a few supplementary features to characterize the general trend of the religious mind.

The religion of fear shows a tendency to reduce prayer and the sacramental life to a code of ritual prescriptions. In the *Izmaragd* one finds little preoccupation with the exterior side of religion. It is assumed to be present but it is not in-

---

[178] *Izmaragd* I, ch. 25 (and II, ch. 12).

[179] It is significant that the *Izmaragd* omits a detail found in the "Life of St. Niphon" where the song of singers contained "foul words inspired by the demon."

sisted upon. This will be clear from a consideration of the teaching on prayer.

One of the chapters borrowed from Chrysostom protests against the external formalism of prayer: "You move your lips and bend your knees but your thought flies without . . . it speculates on purchases, gains, loans, fields, estates, profits." True prayer is "spiritual nourishment," it consists in "conversing with God and invoking him with one's sorrowful soul." The preacher is against "long and protracted words" and suggests "short and frequent prayers." He even goes so far as to affirm, citing "Christ through Paul" (?) that "if you protract the word in length you will relax and give the devil a great power over you." The practical counsels are not unlike those of Prince Vladimir Monomakh to his sons and it is possible that they were borrowed from the same source.[180]

When you are outside church, call "Lord have mercy," do not move your lips, speak with your mind, and God will listen to you, even though you be silent. Prayer does not demand a certain place, everywhere prayer is good provided it comes from the soul . . . When you stand before an enraged judge who tortures you, or fall into the hands of soldiers, pray to God, for God is always with you, assisting you.[181]

The instruction on night prayer is composed in the same spirit. The night prayer is a very important feature of ancient Russian devotion since it was really practiced for centuries, from Monomakh to Avvakum.[182] This form of prayer is readily susceptible to ascetic-ritualistic degeneration. But the

---

[180] Fedotov, *RRM*, I, 250.

[181] *Izmaragd* I, ch. 43 (from St. John Chrysostom). Printed in *PG*, vol. 52, col. 458.

[182] Fedotov, *RRM*, I, 250, and G. P. Fedotov, *A Treasury of Russian Spirituality,* New York and London, 1950; Harper Torchbook (TB 303), New York, 1965.

selection incorporated into the *Izmaragd* is sublime in its religious inspiration:

My brothers, night is given to us not for perpetual sleep and idleness. See how manual workers, plowers, and merchants get up at midnight; you too arise as good churchmen do. Go out of your house, see and hear the deep silence without a sound, admire God's creation — at that time your soul is purer and your mind lighter, let the darkness and the silence incline you to repentance. If you look up to the stars you see the sky adorned as with innumerable eyes. Reflect where those are who were so noisy by day, laughing, enjoying themselves, bustling about, busy with vanities, robbing and struggling against innumerable evils. They are not better now than the dead in their sleep. Sleep is the image of death . . . You see all lying as in coffins, and that will help you to awaken your soul and strengthen it through meditations on the vain striving of this world . . .

Let men also and not only women, meditate thus, let your house be as a church made up of husband and wife. If you have children wake them too and have them arise, that your house may be like a church by night . . . If they are very young and cannot overcome sleep, let them get up for one prayer or two, and then put them to bed again, only make certain to get them up, teaching them to act thus.[183]

Whether liturgical prayer was considered a higher form than private or night prayer is difficult to determine. On the one hand there are, especially in the second version of the *Izmaragd,* strict injunctions to attend church on Sundays and feast days. Stories are told of the divine reward for church-goers; a youth, who passing by a church entered it for prayer, was saved from death;[184] a cobbler, a zealous attender of church services, became rich.[185] Attendance at Matins is required; whether it be daily or on feast days only is not made

---

[183] *Izmaragd* I, ch. 459 (and II, ch. 31). Printed in Arkhangelski, IV, 137. There is a variant in Ponomarev, ed., *Pamyatniki,* vol. I, no. 23.

[184] *Izmaragd* II, ch. 38. Printed in Kostomarov, ed., *Pamyatniki,* I, 82.

[185] *Izmaragd* II, ch. 134. Printed in Kostomarov, ed., *Pamyatniki,* I, 87.

clear, and this under the penalty of a penitential exercise:
"If, from laziness, you do not arise to go to Matins, you
must not give to your body to eat until evening." [186] Some
precepts insist on decorous conduct in church — "no talking,
no whispering, no laughing" — even "no singing with vanity." [187] These warnings are corroborated by one of Chrysostom's philippics against transgressors: "Women assembling in the church paint themselves immoderately . . . If
a man desires to buy something he deliberates on it in
church. Many who come to church quarrel, and if you wish
to hear about domestic economy or news of war or medicine
— all this you will hear in church . . ." The very practical
suggestion of the preacher is: "If you cannot keep silence go
out of the church so as not to disturb the others." [188] This
simple motivation is offset by another mystical one: "The
angels sing together with us; when one starts to talk or to
laugh, holy angels, ceasing their song, mourn over him."
From the "Life of St. Niphon" the *Izmaragd* took the idea
that "if a man visits churches by night or by day his feet
are venerated by holy angels. [189] According to a legend attributed to St. Basil, two angels at the entry to the church
write down on their scrolls the names of worthy and unworthy worshippers. This last idea was so familiar in Russia
that in most monasteries one sees the two writing angels
painted on the gate walls.

An ethical approach to the liturgy is a prevailing feature:
"Let us celebrate the seventh day assembling in the church
for prayer . . . having no resentment against any one nor
anger nor envy . . . having mercy on the poor and beg-

---

[186] *Izmaragd* I, ch. 71.

[187] *Izmaragd,* I, ch. 50 (from the Life of St. Niphon). Printed in Sreznevski, ed., *Drevnie pamyatniki russkago pisma i yazyka X–XIV vekov,* p. 608.

[188] *Izmaragd* I, ch. 51. Printed in Arkhangelski, IV, 169.

[189] *Izmaragd* I, ch. 50 (from the Life of St. Niphon).

gars." [190] Hearing the word of God is indicated as the aim of public worship. It is compared with the reading of an emperor's missive. The difficulty of comprehension requires an interpretation by a preacher. In contrast to the Byzantine and modern Russian attitude the sermon is considered an essential part of the service: "Do you not understand what is sung? I shall try to teach you if you will but listen and desire to learn; if you do not I shall cease and you will be damned because you have a teacher and do not listen . . ." The word of God, in its correct interpretation, is called "spiritual honey." [191]

A sermon considers the reformation of life as the only justifiable fruit of the liturgy: "What do you gain by coming to church from childhood, what spiritual profit? What evil habits have you abandoned? . . . [if you go to church] for idle talk and not for God's sake, not in sorrow for your soul, you might better go to the market or for visits or not leave your home at all." We must go to church "that we should sigh over our sins and better ourselves." [192]

On the whole the *Izmaragd*, in matters of liturgical theology as in other issues, maintains an ethical course which inclines slightly toward ritualism on the one hand and mysticism on the other. The presence of angels in the church is but a weak echo of Byzantine liturgical mysticism. Mysticism was not unknown in medieval Russia but one has to look for it elsewhere than in the *Izmaragd*.

The doctrine of the sacraments, found in the *Izmaragd*, tends to the same conclusion. We have already stated that in penitence the moral attitude is emphasized at the expense of the sacramental. As to the Holy Eucharist, the scant refer-

---

[190] *Izmaragd* I, ch. 49. Printed in *Pravoslavnyi Sobesednik,* 1859, p. 465.
[191] *Izmaragd* II, ch. 39. Printed among the works of St. Cyril of Turov.
[192] *Izmaragd* II, ch. 100. Printed in part in Arkhangelski, IV, 64.

ences to it serve a disciplinarian and preventative end, rather than encouraging and promoting a mystical union with Christ. At all times the terrible mystery of the divine Flesh and Blood restrained the longing for mystical union. Fear and love entered inseparably into the attitude toward this sacrament. In the *Izmaragd* as in most Russian medieval documents one finds an abnormal overgrowth of fear, and often the complete absence of love, as motivating forces in the doctrine of Communion.

The only sermon on the Eucharist in the first version of the *Izmaragd* (the second version has none) begins with a call to Communion only to mention at once the spiritual impediments and dangers involved:

Let us, my sons, all together, the grown up as well as the little ones, with pure hearts free from shame approach the terrible God when even angels, though free of sin, tremble, and we who sin every day, how shall we partake without fear of his most pure Body and precious Blood? . . . If you have committed fornication or another evil or quarreled with someone and have not been reconciled with him or *talked with someone in church of secular things* during the Divine Liturgy — do not approach the holy Body and Blood of Christ . . . If someone of you nourishes anger against another man do not enter the church without reconciliation and do not approach the Holy Communion lest you may be condemned to eternal suffering.[193]

A very popular sermon attributed to St. Basil emphasizes the terrible cosmic effect of the sacrilege of unworthy Communion: "The nether world with stone and heavenly powers will tremble." Far from encouraging, admonitions of this kind could only terrify and deter people from Communion. Such was certainly not the intention of the preachers; they simply subordinated purely religious values to moral ones. For them as for their flock penitence had a more palpable and utilitarian significance. The two sacraments, probably

---

[193] *Izmaragd* I, ch. 35.

even in Kievan times, were inseparably united. The Russian, finally, created a particular word to designate participation in both sacraments (*govenie*). And we can hardly be in error to presume that for most Russians, even at present, the main emphasis is on penance, as an annual purification or spiritual bath. The Eucharist became a sign of pardon, a visible seal of the reconciliation of the sinner with the Church. Whether or not this attitude toward the Eucharist was the only one in the Middle Ages we shall see in the next chapter. Let it suffice now to say that this was the attitude of the *Izmaragd* and that it is in harmony with its general moralistic trend.

The moralism of the *Izmaragd* is almost equally divided between two poles of attraction: fear and love. The first version of the *Izmaragd* presents as its first item the famous "Hundred Chapters" of Pseudo-Gennadius. In the Greek moral catechism the predominance of fear is undeniable, but the Russian compiler, obviously taking the Greek masterpiece as his model, succeeded in restoring a fairer balance between the two religious principles. In this respect no difference between the two versions of the *Izmaragd* can be detected. Charity and the fear of God are thus offset in the second version as they are in the first. The second was produced in a desire to enrich and expand rather than to expurgate. It added some articles against adultery, but this was the result of a genuine lack in the first edition. It omitted theoretical articles on charity but they were dialectically contradictory in character and this omission does not give evidence of an anticaritative tendency. Some found an anti-rationalistic tendency in the omission of some articles on book-reading.[194] But this conclusion is incorrect. The omitted chapters are replaced by others with the same tendency and spirit although we are unable to see the reasons for the substitution. Yet, there is one point in which a definite tendency guided the

---

[194] Sedelnikov, I, 128.

pen of the second compiler. He omitted the very important and eloquent chapter 71 on "False Teachers" and the doctrine of the universal right of teaching. At the same time he inserted a chapter entitled "On Not Judging Priests Who Judge." The meaning of this change in the frame of the events of the time will be clarified in the next chapter.

III

THE FIRST RUSSIAN SECT

*T*HE generation that left us the first extant manuscript of the *Izmaragd* (the end of the fourteenth and beginning of the fifteenth century) saw the rise and decline of the first Russian sect known by the pejorative name of the *Strigolniki*.[1] The birth of the first Russian heresy is in itself a significant fact. It witnesses to the ardor of religious interests and the awakening of independent theological thought. Kievan Russia knew neither sects nor heresies, but at that time this meant that Christianity in Kiev did not have deep enough roots in the masses and that the new Christian intelligentsia lived on borrowed Byzantine capital. In the Mongolian period, in spite of the lowering of the general cultural level, Christianity became truly popular, a national treasure which seriously deserved a spiritual exploitation.

The factual development of the first sect in Russia is little known. Under 1375 (or 1376) the *Chronicle of Novgorod* has the following entry: "In this year in Great Novgorod the perverters of the Christian faith were killed: deacon Nikita, Karp the deacon, and a third man with them; they were thrown down from the bridge (over the

---

[1] Two basic works, dealing with the Russian sectarian movements of the fourteenth and fifteenth centuries, have appeared in recent years: N. A. Kazakova and Ya. S. Lur'e, *Antifeodalnye ereticheskie dvizheniya na Rusi XIV — nachala XVI veka* (Anti-Feudal Heretical Movements in Rus from the 14th to the Beginning of the 16th Century), Moscow and Leningrad, 1955, and A. I. Klibanov, *Reformatsionnye dvizheniya v Rossii v XIV — pervoi polovine XVI vv.* (Reformation Movements in Russia from the 14th to the First Half of the 16th Century), Moscow, 1960. The first of these works includes a critical edition of the major texts cited by Fedotov. Both attempt to explain the Russian sectarian movements exclusively by the social conditions of the "feudal" world. Numerous secondary bibliographies, recently published in Russia, are referred to in their works. J. M.

Volkhov river)".[2] Other documents give the name of *Strigol-niki* to the executed heretics, such as Karp, the deacon and the leader of the sect, but otherwise they add no details to the story of the sect and its repression. The name of Strigolniks is differently interpreted by historians. It is, beyond doubt, connected with the Russian word *strigu* (I shear). It may have designated professional barbers or clerical "tonsurers," may have contained an allusion to the professional activity of the leaders or simply may have expressed a contempt for their low social status. Certainly it has nothing to do with the doctrine or religious practice of the sectarians.[3] The execution by drowning shows that it was not performed by order of the ecclesiastical court; the Russian Church by this time objected, as we will see, to the capital punishment of heretics. Drowning was a usual form of execution practiced, in a rather turbulent fashion, by the peoples' assembly (*veche*) of Novgorod. Novgorod and Pskov, its vassal city and "younger brother," are the only places where the presence of the sectarians is evidenced by documents.

The execution of 1375 did not put an end to the sect. Just after this date begins the literary polemic against the Strigolniks of which we possess the following documents: the missive of the Patriarch Nilus of Constantinople dated 1382, that of Bishop Stephen of Perm dated 1386, and four letters of Metropolitan Photius from the years 1416–1429.[4] The last letters, addressed to Pskov after a period of almost forty

---

[2] The Novgorodian Third Chronicle (1376). Compare E. E. Golubinski, *Istoriya russkoi tserkvi* (History of the Russian Church), 4 vols., Moscow, 1880–1907.

[3] As opposed to the interpretation of V. F. Botsyanovski, *Bogoiskateli* (The Seekers after God), St. Petersburg, 1911.

[4] "Pamyatniki drevne-russkago kanonicheskago prava" (Monuments of Ancient-Russian Canon Law) in A. S. Pavlov, ed., *RIB*, vol. VI. St. Petersburg, 1880, nos. 22, 25, 42, 51, 55, 56. The chronology was corrected by Golubinski, *Istoriya russkoi tserkvi*, I, 406n4.

years, prove the long survival of the Strigolnik movement, at least in Pskov. The public reaction of 1375 presupposes an incubation period beginning about the middle of the fourteenth century, which suggests that the movement survived for at least seven decades. It is generally supposed that a new persecution in Pskov, in 1427, put an end to the sect. In his first two letters Photius as well as Patriarch Nilus before him, suggested only the spiritual punishment of the sectarians — their excommunication and separation from social life (communal eating and drinking). In his last letters Photius required measures by the civil authorities, "except death and bloodshed," and particularly imprisonment. The Pskovians seem to have been all too glad to get rid of the heretics. At least in 1427 they wrote to the metropolitan that they had searched for the heretics and punished them; but one part of them fled from the city, and those remaining in freedom (probably after punishment) stubbornly held to their convictions. The silence of our sources about the Strigolniks after 1427–1429 can be taken as proof of their gradual disappearance.

Although we do not possess any writings of the Strigolniks themselves,[5] their opponents seem to give a consistent and fair account of their doctrine; yet, our curiosity is only half satisfied with the too scanty statements of the Orthodox prelates. They use rather sharp theological language but, while comparing the Strigolniks to Arius, Macedonius, and other famous heresiarchs of antiquity, they do not accuse them of any dogmatic errors or of immoral conduct. In their

---

[5] Bishop Stephen says that Karp "copied book-writing for the support of his heresy," which seems to indicate a collection of ancient texts rather than an original work. Pavlov, ed., *RIB,* vol. VI, col. 214. Later A. D. Sedelnikov found traces of Strigolnik literature or, rather, their tendencies in some ancient Orthodox manuscripts. See "Sledy strigolnicheskoi knizhnosti" (Traces of Strigolnik Literature) in *Trudy otdela drevne-russkoi literatury, Akademiya Nauk SSSR* (Works of the Section on Ancient-Russian Literature, Academy of Sciences USSR), Leningrad, 1934, I, 121–136.

descriptions the Strigolniks appear not as heretics but only as schismatics. Using the words of Patriarch Nilus they "separated themselves from the Catholic and Apostolic Church on the pretext of piety believing that they guarded the divine Scriptures and the exactitude of sacred canons." This suggests the idea that their opposition to the Church originated from within conservative circles which were inspired by canonical zeal. Its *raison d'être* is thus represented by the patriarch: "They believe that the bishops, priests, and all the clergy, and other Christian people are heretics since they ordain and are ordained for money, and that they alone are orthodox." [6] That means that the schism originated as a protest against the supposed simony of the clergy.

The protest again simony is mentioned in all anti-Strigolnik literature. But Bishop Stephen, to whom we owe most of our knowledge about the sectarians, provides some other motives for their anticlericalism. "You Strigolniks say: 'These teachers are drunkards, they eat and drink with drunkards and take gold, and silver, and garbs, from the living and the dead.'" [7] Drunkenness and greed are the common features in the incriminations against the Russian clergy in all centuries. Greed, or an acquisitive spirit, was a particularly sensitive point for the conscience of the Strigolniks. It was obviously connected with their aversion to simony, but, on the other hand, this aversion was deepened and sharpened by a vision of the poverty of Christ in the Gospels. "You Strigolniks seduce Christians by Christ's word to the Apostles: 'Get you neither wallet nor brass in your purses.'" [8] The justification of clerical remuneration takes, therefore, a predominant place in this polemic. The Strigol-

---

[6] Pavlov, ed., *RIB*, vol. VI, no. 22 and supplement, no. 31 (Greek text).
[7] *Ibid.*, no. 25, cols. 220–221.
[8] Matthew 10:9–10 (an inexact quotation), *ibid.*, cols. 222–223.

niks were moral rigorists in their demands of the clergy, but their own way of life was on a level with their moral standards. Stephen makes no attempt to hide this. "Some foolish men say of the Strigolniks: 'They do not rob or gather possessions.'" Stephen himself treats them as haughty and righteous pharisees. "Such were heretics: fasters, prayerful, learned hypocrites making themselves pure before men; if people did not see their blameless life who would believe in their heresies?" They cannot be reproached with ignorance either: "You have learned the words of the books whose sounds are sweet to the Christians and have established yourselves as teachers of the people." Upon their learning the laymen or lower clerics based their right of teaching: "You say that Paul ordered even the simple man [layman] to teach."[9]

Such is the portrait of the sectarians as painted by their adversaries. They were not simpletons or ignoramuses, men of lower culture or the lower classes; nor were they critics rejecting a part of Church traditions contained in the Scriptures. They were conservative radicals who insisted upon a strict and literal observance of moral and canonical rules. Schism was the only logical corollary of their intransigent attitude. As Stephen said in ridiculing them: "Tell me, heretics, where do you expect to find a priest for yourselves? If you say the patriarch is unworthy, metropolitans are unworthy, then, according to your words, there is no priest on earth who is ordained without ecclesiastical fees."[10]

Almost certainly, the Strigolniks had no priests in their group. Refusing to accept sacraments from unworthy priests they faced a difficult problem: "No angel will descend to ordain a priest for you," mocked the same polemist. And, thus,

---

[9] These quotations are *ibid.,* cols. 218, 222, 226, 227.
[10] *Ibid.,* col. 217.

these conservatives were forced to enter upon a revolutionary path — to give up the sacraments and the whole ecclesiastical way of salvation.

We have definite information about the sacrament of penance. Karp, the founder of the sect, "did not allow confession to priests, "but from the exposition of Stephen it is quite clear, also, that the Strigolniks voluntarily shunned the Eucharist of the Church. The Devil, through Karp, "separates [his followers] from the communion of the holy, most pure and vivifying mysteries of Christ." [11] The whole structure of Stephen's letter, which is a true theological treatise, is centered around Eucharistic dogma. The bishop begins with the two trees of paradise which he calls the tree of life and the tree of reason. The first gives man immortality, the second death. The lost fruit of the tree of life was restored to us by Christ in the form of his Body and Blood. Participation in them is the condition of life: "If you do not eat the flesh of the Son of man or drink his blood, you have not life in you." [12] But against the will of Christ, the Strigolnik (Karp) orders the avoidance of the tree of life, Communion, considering what is written in books as the tree of reason. Yet writings, used without humility, can kill: "Every one, who reads books without humility and meekness, trying to reproach someone for something, falls into heresy . . . and the commandment given to him for life turns against him unto death." [13]

The Strigolniks, sticking to the Scriptures, gave up the Eucharist. That is, they did not look for any substitute; they did not dare either to create their own priesthood or to consecrate bread and wine by the prayers of laymen. A substitute for sacramental penitence was, however, found, and this

---

[11] *Ibid.,* cols. 214, 224.
[12] John 6:54, *ibid.,* col. 214.
[13] *Ibid.,* col. 227.

is the most interesting feature of the sect. Unfortunately, our only informer, Bishop Stephen, is extremely terse here: "You add also another heresy, Strigolniks; you order men to confess to the Earth." [14] This is the first mention of the rite of confession to the Earth, well known in Russia not only among sectarians. Perhaps this scanty notice can be supplemented by another one, from a letter of Metropolitan Photius: "Looking at the sky [Strigolniks] call to their Father" or "looking up from the Earth to the air call God their Father." [15] The supposed heterodoxy of this invocation can be interpreted in the sense that the Strigolniks renounced their earthly spiritual fathers — the priests — confessing only to the Father in heaven. The emphasis on sky and air indicates praying in the open air; one can indirectly conclude that the sectarians not only abandoned the sacraments of the Church but avoided the liturgical services in churches, usually praying out-of-doors instead of in their homes and prostrating themselves on the Earth to confess their sins to her. Starting with a conservative opposition to the clergy they ended with the most radical rejection of the whole sacramental and liturgical tradition of the Church.

One more detail among the errors of the Strigolniks is known. Karp taught: "It is not becoming to sing [prayers] over the dead or commemorate them or celebrate services or bring offerings for the deceased to the church or make banquets or give alms for the souls of the dead." [16] Now the care of the dead was one of the main sources of enrichment for the medieval church. Twice in his letter the polemist lets the Strigolniks accuse the priests of taking money "from the living and the dead." The mention of banquets and alms (partly given to the benefit of churches) points in the same

---

[14] *Ibid.,* col. 223.
[15] *Ibid.,* no. 56, col. 484.
[16] *Ibid.,* no. 25.

direction: the struggle against the rich and dissolute clergy. In this case, however, another explanation is also justified. As hopes for posthumous prayers bought with money undermined the personal morals of the laity, the Strigolniks ended by denying the efficacy of all prayers for the dead. This would be the final inference from their moralistic attitude.

If the tendencies and the general spirit of the sect are quite clear, its origin demands an explanation. Discontent with the clergy existed in Russia at all times; it did not lead by itself, however, to schism or to separation from the Church. We must therefore look for the specific reasons which led the Novgorod Strigolniks to their daring conclusions.

Some Russian historians have tried to explain the rise of the sect by the influence of foreign heresies: that of the Bogomils from the Balkans, and Geisslers or Flagellants from Germany.[17] These parallels, however, are too far-fetched. The practices of the Russian Strigolniks have nothing in common with the dualism of the Bogomils or with the ecstatic self-scourging of the Geisslers. We can and, consequently, must trace the origin of the Strigolniks to the Russian soil itself, to their own social and spiritual surroundings.[18]

The issue of simony was not raised first by the Strigolniks; it had a century-old history behind it. It was raised initially, as far as we know, in a very sharp form by the Metropolitan Cyril at the Council of Vladimir in 1274. This is the only council of the Russian Middle Ages (including the Kievan

[17] See F. I. Uspenski, "Filosofskoe i bogoslovskoe dvizhenie v XIV veke" (The Philosophical and Theological Movement in the 14th Century), in ZhMNP, 1892, and in a separate edition. See also N. S. Tikhonravov, "Otrechennye knigi drevnei Rusi" (Apocryphal Books of Ancient Russia), in Sochineniya (Works), 3 vols., Moscow, 1898, I, 214 ff.

[18] This is the way already taken by Golubinski and more recently by Sedelnikov to whom we owe the main structure of our chapter.

period) for which the canons are extant. The very first canon of the Vladimir Council begins with the denunciation of simony: "It has come to our hearing that some of our brethren have dared to sell sacred orders, to appoint [the clergy] to churches and to take from them so-called 'fees.' They have forgotten the canon of the holy Apostles . . . Let all hear it clearly: 'He who is ordained by money should be deposed, likewise he who ordained him.'" [19] This first canon is very long. After enumerating a whole series of ancient councils legislating against simony it describes, in detail, a valid procedure for appointing priests and all the qualities which a worthy candidate must possess. Together with fees for ordination it prohibits any undue taxation of the clergy and laity by bishops or their administration. And yet, after all kinds of solemn excommunications, Metropolitan Cyril makes a concession that fits badly with his canonical strictures: "Take nothing from them *except* what I have established in the metropolitan province; the same rule should be observed in all dioceses; let the cathedral officials take seven *grivnas* for the priesthood and the diaconate altogether." [20]

To explain this strange concession one must keep in mind that in the Byzantine Church since the edict of the Emperor Isaac Comnenus (1057–1059) the fee of seven *hyperpyra* (gold coins) was legally fixed for an ordination. [21] The Russian Church could not help conforming to the practice of the Greek Mother Church. Metropolitan Cyril, a Russian by birth, was inspired by a well-meaning intention to effect conservative reforms in the Russian Church which was disorganized after the Tatar invasion. He had

---

[19] Pavlov, ed., *RIB,* vol. VI, no. 6, cols. 86–87.

[20] *Ibid.,* col. 92.

[21] Golubinski, *Istoriya russkoi tserkvi,* II, 2, p. 69. The Russian *grivna* took the place of the Greek *hyperpyron.*

already procured from Bulgaria a new version of the book
of canon law (*Kormchaya*) and was eager to enforce its
strict canons through a Russian council.

We do not know whether Cyril's moderate or com-
promising decision satisfied the Russian clergy. There were,
most probably, bishops who demanded from the candidates
more than the prescribed seven *grivnas*. On the other hand,
the canonical conscience awakened amid the ecclesiastical
intelligentsia could hardly be appeased by a compromise
after the Greek pattern. In any case, the discussion around
the problem of simony continued in the fourteenth century,
with a fervor verging on ebullience.

Metropolitan Peter (1308–1326) in the first years of
his rule was a much more questionable figure. He was supported by the Prince of Moscow, but the Great Prince, who
was at that time Michael of Tver, had another candidate
for the chief ecclesiastical post. Hence various incriminations
against Peter were raised before the Patriarch of Constantinople and before a Russian council. One of the items of
the charges was that of simony. Patriarch Niphon who took
the part of Peter's enemies wrote to the Prince of Tver:
"And the metropolitan does still worse; he takes profit from
ordinations; that means he is a shopkeeper; he sells the
grace of the Holy Spirit or, rather, the wrath of God; the
sacred canons not only depose him for this but excommuni-
cate and curse him." [22]

At the Russian council of Pereyaslavl in 1310 (or 1311),
Peter was acquitted of all the accusations against him, but
the debate on simony was not closed. The doubts raised in
the minds of the zealots were not quenched, and the ambiguous attitude of Constantinople was hardly capable of
quieting them. The patriarch, as we have seen, condemned
simony in the form of obligatory fees for ordination in a

---

[22] Pavlov, ed., *RIB,* vol. VI, no. 16, col. 149.

most solemn way, under threat of excommunication. Yet, one of his successors justified the Greek practice of fixed fees as a voluntary gift covering the expenses for ordination (candles, wine, and so forth). Such is the casuistic argument of Patriarch Nilus in his letter against the Strigolniks.[23] The sophisticated distinctions made by the Greeks were outweighed in Russian minds by the terrible threats for practicing simony and its identification with the heresy of Macedonius the Pneumatomach. This comparison is found both in Nilus' letter and in a canon of the Council of Vladimir: "Macedonius and other pneumatomachs blaspheming the Holy Spirit called him a slave of God; and they (simonians) make him their own slave buying and selling him."[24]

At the time of the struggle around Metropolitan Peter (1312–1315) a monk was sent by the Bishop of Tver to Constantinople to explore the Greek canonical practice on ordination fees. On his return this monk, Akindin by name, wrote a letter to Prince Michael of Tver exhorting him to wage a struggle against simony in his lands. As an eyewitness and the attendant at a Council in Constantinople, he relates the canonical situation in Greece in a not very accurate, but perfunctory way: "The patriarch answered me: 'Even if a *half-hyperpyron* or any trifling amount [were paid], it is the field of blood and potter's field; they are equal to Judas and will have no part in Christ either here or in the age to come.'" The language used by Akindin is as violent as his canonical corollaries are radical. If we possessed some writings of the Strigolniks we should probably find there the same arguments and the same conclusions. "I see the heresy growing and increasing, defended shamelessly by open lips; from our highest bishops to the low-

---

[23] *Ibid.,* no. 22, col. 195.
[24] Canon I of the Council of Vladimir, *ibid.,* no. 6, col. 88.

est [clerics] it started through a godless custom of making the unsellable grace of the Holy Spirit the object of
commerce and of receiving [fees] for ordinations: the
metropolitan from the bishops, priests, deacons, and other
clerics; the bishop likewise from the clergy under him . . .
According to the apostolic tradition both he who is ordained
for money and [the bishop] who has ordained him must be
deposed from their orders . . ." Akindin takes so literally
this ancient canon that he does not even hold necessary the
verdict of any ecclesiastical court: "He who ordains and
receives fees for ordination is already deposed and he
who is ordained by the deposed has no profit, and he who
partakes, wittingly, of the Holy Communion with him will
be condemned with him." At the end of his letter Akindin
comes back to the same idea: "And if however he takes little
for the ordination, your bishop is no more a bishop, and he
who takes communion from him will be damned with him." [25]
The layman, thus, is called upon to be a judge over his priests
and bishops. According to Akindin the whole Russian clergy
is without exception guilty of simony and is *ipso facto*
deposed. If his words are to be taken literally, the layman
has no other way than to separate from the heretic clergy
lest he be damned with them. The whole doctrine of
the Strigolniks is already contained in Akindin's. However,
we had better not take his impassioned language too seriously.

Taking his point of departure from the question of simony, Akindin joins the Strigolniks in a general condemnation of contemporary clergy, and in stating the right and
duty of reason to judge over the hierarchs. He proceeds in
the following way:

In defense of ordination fees he used to hear the argument of the "oppression by the heathens [Tatars]." What

---

[25] *Ibid.,* no. 16, cols. 151, 153.

was meant, of course, was the impoverishment of the Church as a result of spoliation and the necessity of increasing the Church income. Akindin answers not without common sense: "Where the heathen or the thief or the robber sees any wealth he takes great pains to rob or steal or break; but where the *poverty of Christ's humility* is he has no hope for any gain; there he neither violates nor oppresses . . ." Akindin sets up the ideal of a poor and humble Church. "Is it with riches that the Apostles ran over the universe preaching the Word? Had they not counted all things to be lost to acquire Christ?" How far the modern bishops had deviated from the apostolic life is shown in the portrait of the reverse of an ideal bishop given by Akindin: "To be called bishop only by name and adorn oneself with bishops' vestments, to boast of numerous crowds of followers, and to punish without justice, like tyrants and not bishops, responding with hatred to those who accuse them." Thus, the initial protest against simony, based on canonical *akribeia*, is enlarged into an incrimination of the wealthy and ambitious hierarchy with an evangelical background for this denunciation. And the writer ends in a prophetic and revolutionary spirit: "Fear, o bishop, the Lord's visitation, which is predicted by the prophet against you: 'Angels, begin with my saints, slay and do not spare. Because of you the name of God is blasphemed by the gentiles.' " [26]

All the contemporary calamities of Russia, under the Mongol yoke, are ascribed by Akindin (and by Metropolitan Cyril before him) to a neglect of the canons, particularly to the simony of prelates. Akindin does not hope for a reform movement from any member of this decayed order although his own bishop is the leader in the campaign against Peter as a simoniac: "How can they teach us not to take payments? Money is said to blind the eyes of the wise; they

---

[26] *Ibid.,* cols. 155–157.

themselves are blinded with the ordination money." And so
Akindin turns to his prince, though a layman, from whom
Christ will require an account at his Terrible Judgment, if
"he keeps silence before the metropolitan." But to oppose
a sinful bishop is not the privilege of a prince. Every layman
is entitled to it by his reason, the gift of God: "According
to the great Athanasius every man, receiving from God
reason with which to discriminate, if he follows an ignorant
shepherd, will be tormented, as it is said: a blind man leading another blind one will fall into the pit with him, that is
into the abyss." [27]

We have been dwelling at length on the epistle of Akindin because we can learn from him the mood and the way
of argumentation of the future Strigolniks. But, what is
quite unexpected is that Akindin's great adversary, Metropolitan Peter, accused of simony and obviously approving
of the Greek practice of ordination fees, prepares the way
for the doctrine of the sectarians in one point, at least, and
that a more dangerous one. In a pastoral letter addressed to
the clergy he prohibits widowed priests from celebrating the
divine service (on the suspicion of the impurity of their life).
And the prelate concludes: "Whosoever does not obey my
word, and also those who communicate with him, will be not
blessed." [28] Here the laymen are made responsible for
the uncanonical conduct of their priests. They are obliged to
abstain from Eucharistic Communion with guilty priests
under the threat of excommunication. Peter's decision in
the case of widowed priests (a very questionable decision with
no basis in ancient canons), gave additional justification to
the Strigolniks' attitude in the case of simony. The result
was an open schism.

The Russian situation recalls the canonical struggles

---

[27] *Ibid.,* col. 157.
[28] *Ibid.,* col. 161.

against simony and fornication which the Roman Popes and
the reform party of Cluny waged in the Western Church
in the eleventh century. Then too Pope Gregory committed
the imprudent act of calling upon the laity to ostracize unworthy priests and to abstain from communication with them.
One of the results of this reform movement was the growth
of popular evangelical sects in the twelfth century. The
Russian Strigolniks, both in their origin and the tenets of
their doctrine, have their parallel with the Waldensians.
A parallel, however, is not a connecting link. The Strigolniks
simply repeated on Russian soil the religious experience of
the Western sects.

A connecting link can be discovered between the two
centers of the anti-simonist movement in Russia: Tver and
Novgorod.[29] A few years after Akindin wrote his epistle the
principality of Tver suffered a punitive raid by the Tatars.
We are told that masses of the population fled before their
foes and found refuge in the neighboring territory of Novgorod. Books are still preserved in the libraries of Novgorod
which give evidence of this migration. It is only natural
that Tver's canonical ideas should find new roots in Novgorod and Pskov. They were sustained on the new soil by
peculiar events in ecclesiastical affairs which shattered the
bases of Church discipline and the esteem for Church authorities. During the fourteenth century the Archbishop
of Novgorod waged an intermittent war against the Metropolitan of Moscow pleading, unsuccessfully, for canonical
independence before the patriarchal court of Constantinople.
The main object of the dispute was the appellate jurisdiction
of the Metropolitan in the territory of Novgorod. When he
came to Novgorod to exercise justice, the metropolitan heavily burdened the clergy and lay suitors in Novgorod with all
kinds of taxes. Justice was a financial business in the Middle

---

[29] For the following compare Sedelnikov, I, 124–126.

Ages. Thus, in the eyes of zealots and Novgorod patriots, the issue of ecclesiastical autonomy took the form of a struggle against exploitation, greed, and in many cases simony.

In 1385, at the very time of the Strigolnik controversy, the *veche* of Novgorod took an oath (a decision corroborated by religious sanctions) no longer to accept the appellate jurisdiction of the metropolitan. Later on, in 1392, Metropolitan Cyprian proclaimed the excommunication of all of Novgorod, the clergy as well as the laity. The country, probably indifferent to this act of the Moscovite prelate, lived in this state for an entire year.[30] Such a situation could not increase the respect of the laity for Church discipline.

As for Pskov, this city, after having gained its political independence from Novgorod endeavored to crown this with ecclesiastical independence by obtaining its own bishop. Those projects failed as did the parallel schemes of Novgorod. Meanwhile the clergy of Pskov opposed the pastoral visits of the Archbishop of Novgorod as well as his jurisdiction. For a time a kind of presbyterian rule was established in Pskov, a self-government of the clergy which, unfortunately, resulted in a decline of discipline. The letters of Metropolitan Photius to Pskov at the beginning of the fifteenth century describe a very low state of canonical and even moral discipline in Pskov.[31] Both here and in Novgorod the atmosphere was very favorable for the growth of lay anticlericalism already prepared by the doctrinal struggle against simony.

The reflection of these trends can be traced even now in some surviving manuscripts of the fourteenth century, originating in the Novgorod-Pskov area. Although we do not

---

[30] Golubinski, *Istoriya russkoi tserkvi*, II, 306–318.

[31] A. I. Nikitski, "Ocherk vnutrennei istorii tserkvi vo Pskove" (A survey of the Internal History of the Church in Pskov), *ZhMNP*, 1871, V, 1–70; 1873, II, 188–251.

possess any book of a frankly sectarian character, some of the Collections discussed before show undeniable tendencies of the movement. Professor A. D. Sedelnikov, in his essay on the "Traces of Strigolnik Literature" discovered those traces in the first version of the *Izmaragd* and in manuscript no. 1262 of the former library of St. Sophia in Novgorod.[32] Although the *Izmaragd* is not interested directly in the matter of simony, its spiritual tendency, moralistic and rationalistic, is akin to that of the Novgorod sectarians. Many of its "articles" emphasize the importance of Scriptures or books as the primary means of salvation. *Izmaragd* denounces the weaknesses of the priests and enjoins on all laymen the duty of preaching. Two articles in the first version of the *Izmaragd* are of a special relevance to the Strigolnik strife: "The Sermon on false teachers" (c. 71) and "The Sermon on the spiritual observance of feast days and on drunkenness" (c. 24). The last sermon, on the whole a very harmless and commonplace instruction on morals, contains a short digression on "spiritual viands." These viands, becoming to the Sabbath day, are defined as "concealed in the vessels of books, brought down from heaven." Of this nourishment it was said: [This is] "the bread of the angels which man consumes."[33] Now, we have seen that Bishop Stephen denounces as the greatest error of the sectarians that they replaced the fruit of the tree of life, the Eucharist, with the fruit of the tree of reason, the wisdom of books. They ignore the warning of Christ: "Except ye eat the flesh of the Son of man and drink his blood ye have not life in yourselves" (John 6:53). Although Stephen does not use the expressions "spiritual viands" and "bread of angels" it is

---

[32] We quote the *Izmaragd* again after the analysis by V. A. Yakovlev, "K literaturnoi istorii drevne-russkikh 'Sbornikov': opyt issledovaniya 'Izmaragda' " (The Literary History of the Ancient-Russian 'Collections': A Research Essay on the 'Izmaragd') in *ZNU,* vol. 60, Odessa 1893.

[33] *Izmaragd* I, version 24.

very probable that "bread of angels" is equivalent to the "bread which came down from heaven" (John 6:58), and, thus, we have here two interpretations of the same text, one traditional and Eucharistic, and the other referring to wisdom, even if not new,[34] yet popular in the circles of the Strigolniks.

As to chapter 71 of the first version of the *Izmaragd* on "False Teachers," in view of its probable influence on the doctrine of the Strigolniks, we give here its translation at length. It begins with a praise of books and the duty of teaching:

Stand faithfully upon the Word of the Lord, you lovers of Christ and of books. The Lord said: "He who loves me will study my Law day and night," that is, the books. For the books have a memory beyond oblivion. The books are created by the Holy Spirit. He who holds them in his head will not forget those terrifying books of the age to come, of which it is written: "The books of the Judge of judges will be opened . . . Woe to them who do not read the holy books before all men but, like Judas, conceal the talent, that is, the teaching of the Lord . . . and starve other people with spiritual famine. Know, o man, that the books are the mother of all good who feeds her children . . . Sell then what you possess and buy holy books . . . In them the Son of God is concealed, the true wisdom of the Father . . ."

[And here the preacher comes to negligent or ignorant teachers] Woe to you, blind preceptors, who neither learned well nor are confirmed by book wisdom, you adorners of vestments and not of books, you who have abandoned the Word of God and serve your belly, whose god is the belly . . . Of such the prophet said: "There will be in the last days slanderers of books, walking after their lusts; they will be the false teachers who will induce many into perdition and many will follow their teaching, not salutary, but crooked and weak . . ."

Heed the parable: Many shepherds hire paid servants to tend the cattle, while they themselves drink and sleep. In the same way,

---

[34] The "Sermon on Spiritual Observance" was a part of the sermon falsely attributed to St. Theodosius of Kiev. Compare Yakovlev, *ZNU,* vol. 60, p. 15.

shepherds of rational sheep sleep by ignorance or rudeness or inebriate themselves with unrighteous acquisitions and become connivers of the rulers. They do not wish to teach . . . therefore they teach that which is simplest and conceal the mystery which can bring one to reason and guide one to eternal life . . . O woe, the shepherds have already become wolves; they have lacerated the sheep. That is, the priest taught people not good but evil . . . You do not teach your- selves and hate those who teach, saying: "Let there not be many teachers . . . But when shepherds become wolves then sheep must teach sheep . . . If a layman will teach rightly in the absence of the bishop and teacher that is all right."

[Another parable is drawn to illuminate the lesson] If an army is moving against a town whoever, even though it be a simple man, cries out: "flee to the town, people, the foe is coming against you," the sensible men, who hear it, will run into the town to escape the distress. But the senseless ones say: "It is not a prince's man who is speaking, do not flee." And the enemy would come and slay them and conquer the others and the last would be the worst.

But you, my dear brethren in Christ, *if you have reason,* do not listen to evil teachers or keep up friendship with them, for it is forbidden either to eat or drink with such . . . Accept a good teaching if you hear it from a layman and do not accept an evil one even if a bishop is teaching; understand what the Scripture says: "You will know them by their fruit."

One would like to know something about the origin of this remarkable document. Nobody doubts that it is a Russian work. Sedelnikov dates it as fourteenth century be- cause of a quotation he found in it from the *Blasfemia,* a translated treatise which appeared in Russia in the fourteenth century.[35] This would mean that the sermon on "False Teachers" was composed in the very heyday of the discus- sions on simony in Russia.

Both this sermon and that on "Spiritual Observance"

---

[35] Sedelnikov, I, 134. V. M. Izergin, however, dated it as early as the twelfth century. It is found in a manuscript of St. Sophia (no. 1285, fifteenth century), which is a copy of a twelfth-century manuscript. The question needs paleographical reexamination. See V. M. Izergin, "Predislovie k pokayaniyu" (A Preface to Repentance) in *ZhMNP,* 1891, II, 158–159, 176.

are extant in the manuscript no. 1262 of St. Sophia. In the last Collection Sedelnikov found many other items relevant to the Strigolnik controversy, either reflecting their anticlerical spirit or objecting to schism. To the first group among others belong: the *Blasphemia*, which occupies one third of the Collection; the Preface to Repentance; the missive of Joseph of which we shall speak later; and a sermon against paganism "How the First Heathens Believed In Idols."

The "Preface to Repentance," a pre-Mongol document[36] of a very broadminded attitude, raises the question of "whether it is good to confess one's sins to spiritual fathers." The answer is discriminating: "Good and useful but not to those who are not tested. If the priest is rude, ignorant, drunken or proud he will make you wicked, negligent, slothful and relaxed. Of such the Lord said: 'Woe unto you, pharisees, hypocrites . . . Woe unto you, blind guides barring the way to them who seek salvation.'"[37] Bold as this answer is, it is but a literal translation from a Greek canonist of the eleventh century. While in Greece it was a survival of the ancient Church order when private confession, after monastic patterns, was optional for laity, in Russia of the fourteenth century, it had a revolutionary significance: it was a guide with which the Strigolniks could justify, at least partially, their separation from the Church.

The same "Preface to Repentance" raises the question of learning at the very outset. For the author this learning is the main qualification of a good priest.

It is becoming that the bishop be sensible and intelligent and wise in book doctrine . . . Such must also be the priest. Otherwise he ought not to be priest, even though he were a saint; for he is ignorant and senseless. And ignorance is worse than sin . . . Learn

---

[36] G. P. Fedotov, *RRM*, I, 241–243.
[37] Pavlov, ed., *RIB*, vol. VI, cols. 838–839.

books from each other, and God gives reason to whomever he wills — who keeps his commandments.[38]

As to the sermons against popular paganism, mostly stemming also from the pre-Mongol times, they are full of denunciations of unworthy priests. The preacher sees in the clerical vices, their indolence, their greed, the greatest obstacle in the campaign against paganism. That many of these pseudonymous and anonymous sermons were composed by laymen is a very plausible inference especially for those of them which are ascribed in the title to "Christ-lover." It is well known that in Old Russian "Christ-lover" is an honorable appellation of a pious layman.

The sermon on "How the First Heathens Believed in Idols" begins with a quotation from St. Paul on the origin of idolatry (Rom. 1:21–27). And immediately after the sentence on the heathens addicted to unnatural vices the Russian author goes over to the priests. "This is precisely what the priests who obey them [the heathens] do and do not wish to teach them. With silence they have barred their mouths to the perdition of the weak-minded. They do what is pleasing to them, serving their belly and not God. As the Apostle said: 'those for whom God is the belly and who glory in the shame of their face.' How will you stand before the altar of God while stinking with yeasts [beer] and trembling like Cain? And the Lord said: 'Woe unto you, blind guides . . .'" Only then does the author arrive at his proper subject, the origin of pagan cults.[39] The conclusion is clear — the persistence of idolatry is the result of pastoral negligence by the priests. The second half of the same sermon is a literal translation from a *spurium* of John Chrysostom on "False

[38] *Ibid.,* cols. 835–837.

[39] N. Galkovski, *Borba khristianstva s ostatkami yazychestva v drevnei Rusi* (The Struggle of Christianity Against the Remnants of Paganism in Ancient Rus), Moscow, 1913, II, 53–69.

Prophets"[40] where we read the familiar warning against false shepherds: "Do not be astonished if shepherds also become wolves. For the Apostle Paul conversing with bishops and priests said 'From among yourselves shall men arise speaking perverse things' (Acts 20:30). Therefore, let you not be seduced by anyone even if he has an angel's form outside and the demon's within . . . Let nobody seduce you . . . neither a bishop nor priest nor deacon nor psalmist nor any of those who come to you in sheep's clothing, speaking perverse things." A general impression of this sermon lets us suppose that it was directed not so much against paganism as against the contemporary clergy.

The anticlerical tendencies found in one or two of these Collections are not unusual in the writings of this period. While they may have been included through the influence of the Strigolniks, we find them in other manuscripts of this age, which is far from rich in literary remains. Among the few Collections extant from the fourteenth or, perhaps, the beginning of the fifteenth century, students of Russian literature know well and appreciate the so-called Paisius Collection. We find there, amidst other heterogeneous material, the following articles: "What is more useful, to bring one's possession to the Church or to give it to the poor?" "On false teachers," "St. Ephrem on book learning," "The Preface to repentance," and articles against the sins of the clergy and on the usefulness of other people's substitutive prayers.[41]

None of the preserved manuscripts, even by omission, allows us to presume a sympathy with the antisacramental conclusions which the sectarians drew from the common anticlerical premises. The conclusion was drawn by the Ab-

---

[40] PG, vol. 59, cols. 553–563.

[41] Sreznevski, ed., Svedeniya, in SORYaS, vol. XII, ch. 56; and in a separate edition.

bot Akindin but in an irresponsible polemical way; certainly the Abbot of Tver did not mean to secede from the Church which he indicted of simony; nor did Metropolitan Peter think of the far-reaching consequences of his imprudent canonical order. The practical and consistent conclusion was the Strigolniks' own daring act which put them in collision not only with the Church authorities but with all the laity as well. The Church, in the person of Metropolitan Photius, had to protect the sectarians from the capital punishment imposed by the popular governments of Novgorod and Pskov. One can only guess that the withdrawal from the sacraments of the Church was also supported by general tendencies of the age; in penance there was a prevailing of its moral side over the sacramental; in the Eucharist there were both the lack of emphasis upon the salvific value of this sacrament and the veil of awe and terror with which it was surrounded; the emphasis put on the dangers of unworthy Communion rather than those of rare Communion.

It remains for us to elucidate one obscure point in Strigolnik practice mentioned by their opponents. We do not know whether they created any substitute for the Eucharist of the Church, but they did find a substitute for the sacrament of penance — the famous confession to the Earth. This strange religious rite is well known to Russian folklorists. It is in use not only among some sectarians who reject the priesthood, but even among the Orthodox under particular circumstances (in the absence of priests). For the first time in Russian history this rite appears among the Strigolniks.

Studying the origin of this rite, S. I. Smirnov points, as matter of precedence, to confession before sacred objects in churches which was practiced in the Christian East. In Constantinople it was the icon of Christ in the Church of the Apostles which heard confessions and even miraculously granted absolution. In Jerusalem it was the sepulchre of St. Pelagia; in Lidda, a column at the shrine of St. George. Some curious customs were connected with this irregular confession aiming at the confirmation of the expected absolution by the saint. In Russia a few instances of the confession of sins to the relics of saints are known. But these are isolated cases; none of them indicates a widespread custom similar to the ones mentioned in the Christian East. On the other hand, confession to the Earth is thoroughly unknown in the East. In recent times in Russia those Old-believers (*bezpopovtsy*) who have had no priesthood since the end of the seventeeth century have practiced confession to the Earth or before the icon of Christ. As for the Orthodox, the custom is known among them in Siberia, in places where priests are rare. Both the sectarians and the Orthodox give the same explanation for this rite. "If there is nobody else, one can confess even to the grass" (an Old-believer). "What is to be done if illness takes you in field or in wood? To whom if not to the Earth or to a tree have you to confess if there is no man?" (Orthodox). But, of course, the Earth is not just any object chosen at random. If the people choose it (her) for sacred confidence they have their deep reasons.

The sacredness of Mother Earth is the legacy of Russian paganism. In Christian times the Earth preserved the quality of a living or animated being, of a universal mother and even, to a certain degree, of a keeper of the moral law. In this Russian Christians could find some support in the doctrines of the Greek Church. Some Greek Church Fathers (Gregory Nazianzen, Chrysostom) in their Hellenistic rhetorical style call the Earth "the universal mother." [42] The apocryphal vision of St. Paul represents the Earth

---

[42] S. I. Smirnov, *Drevne-russki dukhovnik: Issledovanie po istorii tserkovnago byta* (The Ancient Russian Confessor: Research in the History of Church Life), Moscow, 1913, p. 266n3, after A. Dietrich, *Mutter-Erde,* Leipzig and Berlin, 1905, p. 69.

together with the Sun and the Moon as complaining to God of the sins of men and imploring for their punishment. Even in a liturgical text of a very solemn significance, in the Vesper prayers on the feast of the Holy Trinity one hears the words: "and against thee, Mother Earth, I have sinned with my soul and body." [43]

These Greek ideas expanded profusely on Russian soil or rather fused, for theological justification, with the indigenous cult of Mother Earth. The Russian people call the Earth "holy," kiss her and confide to her their heart's woe; they sometimes ask pardon from the Earth (as well as from their kinsmen and acquaintances) before ecclesiastical confession. One step more in this semi-Christian cult, and the Earth takes the place of the absent priest, hearing the confession of the sinner herself. Among the so-called "spiritual" (religious) songs of the Russian people there is one on this subject. We translate it here with minor abbreviations:

> A lad confessed his sins to the Humid Earth:
> Take my confession Mother Humid Earth!
> I have on my soul three heavy sins;
> The first great-heavy sin on my soul,
> I scolded my father and my mother dear,
> The second great-heavy sin on my soul,
> I lived with my God-sister in Christ
> We begot a little child,
> The third great-heavy sin on my soul,
> I killed in the field my brother by the Cross,
> I have broken an oath upon the Cross.
> Says the Mother, the Humid Earth:
> Thy first sin, God will forgive it thee,
> The second sin, God will forgive it thee,
> But the third sin I *can not* forgive. [44]

---

[43] Golubinski, *Istoriya russkoi tserkvi*, II, 399–400.

[44] Smirnov, p. 280; V. G. Varentsov, *Sbornik russkikh dukhovnykh stikhov* (Collection of Russian Spiritual Poems), St. Petersburg, 1860, p. 16. Compare G. P. Fedotov, *Stikhi dukhovnye* (Spiritual Poems), Paris, 1935, pp. 67–84. "Brotherhood by the Cross" was established by a special rite; it implied eternal spiritual friendship and mutual loyalty.

The date of this song, as is the case with most creations of popular poetry, cannot be determined; certainly it goes centuries back into the past; some scholars go so far as to date it in the fourteenth century and explain it by the immediate influence of the Strigolniks.[45] We cannot follow this daring theory. The content of the sins confessed in this song has a particular feature; all of them are sins against kinship, physical or religious, and, thus, are the survivals of the *gens* (or *rod*) religion that has a very close tie with the cult of Mother Earth. As such, they indicate a very deep, or very low, cultural stratum, that of the "double-faith" (*dvoe-verie*).[46] The Strigolniks, as we know, belonged to the class of the intelligentsia, the most learned circles of the laity. Besides, as Photius writes, certainly in an allusion to their confessional practice: "They looked at the sky, calling to their Father." If we can combine this information with the confession to the Earth, then the Strigolniks blended Earth and Heaven, the Mother and the Father in their rites, and they certainly could not limit their confessions to sins against kinship or any other specific kind of sins.

Yet, qualifying the semipagan character of the Strigolnik confession so much, we cannot help being surprised by the paradox of their attitude. Representing a rationalistic and moralistic wing in the Church, they adopted, after their separation, such irrational practices that they were drawn near to the pantheistic and semipagan cults of the people. Such a dialectic of religious development is not rare in the history of sectarian movements; mystics become rationalists

---

[45] A. V. Markov, "Opredelenie khronologii russkikh dukhovnykh stikhov" (Determining the Chronology of Russian Spiritual Poems) in *Bogoslovski Vestnik* (Theological Messenger), June 1910, p. 363.

[46] On the remnants of paganism that are referred to here, see E. V. Anichkov, *Yazychestvo i drevnyaya Rus,* St. Petersburg, 1914, and N. Galkovski, *Borba khristianstva s ostatkami yazychestva v drevnei Rusi,* 2 vols., Moscow, 1913. Compare also George Vernadsky, *Origins of Russia,* Oxford: Clarendon Press, 1959, pp. 108–173.

and vice versa. Curiously enough, Bishop Stephen in his polemics with the Strigolniks combines his mystical idea of the Eucharist with a thoroughly rationalistic attitude toward Mother Earth. "The Earth is an inanimate creature, it does not hear nor is it able to answer the sinner or to forbid him." In this too common-sense judgment Stephen goes against the religious intuition of the Russian people, Christian and semi-Christian alike. In order to substantiate his conclusion, he should have avoided every moralization about the sacrament of penance, while in fact, he really does not: "As an ill man declares his suffering to a physician and the physician prescribes a medicine according to his suffering . . . so does man confess his sins to his spiritual father and the father orders him to cease sinning and imposes upon him an *epitimia* proportionte to his sin; that is why God remits this sin." [47] The bishop himself makes the validity of the sacrament dependent upon the art of spiritual physician; the sectarians, despairing of the competence of the physicians, referred directly to the mercy of God but through the medium of the God-created elements of nature.

These two attitudes represented by the sectarians and the bishop-polemicist do not exhaust the spiritual movements of this fruitful time. We have already mentioned the "Missive of Joseph" as a document of anticlerical trend. Yet its import is much greater than this. It is a very eloquent criticism of the exterior forms of devotion and a call to mystical union with Christ in the Holy Eucharist. Nothing is known about the author, although his Russian origin is quite certain; there is nothing which would date him in the fourteenth century when the first manuscript of his letter occurs. As a teacher of monks he may have been an abbot in one of the Russian monasteries of that time. The

[47] Pavlov, ed., *RIB*, vol. VI, no. 25, cols. 223–224. *Epitimia* is the penance imposed by the Church for sin.

problems discussed by him lead to the same ideological circle where the Strigolnik movement developed. But the
spiritual position of Joseph is peculiar; he is liberal and
mystical at the same time. He shares both in the criticism
of the clergy by the sectarians and in the defense of the
Eucharist by Bishop Stephen.

Joseph[48] begins with one particular form of devotion,
very popular in Russia as in the whole of Christendom: the
pilgrimage to the Holy Land. Hearing that some of his
spiritual children are going to undertake this journey, he
expresses, at first, his joy at their intention of "seeking
God." But his afterthought is rather a serious warning:

> God does not commend us to seek salvation with our feet, but
> with an immortal thing, an image of the Holy Trinity, a rational
> talent dwelling in us, that is with word and soul. And if some one
> buries his rational talent . . . in the earth of corruptible things and
> begins to seek with his feet God who is not in Jerusalem but holds
> in his palm the whole universe, he labors in vain; he must know that
> he is ailing with a devil's sore.

The devil seduces him with "the pretext of piety" to seek
God in Jerusalem where signs and miracles are being
wrought. But the seeking of miracles is condemned by the
"terrible answer" of the Savior: "The men of Nineveh and
the Queen of the South will condemn those who seek signs
and miracles" (Matt. 12:41–42).

Thus, not pilgrimages alone are rejected by the Russian
author but also the whole medieval approach to religion.
He opposes it in another way both mystical and sacramental:
"Having found God you ought not only approach him but
to eat his food and to see that the 'Lord is good'; He is
sweetness itself and unsatiable desire and joy and ineffable

---

[48] Edited by N. K. Nikolski in "Materialy po istorii drevne-russkoi
dukhovnoi pismennosti" (Materials on the History of Ancient Russian Religious Literature), in *SORYaS,* vol. 82, St. Petersburg, 1907, sec. 4, pp.
135–140.

beauty; and you do not wish to communicate in this joy *frequently* . . ." You should thirst "as the heart panteth after the brooks" to cool the burning poisons of serpents with them; so should we cool the poison of rational serpents from Christ's spring of life. Those who withdraw from it will perish. With many authorities Joseph tries to corroborate his call to frequent Communion. He is not particularly felicitous in his quotations; but behind their inexactness one feels a powerful spiritual intuition which tries to grope its way through doubtful canonical and legendary ground. Joseph quotes John Chrysostom (in fact the quotation is from St. Basil) who recommended that monks communicate five times a week, giving the following answer to the popular argument of "unworthy Communion." The unworthy is always unworthy if he does not wish to clean himself, and the worthy is always worthy. The unworthy, if he communicates, resembles Judas. And the worthy, if he does not communicate, becomes another Judas because he sells the Kingdom of Heaven "for miserable things."

A legendary reference is taken by Joseph from the Egyptian patericon (*Lausaikon*). St. Macarius once returned to human form a woman who was transformed into a horse because of her guilt: "She changed her custom of communicating every week and out of laziness did not communicate for three weeks. Therefore, she brought this trouble upon herself."

The main obstacle to frequent Communion, according to Joseph, is the modern priests who do not favor this practice. Against them he turns the power of his prophetic wrath:

Woe to the blind fools who, holding the key to understanding, do not themselves enter the doors of life and close them to those willing to enter . . . Now this power is held by priests who communicate themselves but forbid those who are willing to to communicate worthily. For them I have no word of my own because they know themselves that Christ has given the hope of salvation to all equally, suffered torments for all, given to all his precious blood and flesh for an imperishable food.

Between Akindin and Stephen (a radical rationalist and a mystical authoritarian) Joseph stands as a mystic radical, alone in his time, so far as we can see. He was the defender of a lost cause. Historical development in the Middle Ages, both in the East and the West, had already decided against frequent Communion and the echoes of the ancient Church tradition were stifled by the dominant religion of fear.

Unfortunately, we cannot draw a clear picture of the Eucharistic practice in Russia in the medieval or in the Kievan period. Canonical norms are contradictory because the ancient canonical Collections continued to be copied at later times when they obviously were out of date. Some Church authorities protested against the use of "bad *nomo-canons*," meaning by this term partly the absurd prescriptions resulting from the unenlightened zeal of private canonists, but, also, partly from the obsolete practice of older times. However, the Russians had as little means of distinguishing between "good" and "bad" canons as between true and apocryphal Scriptures. They possessed the authentic Greek Collections of canons (*Nomocanon*, in Russian, *Kormachaya*) but they needed a complementary development according to national needs, and this development was mostly due to private clerical zeal and not to the official authorities of the Church. This is particularly true in the field of the penitentiaries or canons concerning the *epitimias* for singular sins. We possess scores of these brief penitentiaries, partly contradicting one another but often copied together by the same hand. In these penitentiaries we have to look for indications of Eucharistic practice in Russia. In rare cases where the date of these Collections can be stated with certitude or probability we can observe the stages of development in rules and norms if not in practice. One has to suppose that practice followed the rules with some disorderly variations.

Concerning the frequency of Communion, the oldest and precisely the "bad" Russian canons, probably of the eleventh century, reflect the order of the ancient Church, that of weekly Communion. The so-called "Rule of the Holy Apostles" prohibiting Communion for three months for certain sins (ch. 23), one month (ch. 27) and three weeks (ch. 17) gives indirect evidence that it considers weekly Communion as a norm. The same custom underlies the Rule which bears the name of Maximus, although it is preserved only in manuscripts of the sixteenth and seventeenth centuries. Indeed, canon 10 of Maximus declares: "He who passes forty days without Communion must be called a heathen." [49] But, although even in the first version of *Izmaragd* Communion is once mentioned as the normal act of the Sunday service,[50] in the fourteenth century this was, certainly, a literary survival. We are not even sure that at any time weekly Communion was the rule in Russia. At least, a very ancient pre-Mongol canonical document enumerates a series of feast days in which "it becomes one who is worthy to communicate" (ch. 9). Here are mentioned 23 days, including all the Sundays of Lent.[51] In the Mongol period we meet a general recommendation to communicate on each of the great

---

[49] S. I. Smirnov, ed., *Materialy dlya istorii drevne-russkoi pokayannoi distsipliny: teksty i zametki* (Materials for the History of Ancient Russian Discipline: Texts and Notes), in *OIDRMU,* Moscow, 1912, II, 29–30; VIII, 52.

[50] *Izmaragd* I, ch. 49.

[51] "The precept of the holy Fathers to the confessing sons and daughters" is wrongly attributed by Golubinski to the Metropolitan George (XIth Century), Smirnov, ed., *Materialy,* XIX, 383–395. However, we cannot agree with Smirnov who understands by this period of 23 days the suggestion of a choice for the three Communion days. Any day is suitable for Communion. We see in this list a transitional stage between weekly Communion and Communion three times a year.

yearly fasts: three times at first, and four, after the fifteenth century when Our Lady's fast was introduced. In the "Golden Chain" we read: "A layman who does not communicate three times a year calls himself Christian in vain, he is neither hot nor cold." The same injunction is found in the *Izmaragd*. Metropolitan Photius (1408–1431) prescribes confession and, indirectly, Communion on the four long fasts, and that remained the ideal norm until the end of Muscovite Russia.[52]

Yet this norm was not enforced upon all the faithful. There are canonical documents which consider yearly Communion before Easter as normal.[53] Such is the view of St. Joseph of Volok, a great authority by the end of the medieval period (about 1500).[54] Nowhere do we hear of any penances or punishments for non-communicating. All the threats are directed against unworthy communicants and priests who administer Communion to them.

And this is not all. Since a very early period (which cannot be determined with precision), Russian Eucharistic devotion was regulated by two rules: no Communion without previous confession, and no absolution without penance (*epitimia*). These two rules combined made the Communion of the average layman extremely difficult, if not impracticable.

Numerous penitentials, official and private, give us the widely varying scales of ecclesiastical penances for every kind of sin. These *epitimias* in the Russian Church consisted mostly of fasting and a precise number of daily prostrations for a fixed period of time ranging from three days to one's whole life. During the time of performing the *epitimia* the penitent was not admitted to Communion. Now it is hardly believable that during this probation time he would not

---

[52] Smirnov, ed., *Materialy*, XIX, 166–167.

[53] Smirnov, ed., *Materialy*, XXXVIII, 183.

[54] Smirnov, ed., *Materialy*, XLVI, 225.

commit some new sins, however light ones, which would impose new *epitimias* upon him and thus delay the day of his Communion indefinitely. It is true that some ancient penitentials allowed even persons under penance to communicate once a year, on Easter or before Easter.[55] But all these collections belong to the "bad" *nomocanons* in the eyes of the enlightened canonists of old and modern times.[56] Many "good" canons, on the contrary, punish priests who admit penitents to Communion before the end of their penance.[57]

The penitential times themselves were very long and reveal a tendency to increase through the centuries. Joseph of Volok, at the end of the fifteenth century, writes as follows: "For a minor sin the *epitimia* lasts one year, for some others two or three or four, for others five, six and seven years. For great and heavy sins, fifteen and more, but for others twelve or even three." [58] Joseph tries to graduate the scale not only according to the transgression but also according to persons. And yet he counts only by years. In a group of letters to his spiritual sons he warns them positively against communicating those under *epitimia*. A certain person to whom a four-year penance was assigned he allows only on great feast days to kiss the icons and the cross and eat blessed bread (*antidoron*) — the sinner's substitute for the Eucharist. "And when four years are over, if he observes everything as is written, particularly bodily purity (sexual abstinence) and abstains from every evil, he may partake of the Holy Eucharist." [59]

---

[55] Smirnov, ed., *Materialy*, II, III, XX, XXVII.

[56] Note "Kirik's Questions" (12th century), in Pavlov, ed., *RIB*, vol. VI, no. 75, col. 44. Compare also L. K. Goetz, *Kirchenliche und kulturgeschichtliche Denkmäler Altrusslands nebst Geschichte des russischen Kirchenrechts*, Stuttgart, 1905, and Smirnov, ed., *Materialy*, pp. 284, 302, 397.

[57] Smirnov, ed., *Materialy*, pp. 193–194.

[58] *Ibid.*, XLVI, 225.

[59] *Ibid.*, 227.

It is clear that under such conditions Eucharistic Communion was practically impossible. In fact, it became very rare. We even hear of cases when persons after receiving penitential absolution did not go to Communion fearing either the terrific consequences for the "unworthy" or the obediences imposed on communicants.[60]

If, in spite of all these canonical obstacles, Communion did not die out completely in ancient Russia (as it practically died out elsewhere, for example in Abyssinia) this was due mainly to priestly abuses and to the canonical confusion which prevailed.

Manifold were the devices by which a priest or his spiritual son could circumvent the severe prescriptions of the penitentials. To begin with these prescriptions were not considered to be strictly binding on the confessors. They merely provided the pattern which ought to be applied with discretion. Some of the instructions addressed to spiritual fathers seem to ignore completely the existence of penitential canons, while others enjoin their strict observance.[61] In some cases a particular attenuation of penance was required; by a half for the "orphans," by which name the poor or working people were meant.[62] A great leniency was required also for the "new penitents," that is, for those adult persons who had come to confession for the first time in their lives. They were not to be frightened away from the sacraments, and their penances, insignificant in the beginning, had to be increased gradually until they reached the canonical level.[63] The case of a heavy illness and approaching death dispensed with *epitimias* before receiving Viaticum.

---

[60] Note the sermon attributed to the Metropolitan Peter in N. Kostomarov, ed., *Pamyatniki starinnoi russkoi literatury* (Monuments of Ancient Russian Literature), vol. IV, Moscow, 1862, p. 186: "Whoever wishes to have the Holy Gifts every year must give pledges to obey you [spiritual fathers]."

[61] Pavlov, ed., *RIB*, vol. VI, col. 835; *Izmaragd* I, ch. 73.

[62] Smirnov, ed., *Materialy*, XIII, 20, p. 90.

[63] *Ibid.*, XXXI, 160.

Such were the canonical means of leniency; there were numerous semi- and anti-canonical expedients besides. Some of the "bad" penitentials admit (while others prohibit) the use of hired helpers who perform a part of his *epitimias* for the penitent.[64] Still others, and not only "bad" ones, allow the commutation of *epitimias* for fixed numbers of Liturgies, ordered and paid for by the penitent. The tables of equivalence appear rather favorable for the sinner. Ten Liturgies had the value of four months of *epitimias;* thirty, of the whole year.[65] And, finally, there were always enough weak and corrupted priests who, induced by gifts or fear, admitted sinners to Communion without imposing penance upon them. Those "connivers" are threatened by terrible torments in hell in numerous canonical missives and instructions, but, owing mainly to them, the layman in ancient Russia had a chance to approach the chalice with the Body and Blood of Christ. How often is another question. We hold as too optimistic the estimate of Smirnov who takes, as an average norm, three or four times a year, corresponding to three or four long fasting periods. Perhaps once a year would be nearer the actual state of things. Of course, we know of exceptions on both sides of the average. Biographies of some princes, written in the style of the Lives of saints, inform us that they used to communicate on all the Sundays of Lent.[66] At the other end of the scale one meets people, and that not seldom, who never go to confession or, for that matter, to Communion. If, in the Kievan period, the noncommunicants had to be sought mostly among the heathen or half-heathen population, in the Middle Ages, or

---

[64] "Kirik's Questions," no. 96; Smirnov, ed., *Materialy,* XI, 22; XXX a, lines 20–21.

[65] "Kirik's Questions," no. 76; Smirnov, ed., *Materialy,* XI, 38; XXX b.

[66] The Life of Dimitri Donskoi and the Life of St. Michael of Tver. The latter prince observed this practice on his last journey to the khan where he expected and, in fact, met his death. For the Kievan period see the Hypatian Chronicle (1168) on Prince Rostislav Mstislavich.

in Muscovite times, their number is explained by the ecclesiastical education itself. Based on religious fear and moralism it failed to reveal to the laity the religious value of the fundamental sacrament of the Church. Union with Christ through the partaking of his Body and Blood was beyond the understanding of the average Christian, the clergy included. A Joseph in the fourteenth century was an exceptional personality, who was conscious of his isolation amidst the contemporary clergy, though Bishop Stephen (St. Stephen of Perm) seems to agree with him on the issue of the Eucharist. The sectarian Strigolniks reflected more truly the general state of mind, putting morals above this sacrament. Nevertheless, very few followed them in their rejection of ecclesiastical loyalty. Their schism provoked a ferocious anger among the popular masses. The Russian people loved the Church, with all the beauty and richness of her ritual and the spiritual comfort they found in it. So many sacred things — icons, crosses, relics, holy water, blessed bread — surrounded and nourished them in the Church that they did not miss the sacrament which once had been the core of the liturgical life but had gradually become practically inaccessible or irrelevant to them.

IV

THE FEUDAL WORLD

*T*HROUGHOUT Russian history there has not been any marked difference in the Christian ideals of life presented to the devout laity and to the nonmonastic ("white") clergy. The *Izmaragd* as well as most of the other pious Collections were addressed to the two classes of readers. We have, however, little evidence for determining how far the excellent counsels of didactic writers were followed in real life. Actual practices are better reflected in historical chronicles or annals, but these, of course, must be corrected to take into account social limitations; it is to the clan depicted in the lives of princes and their boyars that there is given conventionally, or rather by analogy with the Western world, the name of feudal society. Here we also encounter an idealization of reality; the pen of the chronicler in this period is less free from local and dynastic allegiances than it was in Kiev. Most of the scribes were official chroniclers at the courts of local princes or, in exceptional cases, bishops (for example, in Rostov). They do not even claim to stand above local interests; local patriotism is their inspiring force. This is what makes their writings the expression of the political and social aspirations of feudal society rather than a vehicle for establishing immutable Christian standards as was the case in the first century of Russian annals. It is regrettable that in the Great Russian northeast the annals lost much of their picturesqueness and much of the richness of descriptive detail that give so much charm to the Kievan chronicles.

The catastrophe of 1237 when the city of Vladimir was burned to the ground, never to be completely rehabilitated, put an end to Vladimir historiography. After the Mongol invasion the annals were continued in the city of Rostov and it was only at the beginning of the new century that the chronicling of history by scribes sprang up gradually in most of the great feudal centers — in Tver, Suzdal, Ryazan, and Moscow. It would be interesting to possess all these local chronicles in their primitive form. Unfortunately, they have not been preserved intact. When Moscow achieved the conquest of all the northeastern lands, she undertook a corresponding unification of national historiography. Local annals were fused in composite compilations reflecting a spirit and tradition that was already Muscovite. Thus, there exist, in fact, apart from the Novgorodian and Pskovian chronicles only the works of the Muscovite editors of the fifteenth and sixteenth centuries. The unification followed political tendencies; judgments unfavorable to Muscovite policies often were eliminated or modified. However, the remainder were usually preserved in their original wording; the compilers did not possess sufficient literary skill to refashion their material into a completely new form. Their annalistic notices are mostly the juxtaposition of separate entries, the local provenance of which is easily perceived. It would be quite feasible, though not an easy task, to reconstruct out of these fragments the outlines of the original local annals, a task parallel to that which Shakhmatov has performed for ancient Kievan historiography. This work would require, perhaps, the whole life span of a well-trained critical historian.[1] Meanwhile, one must depend on one's own critical sense in trying to single out the primitive local traditions from the later Muscovite versions. This is precisely the task of the present chapter. It would be senseless to handle all the medieval chronicles as if they were the work of the same hand. Despite the leveling primitivism of the medie-

---

[1] Professor M. D. Priselkov reconstructed the Troitskaya Chronicle in a work posthumously published, *Troitskaya letopis* (The Trinity Chronicle [of 1408]), Moscow and Leningrad, 1950.

val mind an outspoken contrast of moral attitudes can be
detected. Not that every local political center elaborated its
own moral and religious character; the line of demarcation
ran between Moscow on the one hand and most of the other
principalities on the other. Only in regard to the latter can
one speak, in a limited sense, of feudal spirit and ethics.
Without anticipating the content of subsequent chapters we
can already emphasize here the uniqueness of the political
outlook of Moscow; it was dominated, in the decisive period
of its development by two forces: the Tatars, whose allies
were the princes of Moscow up to the time of Dimitri Donskoi (1362–1389) and the ecclesiastical government in the
person of the metropolitans of Kiev who made their residence
in Moscow from 1328. The fusion of ecclesiasticism and
Orientalism, strange as it may seem, became the earmark of
Muscovite culture for centuries. Quite apart from both the
feudal world of the principalities and authoritarian Muscovy
stood the Western democratic system of the two city-states,
Novgorod and Pskov, possessing their own rich historio-
graphical and ecclesiastical tradition.

Although the Northern annals were a direct continuation of those of Kiev, and all of them began as literary
replicas of the ancient works, a change both in style and basic
ideas gradually appeared at the end of the thirteenth century.
However, too radical a change ought not to be expected. It
consisted mostly in a shift of emphasis and in new shadings
rather than in new ideas.

The obituary portrait of the prince, which was so typical
of the Kievan annals, became a rarity in the fourteenth century; only Tver, a great rival of Moscow, has preserved for
us the whole gallery of its princely forbears. In compensation, we can avail ourselves of half a dozen excellent, though
idealized, biographies in the lives of holy princes. The Rus-

sian Church retains in its calendar commemorations of about fifty canonized Russian princes. Some of them belong to the ancient period, like St. Vladimir, his grandmother Olga, and his sons, Boris and Gleb. Yet by far the greater number of canonized princes belong to the first century of the Mongol occupation. This was a troubled time when there was more need of the sword of a defender-warrior than of the prayers of an ascetic monk. True, many holy princes died violently either in a battle with the Tatars or at the khan's court, victims either of his wrath or his sense of justice. They could be commemorated as martyrs in a larger sense, but others were revered precisely as the protectors of their lands. No particular ascetic virtues were attributed to them; they remained personifications of the feudal virtues of their social state, pious laymen of military calling. Moreover, the strict line between canonized and noncanonized princes is not easily drawn. Most of the princes of Tver, whose biographies are preserved, were venerated in their own city, but victorious Moscow did not accept their canonization, except for the greatest of them, St. Michael.

Many biographies of canonized and noncanonized princes found their way into local annals along with short notices about the others. They display the same moral and religious ideals and are even composed in the same style. We are, therefore, entitled to use them as representative of the heroic virtues of the feudal ruling class.

At the very outset of the period that we are considering, in 1238, we find in the chronicles the eulogy of young Prince Vasilko (Konstantinovich) of Rostov, who was captured and murdered by the Tatars after the battle of the Sita River. It is a vivid portrait of a medieval prince revealing in its secular section the pen of a military man (*druzhinnik*). "Vasilko was handsome of face, bright of eye and dread of countenance, courageous to the extreme and light of heart; whoever served him, or ate his bread and drank of his cup, could not, because of his great love, live with or serve any other prince; for he loved his servants extremely; courage and wisdom dwelled in him, justice and truth walked with him; he was skillful in everything" (*Lavr.*).[2] Although in later biographies of Alexander Nevski these characteristics were transferred to the greater hero in their entirety, the portrait of Vasilko still belongs to the Kievan period. The physical beauty of a prince ceased to be a stock feature under the Mongols. One trait is particularly precious but needs some comment; "lightness of heart" is not the same as the English "light-heartedness." It implies kindness toward people, gaiety of mood, and quick forgiveness of wrongs; the heavy heart is rancorous. Kindness and cheerfulness are counterbalanced by the "dreadfulness" of an awe-inspiring glance. Rarely mentioned in ancient times, after the thirteenth century this trait becomes the usual attribute of a lord, not yet associated with despotism or cruelty as later when the same epithet (*grozny*) is applied to Tsar Ivan IV.

The secular features in Vasilko's portrait are supplemented by his predominantly Christian virtues, which are enumerated on the occasion of his funeral. "A multitude of Orthodox people beheld in death the father and sustainer of orphans, the great comfort of the afflicted, the light-giving star to the darksome oppressed. For he won the hearts of the whole ecclesiastical state; he was like a beloved father

---

[2] The various collections of annals are gathered in the *Polnoe Sobranie Russkikh Letopisei* (Complete Collection of Russian Chronicles), edited by the Arkheograficheskaya Komissiya (Archeographic Commission), St. Petersburg, 1846, and frequently abbreviated as *PSRL*. The individual chronicles are abbreviated as follows: *Sim.* (*Simonovskaya*); *Nik.* (*Nikonovskaya*); *Rog.* (*Rogozhskaya*); *Voskr.* (*Voskresenskaya*); *Lavr.* (*Lavrentievskaya*); *Tver.* (*Tverskaya*); *Troits.* (*Troitskaya*); *Sof.* (*Sofiskaya*).

to all the clerics and beggars and the sad; but particularly
was he generous in almsgiving remembering the words of
our Lord . . ." (*Lavr.*).

This is the most comprehensive and detailed characterization of the medieval prince. Its separate features are
found, scattered in various applications to other worthy
personalities. As was once true in Kiev, one virtue is never
lacking, charity to the poor and the clergy. The clergy take
God's place in the diune formula of Christian love toward
God and man. So it happens that in some panegyrics, even
those not signalized by any particular brevity, charity alone
is spoken of, as in the commemoration of Prince Gleb of
Rostov (*Sim.* 1278): "He comforted the sad, distributed
food and drink unsparingly to the needy . . . [a long development follows], he built many churches and adorned
them with icons and books, and he much esteemed the state
of priests and monks; he was loving and merciful to all and
he was humble; for he loathed pride and turned from it
as from a serpent . . ." Humility alone accompanies charity
in this panegyric, as in a very similar portrait of Prince
Basil Yaroslavich (*Nik.* I, 1276).[3] We interpret these characteristics not as testimonies of the level of Christian life but
only as a standard of the Christian ideal. Ecclesiastical exaggeration is as obvious in the instance cited as it is becoming.

The religious devotion of a prince is exemplified not
only in the building of churches and the care of the clergy,
but also in the description of his most personal and intimate
act of repentance at the approach of death. The last days
of a prince are often described in details that reveal the
pen of an eyewitness. Prince Dimitri Svyatoslavich died as
a monk, in a *skhema*, or monastic garb, tonsured by Bishop

---

[3] See also the portraits of Prince Yuri of Vladimir (*Lavr.* 1239), and
Michael Alexandrovich of Tver (*Rog.* 1399).

Ignatius of Rostov, in the presence of Prince Gleb Vasilkovich and his mother who sat near him. He had lost his speech
but he spoke again. Looking at the bishop with cheerful eyes
he said: "My Lord and father, God has completed your
labors for me; you have girded me for a long journey, for
eternity, having crowned me as a warrior of the true king,
Christ, our God." Thereupon he gave up his soul, humble
and meek (*Sim.* 1269). Prince Theodore of Yaroslavl
(+1299) was canonized as a saint. The most ancient of
his *vitae*, composed by his contemporary, is an account given
entirely by an eyewitness of the prince's tonsure on his
deathbed. The dying prince was carried to a neighboring
monastery and, after the rite of tonsuring, was left in the
abbot's house for the last night of his life. Leaving his palace
was an indication of the seriousness of his renunciation to
the world.[4]

The custom of monastic profession on the deathbed,
which had started in Kiev,[5] no longer encountered any
ecclesiastical objections. Occasionally, opposition came from
the prince's family, for example, in the case of Boris Vasilkovich, who was prevented from taking the tonsure by his
wife Mary, who still hoped for his recovery (*Nik.* 1299).

None dared to dissuade the Prince of Tver, Michael
Alexandrovich, from a similar act "for he was a dreaded man
and had a heart like the heart of a lion." He took the tonsure during his last illness, although not in his last hour.
After the rite of tonsure he lived for many days, frequently
receiving Holy Communion and being anointed with sacred
oil, obviously in the hope of recovery. But his first act as a
new monk was to give a banquet, quite in Kievan style, "for
the bishop and clergy and for the invalids, in order to dis-

---

[4] N. I. Serebryanski, "Drevnerusskiya knyazheskiya zhitiya" (Ancient
Russian Lives of Princes), in *OIDRMU*, Moscow, 1915, III, texts, pp. 90–92.

[5] Compare with the discussion of Prince Rostislav of Smolensk (+1168)
in Fedotov, *RRM*, I, 274–275.

tribute much money to the priests and the poor" (*Rog.*
1399). The real motive of this deathbed charity is revealed
by the addition: "He distributed with his hands much
money for memorial services (*sorokoust*) and had his name
inscribed in his own presence for the commemorations." The
author of this obituary asserts that Prince Michael "for
many years had burnt in heart with the desire for sacred monastic orders and used to express with tears his longing for
the religious life." [6] Yet there is nothing ascetical about this
"dreaded" and "lion-hearted" man, even in the description
of the same annalist. Either this longing for tonsure is to
be rejected as rhetorical exaggeration or it is, rather, a simple expression of a high esteem of monastic life which was
general and not personally binding; this ideal esteem inter-
fered little with practical life and its secular ethics. Cases of
princes retreating to a cloister on other occasions than on
the deathbed are exceptionally rare; in the Russian Middle
Ages they occur even more rarely than in Kiev. The reason,
probably, is to be found in a fuller appreciation by the
Church of the secular virtues of a prince whose sword was
vitally necessary in those troubled times. This is proven by
the frequent canonization of princes and the characteriza-
tions of their lives.

As has been proved by literary criticism[7] the numerous
Lives of St. Alexander Nevski are based upon two ancient
(thirteenth-century) biographies, one belonging to a monk
of the city of Vladimir, another to a warrior, a retainer of
the prince. It is noteworthy that both authors highly praise
the courage and military valor of Alexander Nevski and
even make this virtue the main feature of their biographies.

---

[6] Note the same claim for Prince Alexander Nevski in Serebryanski, p. 119.

[7] Compare B. Mansikka, *Zhitie Aleksandra Nevskago, razbor redaktsi i tekst* (The Life of Alexander Nevski: An Analysis of the Editions and the Text), in *PDPI,* vol. 180, St. Petersburg, 1913.

Particularly eloquent is the voice of the secular author. He
begins with a comparison of the Russian hero with the heroes
of the ancient world: "The namesake of the King Alexander
of Macedonia was similar to the King Achilles, strong and
valiant . . . He was prince over princes and chieftain over
chieftains. His voice was dreaded like a sounding trumpet."
Alexander was victorious everywhere and invincible himself, like Akritas, who alone, by his strength, could defeat
armies and could never be defeated.[8] The monastic hagiographer did not infringe upon this heroic style; he merely
substituted the heroes of the Bible and Flavius Joseph for
the pagan glories: "His stature was greater than that of
other men, his voice was like a trumpet amidst the people,
his face like Joseph's . . . his strength, a part of the
strength of Samson the valiant, his wisdom like Solomon's,
his valor like that of Vespasian, the Roman King."[9] The
bulk of both Lives consists of the description of the two
battles that made the name of Alexander famous — with
the Swedes on the Neva river and with the German knights
on the ice of Lake Peipus. In both struggles Alexander took
part personally and covered himself with glory. To the
Neva he hurries "with a small force of retainers without
waiting for his great army . . ." During the battle "he
slayed a multitude of foes and made a sign on the face of
the king with his sharp sword." The courage of his warriors
is also celebrated on this occasion, "Their hearts were like
lion hearts." Six minor heroes distinguished on the Neva are
mentioned by name with an account of their exploits.[10]

In the city of Pskov, Prince Dovmont of the thirteenth
century was revered as a saint. He was a heathen Lithuanian
by birth, who, as the result of certain tribal disturbances

---

[8] Digenis Akritas, a hero of the popular Byzantine epic, whose story was
translated into Slavonic. See Serebryanski, p. 121.

[9] Serebryanski, p. 111.

[10] Serebryanski, pp. 113–114.

(after having killed his father he found refuge in the Russian city), was baptized and became a valiant and successful defender of his new country against his native countrymen and the Germans. His ancient Life, destined for liturgical use (fourteenth-century) is a very brief document, of less than a score of lines, and the eulogy of the saint begins as follows: "He was a dreaded warrior having shown in many battles his valor and pious customs." These customs are specified, in the usual way, as piety and almsgiving.[11] A later, more extensive Life, composed on the basis of the annals and other princely biographies is nothing but an account of Dovmont's battles and military expeditions. All his exploits, of course, are accompanied by prayers and they are presented as acts of faith. In connection with one of Dovmont's wars against the Order of German Knights an unusual ritual is mentioned, which was otherwise unknown in Russia but general in the West, the blessing of the sword. This is the text of the Life, substantially identical with that of the annals:

The blessed Prince Dovmont, hearing of their [the German] advance, with great resolve but without God, entered the Cathedral Church of the Holy Trinity, laid down his sword before the sanctuary and falling upon the ground began to pray in tears; after having prayed long he rose and the Abbot Isidore of St. Savior took his sword, and all the priests together with him, invested the Prince with the sword and let him go.[12]

There can be little doubt that this religious rite was borrowed in Pskov, a borderland city, from Catholic Germany. Incidentally, the sword of Dovmont, until recently, hung in the Holy Trinity Cathedral, over the tomb of the Prince. It was the work of a Western master and had a Latin inscription expressing the military spirit of Catholic knighthood: "Honorem meum nemini dabo."

---

[11] Serebryanski, pp. 138, 139–143.

[12] Serebryanski, p. 141.

The canonized princes are, certainly, not the only subjects whose courage and military deeds are praised by contemporaries and posterity. Many princes of the Middle Ages share in their renown. A few examples will suffice. "The Great Prince Andrew of Suzdal, having strained his strength and fearing not their threat . . . broke through the hosts of the Tatars who fought against them" (*Rog.* 1361). The Prince of Berezky was killed by the Lithuanians "who had formerly shown great courage in wars and great valor in battles and so he laid down his life loyally serving his Prince [of Moscow]." A version of the annals (of Tver) adds to this entry: "To this hero is due glory" (*Sim.* and *Rog.* 1370).

The last quotation shows that the ideal of personal glory and honor did not die out in medieval Russia, though it is expressed much less frequently than in the Kievan Chronicles. We find similar sentiments on the lips of a Prince of Tver as late as 1408, speaking of his unfaithful ally Basil of Moscow: "He has dishonored my name in all countries" (*Tver.* 1408).[13] Yet a great change as compared with the pre-Mongol past is obvious. Gratuitous, adventurous valor lost its general esteem; courage is appreciated only insofar as it serves society. The prince is the defender of his people; he wields his sword not for his personal pleasure or honor. Vain valor even elicits severe reproach as in the case of Prince Andrew, a generous brother of Nevski: "Although he was adorned with nobility and courage still he considered it a small matter to govern his state, taking rather to hunting and heeding young and unwise councilors" (1253).

If war is viewed as a public service, as an action of self-sacrifice pleasing to God, then any opposition between military and monastic ideals disappears. All princes desire to take the monastic tonsure before death because tonsure, like

---

[13] *PSRL,* XV, col. 476.

baptism, effects the remission of sins and not because they feel any particular ascetic contempt for worldly political activities. Thus, there are cases that most probably would have been impossible in Kiev of monks who return temporarily to the work of the sword in good conscience, convinced that they are doing the will of God. True, the two recorded instances pertain to wars against the heathen. The first involves Voishelk, son of a Lithuanian heathen, Prince Mindovg, who was a monk in one of the Russian monasteries. After the violent death of his father at the hand of his own sons, Voishelk decided to avenge this misdeed. "He took off his monastic vestments, having promised to put them on again in three years and in no way changing his monastic rules. He gathered many warriors . . . and went against the pagan Lithuanians and Chuds and made prisoners of all the people he found there . . . and he erected many crosses and churches and monasteries and returned to his monastery." The observation of all his monastic rules (that is, those of fasting or prayer) atones for the bloodshed; a war of personal revenge is represented as holy, and, that there may be no doubt of his approval, the chronicler puts into the mouth of the prince-monk the following prayer: "Thou, o Lord, see this and glorify Thy name so that the iniquitous should not boast in their unrighteousness . . ."

The other instance, which is better known, exerted great influence. St. Sergius assigned to Prince Dimitri two of his monks, the former boyars Peresvet and Oslyabiya, to fight with him at the battle of Kulikovo. Legends make great capital of this historical fact, though they describe in different ways the character of the two monk-heroes. Their graves were venerated in Moscow up to the Revolution, and in the eyes of the Muscovites as well as of present-day Orthodox Russians generally, their example justified the concept of a "holy" war and the participation of the clergy therein. On the other hand, the pre-Mongol Russian attitude can be gauged from the fact that most contemporary anti-Roman polemics cited as a specifically Western abuse the participation of bishops in armed combat. Certainly, the Christian horror of bloodshed at the hands of monks and the clergy did not disappear completely but abated considerably during the medieval period.

Returning to the portraits of medieval princes we see how differently they appear in the light of a double ethical standard: Christian charity and military valor. The two opposed characteristics are mild (*krotki*) and dreaded (*grozny*). It is not accidental, perhaps, that the former feature is emphasized for the most part during the first Mongol century. "In 1276 there passed away Basil the Youngest, the Great Prince of Vladimir . . . he was of no malice and forgiving of those who sinned against him." "In 1303 there passed away the Prince Dmitrievich of Peryaslavl, pious and humble, mild and tranquil."

But as early as the life of Alexander Nevski (thirteenth-century) his "dreadfulness" in the eyes of his enemies is emphasized even at the expense of historical truth. "His name was dread in battle." "Dreaded was his coming" [to the Tatars], and the Moabite women began to frighten their children by saying: "Alexander is coming! . . . And all the land was glorious in the fear of his wrath and his valor."

Prince Dovmont of Pskov "was a dread warrior" in the words of his brief ecclesiastical Life (from the Lectionary). The same "dreadness" is a usual feature of the princes of Tver in the fourteenth century. Although Prince Michael Yaroslavich died as a martyr at the court of the khan his portrait begins like a hero's: "He was taller in stature and stronger than other men, very noble and wiser than most; he had a dread glance . . . fearful to the warriors . . ." And

in the long panegyric of his grandson, Michael Alexandrovich (1399), one reads: "Nobody dared to say anything
against him; they were afraid of him, for he was a fearful
man and his heart was like the heart of a lion."

As we see in attributing these characteristics — mildness
and dreadfulness — no special attention is paid to personal
holiness as it was expressed in the proceedings of the canonization of a prince. Both could exist side by side in a holy
prince. As time passed, mildness decreased in esteem, and
"dreadness" became the more admired virtue. And we come
to the Muscovite ideal of the ruler when "dread" becomes
an epithet of both Ivan III and Ivan IV.

However, during all of the Russian Middle Ages, there
did exist a line of demarcation between a lawful "dreadness"
on the part of a ruler and cruelty which was universally
condemned. The cruel punishment of the Novgorodian,
whom Alexander Nevski condemned for rebellion, of which
the chronicle informs us (that is, the severing of tongues and
ears) was not alluded to in the *vitae* of the Prince. Describ-
ing the repulsive tortures to which the citizens of Smolensk
put their enemies from Lithuania in 1386, the annalist of
Tver concludes his impression: "They tormented bestially
and inhumanly."

The note of condemnation could be felt also in the description of obscene outrages and cruelties committed by the
citizens of Opochki in 1426 (Pskov province) against the in-
ternational army of Vitovt (Lithuanian). However, in this
instance, the Muscovite chronicler abstains from any overt
protest and places the "shame" on Vitovt, the enemy, who
retreated in ignominy.

This partisanship vitiates the reactions of Christian feeling, and pity for the victims of war finds free expression
mostly from the neutrals or at the expense of the traditional
enemy who is accused of atrocities. We see the eternal mirror

of human weakness. The Tverites had ample opportunities
for the moral condemnation of Muscovite callousness. But in
1373 Prince Michael of Tver captured the town of Torzhok
and committed the usual acts of revenge. The slaughter,
death by fire and in the river, and the sufferings of the
prisoners are eloquently described in the Chronicle of Moscow which concludes: "Who, brothers, does not weep at this,
of the eyewitnesses still living . . . Such an evil was not
done to Torzhok even by the pagans" (*Sim.* 1373). In the
chronicles of Tver the atrocities committed in Torzhok are
covered by hypocritically pious meditations: "All these punishments God sends upon us for our sins" (*Rog.* 1373).

The other opposed pair of virtues, parallel to mildness-
dreadness is humility-honor. Honor and glory, so freely ex-
panding in the twelfth century, out of the cover of Christian
humility, still exist as ideals in feudal circles, although they
are mentioned less and less. Even as late as the beginning of
the fifteenth century (1408) the Prince of Tver, Ivan Mikhailovich, deceived by his ally, Basil of Moscow, referred to
the wrong done to his honor: "I sent my brothers to help
him but he, unbeknownst to my brothers, made my name dishonored in all countries; may God be my judge in this."

We hear more of humility, but at this period, in political
relations, humility is hardly more than a Christian disguise
for other, often not very Christian motives. In 1372 the
Prince of Tver, Michael Alexandrovich, whose lionlike nature was praised by the chronicler, sent "with humility"
this notice to the people of Novgorod and Novotorzhok:
"Whoever has beaten and ravished my people of Tver is to
be extradited to me, and I do not wish anything that is
yours, but you must appoint my governors" (*Tver.* 1372).
Here humility consists only in the readiness of the prince to
enter into negotiations; complete submission by his enemies
is his demand.

About the same time (1371) the Muscovite chronicler describes the war against Ryazan in which the Muscovites were the aggressors. He contrasts the boasts of self-confident enemies to the pious attitude of "ours." "They strengthened themselves with humility and many sighs, confiding in God, strong in battles" (*Troits.* 1371).[14] Here humility simply stands for the force of the stronger and more clever. We shall see that this abuse of the word humility which could already be observed in Vladimir at the end of the Kievan period is typical of the political ethics of Moscow.

Ever since Klyuchevski's investigations it has become the classical approach to contrast the prince adventurer of Kievan Russia, always engaged in battles, in the quest of a better udel, with the sedentary lord of Mongol Russia whose princedom is hereditary and whose personal power is dependent on the economic standard of his udel. This concept is warranted for Kievan Russia, ostentatious in its contempt for wealth, which it deemed fit only for the distribution to the retinue (*druzhina*). But in the historical sources of the fourteenth and even fifteenth centuries survivals of this older, anti-economical outlook are still visible. In a eulogy of Prince Michael Alexandrovich of Tver (1399) one reads: "He was sweet to his druzhina, because he did not love gold, nor precious garb, but all that he had he gave . . . to his druzhina."[15]

On the other hand, the adventurous type of prince, so typical of the *Tale of the Prince Igor* was already condemned in the first generation after the Mongol conquest, in the person of Andrew, Nevski's brother: "Although this prince was endowed with nobility and valor, he deemed the governing of his state as a trifling matter, spending his time rather in hunting and listening to young councilors from

---

[14] Priselkov, ed., *Troitskaya letopis,* p. 393.
[15] *PSRL,* XV, col. 469.

whom came a great disorder, a scarcity of people and the
waste of goods" (1252). Typical of the acquisitive and
economical type of new princes were the rulers of Moscow
of whom we shall speak later.

In an idealized portrait of a prince it is very difficult to
separate personal virtues from social ones. Up to this point,
in trying to remain in the personal sphere, where princely
virtues are not different from those of the military aristocracy in general, we have been forced to enter into the political field. From now on we shall study politics as such from
the point of view of prevalent religious and moral ideas.
We are still in a feudal world except for the democracy in
Novgorod and the growing monarchy in Moscow. Essentially, there is no cleavage with the Kievan tradition, no traces
of political Byzantinism on Russian soil.

It is still a common belief that a prince is appointed by
God,[16] and his assassination by rebelling subjects is a grievous
sin. The citizens of Bryansk who killed their prince in 1341
are called "cursed" and "malicious traitors" (*Rog.* and *Sim.*
1340). But the killing of a prince in a feud with another is
not regarded as a crime. The conscience of a blood relation-
ship among all the Rurikides is lost; the princes of the
Russian land are no longer brothers.

Certainly, there must be a great distance in political self-
consciousness between a great feudal lord like the Prince of
Tver and a small princely landowner with a limited political
horizon and predominantly economic interests. Yet, the idea
of public service remains as the predominating ideal of this
period; neither despotic rule in the Byzantine pattern nor
exploitation for the sake of private interest, as was natural
·in the small udels, was considered justifiable. A good prince
serves his land and people but does not dominate them.

---

[16] See the letter of St. Cyril of Belozersk in *Akty Istoricheskie: 1334–1700*
(Historical Annals: 1334–1700), St. Petersburg, 1841–1842, no. 16.

Even the Lives of St. Alexander, which try to exalt him to the level of the ancient heroes and the Roman emperors, emphasize his self-sacrificing service to his people.

Alexander did not abandon the way of his father, for his people's sake: for them he suffered much oppression. He did deny himself in great honor, giving away all his wealth, all his fortune to the aliens. Nor did he spare the offspring of his heart. For the sake of the Christians he gave him unto the aliens ransoming men from woe and grief and captivity.

Even as late as the beginning of the fifteenth century (1399), in the threnodies of the citizens of Tver for their Prince Michael, they are far from servile or even submissive in their feelings toward "the dread man":

Where are you going . . . Tver's great freedom, the honored glory of the sons of Tver, great guardian of our city, who always protected it like an eagle its nest; through you the sons of Tver enjoyed honor and were unmolested in strange countries.

Of the three social forces which limit the power of a feudal prince the popular assembly or *veche* is no longer a constitutional factor. The aristocracy of boyars and the druzhina retained all their influence. Yet, most dominant, because morally it was the most justifiable, was the influence of the Church in the person of the metropolitans and the bishops. In an obituary of a Great Prince of Vladimir (1276) one reads: "As in the early times, the prime political function of the bishops is to keep peace among the princes." In 1296 when political discord threatened to result in war "the princes were moved to love by the Bishops Simeon and Ismael" (*Voskr.*). During a quarrel between the city of Novgorod and its Prince Yaroslavl (1270) the prince turns to the Metropolitan Cyril asking for his mediation: "It is your duty to bring all to peace, especially us, the children you know so well." And the metropolitan accepts this commission, insisting, in his missive to Novgorod, not so much on the privileges of the prince as on his own authority.

> The Lord God, in lieu of himself, gave the apostles the power of binding and loosing and, after them, their successors. And we are the successors of the apostles, bearing the image of Christ and holding his power. And I, the chief pastor of all Russia, teach and instruct you in the Lord: "Fear God and honor the prince, and do not wage war in vain, nor shed blood. There is penance and pardon for every guilt and every sin. Insofar as Prince Yaroslavl Yaroslavich was wrong toward you, he repents and asks forgiveness in all . . . and I pledge to you for him. Receive him with fitting honor."

The letter ends with a threat of spiritual punishment in the event of disobedience. For our purpose it is interesting that the metropolitan does not require unconditional surrender to the prince, as the authority ordained by God, but indicates the prince's remorse for his wrongs toward the city.

A century later (1366), we see a Bishop of Tver acting as arbitrator between the Great Prince of Tver and the junior princes in a suit concerning lands. However, it is true that it was done at the order of the Metropolitan Alexis who at that time was a regent of Moscow.

We should not expect that in all cases the bishop could stand above personal partisanship or fear. The same Bishop of Rostov, Ignatius, who was praised in a chronicle as peacemaker among princes and brothers, was severely rebuked and all but deposed by the metropolitan for a posthumous crime against a prince a year before. Nine weeks after the death of Prince Gleb, the bishop ordered that his body be removed from the cathedral church where he was buried. As the metropolitan says: "You have condemned the dead man before the judgment of God; and during his life you were intimidated by him, taking gifts from him and eating and drinking with him" (*Sim.* 1280).

And yet in the Middle Ages instances of bishops taking

princes to task for moral or political transgressions are not rare. Not only did bishops assume this role but even on occasion so did simple abbots who were renowned for saintliness of life. Some letters (dated 1427) have been left from St. Cyril of Belozersk addressed to certain feudal princes, sons of Dimitri Donskoi, which present not only spiritual counsel but in at least one case advice on internal politics. However, it is true that St. Cyril does not make a distinction between private and public ethics as is evident in his letters to Prince Andrew Dimitrievich of Mozhaisk (dated 1408 and 1415): "And you, my lord, consider it in this light; you are a lord in your domain, appointed by God in order to restrain your people from evil customs." Then follows an entire political program based on general moral principles:

> You should, my lord, judge right judgments, as before God; without slander; without false evidence; the judges should not take bribes, and should be content with their lawful share . . . And you, my lord, should pay heed that in your domain are no pot-houses; for, my lord, they are a great peril to souls; those who frequent them ruin themselves with drinking and their souls perish. Neither, my lord, should you have customhouses, for they provide, my lord, unrighteous revenue; where a ferry exists, there it is just to pay for the labor. Also, my lord, there must be in your domain, no brigandage and no stealing. And if they do not stop their evil-doing make them subject to your punishments of which they are worthy. And also, my lord, restrain your subjects from foul words and abuse, for all this angers God. If you do not endeavor to correct all this, it will be exacted from you, because you are the lord of your people, ordained by God. And you should not be loath to give judgment to Christians in your own right. This will be imputed to you by God even more than prayer or fasting. You should abstain from drunkenness and give alms according to your means; for, my lord, you are unable to fast and are lax in praying, and thus, alms, in their place, will make up for your deficiency.

The suggestion that the Prince go to church frequently and

"stand there with fear and trembling" concludes this interesting missive.[17]

There are some points which appear utopian to us; as, for example, the abolishment of taverns and customhouses. Yet, it would seem that during the Russian Middle Ages these were the chief forms of concrete social evil which were especially attacked by the social reformers.[18] In the obituary of Michael Alexandrovich (1399), Prince of Tver, we read: "During his time inn-keepers, and publicans and market customs were abolished." The divinely ordained power of the prince is always regarded in terms of his responsibilities, and despite the ever-repeated "my lord," which serves to mitigate the bitterness of the spiritual medicine, the prince appears as a bad boy before his teacher.

Cyril begins his instruction with the necessity of justice, in the prince's courts. In the Middle Ages just as in Kiev, justice was a highly honored virtue; perhaps the emphasis grew even stronger. In the chronicles it is praised in the Great Prince Yaroslav (1238) and in Michael of Tver (1399) who is called, in Slavonic liturgical style, a "justice unoffendable." But the most interesting documents are two works of the fourteenth century — "The Instruction to Princes," and "The Instruction of Simeon, Bishop of Tver." Both insist on the duty of personal judgment by the prince and his responsibility for his *tyuns* (administrative and judicial officers). The instruction to the princes begins with biblical references such as "God, give thy judgment to the King" (Ps. 71:1) and a rather original turn of an old saying: "A prince who loves justice and righteousness is a heaven on earth" (usually this is the definition of the Church). Yet when they abandon these ideals, the princes prepare a dreadful future for themselves:

---

[17] *Ibid.*

[18] In Kievan Russia the corresponding evil was *izgoi.*

Having been gods you will die like men and will be led like dogs to hell. [And why?] You appoint in your place governors and tyuns who are ungodly . . . perfidious, who do not understand judgment and do not examine righteousness, who sit drunken in the courts and hasten the proceedings . . . robbers and venal men . . . He who is in the right is condemned by them as guilty. When he implores the prince, the prince does not listen to him . . . People cry out to you, prince, and you do not avenge them, deeming truth an injustice, loving lawless profits; this is why thou hast sent evil judges over the people. It is written: it is not good to behold a fox among the poultry; it is absurd to make a lion a shepherd of sheep; one ox will trouble the whole row; one thief stinks in all directions; under an unrighteous tsar, all servants are lawless.

This instruction on the lips of Simeon, Bishop of Tver, takes a wittier form.[19] This bishop was invited to a banquet given by a prince of Polotsk who, wishing to reproach his tyun in some matter, said to the bishop before all present: "My lord, where will the tyun be in the next world?" Simeon answered: "Where the prince will be." The prince, in displeasure, said to the hierarch: "The tyun judges wrongly, takes bribes, sells people, tortures them, does every evil and what do I do?" The bishop said:

If the prince is good and pious . . . he appoints as tyun or governor a good and pious man . . . If the prince is in paradise, the tyun too will be in paradise. If the prince be without the fear of God, without pity toward Christians . . . he appoints as tyun a malicious man . . . with the sole purpose that he amass profits for the prince; it is as if he were to let loose a madman against the people . . . if the prince will be in hell, the tyun, too, will be in hell with him.

What appears from these documents is, on the one hand,

---

[19] This is the same Simeon (+1288) of whom the chronicler remarks: "He was edifying and strong in books; he would argue without fear of the prince or the lords" (*Sim.* 1288). His instruction was included in the so-called *Merilo pravednoe*, M. N. Tikhomirov, ed., *Merilo pravednoe po rukopisi XIV veka* (*Merilo pravednoe* according to a manuscript of the 14th Century), Moscow, 1961, pp. 128 ff.   J. M.

the wide extent of judicial corruption and the connivance of the princes with the judiciaries, but, on the other hand, we see well the strong protest of the Church and the general Christian conscience against evil. We are still far from the social pessimism and despondence that characterize Muscovite Russia and, in some measure, even the modern soul.

But justice as a virtue is larger than its judicial aspect. The Russian word *pravda* is particularly rich in meaning; "justice," "righteousness," and even "truth" can be expressed by this term. And one encounters it indeed in its opposite *nepravda* (injustice) at every step in the annalistic account of interprincely relations and feuds. "Why have you lost justice?" asks the Prince Oleg of Rylsk (in 1284) of Prince Svyatoslav, his former ally, before beginning war against him. Prince Dimitri, the son of Nevski, on being attacked by his brother Andrew in 1282, "looking up to heaven sighed, shed tears and said: 'See, o Lord, this injustice, I did not commit any wrong against them.' And thus, after having wept a little, mounted his steed and went against them with his warriors."

Sometimes the chronicler himself cannot abstain from the moral condemnation of a political action. "Prince Dimitri Borisovich took away the lands of Prince Michael Glebovich [of Belozersk] in sin and injustice, and thus he offended and injured his brother. O evil human insatiability and cursed pride!" (*Sim.* and *Nik.*). Or, condemning the annexation of Nizhni Novgorod by Basil I of Moscow in 1393: "He took Nizhni Novgorod with gold and silver (given to the khan) and not in justice" (*Sim.* and *Rog.*). In 1408 the old rivals Ryazan and Moscow proceed against the Prince of Pronsk, vassal of Ryazan, "not according to justice," says the Chronicle of Tver. "The Prince of Pronsk looked up to heaven and said 'See, o God, and look at the face of thy justice and judge my contest with those who rise up against me.' And he said to his retainers: 'Let us be content, o druzhina, for God does not like the power of horsemen, nor the force of men but he saves those who confide in him.' "

Certainly not all of these judgments are free from partisanship. In this period all chroniclers are patriots of their cities and principalities. One could not find (as it was possible in the eleventh and twelfth centuries) a direct condemnation of the political action of a prince by his own chronicler. But a moral conscience which is bound by patriotism frees itself when it is disinterested or judges the actions of strangers. Still, the need of moral justification reflects itself in these meditations. Local interest is not sufficient even though it is not abandoned. The situation is not unlike that of European diplomacy in the nineteenth century. To define it as cynicism would not be fair.

The general concept of justice assumes different political forms. The Russian Middle Ages, in common with Kiev, possess the standard ideas of peace and the keeping of pacts sanctioned by a common kissing of the cross, but the third dominant ideal of Kiev, charity among blood-relations, was completely absent from political considerations and replaced by a new concept.

We have seen that the higher clergy still considered it their duty to maintain peace. This ideal is, however, not mentioned as often as in the Kievan chronicles. We even know of a case where its mention serves as a cover for quite the opposite attitude. In the tale of the invasion of Edigei (1409) the Tatars' motive for their aggression is described thus: "The Tatars learned that the Russians do not like bloodshed, but are peace-loving and expect justice . . ." This idea, familiar to nationalists of all times and nations, means, in a frank speech, that the love of peace is a weakness that attracts aggressors. One reads also the Old Testament sentence, "A glorious war is better than a shameful peace"

(*Lavr., Sim.* 1239), which was familiar at the end of the previous period.

Kissing the cross is far more frequently mentioned in connection with its breach or even in circumstances when the ritual is performed with the malicious intention of violating it, as was the case with the Princes of Nizhni Novgorod, who came with the Khan Tokhtamysh against Moscow and declared: "We kiss your cross as a sign that the tsar (khan) wishes to grant you his grace" (*Tver.* 1382). A new expression appears which seems to justify the breaking of an oath: "to cast aside from oneself the cross-kissing." When a prince or a city finds it burdensome or impossible to keep a solemn promise, they simply declare in a one-sided act that the oath does not bind any longer (*Rog.* 1375, 1392). At the end of this period one even meets an abbot who suggests to a prince that he break or "cast aside" cross-kissing. During the long fratricidal war among the family of Princes of Moscow, Basil I, who was blinded by his cousin Shemyaka and gave up his power and territory to save his life, found refuge in the monastery of St. Cyril (1447), and here "The Abbot Triphon, with all the brethren, blessed the Great Prince Basil and his sons in their resolve to take back the great principality," speaking thus: "Let the sin be upon me and upon my brethren's heads that you have kissed the cross and given oath to Prince Dimitri; go, my lord, with God and your just cause to Moscow, take your domain and Great Princedom."

In ancient Russia the clergy sometimes blessed a prince to break an oath and took this sin upon themselves, but they did it in the interest of peace; Abbot Triphon sends Basil to a new civil war, thus violating an oath on the cross. The great distance between the twelfth and the fifteenth centuries cannot be better demonstrated.

Small wonder that in view of the frequency of political

perjury some conservative minds attributed the cause of the widespread fires to them. In connection with the great fire of 1371 in Novgorod a chronicler remarks: "Many fires happen because of our sins . . . And what can be worse than to walk before God violating our oaths, to kiss the cross and then to transgress against it, and this evil is often committed among us" (*Sim.* and *Rog.*).

The new political and social order undermined the idea of the sacred blood-unity among the Rurikides as the basis of the unity of Rus. The princes ceased to exchange their cities and states in accordance with family seniority. Their lands and principalities became hereditary *otchina* and *dedina* (literally, the legacy of fathers and grandfathers). A new principle of political morality, corresponding to private-property holding, is formulated for the first time (to our knowledge) by the contemporary (secular) biographer of Alexander Nevski. In his prayer before a battle he addresses God "who has set the frontiers of nations and has commanded us to live without transgressing upon another's holding." [20] The same principle of the inviolability of frontiers is applied both to relations among nations and among the princes of the Russian land. The annexation of another's lands was considered a "sin and great injustice" (*Voskr.* 1279). Defensive war is always justified, and to defend one's "heritage" (*otchina*) is not only the right of a prince but also his duty toward inhabitants of his lands. This is the significance of the praise of Prince Constantine Vasilievich of Suzdal (and Nizhni Novgorod): "He defended his heritage [land] with honor and awe-inspiring valor against strong princes and Tatars" (*Nik.* 1355).

The "strong princes" understood here are those of Moscow. "The assemblers of Russian land" could achieve their historic feat only by violating the hereditary right of other

---

[20] Serebryanski, p. 112.

Russian princes. Tver, Suzdal, Ryazan, Rostov — all feudal principalities — had to oppose their aggression, and local chronicles, although distorted by later Muscovite hands, reflect these bitter feelings. On the construction of new fortifications in Moscow a chronicler of Tver remarks: "In Moscow they have begun to build the fortress [Kremlin] of stone and, assured of their great strength, they have begun to compel Russian princes to conform to their will, and whosoever does not conform they attack maliciously" (*Rog.* 1367).

Thus, the idea of a just war remained firm in medieval Russia, and people did not want for heavenly patrons in their just or even unjust wars. As a pale remnant of ancient times the Cross, or the power of the Cross, is sometimes mentioned as a victory-giving force. Yet, it pertains rather to the conception of war as a judgment of God and a high standard of political morals. A chronicle expresses this idea: "The power of the holy Cross always overthrows those who commit injustice" (*Voskr.* 1262). Most frequently the power of the Cross appears in conjunction with other divine or holy forces, mostly of local significance. The dedication of the cathedral of the capital city reveals, of course, the patron of the city and the whole principality: "St. Sophia" in Novgorod, "Holy Trinity" in Pskov, "St. Savior" in Tver, the "Mother of God" in Moscow. The "Holy Trinity" appears in all the battles of Dovmont, Prince of Pskov, not as the supreme Christian name for the Deity but as a local sanctuary. This is clear in the following enumeration where the Trinity does not occupy first place: "By the power of the precious Cross and with the aid of the Holy Trinity and the prayers of our most holy Lady, the Mother of God and Ever Virgin Mary," Prince Dimitri defeated the Germans (*Voskr.* 1268). Our Lady is very often associated with the name of God even where there is no reason for her invocation in the local cult.

The dedication of cathedral churches reveals a great similarity of names. The cult of St. Sophia remains practically limited to the city and region of Novgorod. St. Sophia of Polotsk was outside Great Russia and Novgorod seemed to be loath to propagate the great name in dependent cities. This situation gave rise to the saying: "Where St. Sophia is, there is Novgorod." The case was quite the same with the name Holy Trinity which, ever since the twelfth century, had been associated with the Cathedral of Pskov until the moment when St. Sergius, in the middle of the fifteenth century, dedicated his monastery to the Trinity. Thus, the Savior and Our Lady remain as practically the only possible dedications, again, however, within interesting geographical limitations. Cathedrals of St. Savior prevail in Novgorod's sphere of influence, that is, in the West and in a half-arch from the North which takes in the Muscovite center; we find them in Torzhok, Pereyaslavl, Yaroslavl, and Nizhni Novgorod. Our Lady prevails in the sphere of old Vladimir and young Moscow, its heir. All churches of the Savior were dedicated to his Transfiguration (all dedications to Christ and Our Lady had to be in specific relation to one of their feast days). The reason is probably found in the fact that one of the oldest churches of Novgorod was that of the Transfiguration. The Kievan Chronicle relates that one of the victories of St. Vladimir over the Pechenegs was won on this day (August 6, 996). If we were to make a detailed map of the main churches in Kievan cities this map could be used to indicate the comparative influence of Novgorod and Moscow. In the famous Solovki monastery, on an island of the White Sea which was colonized both from Novgorod and the Muscovite South, by the fifteenth century there were two cathedrals, in honor of Our Lady and the Savior-Transfiguration (*Spaso-Preobrazhenie*).

Simple saints probably never enjoyed the honor of the

dedication of cathedral churches and, thus, if they appear as patrons in battles it is for one of two particular reasons: either they are the calendar saints of the day of battle or the patron saints (namesakes) of the victorious prince. St. Leontius, to whom Dovmont prays before battle and to whom the victory was ascribed in part, is such a calendar saint.[21] If St. George grants him another victory (after God *and* the Holy Trinity) it is because, as the chronicler himself explains, "this happened on April 23rd, the day dedicated to the memory of the holy and glorious victory-giving martyr George" (*Voskr.* 1271). The Archangel Michael is the patron of the Prince of Tver, Michael Alexandrovich, who associates him with other divine powers in his prayers in war. "The Great Prince, Michael Alexandrovich strengthened himself with the power of the Cross and put his hope in God and his most pure Mother and in the help of the Great Archangel Michael" (*Rog.* 1372).

In addition to canonized saints, departed ancestors with their prayers for the living, were considered as patrons and helpers in the hour of danger. Two groups among them figured as powerful protectors, princes and bishops (the latter includes the clergy in general). This imperceptibly began to include living bishops and priests whose prayers and sacramental actions exerted great power. By way of example let us consider the enumeration of the spiritual powers which, according to the chronicler, saved Novgorod from the hordes of Baty: "Novgorod, however, was protected by God and St. Sophia, the Catholic and Apostolic Church, the holy great Cyril, Archbishop of Alexandria and the prayer of the holy Orthodox archbishops, the holy princes, Orthodox monks and a multitude of priests" (*Troits.* 1238). Another

---

[21] *Voskr.* 1265: "Then came the day of the great martyr Leontius, and Prince Dovmont said: 'Holy Trinity and great Holy Captain, Leontius, help us in this hour.'"

instance can be seen at the end of this period, in Muscovite territory, that is, the "chart of cursing," formulated
(1448) by Dimitri Shemyaka with the invocation of all holy
powers who will wreak vengeance on him if he is guilty of
perfidy:

> Then there will be no longer with me the grace of God and His
> most holy Mother and the power of the precious and life-giving
> Cross and the prayers of all the saints and thaumaturges of our
> land, the Lords-Metropolitan Peter and Alexis and Bishop Leon-
> tius the Wonder-Worker and the Abbot Sergius, the wonderworker,
> and others; and there will be no longer upon me the blessing of all
> the bishops of the Russian lands — and all the priestly orders under
> them (*Sim.* 1448).

And if, despite such powerful heavenly protection, the
battle was lost, the pious chronicler saw it, if not as the will
of God, at least as being permitted by Him, even in wars
against nonorthodox enemies where the justice of the cause
was beyond question. "With the sufferance of God the Germans prevailed and the Pskovians hastened to flee — because
of our sins" (*Tver.* 1408). In the same way the defeat of the
Russians at Suzdal at the hands of the Tatars is explained
through "the suffrance of the Lord Sabaoth" (*Sof.* I, 1445).

The sins punished in these wars are not specified except
in one case, pride. The defeated are charged with confiding
in their own strength; the victor is often praised for his
humility before God. It is clear that, as these contradictory
states of mind are not open to the observer-chronicler, his
judgments when they are not dictated by mere partisan feelings are based on the result itself.[22]

In speaking of war we ought to consider the problem of
the enemy and, particularly, the Tatars. Did the Middle
Ages make the same distinction between internal feuds and
external wars as was made in Kiev? The answer is negative.

---

[22] Compare the Muscovite interpretation of the victory over Ryazan.

Certainly, religion (Orthodoxy) made a certain difference
between a Russian and a German or a Tatar, but wars between Russians ceased to be viewed as civil or fratricidal
wars. Peace is always preferable, but a war for a good cause
was justified, even against Russian princes or cities. Local
patriotism received powerful support in local cults and from
local hierarchs.

The holy war against the heathen-nomads, the only one
which was always urged by the Church, had now changed its
objectives and meaning. It seems now that the only sacred
war that united all Russia in undivided feelings was the war
against Christian-Catholics, Germans and Swedes. At the
very beginning of this period, at the same time as the conquest by Baty, the Teutonic Order and Sweden made an effort to subjugate the Russian West, which was still free from
the Mongol yoke. The campaigns of Alexander Nevski and
Dovmont of Pskov had solemn religious aspects, were
shrouded in legends, and resulted in the canonization of the
victorious defenders of Russian soil. True, the origin of
these wars was national, not religious. But it was probable
that as the result of the victory of the Order Pskov, and perhaps Novgorod, would be forced to recognize the Roman
pope. In Novgorod itself one still sees no trace of anti-
Catholic feelings. Foreign merchants live there as formerly,
a self-governing Hansa colony, with two Catholic churches,
although it is true that they are isolated from the native
population. The foreigners, that is, Catholics, were under
the protection of the Archbishop of Novgorod, who defended them from the mob in frequent popular riots. On one
occasion at the end of the fourteenth century, the city, in
bargaining with the patriarch of Constantinople for privileges for its archbishop, threatened to go to Rome as a
final argument. This threat was not serious and did not fail
to elicit a severe rebuke from the patriarch but, up to the

time of the loss of their independence, the Novgorodians saw no objection against a political alliance with the Catholic kings of Lithuanian Poland.

With regard to Lithuania, Tver had the same attitude, after the Christianization and civilizing of the Lithuanians in the fourteenth and fifteenth centuries. In 1408 a Prince of Tver, Ivan, states as the traditional principle of their policy: "Our fathers and grandfathers always were at peace with Vitovt [Prince of Lithuania], at I was myself" (*Tver.* 1408). Standing between the Russian East and West, a relentless foe of the Tatars, Tver had to seek political alliance with Lithuania, whose population was in the majority Orthodox and Russian, although the princes and part of the aristocracy accepted the Roman confession.

It was not the same in Moscow. For her the Lithuanians, not the Tatars, were the archenemy. The great historical problem was whether Lithuania or Muscovy would achieve the unification of the Russian lands. The participation of the two Lithuanian princes in the battle of Kulikovo, where all stronger princes of Russia were most conspicuous by their absence, did not change the fundamental antagonism between Moscow and Vilno. From this political situation a fanatical anti-Romanism developed in Muscovy. In the Lives of the Muscovite saints of the fifteenth century even demons wear "Lithuanian conical hats," and already a conviction which would have been impossible in Kiev was rife, finding its expression in the "Story of Metropolitan Isidore" in these words: "The Latins [Romans] are not Christians; how can they be Christians?" [23] Isidore of Moscow accepted at Florence the so-called "Union" with Rome, following the

---

[23] A. A. Popov, ed., "Slovo na Latyni i o izverzhenii Isidora" (Sermon on the Latins and on the Ejection of Isidore), in *Istoriko-literaturny obzor drevne-russkikh polemicheskikh sochineni protiv Latinyan* (Historical-Literary Survey of Ancient-Russian Works Against the Latins), Moscow, 1875, p. 368.

majority of the Greek hierarchs. The Muscovite "story" judges his case (in absentia): "The holy canons of the divine law of the holy Apostles command that such a man, a perverter of the Church, be burnt in fire and be buried alive in the earth." [24]

And now the Tatars.

Except for the very first years of the Mongol Conquest (1237–1240) the Russian political conscience was always divided on this primordial national issue. Pro- and anti-Tatar groups, princes and cities, always existed, and both found their defense in the pages of the chronicles. That the pro-Tatar faction policy was not dictated by base motives alone is seen not only in the great figure of Alexander Nevski but also in an obituary of Prince Gleb Vasilkovich of Rostov. His father was martyred by the Tatars in 1437, but Gleb "from his youth . . . began to serve the Tatars and ransomed many Christians, who were oppressed by them, comforting the sorrowful, not sparing his food nor drink." The motive of prudence and expediency opposed that of honor and freedom and brought about many dramatic conflicts.

The first scandal of dissension was made by the two sons of the Great Prince Yaroslav, Alexander (Nevski) and Andrew. Alexander decided to bow before the overwhelming force, but when he was already under the power of the Horde, Andrew stirred up a revolt. A friendly chronicler puts these words into his mouth: "O Lord, why is this? How long must we quarrel among ourselves to bring the Tatars against one another? It is better for me to flee to a foreign country than to be friends with Tatars and to serve them" (*Nik.* 1252). Routed by the Tatars ("for our increasing sins") he actually did flee abroad (to Sweden). But another chronicler, a representative of the Alexander faction, sees fit to be ironical at the expense of the prince-émigré: "Prince

---

[24] *Ibid.*, pp. 378–379.

Andrew with his boyars decided rather to flee than to serve the tsars of the Tatars and fled to an unknown country . . . The result was the devastation of his land" (*Lavr.* and *Sim.*).

Ten years later, still in Alexander's lifetime and during his absence in Mongolia, a spontaneous revolt burst out in Rostov and other Northern cities mostly on the Volga river. Despite the hopelessness of these uprisings most of the chronicles hail them as acts of God's will: "God rescued the people of the land of Rostov from the cruel oppression by the Moslems, through the prayers of the holy Mother of God, and he inspired fury in the heart of Christians; they could not bear any longer the violence of the heathens, and summoning the *veche*, expelled them from the cities" (*Voskr.* 1262).

In 1282 the feud between two sons of Nevski, Andrew and Dimitri, caused them, as was often the case, to seek support from the Tatars. In the account in the Nicon Chronicle the innocent and wronged party was Dimitri. When he is slandered to the Horde by his brother, he prays to God with tears professing the justice of his cause. Overwhelmed by Andrew he fled to a rival Horde, to the Tsar Nogai, "told him everything with tears and gave many gifts to him and his princes." Tsar Nogai listened to him and "held him in honor." Here a Tatar khan appears as the defender of innocence. Even in the story of the martyrdom of Prince Michael of Tver the Khan Uzbek is not a villain. The guilt of murder is borne by Yuri, Prince of Moscow, and his Tatar friend, Kavgadi. The Uzbeks' desire was to give the rebellious Prince of Tver a fair trial. "Do what you like provided you judge righteously, by my justice, for the king's justice must be righteous" (*Nik.* 1319).

For almost all of the fourteenth century Tver and Moscow took opposite stands toward their Tatar overlords. Tver received greater honor, Moscow, more political benefits. But even chronicles friendly to Moscow do not dare to justify all the political misdeeds of her princes. Neither the devastation of Russian provinces by Yuri in alliance with the Tatars, nor the murder of Michael of Tver in the Horde found any defenders. But the similar, though more prudent, policy of his brother Ivan (Kalita) finds a complete justification in the Chronicle of Moscow: "And then there was a great raid of the Tatars . . . And Prince Ivan Danilovich of Moscow was with them. And going into war they captured Tver, Kashin and other towns. Christian blood was shed by the pagan Tatars . . . But the great and merciful Savior, our Lord, protected with his grace our pious Prince Ivan Danilovich and for his sake Moscow and the whole of his land from the pagan foreigners, the Tatars" (*Sim.* 1328). In this notice we can observe a tendency to absolve Prince Ivan from the shedding of Russian blood as well as an unwillingness to whitewash his allies, the Tatars. In 1319 we find Yuri of Moscow as accuser and even executioner of St. Michael of Tver at the Horde. In 1339 when Michael's son, Alexander, came to the khan under the peril of certain death he found his enemies there, the princes of Moscow, Simeon and Ivan. This is the cautious manner in which the Chronicle of Moscow describes the crime which took place at the Horde: "At the Horde they [impersonally, the Tatars are meant] killed Prince Alexander Mikhailovich of Tver and his son Prince Theodore, and they were rent asunder, joint from joint; Prince Simeon and his brother were permitted to go to Russia, with love, and they returned from the Horde to Russia rewarded by God and the tsar" (*Sim.* 1339). The identification of the will of God and that of the khan (tsar) is a striking pro-Tatar feature.

However, Moscow was not the only principality which preserved such lasting ties with the Tatars. Ryazan, which offered the strongest resistance to Baty and was completely ruined by him, was of all the Russian lands the most exposed to Tatar raids because of its geographical (southern) situation. Thus, their princes could not take part in the campaign of Dimitri Donskoi when Moscow at last changed its policy. The princes of Suzdal-Nizhni Novgorod, Moscow's rivals at the end of the fourteenth century, faced precisely the same situation. Still, in 1361, during troubles in the Horde, Prince Andrew of Suzdal faced the Tatars on the battlefield. The chronicle relates his bold exploits in an epic style which recalls the Igor tale: "Prince Andrew, sharpening his strength and not fearing their thunder rushed suddenly and broke through the Tatar armies, fighting with them" (*Rog.* 1361). But his sons were despoiled by Moscow and his grandsons, deprived of their lands, wandered over the steppes, concluding an alliance with the Tatars in their raids of revenge against the Muscovite victors.

We must not think that the battle of Kulikovo radically changed the relations of Moscow itself to the Tatar khans. Very soon afterward the old subjection was reestablished. Two years after Kulikovo, Khan Tokhtamysh captured Moscow and Dimitri did not resist him. The Chronicle of Moscow, as if to justify Dimitri, says: "He did not raise his hand against Tsar Tokhtamysh" (*Sim.* 1382), thereby suggesting that the khan was a legal tsar, ordained by God, against whom resistance would be sinful. It is remarkable, indeed, that in contemporary Russian sources the Tatar monarch is never called khan but always tsar, the title which was formerly reserved, except for biblical kings, for the Emperor of Byzantium, the head of the Orthodox world. We have seen that the idea of justice and law was not alien to the khan of the Tatars. In the story of the martyrdom of Michael of Tver the Tatar princes ask the khan: "What will your word order, the word of the *free* tsar?" A hundred years later this epithet is used by the Muscovite ambassador in addressing the khan: "Lord, free tsar." He repeats this word many times, emphasizing that "you are free in your land," whereas the rival of Moscow bases his claim upon "the dead character of your father and not upon your grace, that of the great tsar" (*Sim.* 1432). The freedom of the khan has all the connotations of the future autocracy of Ivan IV, absolute arbitrariness as opposed to written law. Even the despotism of the khans, under the name of freedom, found its admirers in Russia.

For more than a century the higher clergy, enjoying the privileges granted by the khan's *yarlyks* (charters), belonged to the Mongol faction. No wonder that in the Church calendar we find at least two canonized princes of pro-Tatar orientation.

One is Peter, a tatar himself and even a relative of Baty ("Tsarevich of the Horde"). In the first generation after the conquest this young Tatar prince was converted to Christianity by the Bishop of Rostov, Cyril. The motives indicated are a healing performed by Cyril at the Horde and the beauty of the cathedral church in Rostov. Being baptized he remained in Rostov as a private layman, married (to a Tatar bride, it seems) and built a church and monastery in Rostov. After the death of Peter, twice his sons and later grandsons were . . .[25]

---

[25] This chapter was left unfinished by G. P. Fedotov.

V

THE REPUBLIC OF ST. SOPHIA

*E*ven liberal Russian historians, such as Soloviev and Klyuchevski, on the whole have been so overwhelmed by the fact that the Moscow kingdom was the creator of the Russian Empire that they have allowed Moscow to crowd out all the five preceding centuries of an ancient way of life which was incomparably richer than it in culture and spirituality.[1]

Of course the Grand Prince of Moscow had been crowned tsar only in the sixteenth century (1547). At one time Basil I, the son of Dimitri Donskoi, stated, "We have the Church, but we have no emperor." Although the Patriarch of Constantinople corrected him by warning, "It is impossible to have the Church and not to have the emperor,"[2] this Byzantine viewpoint had few supporters in Russia. In fact,

---

[1] A chapter on Novgorod was a part of Fedotov's original plan for this volume but it was never written. This short sketch is translated from the little known periodical *Narodnaya Pravda* (The People's Truth), nos. 11–12, New York, 1950, pp. 21–33, and gives the general direction of Fedotov's thinking concerning Novgorod, one of the most original and creative centers of Russian medieval civilization. The absence of a real study on the subject by Fedotov is highly regrettable; it may well reflect the difficulty he undoubtedly found with the projected chapter and the reason why he may have postponed its composition. This difficulty stems from the lack of a complete survey or monograph on medieval Novgorod, a gap that, today, has been filled — although only partially — by V. N. Vernadsky, *Novgorod i novgorodskaya zemlya v XVom veke* (Novgorod and the Novgorod land in the 15th Century), Moscow and Leningrad, 1961. Individual aspects of Novgorod's civilization are described in A. I. Nikitski, *Ocherk vnutrennei istorii tserkvi v Velikom Novgorode* (A Survey of the Internal History of the Church in Novgorod), St. Petersburg, 1879, and V. N. Lazarev, *Iskusstvo Novgoroda* (The Art of Novgorod), Moscow and Leningrad, 1947. For a report of more recent archeological research in Novgorod see A. V. Artsikhovski, "Raskopi 1952 goda v Novgorode" (Excavations in Novgorod during 1952), *Voprosy Istorii*, 1953, no. 1 pp. 113–124. J. M.

[2] F. Miklosich and G. Müller, eds., *Acta et diplomata graeca medii aevi sacra et profana*, 6 vols., Vienna, 1860–1890, vol. II: *Acta Patriarchatus Constantinopolitani, 1314–1402*, Vienna, 1862, pp. 188–192. Reproduced also in *RIB*, vol. VI, prilozheniya, cols. 272, 276. J. M.

according to the Byzantine theory of a universal empire, all Christians in the world were the subjects of one emperor. All Orthodox peoples were his vassals. Russian princes were only granted secondary titles by the Byzantine court. It is understandable that the Russians ignored these theories, which were humiliating for their national pride, and no Greek metropolitan in Russia could really impose them. The Greek emperor was for the Russians only an ideal center of the Christian world, as the (German) Holy Roman emperor was for France and England. On the other hand, no one else could lay claims to his position. Although the liturgy of the Church was permeated with Byzantine theocratic ideas, and echoes of them sound in the precepts of the Church, not a single Russian prince claimed autocratic power. The prince's authority was limited by various social forces, such as the *veche*, the boyars, and the bishops. This situation held too many advantages for the Church, especially ecclesiastical privileges, for the Church to destroy its own freedom. If a bishop was offended by a prince, he sought justice from the Metropolitan of Kiev, and this metropolitan, appointed in Byzantium, could be judged only by the Patriarch of Constantinople. For this reason the metropolitan stood high above local authorities, including the prince, even if he played no active role in politics. There is substance to the statement of one of the twelfth-century metropolitans to the Kievan Prince that "we have been appointed to restrain you from bloodshed."

The relation between Church and state in Great Novgorod was set up differently from the relation that prevailed in the principalities. But first we must refute the common misconception that Novgorod was only an isolated city and that, consequently, when we speak of Russia as a whole, the peculiar fate of Novgorod may be passed over in silence. The territory of Novgorod was immense; all Northern

Russia as far as the Urals and even a section of Siberia lay under her authority and her law. Even after Moscow had swallowed up all the independent principalities (the so-called *udels*), Novgorod's possessions were more extensive than Moscow's. True, the greater part of these lands were deserts, forests, and tundra, populated by alien tribes, with settlements of Russian colonists scattered through them. In the West, though, quite a few important towns belonged to Novgorod: Torzhok, Ladoga, Staraya Rusa, even Pskov itself at one time. Here the most famous Russian monasteries arose, Valaamo, Solovki, Kirillov, Ferapontov on the White Lake. In the history of medieval Russian art (thirteenth to fifteenth centuries) Novgorod holds first place. Here the Great Russian characteristics were formed and conserved in their greatest purity, far from Tatar bondage and the slavery of serfdom. Here, even today, folklorists find the best songs and heroic ballads, ancient costumes, and the most interesting remains of wooden construction. And finally, Novgorod, in its trade with the Hanseatic League, was the chief window in Russia opening on Europe. When Peter the Great cut this window through once more, he was acknowledging that he was returning Russia to Novgorod's ancient frontiers. Prince Alexander Nevski of Novgorod, the victor over the Swedes and Germans, was to become the guardian angel of the new Western-looking empire.

In summary, Novgorod was not an outlandish growth in Russian life but the most Russian element in it, the element which was most free of Tatar admixture, and in addition contained, as it were, the possibility for a free culture to develop in the future.

Was Novgorod a republic? Yes, at least for three and a half centuries of its history, from the twelfth to the fifteenth centuries. The fact that a prince held authority in Novgorod should not deceive us. From the time when Russia actually lost her political unity, on the death of Vladimir Monomakh (1125), and the decay of the Kievan monarchy, the authority of the Prince of Novgorod was neither hereditary nor life-long. At any time the popular *veche* could "show the prince his road" out of the city. The prince, on the other hand, was not an all-powerful master in Novgorod, not even the chief official in the administration. His main task was military; he was temporary commander of the armed forces. And even this military command he shared with the *tysyatski*. As a judge, he shared authority with the *posadnik* (deputy or mayor) and others. He was not even nominal head of the city-state. Decrees were not written nor treaties concluded in his name. As he was subject to the invitation of the veche and lacked dynastic rights, like the *podestas* of the Italian medieval republics, the prince was easily included in the system of republican authorities or "masters" who ruled Novgorod. Consequently, Novgorod was really for centuries a republic in fact, or, as N. I. Kostomarov expressed it, a government by the people.

True, from the end of the fourteenth century, Novgorod stopped electing and changing its princes at will. The Grand Prince of Moscow, by virtue of his position, was also recognized as Prince of Novgorod. But this did not yet increase his rights and authority in Novgorod territory. As he did not live in Novgorod, he was represented there by his deputy, who confined himself to the monetary receipts and jurisdiction as strictly defined by treaty. It was to Novgorod's advantage to have the strongest prince of the great Russian state as its protector. In particular, peaceful relations with him ensured unobstructed trade with "lower" Russia. Without the supplies of wheat from the South, Novgorod could not have existed.

Supreme authority in the Novgorod republic belonged, of course, to the veche, or the assembly of all free citizens.

The veche elected the entire administration, not excluding the archbishop, and had the power to check on it and judge it. This was a direct, not a representative, democracy like the republics of the ancient world. Only those who participated in the public meetings could exercise their political rights. An immense territory was administered by the inhabitants of this single city. This was the weak spot in the republican systems of both Athens and Rome; the *agora* and the forum could not rule empires.

In regard to Novgorod the reports of disorder and lack of organization in the veche administration are usually exaggerated. We know little about the normal course of affairs; the chronicles tell only of departures from it. The traditional image of Novgorod self-government, the battles on the Volkhov Bridge, was actually a comparatively rare occurrence. For the most part the "masters" were able to reconcile the hostile parties before bloodshed occurred. We tend to forget this "council of masters" (*sovet gospod*), the upper house which conducted all current affairs and prepared the most important proposals for the decision of the veche. This house consisted of leading officials who had been elected by the veche, those presently in office and former incumbents; the presidency was held by the archbishop, not the prince. It is entirely probable that the popular veche had difficulty conducting affairs in an orderly manner. The struggle among the parties easily led to civil war. This is the usual price that democracy pays for freedom. The wars among the princes, fighting each other elsewhere in the territories of Russia, shed more blood and tears than the fights on the Volkhov Bridge. And, of course, less innocent blood was shed within the walls of Novgorod in all the centuries of its existence than in the few days that Ivan the Terrible visited it in 1570.

But let us return to the Novgorod state. It is noteworthy

that the president of the council of masters was the archbishop. In effect, he was the one who was "president" of the republic, to draw a modern analogy. The *posadnik* was prime minister, the head of the victorious party. The archbishop stood above parties and expressed the unity of the republic. To make him really independent, his name was drawn by lot from those of the candidates elected by the veche. The three lots on the altar in the Cathedral of St. Sophia symbolized the divine will for the fate of the city-state. In the political symbolism of Great Novgorod its sovereign, the bearer of supreme authority, was St. Sophia itself. St. Sophia was not only the name of the whole territorial Novgorod Church, as expressed in the formula, "The Holy Catholic and Apostolic Church of St. Sophia"; it was the name of the republic itself. In that sacred name treaties and ceremonial charters were written; princes and officials took oaths of allegiance to it. It was considered to be the possessor of the Novgorod lands, especially of the Church ("the house of St. Sophia"). The popular will found in it a heavenly symbol, not subject to its fitful caprice.

Novgorod was not the only city in which medieval democracy was practiced through the medium of divine symbols. We see the same concept in the city-republics of Italy. Milan was the city of St. Ambrose, Florence of St. John the Baptist. We cannot assume any reciprocal influence between Italy and Novgorod; it seems rather that a common theocratic conscience, thirsting for a religious sanctification of political life, assumed similar forms in both the Catholic and the Orthodox republics of the Middle Ages.

It is doubtful whether the ordinary citizen of Novgorod, or even many of the local clergy, had a clear idea as to what or who St. Sophia was. Novgorod, which gave so much to Russian art, left no theological works. In this it did not differ from the other domains of medieval Russia. The Novgorod

Cathedral was named in the eleventh century after the churches of Kiev and Constantinople. The Greek bishops knew, of course, that Sophia, the Wisdom of God, was one of the names of Christ. The more scholarly of the Russian scribes also knew this; at least, in some Russian manuscripts we encounter such an explanation. But in all cases known to us of oaths of allegiance, the citizens of Novgorod kissed the icon of the Virgin. This leads us to think, first, that in the Middle Ages there was not yet an established iconographic image of St. Sophia as a fiery angel, and, secondly, that in Novgorod a virginal or feminine conception of Sophia was dominant, anticipating the idea of Sophia held by contemporary Russian theologians of Soloviev's school.[3]

However the Novgorodians envisaged St. Sophia, it was the mistress and protectress of the city and the state. On earth it was represented by the archbishop, who was elected by all the people. As the true president of the republic, immense wealth and even military force were concentrated in his hands. "The House of St. Sophia" was the largest economic unit in Novgorod, and "the Bishop's Troops" were a notable part of her civil guard. In the eleventh century the Novgorodians made great efforts to make their church completely independent of Kiev, but the Patriarch of Constantinople would not agree to the partition of the Russian Church. Actually, the privileges of the Metropolitan of Kiev largely amounted to monetary requisitions, connected with the operation of the ecclesiastical court. The Novgorodians tried to keep the metropolitan, who later moved to

---

[3] Recent research does not confirm Fedotov's view on the Novgorodian conception of Sophia. It seems likely that until the sixteenth century the identification of Sophia with Christ was generally accepted as self-evident. See A. M. Ammann, "Darstellung und Deutung der Sophia im Vorpetrinischen Russland," *Orientalia Christiana Periodica* 4:120–156 (1938), and J. Meyendorff, "L'iconographie de la Sagesse divine," *Cahiers Archéologiques* 10: 259–277 (Paris, 1959), J. M.

Moscow, as far from Novgorod as possible. If relations with Moscow became too strained, as in the fifteenth century, an archbishop could be consecrated without going to Moscow. Consecration could be performed in Lithuania by the Orthodox metropolitan of Western Russia. St. Euphimius, one of the best Novgorod bishops, was consecrated in this way.

It is frequently stated that the archbishop elected at the veche lacked sufficient independence and could be removed from his seat, as could the posadnik and the prince. The facts do not support this theory. Throughout the history of the Novgorod Church, we see one troubled period, the first twenty years of the thirteenth century, when the struggle between *Suzdaliya* and the patriotic parties became extremely sharp. Then the archbishops, on one side or the other, had to leave their thrones more than once, only to return to them again. But this was an exceptional period. Freedom of the person could easily be crushed in the medieval theocratic republics, but freedom of the Church at any rate was better protected in the Novgorod republic than in autocratic Moscow, where, after the late fifteenth century, it became the rule rather than the exception to remove metropolitans at the wish of the grand prince and the tsar.

The bishops of Novgorod defended not only the freedom of the Church but the freedom of the "city" as well, that is, of the republic. The Lives of the last canonized Archbishops, Euthimius and Jonah, who held office just before the fall of Novgorod, bear witness to this. For example, Jonah, when he was already very old, journeyed to Moscow to repel the threat against his native land. He exhorted the Grand Prince, Basil II, "Look with calm eyes on your subjects, and do not start to turn free men into slavery." In a spirit of prophecy he promised for his heir, Ivan III, "freedom from the ruler of the Horde in return for the freedom of my city." But if the prince encroaches on the freedom of innocent men, he will see in his own children "the eye of envy" and division between them.

Unfortunately these expressions of the religious ideal of freedom in Orthodoxy were not developed in canonical treatises. The spirit of freedom was left to the pages of the ancient chronicles and in part to local cults. The local miraculous icon, the "Miracle" of the Virgin, remained linked forever to the memorable miracle of 1170. According to the Novgorodians, it was the icon itself which put to flight a coalition of princes headed by Andrew Bogolyubski and saved their freedom. The icon of the "Miracle" as well as the symbol of St. Sophia and the names of the canonized bishops, John, Euthymius, and Jonah, remained in the memory of the Novgorodians as religious symbols of political freedom.

VI

ST. SERGIUS OF RADONEZH

*T*HE ascetic or monastic vocation is the high point in Eastern Orthodox, as well as in Roman Catholic Christian life. No one in ancient Russia ever doubted that Christian perfection was attainable only in the angelic *skhema* of a monk. The typical saint, canonized by the Church, was the ascetic hero. Thus, it is all the more surprising that in the first century after the Mongol conquest, Russia produced almost no saint of the type that the Greek Church designates by the particular name, *hosios* (Russian *prepodobni* — "similar to Christ"). This fact must especially puzzle those who believe that religious revivals inevitably follow in the wake of political and social catastrophes. A religious response to the challenge of history, certainly, could be detected in the Russian society of the fifteenth century; ecclesiastical preachers and chroniclers as well saw in the horrors of Tatar domination punishment from God for the sins of the nation. Yet, the physical destruction and the hardships involved in mere existence were so great that a general brutality and a disorderliness of life were the natural result. A unique type of the holiness canonized by the Church at this age is found in the noble and dignified service to society by the princes, and in some measure, the bishops. The need to protect a Christian people from absolute destruction relegated purely spiritual vocations to a secondary plane. It was necessary that the initial lethargy after the cataclysm pass away and that a peaceful course of life be restored before a spiritual thirst, which would preclude thoughts of the world, could be aroused. This change was not realized until the dawn of the new century.

The new monastic asceticism, which can be dated from the second quarter of the fourteenth century, is essentially dif-

ferent from that of ancient Russia.[1] It is the monasticism of
the "desert." All the known monasteries of Kievan Russia
were built in towns or the suburbs of towns. Most of them
survived the pillage of Baty or were later restored like the
Monastery of the Caves in Kiev, but the disappearance of
the ideal of personal sanctity betokens an inner decay. Urban
monasteries were still built during Mongol times, for example, in Moscow. Yet, most of the saints of the age left
the towns for the virgin forests. We can only conjecture as
to the actual motives of this new trend in the monastic movement. One possible explanation is that it reflects the difficult
and turbulent life in the cities, which were still subject to
occasional devastation by new Tatar raids. On the other
hand, however, the very decadence of the urban monastic
houses prompted the zealous to search for new ways, ways
that were already indicated in the classical tradition of the
desert monasticism of Egypt and Syria. Russia did not have
any "desert" in the literal sense, but monks still could escape
both men and civilization: the vast Northern *forest* thus
became the "desert" of the Russian monks. In their fervent
choice of the wilderness these pioneers revealed a greater
detachment from the world and its destinies than the monks
of Kiev; of course, this could also be the result of the social
unrest of the Mongol period. But, still, in taking upon themselves a harder task — one necessarily connected with contemplative prayer — they elevated spiritual life to a height not
yet achieved in Russia. This is the age, more than any other,
when one may speak of Russian mysticism.

The head and teacher of the new "desert" monasticism
was without any doubt Sergius of Radonezh, the greatest

---

[1] An inexhaustible source of factual and bibliographical information on
Russian monasticism is now to be found in Igor Smolitsch, *Russisches
Mönchtum, Entstehung, Entwicklung, und Wesen, 988–1917*, Würzburg, 1953,
which is based on *Das Altrussische Mönchtum 11–16 Jahrhunderts*, Würzburg, 1940. J. M.

among the saints of ancient Russia. Most of the saints in this period, before and after 1400, are his disciples or his "collators" or "interlocutors," that is, those who experienced his spiritual influence. Nevertheless, we must recognize that the new ascetic movement seems to have sprung up simultaneously in various places and that St. Sergius only seems to have been its guiding spirit. The traditions of some four Northern (Transvolgan) monasteries set the date of their foundation in the thirteenth century or in the even still more distant past. One of them, St. Savior on the Rock, on Kuben Lake became prominent as a school for spiritual life and as a metropolis of ascetic colonies in the fifteenth century; similar reputations were enjoyed also by the monasteries of St. Sergius and St. Cyril of Belozersk. However, the legend which links the unclear beginnings of St. Savior with the person of Prince Gleb of Belozersk (1260) tells only that the prince, driven onto the island by a storm, found some monks there who had fled from the woes of their time; nothing is said about a monastery or a church on this spot. Dionysius, who was the monastery's first abbot, was elected under Prince Dimitri Donskoi (1359–1389). These Northern monasteries remain unknown to us for a long time. Yet, beginning with the third decade of the fourteenth century we know the names of some saints who sought out the wilderness either with Sergius or independently of him. It is probable that around 1316 a St. Cyril (one of many saints of this name) began an eremitic life in the Kargopol district where a monastery, that of Khelma, was built after his death on the spot where his hut stood. In 1329 a Sergius (also a namesake) came to the island of Valaamo on Lake Ladoga and this, most probably, is the historically accurate, although disputed, date of the origin of the famous monastery. Both cloisters were built in the territory of Novgorod, which had experienced neither the Tatar devastation nor any hiatus in its cultural tradition. However, the portraits of these Novgorodian saints are only pale sketches in the late legends which tell about them.

A citizen of Vladimir, St. Pachomius, who died in 1384, founded the monastery of Nerekhta in the forests of Kostroma. The Bishop of Nizhni Novgorod, St. Dionysius, built his Monastery of the Caves following the pattern of that of Kiev, and no direct influence from St. Sergius could have been felt by him before 1365 when the Abbot of Radonezh came to Nizhni with a political mission from the metropolitan. St. Stephen of Makhrishchi and St. Dimitri of Priluki were contemporaries of Sergius and his undisputed "interlocutors." It is difficult to determine in what measure their choice of the wilderness as the place for monasteries they founded was the result of his direct influence.

Although a rarity for the fourteenth century, we possess a contemporary Life of St. Sergius, which was composed by his disciple Epiphanius, surnamed the Wise. Epiphanius was a monk at the Holy Trinity monastery during the life of Sergius and for some twenty-five years after the death of the saint (1392) he gathered notes and materials for his full-scale biography. Despite its prolixity, excessive scriptural quotations, and "rhetorical word dressing," it is rich in factual content and quite reliable. His pen being inadequate to depict the spiritual experiences of the saint, he has given a true-to-life, exterior portrait, which is, however, permeated with the invisible inner light. With all his deficiencies, Epiphanius is an excellent writer, one of the best in ancient Russia. But the immoderate length of his work was the reason for its skillful abridgment by a learned foreigner and a contemporary, the Serb Pachomius, who edited the original text of Epiphanius for future generations.[2]

---

[2] Recent critical research has focussed attention upon a great number of different versions of the Life of St. Sergius. See V. P. Zubov, "Epifani

St. Sergius was born (ca. 1314–1320) in the territory of Rostov, once the political center of northeastern Russia, which by that time had lost all its ancient power and had fallen more and more under the influence of Moscow. Sergius, or rather Bartholomew (for this was his lay name), was the son of a Rostov boyar Cyril, who had become impoverished and lost his social prominence as a result of the disasters of the time. Epiphanius describes these gloomy events in detail: frequent inroads of the Tatars, heavy tributes paid to them, repeated journeys to the Horde with the Prince of Rostov, bad harvests as the result of political troubles. But Rostov suffered worst of all when the period known as "the violence" began, that is, when the great princedom together with the principality of Rostov fell to the lot of Ivan Danilovich (Kalita) of Moscow.

Woe, woe, above all to the princes (of Rostov) when the power and the princedom, fortune and honor were taken from them . . . A certain governor, Basil by name, was sent from Moscow to Rostov and Mina with him. And when they came to the city of Rostov they subjected the city to great oppression . . . Not a few Rostovians were compelled to surrender their property to those of Moscow and received in exchange strokes of the lash on their bodies and went away empty-handed.

The most eminent of the boyars, the former governor of Rostov, was whipped and hung by his feet. Before this terror,

Premudry i Pakhomi Serb: k voprosu o redaktisiyakh 'Zhitiya Sergiya Radonezhskogo,' " Epiphanius the Wise and Pachomius the Serb: on the Question of the Editions of the 'Life of Sergius of Radonezh'), in *Trudy Otdela drevne-russkoi literatury, Akademiya Nauk SSSR* (Works of the Section on Ancient Russian Literature, Academy of Sciences USSR), vol. IX, Moscow and Leningrad, 1953, pp. 115–158. Some of these versions have been published by N. S. Tikhonravov, ed., *Drevnie Zhitiya Sergiya Radonezhskago* (Ancient Lives of Sergius of Radonezh), Moscow, 1892 (1916); by the Archimandrite Leonid in *POPI*, vol. 58, Moscow, 1885; and in the *Velikiya Minei Chetii* (The Great Menologion), vol. I, St. Petersburg, September, 1868, cols. 1404–1578. There is a shortened English translation of the Life in G. P. Fedotov, *A Treasury of Russian Spirituality*, New York and London, 1950; Harper Torchbook (TB 303), New York, 1965, pp. 54–83. J. M.

Cyril, together with many of his countrymen migrated from Rostov to Radonezh, a small town or village in the territory of Moscow itself, which had just become a separate feudal principality. The new Prince Andrew, the youngest son of Prince Ivan, endowed Radonezh with privileges in order to increase colonization; and thus the family of Cyril, fleeing from Muscovite oppression, found refuge in Muscovite territory. This migration took place while Sergius was still an adolescent and, although he was a Rostovian by birth, he became a Muscovite in the most receptive years of his life. This was significant for the future attitude of St. Sergius, who became a spiritual guide and political helper to the Prince of Moscow. His biographer was not so oblivious of the past and he reveals a strong anti-Muscovite sentiment in both his hagiographical works.

The childhood of Bartholomew (Sergius) is immersed in legends. Some of these merely exemplify traditional features of Eastern hagiography. Such is the legend that tells of the ecclesiastical fast by the infant who did not take his mother's milk on Wednesday and Friday or at any time that his mother happened to eat meat (prohibited to the Eastern monks). Yet, many characteristics were gathered by Epiphanius, obviously, from family traditions, most probably from Sergius' brother Stephen and the latter's son Theodore. Among these characteristics there are two, the best known in the saint's life, which bear a great symbolic significance.

The first is the mysterious consecration of Sergius to the Holy Trinity even before his birth. The family tradition, certainly enriched by the reminiscence of the Gospel (Lk. 1:41), relates that when his mother, Mary, was pregnant with him, once, during the Divine Liturgy, the infant shouted three times in his mother's womb at the three most solemn moments of the service. The priest who baptized the child, in referring to this miracle, predicted his future: "He will be God's elected vessel, the mansion and the servant of the Holy Trinity." This episode dominated the thinking of Sergius' brother Stephen when he proposed to dedicate their first forest chapel to the Holy Trinity and must also have influenced the bishop who consecrated it. Consecration of a shrine in honor of the Holy Trinity was rare in Russia at that period;[3] Sergius made it almost as popular as that of Our Lady in church dedications all over Muscovy.

The second mysterious event in Bartholomew's childhood was his miraculous gift of learning. By nature the boy lacked even ordinary abilities as well as interest in and application to studies. Two of his brothers, Stephen and Peter, had learned reading successfully, "but this lad . . . paid no attention and had no talent; he was not equal to his comrades. For this reason he was much berated by his parents and punished still more by his teacher." He was humiliated by his deficiencies and prayed to God for the gift of understanding "letters." His prayer was answered in a miraculous way and here again a slight reminiscence of the Bible seems to be intermingled in the family traditions. Sent (like Saul) by his parents in search of some lost foals he met a stranger, an aged monk under an oak tree, who was "beautiful with holiness and angellike." To his question, "What do you seek, my child?" Bartholomew complained not of the lost foals but of his backwardness in letters, whereupon the old man gave him a piece of eucharistic bread (*prosfora*) as a "sign of God's grace for understanding the Holy Scripture." That day Bartholomew "suddenly grasped the whole of letters" and "whatever book he unfolded he read well."

The miraculous nature of this episode is significant because it implies a sanctification of culture. Its supernatural

---

[3] In spite of the fact that the main (cathedral) church in Pskov was that of the Holy Trinity (since the twelfth century).

character in Sergius' case gives it more significance than the
simple praise of natural gifts in St. Theodosius or St. Abraham of Smolensk.[4] With regard to the learning of her saints
ancient Russia maintained both approaches of positive appreciation, natural as well as supernatural. She is thoroughly
unaware of the ascetic repudiation of culture so emphasized
in Oriental monasticism.

We must realize, however, that the learning of St.
Sergius did not transcend mere skill in reading. His biographer does not credit him with *grammatika* (real scholarship is attributed by Nestor, whether rightly or wrongly, to
St. Theodosius in the twelfth century). The difference is
characteristic not only of individuals but of the times as well.
Unlike Theodosius, Sergius was not a writer; not a single
written line of his has been preserved; this is why one must
depend exclusively on Epiphanius in the attempt to analyze
his spiritual ethos. The eulogy of the youth offers more than
a merely cumulative list of Christian virtues; it presents an
individual and consistent portrait: "stillness, meekness, silence, humility, wrathlessness, simplicity without sophistica-
tion, equal love to all men." Calmness and silence are
particular Sergian features in this kenotic type. Obviously,
Bartholomew was a contemplative child, a lover of solitude.
Even his smile was reserved and "chaste." He was rather
prone to tears and liked to recite the Psalter, which he knew
by heart. After all the disappointments they had experienced
the family was a devout one.

A longing for the monastic life awakened in Bartholomew early; he did not marry as his two brothers did, but
still he was unwilling — unlike St. Theodosius — to grieve
his parents. They did not oppose his purpose but asked him
to postpone its fulfillment until after their death. Shortly
before that time, however, both father and mother accepted

---

[4] Fedotov, *RRM*, 278.

the "tonsure" themselves as did the eldest brother Stephen who, in the meanwhile, had become a widower. Thus, Bartholomew was overtaken on his chosen path by three members of his family. It was only after having buried his parents and having left his share of his inheritance to the third brother, Peter, that Bartholomew could realize his heart's desire. But instead of joining his brother in his monastery, Bartholomew persuaded him to leave the cloister and go together with him into some "desert place." The influence of the "meek and quiet" younger brother prevailed upon the older; they both seem to have thought but little of monastic stability and regulations. Somewhat later Bartholomew explained his ideal to the abbot who "tonsured him": "For a long time I have been yearning to live in the desert alone, without any man." Not monastic life as such but complete solitude attracted him.

In the tradition of ancient monasticism (Egypt, Syria) the life of an anchorite or hermit was deemed more perfect than that of a member of a cenobitic community. Yet, in view of the spiritual dangers of solitude, it was permitted only to those who had already acquired experience in the school of a religious community or who were at least under the direction of a spiritual guide (elder, starets). Bartholomew, in his youth, could hardly have acquired a deep knowledge of literature and of the restrictions imposed upon the anchoretic life. Neither could ancient Russia offer him any model for this life. He simply followed his inner drive without any guide or authoritative blessing. He took an enormous risk without being aware of it and won his victory.

The adventurous brothers roamed long through forests before they found a place to their taste. It was a true "desert," infested with wild beasts, although it was only some ten miles distant from Radonezh, their family home, and seven miles from the Khotkovo monastery where their parents had died. The brothers at once set about the hard labor of pioneers; they cut wood and built not only a log cabin for their cells, but also a small chapel. Russian hermits could not conceive of an ideal solitude without liturgical consolation. The chapel was consecrated in the name of the Holy Trinity, in remembrance of the miraculous sign, but as neither brother was ordained, the Divine Liturgy was celebrated only from time to time by some visiting priest. Other services could be "sung" or chanted by the hermits themselves. We may suppose that the most frequent visiting priest was the same Abbot Metrophanes who tonsured Bartholomew and changed his name to the Sergius by which he is known in history. According to Epiphanius' calculations, Sergius was then only twenty-three years old.

In spite of his extreme youth he was left quite alone in his wilderness; Stephen could not endure the difficulties of the desert life and moved to a monastery in the city of Moscow where he had a distinguished ecclesiastical career. For years Sergius was able to experience both the joys and the dangers of his beloved solitude. About the latter, and only the latter, his biographer is very eloquent: "The scarcity and want of everything; whatever you mention is lacking . . . the hosts of demons . . . the packs of wolves, howling and roaring, sometimes even bears." Epiphanius does not conceal that Sergius was frightened "as man" but wild beasts did not do him any harm. Epiphanius has a dogmatic interpretation of the power of a holy man over the irrational creatures: "No one ought to be amazed . . . when God is living in a man and the Holy Spirit is dwelling in him, everything is obedient to him as once to Adam, the first-created, before his transgression of the divine commandment." This is, of course, a *locus classicus* for the Orthodox doctrine of mystical life of which Epiphanius was fully cognizant. Only the restoration of the image of the first-created man in Sergius is represented as already perfect since the beginnings of his struggle.

More realistic and more earthbound is the picturesque description of the friendship between the hermit and a bear. The beast "formed the habit of always coming to the saint and the latter, knowing it, would bring out of his cabin a small crust of bread and put it upon a log or stump . . . But when bread was lacking and the bear came as usual he would not go away for a long time but would stand looking here and there, waiting as a merciless creditor for his debt. If the saint happened to have only one crust, he was obliged to divide even it into two parts."

Demons were more terrifying though not more dangerous. Their frequent intrusions aimed only at intimidation, as in other lives of Russian saints. The pattern of St. Antony of Egypt[5] was reproduced with some new local details. "When Sergius entered the chapel by night to sing Matins the wall would open all of a sudden and the devil would enter with a host of demons . . . They wore Lithuanian cloaks and hats[6] . . . threatening to murder him." They shouted: "Flee, run away from here and don't dwell any longer in this place." These noisy disturbances and jeering commands also haunted Sergius' cell by night but caused no real harm. Epiphanius' demonology is as optimistic as Athanasius' in the life of St. Antony.[7] "This is the custom of the devil and his pride; when he sets about boasting or menacing

---

[5] St. Athanasius, *Vita S. Antonii,* ch. 9, in Migne, ed., *PG,* vol. 26, cols. 837–976.

[6] Lithuanian garb in demonic visions in the Lives of Russian saints appear since the fifteenth century as evidence of growing bitterness in the relations between Lithuania and Moscow. Before becoming Lithuanians the demons appeared as Ethiopians, Moors, or Egyptians in Greek hagiography, or as Poles in the hagiography of Kievan Russia.

[7] *Vita S. Antonii,* ch. 6, 23–24.

anyone, he threatens to consume the earth and dry up the
sea, and yet he has no power even over pigs." [8]

As in the life of Theodosius and other Russian saints
the obvious purpose of demonic illusions is to frighten the
ascetic from his path, not to tempt him with sinful desires.
Of fleshly temptations one hears almost nothing; a wise
reserve, or probably over-reverence restrains the pen of the
hagiographer from these treacherous themes. And yet, in
the case of Sergius — this is also typical of most of the Russian saints — we are reminded of his physical strength. [9] Despite his contemplative mind and the shyness which drove him
away from human society, it would be quite false to represent
him as an emaciated and sickly youth, which is the Western
or romantic idea of the mystical temperament.

Epiphanius does not deny the fact of Sergius' fleshly
temptations. But he mentions them casually, and fasting
seems to be the only ascetic weapon in the struggle with the
enemy. [10] No artificial means of voluntary suffering, except
fasting, are alluded to; not even the stings of the mosquitoes
which Theodosius once had braved. The difficulties of life
alone are emphasized. In Sergius, burdensome manual labor
replaces all the refinements of ascetic devices. The "works
of St. Sergius," in a truly peasant spirit, have been imprinted
deeply in the memory of Russian people and in religious art.
In the work of Epiphanius they are mainly represented in
the framework of nascent community life.

As to the duration of Sergius' blessed isolation Epiphanius
himself cannot tell ("two years — perhaps more or less").

---

[8] An allusion to Matthew 8:31.

[9] Epiphanius says: "He was young and strong of body . . . could do the
work of two men."

[10] This is all that Epiphanius says of the temptations of Sergius: "The
devil wished to wound him with the arrows of lust, but the saint realizing
the onslaught of the foe restrained his body and enslaved it with fasting,
and thus he was rescued by the grace of God."

But at last some monks began to gather around the hermit. This was obviously against his will: "Not only did he not accept them but he forbade them," with no success. He could not frighten them away with the hardships of his way of life and finally had to yield. "They built each one a hut for himself and began to live according to Sergius' divine way, trying to imitate him in accordance with their own strength." He was neither their abbot nor elder teacher. The only influence he exerted on them was by his example.

Sergius seems to have particularly excelled in or was at least fond of the art of carpentry. After the appearance of the new brethren he himself built three or four cells for them, surrounded the small settlement with a fence, and added to his many labors; he had to cut wood and carry water up the hill from the well, clear the thicket and plant a kitchen garden, cook scanty food and bake bread. Not only this, but he even had to make clothes and footwear for the brethren although no community life as such yet existed. Every monk had to take care of himself and of his own subsistence, as was the custom in most Russian monasteries at that time and later. Sergius alone assumed more than his own share in manual labor in an endeavor to alleviate the burdens of his disciples.

It goes without saying that the chapel took much time during the day and even the night. The brethren met seven times daily for the chanting of Matins, Vespers, and the other canonical hours. Only the Divine Liturgy could not be celebrated by them; it was celebrated as before by some itinerant priest or by their nominal abbot, Metrophanes.

After the death of Metrophanes, the brethren, who numbered twelve at that time, insisted that Sergius assume both the abbacy and priesthood. Their motives, at least those indicated by the biographer, are purely liturgical: "We wish to come to you for confession and to see you celebrating the

Divine Liturgy each day, and to communicate from your venerable hands." There is no question of government or discipline. The community lives and will live in a complete freedom.

Yet every idea of rank or distinction was loathsome to Sergius. He used to say: "I wish rather to live under others' will than to have others under mine." With regard to the abbot's post he even went so far as to affirm that: "To seek abbacy is the root and beginning of ambition." This was, certainly, more than a gesture or an affectation of ecclesiastical good manners. The man who declined in his old age the rank of the supreme hierarch of Russia can be credited with the absence of all kinds of ambition. He even dared resist the bishop who tried to enforce the dignity upon him, eliciting thereby these words of reproach: "My beloved, you have acquired everything but in obedience you are deficient." Once more it becomes evident that kenotic humility has roots other than the monastic virtue of obedience.

Sergius yielded at last and was ordained priest and abbot at the same time, but, except for the liturgical services, it meant little change in his life. Sergius' manual works were increased with the growth of his religious settlement since he wished to fulfill the Gospel commandment literally — "to be the smallest of all and the servant to all." [11] The relations between the abbot and his monks as well as the economic conditions in the monastery are eloquently attested to in the following episode.

Their poverty was so extreme that in the chapel instead of candles birch torches were used, as in old Russian peasant huts. The scarcity of provisions was aggravated since the abbot forbade the monks to go out and beg for alms; the brethren had "to sit patiently . . . looking for alms from

---

[11] A paraphrase of Luke 22:26.

God." We must remember that there was no communal refectory, and each monk was dependent on himself, the abbot included.

Once Sergius was without any food for three days. On the fourth day "he took an axe and approached one of the monks . . . whose name was Daniel and said to him: 'I heard, father, that you wish to build a porch in front of your cell, and I came for that . . .' 'Yes,' answers Daniel, 'I am much concerned about it but I am waiting for a carpenter from the village; I am afraid that you may demand too high a price . . .' Sergius: 'I do not ask a very high recompense from you; have you some moldy bread?' Father Daniel brought out a basket of molded loaves." Sergius began to work, to hew out planks and pillars, toiling until the evening. Only when the porch was finished did he begin to eat with water only — there was neither soup nor salt. Some of the brethren seeing Sergius toiling the whole day admired his patience, but one of them who did not eat himself for two days came to the abbot and began to vituperate him in his presence: "Moldy loaves! And we may not go out to the world to ask for bread? . . . We are perishing of starvation while obeying you. Tomorrow early we leave this place . . . and we will never come back again." Sergius quelled the nascent revolt with a lesson of Christian patience and hope. "Confide in God. Who having placed his hope in God was ever confused? . . . In the evening tears; in the morning joy."

Sergius' faith in Providence was immediately justified. Some unknown benefactor sent the monastery a whole cart of fresh baked loaves. The unexpected appearance of the rescuers, the anonymity of the gift, and the extraordinary quality of the bread, "honey sweet and fragrant" makes the whole episode strange and mysterious. It is not said positively that the extraordinary loaves came directly from heaven, but a light aura of the supernatural surrounds the factual kernel of the story.

Many times the community must have been saved from starvation by known and unknown benefactors but the life was difficult and was one of extreme poverty. This period of hardship, according to the computations of Epiphanius, lasted for fifteen years. After that peasant pioneers began to settle down in the surrounding woods, felled and burned them for fields for ploughing, built farms and villages. This was the beginning of prosperity for Holy Trinity but the end of the desert solitude. "They deformed the wilderness without pity" is the complaint of the ascetically minded Epiphanius.

The growth of wealth, of worldly influence, and even of architectural beauty in newly built churches did not find their chronicler in Epiphanius. His asceticism was of a quite different kind. Together with Sergius he was enamored of holy poverty. This was a part of the general kenotic ideal based upon the imitation of the humiliated Christ. "In all things and at all times he (Sergius) imitated his Master Jesus Christ our Lord . . . eager to imitate him and follow him," it is said in connection with Sergius' humility. A social expression of this kenotic following of Christ is seen in Sergius, as in all typical Russian saints, in the uncouthness of their garb.[12]

Our author dedicates a whole chapter to this engaging subject. He knows from the old men in the monastery that Sergius never wore a new soft cassock, least of all one made of foreign or colored cloth (we learn thus, incidentally, that colored mantles were not uncommon among the monks of that time). His cassock always was of the simple homespun cloth like that worn by peasants; it was often old and dirty

---

[12] Compare Fedotov, *RRM*, p. 116.

at that, patched and soaked with sweat. It once happened
that a piece of cloth was found in the cloister of such miserable quality that none of the brothers wished to take it.
Sergius took it for himself, cut and sewed a cassock of it,
and wore it for a whole year until it became torn and ragged
on his body. The significance of this taste for the lowest and
the worst, which so disgusts modern man, is clearly comprehended by Epiphanius. Sergius did it "for humility's sake"
desiring to "walk in a beggarly appearance."

A savory story illustrates the social aspect of Sergius'
kenoticism and recalls analogous episodes in the life of St.
Theodosius.[13] The incident occurred at the time when Sergius
stood at the summit of his fame, when his monastery had
become a center of pilgrimages with princes among its guests.
A simple-minded peasant came from afar, along with other
pilgrims, to see the holy man. Sergius was at the time occupied with one of his favorite labors; he was digging the
soil in the vegetable garden. The guest was asked to wait
until the abbot had finished his work, but the curious peasant
looked through a hole in the fence and could not believe that
the man in dirty clothes toiling by the sweat of his brow was
the famous abbot. When Sergius came out of the garden
and was shown to the visitor the latter thought he was the
victim of a practical joke and gave vent to his indignation:
"I came to see the prophet and you show me a peasant."
The brethren were going to turn the impudent peasant out
of the monastery but Sergius, who had heard his words, did
not allow it. "He prostrated himself before him and greeted
him with the true love of Christ; when he had blessed the
peasant he praised him for judging about him so rightly . . .
As the proud rejoice in honors and praises so the humble
rejoice in their dishonor and reprobation."

The end of the story is, of course, the confusion of the

---

[13] *Ibid.*, p. 121.

boor and the triumph of the true hierarchy of values. A prince comes to the monastery and prostrates himself before the saint, whereas his servants push the peasant from his place in the refectory on the right hand of Sergius. The poor man asks for pardon and, in the course of years, returns to the Holy Trinity to take monastic tonsure.

The supreme act of Sergius' kenotic humility was his repudiation of the metropolitan see. He was old at the time and was known even in Greece as one of the outstanding and most worthy personalities in the Russian Church.[14] Metropolitan Alexis, an old man himself was concerned with the nomination of his successor. He as well as Prince Dimitri wished to see a Russian and not a Greek in the See of Moscow. Alexis called him to the Abbey of the Holy Trinity and, as a symbolical introduction, gave him a golden cross with jewels to wear upon his breast. Sergius declined the unusual gift: "Pardon me, my lord, from my youth I never was a wearer of gold, and in my old age all the more do I wish to live in poverty." When the metropolitan disclosed the purpose of his summons, Sergius "was very grieved, as if considering this a great vanity for himself." He refused flatly. "Pardon me, my lord, what you speak of is beyond my measure; never will you find this in me; who am I, the most sinful and despicable of men?" For all his humility he sounds a note of dignity and firmness in defending his ideal of holy kenosis: "My saintly lord! If you do not wish to force me to remove my poor self from listening to your holiness, cease to speak about this to my unworthiness, and do not let any other do it, for nobody can find it in me." The persuasions of the prince had no better effect. Sergius remained "firm and adamant."

---

[14] Compare the letters addressed to him by the patriarch and by the Metropolitan Cyprian in A. S. Pavlov, ed., "Pamyatniki drevne-russkago kanonicheskago prava" (Monuments of Ancient Russian Canon Law), in *RIB*, vol. VI, St. Petersburg, 1880, nos. 20, 21, pp. 174–190.

This negative attitude toward rank and power even in the ecclesiastical realm was shown by Sergius with regard to his disciples as well. One of them, his own nephew Theodore, made a brilliant career in the Church. Elected by the prince as abbot of the new monastery in Moscow (Simonov) he received from the patriarch the title of first archimandrite of Russia and ended his life as Archbishop of Rostov. Following his varied career Sergius "complained much about his honors and glory and prayed unceasingly to God that he might fulfill his high course without stumbling."

That the kenotic ideal, lived to its extreme, is hardly compatible with the qualities of a ruler was experienced already by St. Theodosius, the abbot of the first real Kievan monastery.[15] Sergius behaved toward his flock as their equal or, rather, as inferior and servant of all. We have seen how free they were in expressing even their rebellious sentiments. This freedom once led to an open revolt and split in the monastery. This story is told, with some reticence and softening, in connection with the introduction of the cenobitic rule.

We read in the Life that Sergius received a missive from the Patriarch of Constantinople who, after paying him compliments and bestowing his blessings, suggested the necessity of introducing the "communal life." Sergius consulted the Russian Metropolitan Alexis (who, most probably, was the initiator of this reform) and accepted a cenobitic rule for his brethren. The only Greek rule known and used in Russia, infrequently and with difficulties, was that of the Studion of Constantinople. This one was now introduced into the Holy Trinity monastery.

In practice it meant, first of all, the abolition of private property: "Not to acquire anything for oneself nor call anything one's own but to have all in common." The common household required orderly administration and many monastic

---

[15] Fedotov, *RRM*, I, 123.

officers were appointed. It is in these years after the reform
that we are inclined to ascribe to Sergius the habit of passing
by the doors of the cells at night and of listening to what
was going on within. This inspection as well as the mild rebuke on the following morning are related of St. Theodosius
as well. This conduct was in conformity with the Studion
rule.

That a missive from the Patriarch was required for the
reform indicates by itself that the communal life and the
Studion rule were out of use in Russia at that time. In trying
to discover the reason why the keeping of this rule was so
difficult and intermittent in Russia, we dare venture that the
cause was not so much the love of property as the habit of
independence and dislike of discipline. A chronicle which
better preserves, though in abridged form, the original text
of Epiphanius tells that after the introduction of the rule
"whoever disagreed secretly left the monastery." [16]

Epiphanius' editor, Pachomius, without giving the reason
for the discontent, indicates that its gist was the "dislike of
Sergius' leadership." As he tells it, the instigator of the tumult
is Sergius' own brother Stephen who had returned to the
Holy Trinity from his Moscow monastery. We learn that he
even brought with him as a novice his younger son. On the
trifling pretext for a liturgical or ritual misunderstanding he
began to complain in the church: "Who is the abbot in this
place? Was it nòt I who was sitting before in his place? and
other things he said that it was unfit to say."

The reaction of Sergius was striking and characteristic.
He said nothing but on the next morning left the monas-
tery "in secret" and went a few miles away to his friend the
Abbot of Makhrishchi. After awhile some brothers of the
Holy Trinity, loyal to Sergius, began to gather around him,
and a new monastery was created, with the blessing of Metro-

16 *Nik.*, in *PSRL*, IV, 225.

politan Alexis. When the opposition began to ebb, its members acted through the intermediary of the same Alexis and effected the return of the abbot. The reconciliation is described in most glowing colors. His spiritual sons kissed his hands and feet. "And what about the father? He also rejoiced in spirit seeing his children gathered around him."

This and other episodes are apt to create a none-too-favorable impression of the religious and moral life in Holy Trinity monastery. Yet, on the other hand, one reads of the true disciples of Sergius whose lives were models of holiness. No less than eleven of them were canonized after their death. As in the case of the Kievan Monastery of the Caves, instead of a common level we see, rather, the extremes. The best among the brethren found a great spiritual guide in Sergius and developed their personalities and their gifts. The weakest, perhaps the majority, were not restrained by the rule of a well-organized community. This picture is typical of most Russian social institutions.

Even during Sergius' lifetime some of his disciples were appointed to be the heads of newly founded monasteries in the city of Moscow and in surrounding towns. Holy Trinity became a center of monastic influence that radiated throughout a vast area. But, as one can foresee, the initiative did not stem from the kenotic abbot. It was Metropolitan Alexis, his friend and patron, and the princes of the Moscow dynasty who used Holy Trinity as a seedbed for their new monastic foundations. Sergius gave his blessing, sometimes not without anxious afterthoughts, as we saw in the case of Theodore. His best disciples and the most faithful to his spirit he retained at his side.

The kenoticism of Sergius, as well as that of Theodosius, was inseparable from charity. In Sergius' case it was not altogether obvious; a contemplative lover of solitude could easily immure himself and his monastery from the world. The

remarkable thing is that Sergius did not. Once having acknowledged his failure in securing holy solitude, he reopened
his heart to suffering humanity. According to Epiphanius,
Sergius took as his spiritual guides the great Eastern ascetics
"who had lived an angelic life upon earth": Antony the Great,
and the great Euthymius, Savva the Sanctified, Pachomius
the angel-like, and Theodosius Coenobiarchus. Enumerating
their virtues the panegyrist ends with these characteristics:
"bountiful protectors of the poor, nourishers of beggars,
inexhaustible treasure for widows and orphans." If this
collective portrait seems inadequate with regard to great
monks of the East, it is all the more significant for the
Russian ascetic ideal and for Sergius himself. After the acceptance of the Studion rule, he ordered that rest and refreshment be given to the poor and wanderers and that alms be
given to the needy although this was not at all in accordance
with the Studion rule[17] and could have provoked an invasion
of the monastery by crowds of lay people. But even on his
deathbed Sergius reminded his disciples of their duty in the
words of St. Paul: "Forget not to show love unto strangers."
With the realization of this duty he prophetically linked the
future prosperity of his cloister.

The same trends are discernible in the stories of the miracles of the saint. They are not numerous and not overawing.
Sergius was not a professional healer. Though possessing
great spiritual gifts, that of clairvoyance, for example, and
an extraordinary power of prayer, he shrank out of humility
from the manifestation of his power. The story of the "resurrection" of a child is very instructive in this respect. A father
set out with his sick boy for the monastery so that Sergius
might pray for him. When he had reached the end of his
journey the child had died or at least the father believed it
already dead. The grieving father went to make a coffin while

---

[17] Compare Fedotov, *RRM*, I, 133.

Sergius, who pitied the father, took the child into his cell and prayed for him. When the father returned he found his son alive and Sergius addressed him in a tone of kindly reproach: "Why are you troubled, man, for nothing? Look here, your son did not die; he is alive." The father believed it a miracle but Sergius tried to dissuade him: "You are under an illusion, man, you do not know what you are speaking of: your child, while you were carrying him here, was frozen and fainted, and now, in the warm cell he has recovered, and you imagine him resurrected. Nobody can be called back to life until the general resurrection."

One of Sergius' miracles seems to have had a punitive character, but on closer examination it reveals itself as a work of love rather than justice; or, at least, justice is put at the service of mercy. This is always the case in the vindication of the rights of the poor. A rich landowner, of greedy and acquisitive mind, wronged a poor peasant, his neighbor, "as it is the habit of powerful men to wrong the poor." He took the peasant's pig without payment and slew it. The poor man came to complain to Sergius, and the abbot called the wrongdoer to his spiritual tribunal. "My son," he said, "since you believe that God exists . . . He is the father of the poor, orphans and widows, who is ready for vengeance, and it is a fearful thing to fall into the hands of the living God . . ." The terror-stricken landowner promised to pay the poor man for his damage but when he returned home he repented of his generosity and did not keep his word. Then the punishment came, and a very mild one indeed. The meat of the robbed pig turned suddenly rotten and full of worms. Even dogs would not eat it.

Like most Russian kenotic saints Sergius altered his habitual mildness only against the mighty of this world. One can discern a covert democratic bias in the presentation by his disciples of the healing of a "possessed" grandee. He was led to the monastery in chains raging dangerously and at the sight of Sergius' cross "roared in a loud voice and fell into a mire." This humiliating detail of the exorcism scene appears to have been merited by nothing but the high rank of the patient.

So far we have seen in Sergius for the most part the traditional traits of Russian kenoticism. The model of Theodosius is manifestly reflected in him, only more refined and spiritualized. Yet in this ancient image of the Russian saint some new features can be discerned. Simplicity and openness are characteristic of Theodosius' spiritual life. Sergius' simplicity without guile leads to the verge of a mysterious depth that his biographer is not able to penetrate, but that bespeaks itself, however, through visions which were unheard of in Russia before Sergius. Ancient saints often had visions of demons, which did not spare Sergius either. But it was only to Sergius that the celestial powers spoke, in symbols of light and fire. Some of Sergius' disciples were also partakers of these visions — those who formed a mystical circle around him, Simon, Isaac, and Micah. Once when Sergius was celebrating the Divine Liturgy together with two other priests, Isaac and another disciple saw a fourth man concelebrating in a brilliant vestment radiant with light. At the insistent questioning of his disciples Sergius revealed his secret: "O, my beloved sons, if the Lord has revealed it to you how can I conceal it? He whom you have seen is the angel of the Lord, and not only today but always, by the grace of God, I unworthily celebrate with him; but do not tell anybody what you have seen as long as I am in this life." The same Isaac asked Sergius' blessing for keeping perpetual silence. When the teacher was blessing him he saw "a great flame which issued from him and surrounded all of Isaac's body." Another disciple, Simon, related: "While the holy man was celebrating I saw fire moving upon the offertory table, spreading over the sanctuary and surrounding the altar; and when the saint was going to communicate the divine fire folded up, like a cloth and entered the holy chalice and thus the saint communicated."

Two visions pertain to Sergius himself, although his mystically oriented disciples also took part in them. One night, after praying for the brethren of his monastery, the abbot heard a voice calling him by name: "Sergius!" Opening the window he beheld a great light in the sky and flocks of beautiful birds over and around the whole monastery. The heavenly voice gave him the promise: "Like these birds that you see the flock of your disciples will multiply . . . if they choose to tread in your footsteps."

The same concern for his disciples is reflected in another vision of Sergius', and is of quite unique significance. Sergius was the first Russian saint to behold a vision of Our Lady. This is Epiphanius' narrative.

One evening Sergius was praying, as usual, before the icon of Our Lady. Having finished chanting the "canon" to the Virgin, he sat down to take a little rest and said to his disciple Micah: "Be sober, my son, and alert, for a wondrous and awe-inspiring visitation awaits us." And immediately a voice was heard: "Lo, the Immaculate One is coming." The saint, hearing it, hurried from the cell to the anteroom. At this moment a great light fell upon him, brighter than the sun, and he beheld the Immaculate One with two Apostles, Peter and John, shining in an ineffable radiance. He fell upon his face, being unable to endure this unbearable dawn. And the Immaculate One touched the saint with her hands saying: "Do not fear, my chosen one, I come to visit you. Your prayer for your disciples . . . and your monastery has been heard. Do not be anxious any more because the monastery will abound in all things; not only during your life but also after your departure I will be inseparable from your mansion, giving it unsparingly what is needed, providing and

protecting it." And with these words she became invisible
. . . The saint, in an ecstasy of spirit was stricken by fear and
trembling. Coming gradually to himself he found his disciple
lying as though dead and raised him up. Micah prostrated
himself before the starets and said: "Tell me, father, what
was this wondrous thing, for my spirit almost parted from my
body because of this luminous vision." The saint was rejoicing
in his soul, even his face was blooming with joy, but he could
answer nothing except: "Wait a little, my son, for my spirit
also is trembling because of this wondrous vision . . ." Then
he said to his disciple: "My son, call to me Isaac and Simon."
And when they came he related all in order to them.

True, these visions of St. Sergius and his disciples cannot
be proved as historical facts in their details. On the other
hand they cannot be dismissed as mere legends. For two of
them, connected with liturgical mysteries, there are analogies
in the Life of Euthymius the Great, one of Sergius' models.
Even here, however, it would not be fair to speak of a simple
literary borrowing. These episodes are tied up too closely with
other visions of a similar kind. Undoubtedly the tradition of
these visions was preserved by the mystical trio among
Sergius' disciples, Isaac, Micah, and Simon. Although Isaac
and Micah died before Sergius and were bound by the injunction of silence until his death, from the third, Simon,
Epiphanius could learn the secrets that were hidden from
the other monks. The essential fact is that before St. Sergius
visions of this kind were unknown in Russian hagiography.

One is entitled then to consider these visions in the light
of Sergius' longing for solitude which, lacking specific ascetic
severity, is to be explained only by a contemplative frame of
mind and in the light of the dedication of his entire life to
the Holy Trinity, which in a theologically poor Russia
was neither before nor after Sergius the object of speculative
thought. One, thus, is forced to the conclusion that Sergius

was the first Russian saint who can be termed a mystic, that is, the bearer of a peculiar, mysterious, spiritual life that was not limited to asceticism, love, and continual prayer. The secrets of his spiritual life remain hidden from us. The visions are but signs marking the unknown.

As for the evidence of these visions, however, it is thoroughly legitimate to point out the affinity of Sergius' inner life to a contemporary mystical movement in the Orthodox East. This is the well-known movement of the Hesychasts, the practicers of "spiritual activity" or "intellectual prayer," which was revived by St. Gregory of Sinai in the middle of the fourteenth century and spread widely throughout the Greek and Slavic world. Gregory Palamas, Archbishop of Thessalonica; Euthymius, Patriarch of Trnovo; and many patriarchs of Constantinople were its adherents. In theological interpretation this mystical practice was connected with the doctrine of the "light of Tabor" and divine energies.

A revival of Greek and South Slavic influence in Northern Russia is perceptible after the middle and particularly at the end of the fourteenth century. During Sergius' lifetime, in one of the monasteries of Rostov, Greek manuscripts were studied by St. Stephen of Perm. New translations of the Gospels were made by Russian scholars or scribes in the same century.[18] Sergius himself received in his monastery a Greek bishop and was the addressee of a letter of the Ecumenical Patriarch. One of the disciples of St. Sergius was his namesake, Sergius of Naroma, who is said to have come from Mount Athos, and there is every reason for identifying Athanasius, abbot of Serpukhov, the disciple of Sergius, with that "Athanasius the Russian" who in 1431 transcribed on Athos, "under the very wings of St. Gregory Palamas," a

---

[18] Compare A. I. Sobolevski, *Perevodnaya literatura Moskovskoi Rusi, XIV–XVII vekov* (Translated Literature of Muscovite Russia, 14th–17th Centuries), St. Petersburg, 1903, pp. 4, 26–31.

hagiographical collection for the Russian monastery of the Holy Trinity. The library of Holy Trinity contained Slavic translations of Gregory of Sinai dating from the fourteenth and fifteenth centuries.[19] In the fifteenth century there were copied in the same place the works of the Greek mystic Simeon the New Theologian. All this still does not establish the direct impact of Greece upon Sergius' religious life, but it makes it highly probable. Besides, the ways of spiritual influence are not limited to direct discipleship and imitation. Striking correspondences are frequent occurrences in history; simultaneous and apparently independent trends of spiritual and cultural life, consonant with each other, arise in different areas of the globe. In the light of the mystical tradition that affirmed itself among the disciples of Sergius, his own mystical experiences, illumined for us only by his visions (one can compare the vision of light by Sergius with the Light of Tabor of Hesychasts), acquire a greater degree of preciseness.

From mysticism to politics is a long step, especially in the Eastern world. Yet Sergius in Russia took it as did Bernard of Clairvaux and so many medieval saints of the West. It can be rightly believed that this step was not easy for the lover of solitude to whom even the communal life within the walls of a monastery was a burden. As in the case of the abbacy, charity in the form of patriotism must have been the moral lure that enticed the hermit into the national political field. The interference of Sergius in the destiny of the young Muscovite state was undoubtedly one of the reasons why Muscovy and, afterwards, the whole of Russia venerated Sergius as its celestial patron. In the mind of the Muscovites of the sixteenth century he assumed a position beside St. Boris and St. Gleb as a national patron of Russia. The interpretation of Sergius' political activities offers a great problem as to their motives as well as their religious value.

---

[19] *Ibid.*, pp. 15–16.

This problem was overlooked by most Orthodox people in Russia because of their incurable inability to separate religious and national interests. Pursuing this trend to the limit, modern Soviet writers include Sergius in their selection of national heroes by turning him into a political agent for the Prince of Moscow. Did Sergius deserve such dishonoring rehabilitation?

In our attempt at an evaluation we proceed from a conviction that the integrity of Sergius' moral character is warranted by all historical sources. On the other hand, however, one has to consider the contemporary world of Sergius, so dissimilar from the later Muscovy, with quite different political standards. These standards of ancient feudal law were being trodden down by the Moscow princes in their struggle for power. The immorality of their politics was seen and condemned in all Russia, except perhaps, in the Moscow principality itself. A contemporary annalist telling of the Moscow fortress, the Kremlin, rebuilt in 1367, makes the following remark: "Certain of their great might they [the princes of Moscow] began to bring Russian princes under their will and maliciously retaliate against those who disobeyed them." [20] The Prince of Moscow was so unpopular and isolated in Russia that in the moment of greatest national danger, he stood alone with his vassal princes on the battlefield of Kulikovo.

In this national conflict Sergius undoubtedly stood on the side of Moscow. Princes of the house of Kalita visited him at Holy Trinity. He himself left his monastery on frequent visits to Moscow. He was godfather of the sons of Prince Dimitri Donskoi and he took upon himself certain political commissions. About his political actions we are informed only by the Chronicles; his biographies preserve a complete silence in the matter.

[20] *Rog.*, a. 1367

One of these commissions has full moral justification since it was an act of peace-making. Sergius was sent to Prince Oleg of Ryazan an old and mighty enemy of Moscow, and "with his mild words and lowly speeches" persuaded him to accept a pact of "eternal peace" with Dimitri.[21]

Another case of Sergius' political interference is not so easy to dismiss. This was the mission of Sergius to Nizhni Novgorod in 1365. The principality of Nizhni Novgorod (now Gorki, on the Volga) became for a short time a dangerous rival of Moscow in the struggle for the title and power of Great Prince. Its old capital was Suzdal, one of the most ancient cities of Russia, but Nizhni Novgorod was a new, growing, and prosperous center. Two brothers, the elder Dimitri and the younger Boris, held Suzdal and Nizhni respectively. Dimitri (not to be confused with his rival at Moscow) succeeded in getting the *yarlyk* (charter) for the Great Principality from the khan of the Golden Horde. Yet, when he returned from the Horde with this title he was faced by a new situation. Dimitri of Moscow, who was stronger in military force, disregarded the decision of the khan and by threats forced the Prince of Suzdal into an act of renunciation. Moreover, Dimitri of Moscow took from his rival the city of Suzdal and offered him as a compensation Nizhni Novgorod, the seat of his brother, who had to be content with a still smaller town. At the same time the Metropolitan Alexis hurried to complement this political act of spoliation by a corresponding ecclesiastical action; he "detached" from the Bishop of Suzdal the towns of Nizhni Novgorod and Gorodets, annexing them to his own diocese. It still remained to persuade Prince Boris of Novgorod to yield to this violent annexation and cede his town to his elder brother. But he refused. At that moment of political tension Abbot Sergius was sent as an "envoy" to Prince Boris "calling him to

---

[21] *Sim* and *Rog.*, a. 1385.

Moscow." It had already become a custom in Moscow to arrest and keep in prison the princes, formerly quite independent of Moscow authority, who were naïve enough to fall into such a snare. There is nothing astonishing in the fact that Boris "disobeyed and did not go to Moscow." Then Sergius, "according to the order of Alexis and the Great Prince Dimitri, closed all churches in Nizhni Novgorod." Closing churches was an act of interdict very common in the West but having no justification in Eastern canon law. This measure was, however, applied in the fourteenth century by the metropolitans of Moscow in their strife with the Archbishop of Great Novgorod but without either popular support or success. Even Sergius' name produced no greater effect. The Prince of Moscow had to send an armed force to aid Dimitri of Suzdal against his brother and only when threatened by military defeat did Boris give up his town.

This is the story told by the chroniclers, even those of Moscow origin and pro-Muscovite tendencies.[22] It is scarcely edifying. The issue in question was of at least dubious moral and juridical intent if not a direct act of aggression and injustice. The ecclesiastical support of this aggression was a scandal to the nation. Interdict was canonically unlawful. And, finally, it produced no effect at all. Thus Sergius' mission was a complete mistake and failure. No wonder that Epiphanius in his Life does not mention this episode or Sergius' mission to Prince Oleg.

The clue to an explanation of the situation is given by the mention of Alexis in the Nicon Chronicle. Sergius acted as envoy of his bishop, who is thus responsible for this action. Certainly, the obedience of the saintly abbot to his ecclesiastical superior was not unlimited as we could see in his repudiation of the dignity of the office of metropolitan for himself.

---

[22] The *Sof., Voskr., Nik.,* and *Rog.* Chronicles (a. 1363) give the names of Alexis' two envoys without mentioning Sergius'.

But Sergius could have imagined that in this political mission he acted also as peace-maker in trying to reconcile Boris with his brother.[23] We prefer to ascribe this unhappy action of Sergius to his political naïveté rather than to make him a conscious aide in political machiavellianism.

Both the Chronicles and the Lives, on the other hand, tell of Sergius' role in the battle of Kulikovo, the first successful attempt of the Russians to resist the Tatars (1380). Their narratives agree in all the essentials. Before the battle, when Mamai, the Tatar general and usurper, was advancing against Moscow, Prince Dimitri went to the Holy Trinity monastery to ask Abbot Sergius for his blessing. Sergius blessed and encouraged him, prophesying his victory. These are Sergius' words in Epiphanius' version: "It is fitting for you, my lord, to take care of the Christian flock, committed to you by God; go against the godless and with God's assistance you will conquer and return safe to your homeland with great glory." Epiphanius adds that during the march, when the Russian warriors were seized with a sudden terror before the encounter with the foe, a messenger came from Sergius to the prince with the heartening words: "Go without hesitation, my lord, daringly against their ferocity, do not fear, God will help you in all."

Epiphanius emphasizes throughout this episode the prophetic gift of Sergius. During the battle Sergius, while praying for victory, recounts to his disciples the details of the combat and even the names of the fallen heroes.

The narrative included in the Nicon Chronicle differs from Epiphanius in some interesting details. Before giving the prince his blessing Sergius tries to prevent the military clash and open revolt against the khan by acts of submission and obedience: "Placate the impious Mamai with gifts and honors, that God, seeing your humility, may exalt

---

[23] This motive is given by *Voskr*, and *Sof*. Chronicles.

you and put down his unbridled rage and pride. He [the prince] said: 'I did thus to him, my father, but he still more inflates himself with great pride!' And the holy man said 'If it be so, a final ruin and perdition awaits him and you will have the aid, the grace, and glory from the Lord our God, his Immaculate Mother, and his saints.' " [24]

The same cautious advice with reference to Christian humility was given to Prince Dimitri by the new Metropolitan Cyprian, according to the same Chronicle. One has to remember that the khan of the Tatars was the legal monarch of Russia, called "tsar" in all contemporary sources, and the Church prayed for him in its liturgical services. In the case of Mamai, however, the break of loyalty could be justified by the illegal character of his power; Mamai was not the Khan but a *temnik* (general).

The second addition by the Chronicle to the Life is concerned with two monks of Holy Trinity who took a direct part in the battle. We are told that upon the request of Dimitri, Sergius permitted two monks, Peresvet and Oslyabiya, to go with him; either one or both of them died on the field of Kulikovo. Whether they fought as warriors is uncertain. On the other hand, according to the Nicon Chronicle, Sergius "gave them the uncorruptible weapon, instead of the corruptible one," the cross of Christ sewed upon their *skhemas* (monastic mantles), and ordered them to place it upon their heads, instead of helmets and "fight firmly with Christ against His enemies." This implies that their fighting was spiritual and that they were acting in the battles as the chaplains of the army. On the other hand, the same Chronicle in another passage explains the choice of Peresvet and Oslyabiya: "For they knew the military profession, how to line up regiments; moreover, they possessed great strength, courage and daring." The same Chronicle also

---

[24] *Nik.* 1380.

narrates a personal fight between Peresvet and a Tatar hero in which both fell dead. This means, of course, that a material sword was wielded by the monks. The last version prevailed in later times and has remained very popular in Russia to the present day. It supported mightily the tendency of sanctifying war and wiping out the demarcation line between the Church canons and state laws. According to the canons of the Eastern Church the participation in war by monks and by secular priests is inadmissible, and Greek and Russian polemicists even reproached the Latins for tolerating military activity of the clergy.[25] Some ancient Russian confessors even imposed penances upon laymen who killed enemies in war.[26] Peresvet and Oslyabiya broke with this tradition and foreshadowed the new era when the great monasteries in Muscovy became state fortresses and inscribed some glorious pages in Russian military annals.

The religious loss was obvious. What part in the breaking of the tradition is to be attributed to Sergius is uncertain, as in the case of his diplomatic actions. His political activity stands in contrast with his kenotic personality. He must have proceeded counter to his own personal religious preferences which were dictated by his vocation for what he considered the vital interests of his nation. His actions indicate that he was capable of making concessions to the mighty and venerable power of the Church and of the state but he would not commit himself to anything which he could construe as a betrayal of his religious vocation. One must infer that Russian or Muscovite patriotism was a powerful force in his soul, that

---

[25] A. A. Popov, ed., "Slovo na Latyni i o izverzhenii Isidora (Sermon on the Latins and on the Ejection of Isidor), in *Istoriko-literaturny obzor drevne-russkikh polemisheskikh sochineni protiv Latinyan* (Historical-Literary Survey of Ancient Russian Works Against the Latins), Moscow, 1875, pp. 104, 111 ff.

[26] S. I. Smirnov, *Drevne-russki dukhovnik: Issledovanie po istorii tserkovnago byta* (The Ancient Russian Confessor: Research in the History of Church Life), Sergiev Posad, 1899; Moscow, 1914, p. 244.

this patriotism was vested with religious sanction when it entailed the struggle against the enemies of Christendom; one must infer, too, that Sergius considered the Prince of Moscow a providential leader in this national movement.

All the religious contradictions involved in this attitude were to be fully disclosed in the next century when the kenotic and nationalistic elements in Sergius' heritage clashed in the strife among his disciples and successors.

VII

ST. STEPHEN OF PERM: THE MISSIONARY

*S*T. STEPHEN of Perm (1340–1396) occupies a unique place among the Russian saints of his own as well as of other times.[1] He stands apart from the broad historical tradition, and yet he suggests perhaps some new, as yet undeveloped, possibilities in Russian Orthodoxy. He was a contemporary and friend of St. Sergius, the abbot of the Holy Trinity monastery, but he was not a disciple of his nor did he share Sergius' contemplative and mystical character. Stephen was a missionary who gave all his life to the conversion of a heathen tribe. The weakness of missionary activities is a commonplace in the evaluation of Orthodoxy by outsiders. Even within the Orthodox Church itself people can be found who willingly yield missionary activities to the Western confessions as an external "Martha's" business not very interesting to the Orthodox "Mary". St. Stephen through his life's work refutes such a conception of Orthodoxy. He has, besides, other merits. To the missionary calling he unites a thirst for pure theological knowledge, and in defending his life work — the creation of the national Zyrian (or Permian) Church — he produced a theological basis for the national idea which remained unsurpassed in ancient Russia.

True, one is not able to separate Stephen's ideas from those of his biographer, Epiphanius the Wise,[2] who is also

---

[1] On St. Stephen see P. D. Shestakov, "Sv. Stefan, pervosvyatitel permski" (St. Stephen, First Bishop of Perm), in *Izvestiya i Ucheniya Zapiski Kazanskago universiteta* (News and Scholarly Notes of Kazan University), Kazan, 1868, part I. See also G. P. Fedotov, *Svyatye drevnei Rusi* (Saints of Ancient Russia), Paris, 1931, and S. Bolshakoff, *The Foreign Missions of the Russian Orthodox Church,* London and New York, 1943.

[2] V. G. Druzhinin, ed., *Zhitie sv. Stefana, episkopa permskago* (Life of St. Stephen, Bishop of Perm), The Hague, 1959. This is a photo-reprint of the 1897 edition with an introduction by D. Čiževski.

the author of the Life of St. Sergius. In his work on Stephen he is more personal, loquacious, and free, inasmuch as he is writing about the friend and companion of his youth. Following the accounts of his friend, he considers himself justified in composing long monologues and conversations which are supposed to have taken place in the virgin forests among the savages. He also includes in his biographical record long theological dissertations which serve to justify Stephen's work. As Stephen was the more learned of the two and a man of daring initiative, we are entitled to attribute to him the best part of their common ideas.[3]

Stephen was born in the city of the Great Ustyug on the Dvina River in the Dvina region that just at this time (fourteenth century) was transferring its political allegiance from Novgorod to Moscow. Russian settlements were but little islands amidst a sea of native inhabitants. The surf of this sea reached the suburbs of the city of Ustyug, which was surrounded by villages of western Permians or, as they were also called, Zyrians. It is highly probable that acquaintance with the Permians and their language (one of the Finnish tongues) as well as the idea of becoming a missionary to them may be traced to Stephen's early youth. He was the son of a cleric at the Ustyug cathedral, Simeon by name. Epiphanius tells us of the great and prompt successes of the boy in learning. During one single year he mastered the whole *gramota* and became a reader in the church, "having learned in the city of Ustyug all the literary art and the wisdom of books." One can prudently doubt any wealth of educational means in Ustyug, but the words of Epiphanius are something more than a stereotyped figure of speech on the part

---

[3] On Epiphanius see V. O. Klyuchevski, *Drevnerusskiya zhitiya sviatykh kak istoricheski istochnik* (Ancient Russian Lives of Saints as an Historical Source), Moscow, 1871, pp. 88–112; E. E. Golubinski, *Prepodobny Sergi Radonezhski* (St. Sergius of Radonezh), Sergiev Posad, 1892, pp. 77 ff. Compare D. Čiževski, pp. IX–XVIII.

of the biographer. The subsequent life of Stephen reveals
those unique scholarly talents and the calling that most probably brought the youth into the monastery. His biographer
notes but briefly the growth of ascetic tendencies in the boy
before leading him immediately to the ancient city of Rostov
where he received the tonsure in the monastery of St. Gregory. The choice of place was in itself significant "because there
were many books there." The cloister of St. Gregory, called
the "seclusion," was adjacent to the bishop's palace and situ-
ated in the center of the city, and was cut off by an enclosing
wall from the tumult of the outside world. Bishop Parthenios,
under whom Stephen took his vows, is supposed to have been
a Greek. Together with the old Hellenophile tradition of
Rostov this accounts for the presence of Greek manuscripts
in the library of St. Gregory as well as for the people who
were capable of teaching that language. St. Stephen was one
of the few men in ancient Russia who could read and speak
Greek. With the Russian and the Permian languages this
meant he had a knowledge of three languages which was,
perhaps, not too rare in ancient Kiev but quite exceptional in
the Muscovite North. According to Epiphanius, Stephen
studied also "external philosophy," that is, some elements
of the secular disciplines accessible to him in the Greek original since no Slavic translations could transmit to him this
"external philosophy." The main subject of Stephen's study,
however, was the Holy Scriptures. Epiphanius, who was his
companion (if not disciple) in these exegetical studies, relates some interesting details of the intellectual curiosity of
his friend. Stephen was not content with a "poor study," but
liked to "linger" on until "he understood ultimately and
truly" the meaning of every sentence. Whenever he met some
wise and learned old man, he began to question him, spending with him nights and days in the "eager search for the
desired truth." When jotting down his recollections after

Stephen's death, Epiphanius, one of those who conversed with the saint, begs pardon "for being his annoyer, for arguing with him about some word, or verse, or line" — a curious picture of a theological exegetical seminar in a monastery of medieval Russia.

Greek manuscripts, "with which Stephen never parted," opened to him, as to very few in Russia, the path to the great culture of Byzantium. Stephen, however, barred himself from this path, which was certainly attractive to him, and he did this not for an ascetic life of prayer. The ascetic factor is hardly expressed in his Life. Epiphanius says nothing of his monastic achievements, insisting only that he was a genuine monk, neither does he put on his lips any ascetic exhortations. For the man who wrote the Life of St. Sergius this reticence cannot be casual. Stephen gave up the high career of sacred knowledge for the sake of love, love of the savage heathen. Meeting them in his native Ustyug had pierced his heart with compassion.[4] For them he descended from the scholarly ivory tower and undertook his fruitful kenosis. And in this missionary kenosis he found the ascetic kenosis of Sergius, Theodosius, and of the whole galaxy of Russian saints.[5]

Stephen as a Hellenist was a rare figure in Russia. Stephen as the founder of Zyrian literature was quite unique. He did not wish to combine the conversion of the heathen with their Russification, neither did he wish to approach them with a Slavic liturgy only interpreted by sermons in their vernacular. He did for the Zyrians what Cyril and Methodius had done for the whole Slavic world. He translated the liturgy and the Holy Scriptures — or rather, a part of them.

---

[4] "The servant of God felt a great pity . . . that men created and honored by God were enslaved by His enemy," *Zhitie sv. Stefana*, pp. 8–9.

[5] On *kenosis* as a specific characteristic of Russian piety see G. P. Fedotov, "The Religious Sources of Russian Populism," in *The Russian Review*, I, no. 2, 1942, and *RRM*, I, passim.

First of all, he had to choose or invent a Zyrian alphabet, and a few preserved patterns of the national Zyrian writings show that he did not use for his task either the Slavic or Greek alphabet, but, probably a local system of runes.[6] In this he even abandoned the example of the apostles of the Slavs who had adapted the Greek alphabet to the new idiom.

It was but natural that in his new and daring undertaking Stephen found many adversaries. Some "poor mind" considered it inappropriate to devise a new literature "one hundred and twenty years before the end of the world." This end was actually expected in the year 7000 from the creation, or, according to the accepted Byzantine and Russian computation, in A.D. 1492. The learned Epiphanius himself shared in this belief.[7] The conservatives admitted that, if the translation was needed at all, the Russian alphabet could be used for the newly converted tribes; "for there are literary alphabets which are used by the nations of old, such as Hebrew, Greek, Latin." To these three (in which the inscription on the cross of Christ was composed) the Slavic was added in Russia as a matter of fact. But Stephen received the "blessing" from the highest hierarch then present, the locum tenens of the metropolitan, and left, "as a lamb amidst wolves," for the wild and dangerous country. He certainly had the opportunity to secure in his missionary work the aid of the Muscovite administration, of those military and police officers whose violence was bitterly complained of by the heathen priest in a famous episode of the Life. "From

---

[6] See I. S. Nekrasov, *Permskiya pismena v rukopisyakh XV v.* (Permian Characters in Manuscripts of the 15th Century), Odessa, 1890; P. D. Shestakov, "Chtenie drevneishei zyryanskoi nadpisi" (Readings of the Most Ancient Zyrian Inscription), *ZhMNP*, no. 1, January 1871, St. Petersburg. See also V. Lytkin, *Permskie pismena* (Permian Characters), Moscow and Leningrad, 1953.

[7] "In the last times . . . at the end of the number of 7000 years . . . God raised his saint, Stephen," *Zhitie sv. Stefana*, p. 13.

Moscow can there be anything good for us? Is it not from
there that all kinds of burdens come to us, heavy tributes,
and violence?" Muscovite assistance of this kind could compromise the success of his preaching. Thus, Stephen preferred to go to the land of Perm alone or with a few clerical
attendants.

His missionary trials and successes are pictured in a series of scenes that appear to be taken from nature and are not
devoid of humor; they depict quite vividly the naïve but
kind-hearted character of the Permians. At first we see Stephen within a small circle of already baptized disciples. They
come to him, sit down, and ask questions. And the nonbaptized come also, occasionally. The heathens do not like
him; they stand around with big cudgels ready to strike.
Once it even happened that the heathens, having piled together heaps of straw attempted to burn his house. Later on,
Stephen himself takes the offensive and starts to destroy
idols and primitive wooden shrines. One day, after Stephen
had burnt their main sanctuary, which he had found empty
and not guarded, a huge crowd of Zyrians assembled with
poles and axes. Stephen preached to them at the same time
that he prepared himself for death. No one, however, dared
to attack him.

In Stephen's sermons and exhortations, compiled by his
biographer, one looks in vain for the secret of his extraordinary power of persuasion. Quotations from the Bible can
speak only to those already converted. The denunciation of
idols by biblical and early Christian authors is contradicted
by the veneration of icons as practiced by the Orthodox, and
we shall see that the Orthodox ritual was one of the powerful attractions of the new religion. One is thus forced to the
conclusion that it was mainly the charm of Stephen's personality, together with his higher knowledge and wisdom,
that was able to conquer childish souls. At the same time the

national meekness of the Permians stands out in great relief.
Permians themselves explain in this way the inward opposition they feel toward raising a hand against the Russian
missionary: "He has a bad habit of not starting the fighting"
and they lack the spirit to attack first.

The destruction of shrines was a practical proof of the
weakness of the heathen gods. Those shrines were simple
huts hung with precious furs as offerings to the gods. Stephen
would smash the head of the idol with an axe and, having
shattered it into tiny splinters, burn it together with all the
wealth of furs; he did not wish to take "the part belonging
to the demons."

A positive piece of propaganda for Christianity, speaking
directly to the soul of the heathen, was accomplished through
the beauty of the first church built by Stephen in Ust-Vim,
the main settlement of the Permians. It must have been a
very modest chapel, wooden of course, but the ancient Russians were masters of wooden architecture. Stephen adorned
it with icons and all suitable ornaments "as a beautiful
bride"; he brought liturgical vessels and all kinds of belongings from Moscow or Rostov. Nonbaptized heathen came,
"not yet for prayer, but desiring to see the beauty of the
church," and they went away concluding: "Great is the God
of the Christians." This was preaching through beauty in a
truly Russian style. Permians were charmed as once the envoys of Prince Vladimir had been in Hagia Sophia at Constantinople.

This first church in Permian land was dedicated to the
Annunciation as "the premise of our salvation." Its beautiful
decoration seems not to have fit well with the primitive setting of the life of a solitary missionary amidst a savage tribe.
But Stephen had not severed his connection with Moscow.
He went there from time to time and brought from there
everything necessary for the needs of the growing mission.

Beauty attracted the heathens. For the baptized Stephen offered a more rational introduction into the Christian faith. He made all of them, the children as well as adults, learn the letters invented by him and read his translated books: "the euchologion, the octoechos (daily and weekly order of service), the Psalter, and all the other books." Under "other books" the Gospels and parts of the Old Testament were certainly included, but in this very enumeration the bias to "liturgical theology" is undeniable. In the course of time, after Stephen had received episcopal consecration in Moscow (1379) he ordained his Permian disciples, "some as priests, some as deacons, readers, and chanters . . . he taught them to write Permian books, himself assisting them in this work." Thus, together with the faith in Christ, a hearth of Christian culture was lighted in the wilderness. The learned Stephen carried his scholarship into the denseness of the northern forests.

The dramatic climax in the Life of the saint is his disputation with a heathen *volkhv* (magician), Pam. This is a masterpiece of Epiphanius' literary art in which an attempt is made to paint the religious mind of a Finnish polytheist, or shamanist, in his encounter with Christianity. Undoubtedly, the actual narrations of the missionary form the basis of this episode although the verbal or literary form belongs to the author.

Pam was chief *volkhv* among the Permians and a kind of ruler over the tribe. Stephen had already had many discussions with him: "each one praised his own faith." For Stephen he was not a contemptible adversary, "Whatever I am building, he destroys," was his complaint.

In contrast to the literary Slavic speech of the missionary the *volkhv* expresses his thoughts in a purely Russian popular idiom, sometimes with obvious reminiscences of Russian folklore.

Pam: "Brothers, people of Perm, do not abandon the gods of our fathers, do not forget sacrifices or offerings, do not throw away ancient customs or ancient faith. Do what our fathers did. Listen to me and not to Stephen, a newcomer from Moscow." [Here follows the caustic characterization of Moscow quoted above.] ". . . You should listen to me, an old man and in a father's place before you, rather than to that Russian, Muscovite even — and so young before me that he could be my son or grandson."

The newly baptized people: "We did not conquer, old man, we were defeated, and your gods fell and did not rise again . . . But why do you, old magician, passing over the head, speak to the feet? If you are strong in word vie with him [Stephen], not with us."

Pam: [with anger] "You are cowards . . . That is why this abbot overcame you by his perfidy."

Now Pam turns directly to his mighty adversary.

Pam: "By what power do you do this? . . . You have insulted our gods . . . Those who do this in my court deserve the sentence of death, which you soon will experience at my hand. I shall not fail to work miracles for your destruction and let loose many gods to kill you."

Stephen: "The gods of whom you are boasting have perished . . . The word of Moses has been fulfilled: gods who did not create heaven and earth shall perish."

Pam: "Our gods had pity and did not destroy you . . . From which you must understand that they are kind and merciful."

Here follow three arguments destined to prove the superiority of the Permian faith over the Russian:

[1] You, Christians, have one God, and we, many gods, many assistants, many protectors; they give us the game, all that is in the waters, and in the air, in the swamps and forests — squirrels or sables, martens or lynxes and other game . . . with which your princes and boyars are enriched . . . Is it not the prize of the hunter that is sent to the Horde and reaches the so-called [Tatar] tsar himself? Even to Constantinople and to Germany, to Lithuania, and other towns and countries and remote nations.

[2] Our faith is better than yours because among us one man or two often go to fight a bear and fighting, overcome and fell him, and carry home his hide; whereas among you many people go against one bear, up to a hundred or two hundred in number, and sometimes they bring back a bear if they find him, but sometimes they come back with empty hands . . . which seems to us ridiculous and shameful.

[3] This is why our faith is better; we quickly learn all news; whatever happens in a far-off country, in a foreign town . . . The complete news of it reaches us at the same hour, and you, Christians, cannot learn it . . . For we have many gods aiding us . . .

The last point, somewhat enigmatic, seems to allude to the clairvoyance of the *volkhvy* as part of their magical powers.

Against such arguments how could the persuasions of the missionary prevail when he quoted from Holy Scripture: "beginning from the creation of the world . . . and until the crucifixion of Christ, His Resurrection and Ascension, and until the end of the world" — usual Russian arguments from "historical theology.[8] They were debating the whole day and night, without food or sleep, and all in vain "as if sowing in water."

Then Stephen proposes to Pam a divine trial by fire and water, to pass through a burning hut and to throw themselves into an opening in the ice on the Vichegda river. The *volkhv* at first agrees but loses his courage, and when Stephen drags him by the hand into the fire, he acknowledges his defeat. He is still convinced that the Christian had learned from childhood how to conjure fire and water, whereas he, Pam, does not possess this lore. Stephen's partisans (or rather his biographer) ascribe his victory not merely to God's assistance, but to the virtues of the saint, faith, hope, and love.

It is interesting to note how Stephen used his victory. As Pam refused to be baptized the people demanded his

---

[8] Compare Fedotov, *RRM*, I, 282-384.

death "according to their use and wont." But Stephen rejected this proposal: "Christ sent me not to kill, but to teach,
not to torture but to preach with meekness and admonish
with kindness." However, he condemns the defeated leader
to exile and forbids him to appear in all Christian settlements, so that he "should have no share in common with the
new converted people, should not eat or drink with them
anywhere."

The dispute with Pam is presented as the crowning event
of Stephen's missionary activities. His biographer does not
pursue in detail the growth of ecclesiastical organization in
the new land. Local traditions tell of many churches and
monasteries founded by St. Stephen. Some icons are extant
that are attributed to his hand (he was also an icon painter).
Ust-Vim became the center of the new diocese, that of Perm.
The necessary assistance and assistants Stephen procured
from his native Ustyug as well as from remote Moscow and
Novgorod. But in the struggle between Moscow and Novgorod for the possession of Dvina region Stephen must have
taken no side. We know from the chronicles that he undertook a long journey to Novgorod asking for protection from
the inroads of the Novgorodian pirates who robbed peaceful
Permians. He was received in Novgorod with respect and
was given the necessary letters. Probably on this occasion he
was asked to give his theological counsel on the new sect of
the Strigolniks. In his letters he appears as a skillful polemicist defending not only the authority of the Church but
also the sacramental-mystical sense of religion against the
moralistic rationalism of the sectarians. The doctrine of the
Eucharist as the fruit of the tree of life (as opposed to the
"tree of reason") stands at the center of his polemics.[9]

---

[9] His letter was printed by A. S. Pavlov, ed., "Pamyatniki drevne-russkago kanonicheskago prava (Monuments of Ancient Russian Canon Law),
in *RIB*, vol. VI, no. 25, cols. 211–228.

During a year of poor crops he bought grain in Vologda and distributed it to his starving flock. The closest ties bound him, however, to Moscow. He visited this city not infrequently both for diocesan and general ecclesiastical affairs (for example, for the council of 1390). This, certainly, does not imply a political partisanship in the favor of Muscovite princes; his biographer is frankly anti-Muscovite. Stephen died in Moscow during one of his journeys there, in 1396, and was buried in a monastery within the Kremlin.

The narration of Stephen's death in Epiphanius' work is followed by a highly eloquent *threnos*, or lament, over the deceased hero. Threnody is a poetical form very much loved in Russian folklore, which finds many reflections in written literature.[10] Epiphanius' rhetoric has nothing to do with popular style, but its relation to Russian sensibility is obvious; Greek hagiographical patterns offer no parallels.

The threnody is divided into three parts: the lament of the Permian people, the lament of the Permian Church, and that of the author himself. The Permian people mourn, first of all, their protector who defended them from Russian colonizers, Moscow and Novgorod. "You solicited the prince . . . and the boyars . . . concerning our complaints, our rights, and benefits . . . you often rescued us from violation and enslavement, relieved us from spoliations and hard tributes . . . Even the Novgorodians, pirates and robbers, were persuaded by your words not to fight us . . ." Their particular grief is to be robbed of the saint's grave which is now in the possession of the Muscovites. They do not refer to the expected miracles from the relics; their concern is purely human: "To be for us a great comfort. That is Moscow's justice! It has metropolitans, bishops, but we had only one bishop, and it took him for itself . . . The Muscovites

---

[10] Note the laments of St. Boris in his Life and the laments in the *Tale of Prince Igor*. Fedotov, *RRM*, I, 100, 324.

cannot honor you like we do. We know some people in Moscow who gave you nicknames, called you 'brazen face,' not understanding the power and grace of God."

The Permians owe still more to Stephen for his spiritual deeds; he turned them from a miserable, despised tribe to a Christian nation, among the most ancient and venerable of such.

The bereaved Permian Church mourns the bishop as her husband taken from her and goes so far in her indignation as to suggest the abduction of his body from rival Moscow: "Why do not zealots appear now like those of the sons of Israel who took the bones of Joseph the Beautiful from the land of Egypt and carried them into the promised land?"

In these laments Epiphanius has abundant opportunities to emphasize the idea of the Christian vocation of all the nations of the earth which he had previously developed in connection with the new Permian alphabet. The invention of the new alphabet is considered by him in a vast world-historical perspective. Epiphanius borrows all the facts or myths for his historical scheme from a Bulgarian monk Khrabr, who in the tenth century wrote a short work on "Slavic writings," [11] and from the Russian writers of the eleventh century, the hagiographer Nestor in the prefaces to his Lives of St. Theodosius and Sts. Boris and Gleb, and Metropolitan Hilarion, who in praising Prince Vladimir planted in the Russian national consciousness the Christian idea of vocation.[12] Everything which had been told of Cyril and Methodius and of Slavic and Russian people is now transferred to the Permians and their new apostle Stephen. These are the main lines of Epiphanius' (Stephen's) historical conception:

---

[11] S. G. Vilinski, ed., *Skazanie chernoriztsa Khrabra o pismenakh slavyanskikh* (The Legend of the Monk Khrabra about Slavic Characters), Odessa, 1901.

[12] Fedotov, *RRM,* I, 405 ff.

In the Bible he discovers all in all 72 languages and nations on earth. After the confusion of Babel not only languages were divided but also mores, customs, and laws and arts according to nations . . . The Egyptian nation received geometry as their lot, the Persians, Chaldeans and Assyrians — astrology, magic and witchcraft, the Jews — sacred books . . . The Greeks — grammar, rhetoric and philosophy. Thus the nations, born as they are out of sin and punishment, have a positive justification for possessing a diversity of gifts and callings. A symbol or a necessary means for a national culture is a particular alphabet. Epiphanius even knows from Khrabr the names of the inventors of many of them: Jewish, Greek, Slavic; for the Greek he gives several names of the "philosophers" who each created from two to six letters of the alphabet. Now all Greek philosophers were pagan, and so the Slavic alphabet invented by the two Christian saints is more "honorable." The new Permian alphabet is also the work of a Christian monk, and, what is more, a single one (not two), and thus is even more honorable than the Slavic-Russian. Epiphanius has no scruple in comparing his noncanonized hero to St. Cyril: "Both men were good and wise and equal in wisdom, but Cyril the philosopher was assisted by his brother Methodius . . . and Stephen found no helper except the Lord."

In Christian times all national languages with their alphabets serve a higher end — the mission of the Church. All the nations are called to salvation as David and many prophets had predicted: "I am coming," says the Lord, "to gather all the Gentile tribes and to send salvation to the remote nations . . . who did not hear my name" (Isaiah). From Theodoritus' commentary Epiphanius knows that 51 nations are already baptized, and 29 still persist in pagan errors. A tradition had reached Epiphanius, which he relates with a certain reserve: "I do not know whether it is true . . . when we conquer the whole world then we shall migrate to the grave; that is, the whole world will believe . . . in the last days." Only 120 years are now left until the consummation of time and, thus, this missionary work of Stephen is put into an eschatological perspective.

The tribe of the Permians is now the last converted nation. "We are born after all the others in the bath of the regeneration; we are late . . . as if coming at the eleventh hour, and are less than all baptized nations . . ." The author repeats the words of Hilarion, once spoken of the Russians. But in the Christian order of values the last can be the first, and so the Permians can replace the Slavs and Russians in the famous hymn of Hilarion:

> The Roman country praises two apostles, Peter and Paul; the land of Asia honors and venerates John the Divine; Egypt, Mark the Evangelist; Antioch, Luke; Greece, the apostle Andrew; the Russian land, the great Vladimir who baptized her; Moscow honors Metropolitan Peter as a new miracle-worker; Rostov, Leontius, her bishop. And you, Bishop Stephen, are praised and honored by the land of Perm as her apostle, her teacher, and her leader.

Not only are the savage Permians not outdistanced by the elder Christian nations in the Kingdom of God; they have even a privilege of honor, as we have seen, at least in the person of their apostle and the inventor of their letters. This generous attitude of Epiphanius puts in a true light the nationalistic utterings of the Kievan writers. The corresponding, and partly identical, meditations of Nestor and Hilarion could be interpreted as the manifestation of a young national pride and a concealed Grecophobia. Epiphanius, or rather Stephen himself, whose idea was taken up by his disciple, humbled himself and his own Russian consciousness before the scarcely born national consciousness of another people, and how modest a one! Only now the religious meaning of the national culture, revealed in the work of St. Cyril and

Methodius and inherited by Russia, assumes its deep universal meaning. Every nation, however small, has its own religious calling and its particular gifts. There are no privileged peoples, no messianic nations, in the Kingdom of Christ. The ideal image of the "mourning Permian Church," conceived in the spirit of ontological realism, gives a metaphysical basis for the national idea. Only the Russian thinkers of the nineteenth century, perhaps only Vladimir Soloviev, will develop and philosophically reaffirm the idea of Stephen and that of ancient Russia that was contaminated in Muscovy in the late fifteenth century by the Byzantine dream of the universal Christian Empire.

Coming back from the ideas of St. Stephen to his work, to the national Permian Church, we must acknowledge that this Church was a child without a future. It existed less than two centuries. The Permians remained even after their conversion on such a low level of culture that they could not appreciate and preserve the precious legacy of Stephen — their national language. They became Russified in the course of the Russian colonization as did all their related Finnish tribes in Russian political territory. On the other hand, the Muscovite government and Church, in their nationalistic spirit, could not understand Stephen's idea and did not spare his work. The Permian liturgy was replaced by the Slavic sometime during the sixteenth century.

VIII

THE THEBAID OF THE NORTH

*A*CCORDING to the traditions of the Russian Church
St. Sergius is enshrined in the surrounding galaxy
of his canonized disciples.[1] Some of them enjoyed only local
veneration in the great monastery (Lavra) created by him;
others attained the veneration of the whole Russian nation.
Of the purely local saints of the Lavra only Nicon, Sergius'
successor as abbot, has been preserved in a clear portrait from
the pen of Pachomius the Serb. In this disciple of Sergius,
as in his master, the love of solitude clashed with the duties
of his office. At one point he gave up for years the burden of
the abbacy and then emerged as an exemplary executive, the
rebuilder of the monastery after a fire during one of the last
Tatar raids (1408). It was he, also, who began the acquisi-
tion of enormous land-holdings and agricultural activity for
the Lavra, accepting, as the gift of pious laymen, those domains which Sergius, a lover of poverty, scorned during his
life.[2]

Eleven of St. Sergius' disciples became founders of monasteries, most of them while the saint was still alive. They
carried the spiritual legacy of St. Sergius into all the corners
of Russia and Russian historians compare this flourishing of
monasticism to the ancient "paradise" of the monks: the
Thebaid, in Egypt. With this first generation of Sergius'
spiritual sons the Trinity monastery became a mighty center
of spiritual radiation. It is true that as early as the next generation this rich monastery, heaped with the favors of the
Muscovite princes, and ever closely connected with the capital, ceased to produce both saints and new monastic colonies.

[1] I. Smolitsch, *Das Altrussische Mönchtum 11–16 Jahrhunderts,* Würzburg, 1940, pp. 79 ff.

[2] There is only one donation charter from the time of Sergius and this
has been preserved in the archives of Holy Trinity.

But many of its colonies became, in their turn, centers of radiation and spiritual metropolises. Through them the living succession of Sergius was maintained in Russian spiritual history, at least, to the end of the fifteenth century.

This spiritual stream, issuing from the Trinity monastery, ran in two directions, southward to Moscow — to its urban and suburban monasteries — and northward to the forest fastnesses beyond the Volga. The significance of these two directions is more than a merely geographical one; it is intimately connected, as we shall see later, with the bifurcation of the two main roads of Russian spiritual life.

Leaving aside, for the moment, Muscovite monasticism and the Muscovite type of holiness which prevailed from the end of the fifteenth century, let us study the Northern hermits and cenobites descended from the disciples of Sergius. Here one encounters at the very first glance the great figure of St. Cyril of Belozersk who was a real link between Sergius and Northern monasticism. St. Cyril did not belong to the immediate disciples of Sergius; he did not live at the Holy Trinity monastery. But he did experience Sergius' influence; he was his "interlocutor" in the literal sense of the word. Some others of Sergius' elder "interlocutors" also founded monasteries and hermitages in the North; St. Ferapont (a collaborator of Cyril), St. Dimitri of Priluki (near the city of Vologda) and St. Stephen of Makhrishchi whom we met in one of the dramatic turns of the life of St. Sergius and will meet again in the life of Cyril. But none of them can equal St. Cyril in historical significance.

His Life was composed by the same wandering Serb, Pachomius, who dedicated his pen to panegyrics of the Russian saints.[3] He always wrote at the order of some high benefactor, prince or bishop. This time the command came from

---

[3] V. Yablonski, ed., *Pakhomi Serb i ego agiograficheskie pisaniya* (Pachomius Serb and His Hagiographical Writings), St. Petersburg, 1908.

both the Prince of Moscow, Basil II, and the metropolitan. We might expect a purely rhetorical work, scant in biographical content but we are pleasantly surprised. An abundance of biographical details rendered by eyewitnesses who were the immediate disciples of the saint, the Abbot Cassian and St. Martinian, makes this work of Pachomius his most interesting piece of hagiography.

A native citizen of Moscow (1337–1427), Kuzma (St. Cyril's secular name) was orphaned by the death of both parents and taken into the house of his noble relative, the boyar Timothy Velyaminov, one of the greatest personages in Moscow. Cyril served his lord as treasurer in the management of his domains. Very early he felt the inclination to the monastic life but could satisfy it only by visiting monastic communities on pilgrimages and trying to imitate their life in the world. His benefactor would not consent to let him go. Such was the boyar's arbitrary power and the general fear of incurring his wrath that no abbot dared to "tonsure" Kuzma. At last a rescuer appeared in the person of Stephen of Makhrishchi. During one of Stephens's visits to Moscow, Kuzma, in tears, entreated him to gratify his heart's desire, and after some hesitation Stephen gave him the monastic habit (the first degree of initiation). Velyaminov was angry and reviled the abbot with insults and abuses. Stephen, however, did not betray the young monk, and the wife of the boyar mediated in effecting a reconciliation.

Stephen placed the youth in the biggest monastery in the city of Moscow, namely Simonov, recently founded by St. Sergius himself and the monastery wherein his nephew Theodore was installed as abbot. He gave Kuzma the second degree of monastic initiation with the change of his name to Cyril.

At this point his monastic labors began: fasting, prayer, work in the bakery and the kitchen. Demons wrought terror with nightly knockings and visions, though most of his nights were filled with Psalter reading and prostrations. He lived in the cell of his starets, Michael, to whom he owed a "blind obedience." This is the first of the Russian Lives of saints (which has survived) where the emphasis is put on obedience. Sts. Theodosius and Sergius were very free to discover their own spiritual ways, and obedience was stressed in their monastic orders only as a consequence of the Studion rule, which was not a precise expression of their own spiritual trends. It is characteristic that the obedience imposed upon Cyril was not required to stimulate his ascetic zeal but to moderate it. The starets forbade Cyril to fast beyond his strength; he forced him to take food not once in three or four days, as Cyril desired, but every day with the brethren in the refectory, only not to the point of satiety. Cyril, however, found means to mortify himself. After a night of prayer he would almost faint from hunger. One of his hardest tasks of "obedience" was that in the bakery and kitchen. He spent the nights there, and looking at the flame in the oven he reflected on eternal fire: "Suffer, Cyril, this fire that through this you may escape another fire." He spent nine years in this service, then was granted a short reprieve which he spent in his cell copying books. This new work was much to his liking. He had longed for solitude and silence and prayed to the Mother of God to grant him the favor of continuing this work. Yet, he was soon required to return to the kitchen from which he was not liberated, even after he had received priestly ordination.

Besides obedience and patience another of Cyril's virtues merits praise from his biographer; this was the Russian *umilenie* (attrition or tenderness), which is here taken as synonymous with the gift of tears. He could not even eat bread without tears. And, quite unexpectedly, another feature is added to this traditional pattern of the ascetic saint;

he assumes the role of a fool in order to avoid praise and pride. "Wishing to conceal his virtues" he began to commit some acts "similar to practical jokes and provocative of laughter." We do not know of what these acts consisted but for them the abbot punished Cyril by condemning him to a diet of bread and water for forty days. Cyril repeated his offense and the punishment was extended for six months. The youth was "glad that he fasted not of his own will" and the abbot was disarmed at such humility and at once comprehended the motives of his foolish conduct. This strange combination of humility and daring disobedience is typical of this type of Eastern piety, foolishness for Christ's sake. In Cyril, however, this was but a temporary exercise.

It was also during these years at Simonov that his meeting with St. Sergius occurred. On coming to the monastery to visit his nephew, the venerable abbot — to the astonishment of Theodore and the brethren — would first of all go to the bakery and converse with Cyril for hours "on matters of salvation." These visits must not have been very frequent, but the influence of Sergius was to be transmitted through the monks of Simonov and its abbot. We see, however, from a few details already spoken of, that the general climate of Simonov was more severe than that of Trinity; the authority of the rule and the superiors was more strongly maintained. This was for Cyril a good school of discipline for the monastic community which he was one day to found.

When the Archimandrite (archabbot) Theodore was elected Archbishop of Rostov, Cyril, for a short time, was appointed in his place. The love of solitude, however, was stronger than the call of the community. He immediately rejected the new dignity and immured himself in his cell. But people began to visit him for spiritual guidance, and the envy of the new abbot who succeeded him forced Cyril to abandon the monastery. For a time he "kept silence" in an affiliated cloister, "Old Simonov" (in Moscow) meditating upon withdrawal "far from the world." As he had a particular devotion to Our Lady he did not realize his desire until he beheld her in a vision, or rather her voice confirmed him in his intention: "Cyril, depart from here and go to the White Lake [Beloozero]. There I have prepared a place for you where you can save your soul." Opening the window of his cell he beheld a column of fire in the direction of the North whither the Mother of God was sending him.

A monk from Simonov, Ferapont, who already had been at the White Lake, accompanied Cyril on his journey. After much wandering, in the thick and virgin forest surrounded on all sides by water, Cyril recognized the "very beautiful" place shown him by the Virgin. He erected a cross as a sign for the future chapel.

In many details the story of Sergius repeats itself in the first stages of Cyril's monastery. Ferapont, as once was the case with Sergius' brother, could not bear the "strict and severe" life and founded his own monastery fifteen versts from that of Cyril. Not that the other place was less wild, but "they disagreed in their customs of life."

Cyril was left quite alone in his wilderness. His labors were not without serious dangers, although his biographer mentions neither beasts nor demons which certainly must have been present. Once he had a narrow escape from being crushed by a tree which fell while he slept. Once while clearing the forest for a vegetable garden he kindled some dry branches and unwittingly started a forest fire. His salvation in each case is ascribed to a miracle. After the first incident Cyril prayed God "to take sleep from him." This prayer was granted and he could spend whole nights without sleep. After some time the first disciples put in their appearance, two peasants from the neighborhood and three devoted monks from Simonov. At this stage new dangers threatened, not from nature but from wicked men. A boyar secretly hired a band of robbers to plunder the monastic settlement; he was convinced that the retired Archimandrite of Simonov had brought much money with him. Still earlier a peasant from the vicinity had tried to burn Cyril's cell. In the Lives of saints written in the fifteenth and sixteenth centuries one frequently reads of assaults upon the hermits by the local landowners, peasants, and boyars; the motive of these attacks was the fear that these settlers might be stripped of their lands which would then be transferred to the monastery as a gift from the prince. Such apprehensions were not ungrounded.

The small wooden chapel in the new monastery was dedicated to the Assumption of Our Lady — an indication both of the particular veneration for the Mother of God on the part of the founder and of the ties with Moscow where both the cathedral of the city and the Church of Simonov bore the same dedication. In his monastery St. Cyril ordered and realized strict communal life as was the rule in all monasteries of Sergius' foundation; perhaps in Cyril's it was observed more firmly than in other places. Whatever the brethren received from their friends in the world, whether gifts or letters, they had to bring to the abbot; even to drink they had to come to the refectory. In their cells nothing was allowed but icons and books and water for washing. Particular attention was paid to the complicated order of prayer and chanting in the church, according to the rule of Jerusalem or St. Savvas, which, since the time of Metropolitan Cyprian (1376–1406) replaced in Russia the older Rule of the Studion. In standing and moving, in prostrations before icons or the Gospel, the same strictness of gesture was required. Cyril himself is praised for never leaning against the walls or sitting during long services: "His legs were like columns." Everything was performed according to the "rite" of "the tradition of elders," in silence, both in the church and in the refectory. Once he rebuked his disciple, St. Martinian, who, after a meal, went to another brother for an instrument. Martinian, smiling, tried to justify himself: "When I come to my cell I cannot leave it anymore." But Cyril instructed him: "Do always this. First, go to your cell and the cell will teach you." Another time, seeing the ruddy face of his favorite, Zebedee, he reproached him for his "worldly, non-faster's face worse than that of the glutton's." Although counseling fasting, Cyril, nonetheless, always offered three courses in the refectory. Visiting the kitchen, he took care that the brethren should have as much "comfort" as possible, and helped the cooks with his own hands. Mead and other inebriating drinks (in Russia of that time this meant beer and imported wine) were entirely banished from the monastery. This peculiarity of the Rule of St. Cyril was transplanted also to the famous Solovki. But generally speaking, not severity but vigilance is the mark of life in the monastery of Cyril. One does not hear of any punishments imposed by the abbot. It seems that the spiritual authority of Cyril was sufficient and not questioned.

The abbot himself, like St. Sergius, wore "a torn and much-darned cassock" and was equally mild and pardoning toward his offenders. He says to a monk who has confessed his hatred against the abbot: "All are deceived about me, you alone were right and understood that I was a sinner." He was as great a lover of poverty ("nonpossessor") as Sergius. He did not allow his monks to beg for alms from laymen in time of hunger. They had to hope for aid from heaven. "If God and the most pure Virgin forget us in this place what reason is there for us to continue to live in this life?" He declined all lands offered to him by princes and boyars with this statement of principle: "If we wish to hold lands we shall have many cares which are capable of destroying silence for the brethren." However, he did not refuse alms brought to the monastery. Moreover, the charters preserved from the archives of St. Cyril indicate that the saint sometimes had to yield to the requests of donors, or brethren, and that the monastery even during his life began to acquire land. The impoverished community was still unable to practice charity on a large scale but during a famine it distributed food to the starving. St. Cyril insisted on the obligation of charity and many of his miracles attest to his conviction.

We know very little of the inner, spiritual life of the saint. There is no reason to consider him a mystic. One can only note his particular veneration of Our Lady and the gift of frequent tears as two individual features of Cyril's devotional life. He stands in the center between the mystical and ritualistic currents of his time. A more practical organizer than St. Sergius he yields to him in the abundance of spiritual gifts.

We possess three letters of St. Cyril addressed to princes, the sons of Dimitri Donskoi, which show the abbot as a wise advisor of the laity, knowing no discrimination of persons nor fear before earthly lords. One of these letters containing a whole program of government was quoted in Chapter II.[4] Here we will cite some passages of another letter, to the Great Prince of Moscow Basil I. In the preface the abbot emphasizes the responsibility of supreme power and its dangers.

If one of the boyars sins he does damage not to all people but to himself alone; but if the prince does so he wrongs all the people who are under him . . . Hate, o lord, every power that drives you to evil . . . do not be elated, my lord, by temporary glory . . . for this life is short and death is conjoined with flesh.

He then enters upon the main subject of his letter, the quarrel of the great prince with the princes of Suzdal who were

---

[4] Chapter IV, p. 168.

driven by the violent actions of Moscow to seek security among the Tatars.

We have heard, my lord great prince, that there is trouble between you and your friends, the princes of Suzdal. You, my lord, insist on your right and they on theirs; for this reason great bloodshed is inflicted on Christians. But consider closely, my lord, what are their rightful claims against you, and then humbly make concessions; and insofar as you are right toward them for that stand firm, my lord, as justice says. And if they begin to ask pardon, my lord, you should, my lord, grant them what they deserve, for I have heard, my lord, that until today they have been oppressed by you and that is, my lord, why they went to war. And you, my lord, for God's sake show your love and grace that they should not perish in error amid the Tatar realms and should not die there. For, my lord, no kingdom, nor principality, nor any other power can rescue us from God's impartial judgment.

As we see from this and other letters of St. Cyril, a firm, although mild independence in his attitude to the mighty of this world is a steady characteristic of Cyril as well of his whole school.

After the death of St. Cyril his precept of nonpossession was soon abandoned. His monastery became one of the richest landowners of Northern Russia, vying in this regard with the Trinity monastery of St. Sergius. As one of the signs and fruits of its wealth St. Cyril's monastery possessed a rich library of which the catalogue composed at the end of the fifteenth century is still extant. It is the first known catalogue of an ancient Russian library; it numbers about 400 volumes, all of religious content. In spite of a rapid increase in wealth St. Cyril preserved community life and strict observance of the rule at least until the middle of the next century when the religious life in the Holy Trinity monastery had become completely decadent. This is why the monastery of Cyril, and not that of Sergius became in the fifteenth and sixteenth centuries a center of the radiation of living holiness, which proceeded hand in hand with the setting up of new monastic colonies.

In the course of one century the whole Russian North, up to that time completely wild and barren, was permeated with hermit cabins and monastic settlements. In the same region these points condensed to stellar nebulae. Four big centers of monastic settlements are discernible in the fifteenth century.

The first was formed in the region of the White Lake in the neighborhood of St. Cyril. We have seen that a friend and companion of Cyril, Ferapont, founded his monastery at a distance of fifteen versts from him. The second abbot here was Martinian, a favorite disciple and cell-servant of Cyril who, for a long time was also abbot at Sergius' Trinity monastery. The monastery of St. Ferapont, with its icon paintings and frescoes of the master Dionysius, is one of the most precious museums of Russian art. The walls and towers of Ferapont's monastery as well as those of St. Cyril's monastery, which, in the course of years, was surrounded by a commercial suburb that became the town of Kirillov, represent the most picturesque architectural ensemble of ancient Russia. But in the fifteenth century this was a holy land of hermits. Around the big monasteries cabins and groups of cabins (*sketes*) were built where anchorites practiced silence and kept holy poverty as one of the main precepts of St. Cyril.

The second center of Trans-Volga monasticism, and one not connected immediately with St. Cyril was in the southern region of the Vologda region, the large and wild Komela forest which stretched into the Northern belt of the Kostroma district. Many of its small forest rivers gave their names to the holy men who settled here and the cloisters they founded. The rivers Obnora and Nuroma gave refuge to Paul of Obnora and Sergius of Nuroma, both disciples of great St. Sergius. St. Paul of Obnora, a great lover of silence, who called silence the mother of all virtues, is a pattern of the perfect hermit, not so common a phenomenon in Russia. For years he did not even have a hut for shelter but lived in the hollow of an oak tree. Sergius of Nuroma, his neighbor and himself a great lover of solitude, once found him in the company of a bear and other beasts feeding birds which were perched on his head and shoulders. This picture alone justifies the name of Thebaid given by a Russian hagiographer (A. N. Muravev) to Northern Russian monasticism. But Paul himself could not resist the pressure of disciples and founded a community which became large and rich after his death.

The third spiritual and geographical center of holy Russia was the monastery of St. Savior — the Rock of the Kuben Lake. Long and narrow, about seventy versts in length, this lake links the Vologda and Beloozero regions. Along its shores passed the road from Moscow and Vologda to Kirillov. On a cliff rising from the waves of the rather stormy lake the monastery was built; its story was written at the end of the fifteenth century by the *starets* Paisius Yàroslavov, a friend of Nilus Sorski, and himself a great teacher of "nonpossession." The first abbot known to us came from Mount Athos during the life of Dimitri Donskoi. His disciples founded colonies on the banks of the many rivers flowing into the lake. Some of these monasteries, in turn, became metropolises. One of them, Glushitsa, founded by St. Dionysius, for a century after the death of its founder continued to produce saints and to send forth the nuclei of new monasteries. In the middle of the fifteenth century, Cassian, the abbot of St. Cyril's monastery and a disciple of the holy founder, became the superior of St. Savior on the Rock and thus fused the Russian traditions of St. Cyril with the Greek traditions of the Holy Mountain (Athos). One of his disciples was a young prince, Andrew Zaozerski, who was tonsured under the name of Joasaf and died five years later. In spite of his youth he proved himself a great lover of poverty and a mystic.

Solovki or the Solovets monastery on an island in the White Sea ranked fourth in importance among the monasteries of Northern Russia, an outpost of Christendom and Russian culture in the grim "sea-land," among the "savage Laps." It surpassed by far and was the guiding force in the general current of Russian colonization. One of its two holy founders, Savvatius, came from St. Cyril's, the other, Zosima, was from Valaam, on Lake Ladoga. He brought with him the Western, Novgorodian tradition. The Muscovite South and the Novgorodian West were blended at Solovki in the provenance of the monks and even in the names of the charters (the Assumption and St. Savior). Zosima and Savvatius endured the extremely hard life on the polar island. However, Zosima, the real organizer of the new monastery, emerges not only as an ascetic but as a zealous husbandman who determined forever the character of the Northern monastery. A union of prayer and agricultural, even industrial work and the religious consecration of economic culture remains the mark of Solovki in the sixteenth and seventeenth centuries. The richest landowner of the Russian North from the end of the sixteenth century, a military guard of the Russian coast (a first-rate fortress), Solovki even in the seventeenth century did not cease to give new saints to the Russian Church.

These four main centers of spiritual radiation were not, of course, the exclusive resources of the "holy Russia" of the fifteenth century, the golden age of Russian saints. St. Cyril's influence radiated westward as well. But one can cite many names not connected directly with the monasteries either of St. Cyril or St. Sergius. A special and rich circle of saints is that of Novgorod, which is connected in unbroken succession with ancient pre-Mongol times. St. Savva of Vishera founded his monastery seven versts from Novgorod and among his other ascetic achievements he gave, as far as we know, the first example of stylitism in the true sense of the word. We know no details of his manner of life. Certainly he did not remain on a stone column as his Oriental and Greek prototypes; he used some wooden construction, if not a tree. It is by no means certain that he never abandoned his pedestal. More likely he spent the greater part of the day and night there in prayer, as St. Seraphim did in the nineteenth century. St. Savva the Stylite remains a unique figure in Russian hagiography; but perhaps his example found some imitators who have remained without biographers.

Many retired from monasteries into the wilderness and built tiny huts in which they dwelt alone or with companions; they found food "from the earth and trees," that is, roots and also fruit. They are called *stolpniks; stolp* means the same as the Latin *columna* (column). They supported their narrow small houses with columns raised above ground.[5]

Savva of Vishera was a saint of Novgorod. The best known saint of Pskov of this period was Euphrosynia, the founder of the Eleazar monastery. One reads in his Life, that he was overwhelmingly convinced of the mystical significance of determining whether the word *alleluia* in prayers should be pronounced two or three times, a question which then greatly agitated the society of Pskov. Euphrosynia undertook a journey to Greece and returned a fervent partisan of the double alleluia. The fact, which remained unknown to Euphrosynia, is that in Greece itself there were different traditions about the singing of alleluia. As is well

---

[5] S. Herberstein, *Zapiski o moskovskikh delakh* (Notes on Moscow Affairs), St. Petersburg, 1908.

known, the "alleluia" issue played a great part in the great
schism (*raskol*) in the Russian Church in the seventeenth
century. The Life of St. Euphrosynia, corroborating the
view of the Old-Believers, is one of the earliest signs of the
ritualistic trends characteristic of Muscovite devotional life.

In studying the spiritual trends of Northern monasticism
one is confronted by two important difficulties; first, most of
the lives of the Northern saints remain unpublished; second,
they differ, to their great disadvantage, from the Muscovite
group, in the scarcity of content and the generality of char-
acterizing features. Besides, they were composed mostly in
a subsequent era. However, as a result of the investigations
of Professor A. Kadlubovsky, who studied the unpublished
manuscripts, we can at least glance at the manuscripts, inaccessible to us. From these pages arise the figures of the
great saints once venerated by the whole Russian people but
almost forgotten in the last centuries of the Russian Empire.

All these "Trans-Volgan" groups of ascetics manifestly
preserve, in the greatest possible purity, the legacy of Sts.
Sergius and Cyril; mild humility, voluntary poverty, charity,
and solitary contemplation. These saints easily pardon both
their own offenders and the thieves attempting to rob the
property of the monastery. St. Dionysius of Glushitsa even
smiles on hearing about the theft of community horses. Nonpossession, in the strictest sense of the refusal not only of
personal but also community property, is their common ideal
of life. St. Dimitri of Priluki near Vologda (as well as
Dionysius of Glushitsa) even refused the alms offered by
a layman who suggested that he distribute them to feed his
slaves and serfs who suffered from "thirst and nakedness."
In a similar way St. Joasaph rejected the gifts of a prince:
"We do not need gold or silver." Of course, complete
poverty is an ideal from which even the most severe ascetics
recede unwillingly. After the death of a saint his monastery

becomes rich; but, even though it betrays the precepts of the founder, it at least keeps them before the consciousness of future generations.

In the matter of poverty one has to make a sharp distinction between ideal and reality. The ideal is reflected in the lives of saints, reality, best of all, in the legal charters, of land grants, legacies, purchasing, and so forth. Russian historians, particularly Klyuchevsky, have made a close study of the economic role of monasteries in the colonization of Northern Russia. Their conclusions are that the monastery was a primary factor in this economic expansion. Monastic land-holding surpassed all other categories of land-holdings; those of princes, boyars, or free peasants. In truth, only hermits could practice absolute poverty. The community living on its own work in an uninhabited wilderness was, necessarily, a farming community. St. Sergius or St. Cyril might let their disciples starve while waiting for a miracle. Most abbots, even among their immediate disciples, thought of sustaining their flock as their pastoral duty. To protect their newly planted vegetable gardens and plowed fields from seizure by violent laymen (boyars) they went to Moscow or to other princely residences and obtained charters for large areas of wild, mostly forest, lands with the right of making full use of them. When the monastery became surrounded by free peasants, who settled near it to satisfy their religious needs, the temptation was strong to let them work on the land of the monks. The charters of princes secured the newly built villages for the monks, that is, the right of different services and payments by the peasants. The praying community had been the community of farmers. Now the farming community became one of managers; all or most of the manual work was done by peasants living on the lands of the monastery. All classes of lay society, princes, nobles, commoners, and peasants contributed to the accumulation of monastic property, moved by a powerful religious motive — the post-mortem salvation of souls. In medieval Russia as well as in Western Europe, the monasteries were appreciated by laymen, first of all, as places of eternal prayers for their souls. Of course, liturgical commemoration had to be paid for by a definite sum of money or, in a natural economy, by gifts from the soil. Taxation of different forms existed for these commemorations, scaled according to their efficiency. Through this channel, in the course of ages, enormous amounts of land passed into the possession of monasteries, even those founded by nonpossessors. St. Cyril's in 1582 possessed about 20,000 *desyatins* of arable land alone. Even the community founded by Paul of Obnora, the hermit who had lived in the oak tree, in 1489 was granted a territory of thirty square versts with four villages; half a century later it possessed forty-five villages and hamlets.[6]

But let us return to the hallowed origins of monastic poverty at the beginning of the fifteenth century. Poverty then was real and with it an attitude of independence toward civil powers. Here we find a second feature of the Northern monastic saints which distinguishes them from the Southern Muscovite leaders. A thorough independence from the world gave the saint a boldness with which to judge the world. His usual mildness and humility did not prevent him from appearing as a denouncer and rebuker when the sinner is one of the mighty of this world. This was forever a common feature of the Russian kenotic type of saint. St. Cyril, who left such highly paternal and independent instructions to the princes of the family of Moscow, refused to visit Prince George, the son of St. Dimitri Donskoi; he said, "I cannot

[6] V. O. Klyuchevski, *Kurs russkoi istorii* (A Course of Russian History), Moscow and St. Petersburg, 1904–1922; 2 ed., 5 vols., Moscow, 1937, pp. 281 ff. The first edition has been translated by C. G. Hogarth and published as *A History of Russia*, 5 vols., New York, 1911–1931.

break the monastic rule" that prohibits the monk from leaving his cloister. St. Martinian, his disciple, on the contrary, appeared in Moscow in the palace of Basil II to rebuke the Great Prince, who had arrested and chained a boyar in spite of his given pledge. The author of his Life accompanies this story with a long edifying conclusion: "He feared neither death nor confinement nor the confiscation of lands nor loss of power. But he remembered John Chrysostom who said that the threat of the Emperor is similar to the rage of a lion; and he went and denounced; not only denounced but excommunicated." The third abbot of the Northern group, Grigory of Pelshma, denounced Prince George Dimitrievich and his son Shemyaka when he was convinced that they had seized the great principality unjustly. These conflicts of the saint against the world, however, as well as his encounters with the world in general, are rare and exceptional. The ascetic of the North longed for solitude most of all.

Our biographies are very reticent when speaking of the inner life of the saints. And, yet, A. Kadlubovsky succeeded in making some very valuable observations. From brief and isolated formulae or turns of speech occurring in these documents, not very common in Russian hagiography but inspired by the ascetic treatises of mystical Greece, we can deduce certain implications: 1) Exterior asceticism, in spite of a general severity of life, is subordinate to an inner "working" upon which all attention is concentrated. It is said, for example, of St. Dionysius: "He was never found idle of spiritual working." 2) This "spiritual working" is described as the purification of mind and union with God in prayer. "Make your mind with all zeal . . . seek God alone and pray diligently . . . meditate, seek the celestial realm where Christ is," is the teaching of Dionysius. And his disciple, Grigory of Pelshma, lives "fixing his mind on the Highest and purifying his heart from all tempest of passion." 3)

Finally, in some rare cases, this spiritual working is depicted in terms which are the technical terms for "mental prayer in the practice of the Greek Hesychasts. Their meaning will be clearer when we turn to the doctrine fully developed in Russia by Nilus Sorski. Thus, of Paul of Obnora it is said by his biographer: He lived "purifying his [inner] vision and gathering the light of divine reason in his heart . . . and contemplating the glory of God. Therefore he became an elected vessel of the Holy Spirit." The same words are repeated in a somewhat later Life of St. Joasaph.

Accuracy requires us to note that these last two biographies, with their precise terminology for mental prayer, were composed in the sixteenth century, after the works of Nilus Sorski. Nevertheless, we dare to assert, with a high degree of probability, the continuance of a mystical tradition from Sergius to Nilus. The visions of the celestial world which characterize the Northern saints as opposed to the demonic obsessions of former times can but confirm us in this conviction; such are the visions of St. Cyril (the voice of Our Lady) and the vision of Christ himself to St. Joasaph.

One final remark: mystical concentration, the flight to the wilderness, does not prevent the Northern saints from praising love as "the fountainhead of all virtues." Love is emphasized by Dionysius of Glushitsa and his biographer. It is recommended as "the mother of all virtues" by the Savior appearing to Joasaph. Both the context and explanatory comment leave no doubt that this love includes charity, that it is directed not only to God but also to man.

IX

ST. NILUS SORSKI

*I*ɴ Nilus Sorski (1433–1508) the silent hermitages of the Russian North found a voice. It was he who brought to a close the great fifteenth century, so significant in the history of Russian sanctity. Of all the Ancient Russian saints, he alone wrote on the spiritual life, and in his works he has left a complete and precise guide for spiritual progress. In the light of his writings, the scanty allusions in the ancient *vitae* of the Northern hermits receive their real meaning.

It would seem that, as a price for Nilus' literary bequest, his biography has been lost. It is not even certain that one was ever written; according to tradition, it was destroyed by fire during the sack of the Vologda *sketes* by the Tatars in 1538. St. Nilus seldom left his wilderness for the world and did not frequent princes' palaces; hence, our knowledge of his life is extremely meager.[1]

The noble family Maikov numbers Nilus Sorski among their ancestors. Nilus, who calls himself "Maikov by surname," adds the epithet *poselyanin* (rural inhabitant) which indicates, most probably, his peasant origin. There is a reference that he was, as a layman, a "quick writer" — a copyist of books. In any event he received the monastic tonsure early — "in my youth" in his own words. It is very significant that Nilus visited Mount Athos and "the countries of Tsargrad [Constantinople], where he journeyed with his disciple, St. Innocent Okhlyabinin. In the fifteenth century relations

---

[1] The fundamental book on St. Nilus Sorski is A. S. Arkhangelski, *Prepodobny Nil Sorski* (St. Nilus Sorski), in PDPI, vol. 16, St. Petersburg, 1882. See also B. Grechev, "Prep. Nil Sorski i zavolzhskie startsy" (St. Nilus Sorski and the Transvolgan Elders), *Bogoslovski Vestnik* (Theological Messenger), 1908, no. 2, pp. 57–82; no. 3, pp. 49–66, 327–343; 1909, no. 2, pp. 45–56; F. von Lilienfeld, *Nil Sorskij und seine Schriften: Die Krise der Tradition im Russland Ivans III*, Berlin, 1963; and G. A. Maloney, *The Spirituality of Nil Sorsky*, Westmalle, 1964.

between Russia and the Orthodox East were rather close. Abbot Cassian of the St. Savior-Rock monastery went to Constantinople twice on matters of "ecclesiastical affairs." The well-known starets Paisius Yaroslavov, who lived in the same monastery (he was offered and refused the metropolitan see of Moscow), and St. Nilus at the end of the century were deemed the pillars of life in the Northern wilderness at the same time, representatives of the Greek school of monasticism. Some contemporaries called Nilus the disciple of Paisius, who was the older of the two friends, and, probably, his spiritual father. If Paisius is the addressee of two letters by Nilus[2] it is he and not Nilus who poses a canonical question to be answered by Nilus. Nowhere does Nilus mention his preceptors in the spiritual life. He must have had some because "mental prayer" could not have been learned without a starets, but probably his guides were found at Mount Athos and not in Russia. After his return from Greece he dwelt for some time at the St. Cyril monastery, "having built a cell outside the cloister." However, troubled by lay visitors, Nilus chose a forest place at the river Sora for his *skete*, about fifteen versts from the monastery of St. Cyril, which remained the center of the ascetic colonies of hermits. S. P. Shevyrev, a literary historian who visited Nilus' wilderness in the middle of the century, thus describes its landscape: "Wild, desert and gloomy is the place where Nilus founded his *skete*. The terrain is level but swampy; the forest extends on all sides more coniferous than foliaceous . . . It is hard to find a more isolated place than this desert."

Here some hut-cells were built around a wooden chapel. It was here that the whole of Nilus' life was spent in a solitude broken but rarely by some importunate guests from the "world." St. Nilus opened his doors to them unwillingly:

---

[2] Arkhangelski, letters nos. 7 and 8.

"repelled by me they do not hold me in honor or cease to importune me and this creates our troubles."

In 1489 when Gennadius, Archbishop of Novgorod, waged an energetic struggle against the heresy of the Judaizers, he asked the Archbishop of Rostov whether Paisius and Nilus could visit him to discuss heresies. Evidently, theirs were the most influential names among the Trans-Volgians, but because of their whole religious trend, Nilus and Paisius could not reveal any sympathy for Gennadius' stakes and executions. Both *startsi* attended the council of 1490 which condemned the heretics but treated them rather mildly. The following account of Nilus dates from 1503. At the council in Moscow, convened for a quite different occasion, unexpectedly, "starets Nilus began to declare that monasteries should not possess estates and monks should live in the wilderness and be fed by the work of their hands." He was supported by the hermits of Beloozero. The leaders of the council had to send for Joseph of Volok, who had already left, in order, by his authority and energy to save ecclesiastical land property.

The anchorite of Sora died in 1508. Some manuscripts have preserved Nilus' terrifying testament, which has a precedent in Russia in the will of Metropolitan of Kiev, the Greek Constantine (1159): "Cast off my body in the desert to be eaten by beasts and birds; for it has sinned much before God and is not worthy of a funeral. My striving always was, as much as was in my power, not to take part in the honor and glory of this world; and just as it was in this life so be it also after my death. I beseech all to pray for my sinful soul to pardon me and accept my pardon. May God pardon all of us."

The literary legacy of St. Nilus consists of some letters addressed to his disciples on subjects pertaining to the spiritual life and a vast "monastic" or "*Sketic* Rule" in eleven chapters.[3] The last title, given by editors, is erroneous. It is not a Rule in the proper sense but a treatise, almost exhaustive in spite of its brevity, on Orthodox asceticism. In manuscripts it is entitled: "From the writings of holy fathers *on mental action;* why it is necessary and how it is meet to strive for it." It is always preceded by the shorter "Testament to the disciples," which is a kind of exhortative and personal introduction to the subject. Nilus is an excellent writer. In his letters he reveals his personal side, disclosing both his experience and his ardent love. In the Rule he displays enormous erudition in the mystical literature of Greece and a gift of systematic exposition, rare in Russia.

On closer observation the whole Rule reveals itself to be a mosaic of quotations. But the choice of the quotations and their connecting frame are wrought so artfully that the reader does not feel the heterogeneity of the fragments. Nowhere is a strict line of thought lost. Nilus' method of quotation is neither rhetorical nor ornamental, nor is it merely an exhibit of a compiler's learning. Nilus is eager to show that all his doctrine is based on "divine writings" and not on his own arbitrary ideas.

In the fifteenth century the *Philokalia* was not yet written, the famous anthology of the ascetic and mystical writings of the Greek fathers which was to become a classic in this field in modern Russia. But the *Philokalia* was partially compensated for in the case of Nilus in Collections from the ancient ascetic Fathers composed by Nicon "of the Black Mountain," under the titles *Pandectae* and *Tactikon.*

The following is the list of ancient ascetic writers whom Nilus cites by name and quotes from abundantly: Basil the

---

[3] The Rule has been published by M. S. Borovkova-Maikova, ed., *Nila Sorskago Predanie i Ustav* (The Tradition and Rule of Nilus Sorski), in *PDPI*, vol. 179, St. Petersburg, 1912. There is an English translation in G. P. Fedotov, *A Treasury of Russian Spirituality,* New York and London, 1950; Harper Torchbook (TB 303), New York, 1965, pp. 90–133.

Great, Macarius of Egypt (fourth century), John Cassian, Nilus of Sinai (fifth century), Dorotheus, Barsonophius (sixth century), John Climacus, Maximus the Confessor, Isaac the Syrian (seventh century), Simeon Stethatus, Philotheus of Sinai (eleventh century), Peter Damascene (twelfth century), Gregory of Sinai (fourteenth century). To this list of fourteen individual writers are to be added many ancient patericons and also, possibly, other sources, now unknown, but which can be discovered in subsequent studies. From Cassian Nilus could learn a sense of moderation, from his Sinaitic namesake the spirit of freedom, from Maxim and Isaac the mystical tradition of the ancient Fathers, from Simeon and Gregory the methods of the Byzantine Hesychasts and the poetics of divine love. Let us remember that ancient (Kievan) Russia knew only two of these fourteen ascetic teachers: St. Basil the Great and John Climacus. All the rest are new translations brought from the Southern Slavic countries on the crest of the great mystical and literary renaissance of the fourteenth century.

Embracing the tradition of the Northern Russian eremitism, St. Nilus, however, was not a promoter of total eremitism. He is credited in Russia with founding the *sketic* life, an intermediary one between cenobitism and eremitism. In spite of his contemplative mind Nilus preferred the "medium way, to live with one or two brethren," which is suggested by John Climacus as well. No common household binds the small brotherhood, which is united by liturgical prayer. The proximity of life makes possible relations based on pure love; "each brother helps the brothers." Nilus' service to his community does not bear the character of ruling or teaching. Nilus does not want to be an abbot or even a starets. In his "Testament to the disciples" he directs his "near brothers who are of my spirit; thus I call you, and not disciples. For we have only one Master." In opposition to most authorities

on spiritual life, Nilus appreciates but little human guidance
in this way of life although he also counsels the advantages
of the "conversations of wise and spiritual persons." Yet he
recognizes that now the monks are "very impoverished"
and it is difficult to find an "instructor free of delusions."
This mistrust of monastic obedience stamps the doctrine of
Nilus with a seal of spiritual freedom.

Certainly St. Nilus also demands "the cutting off one's
will for God"; he calls the way of self-will "usury" or "ex-
tortion."

Many times in his letters he complains of the "perversion" of his times when even the zealots of the monastic
ideal, even those who dwell in monasteries under an abbot's
rule, end up by living after their own disorderly will and
not after the law of God. One ought not live "as senselessly
as certain monks who, being in a monastery with brethren,
under a seeming obedience still tend senselessly to their
own will; and retreating to a hermitage they do it unreason-
ably as well because they know neither what they do nor
the principle upon which they stand." [4]

Nilus looks for a trustworthy guide in divine writings.
"Tie yourself up with the law of divine writings and follow
them," he suggests to his disciples. As for all Russian people,
the notion of "divine writings" includes for Nilus not only
divine revelation (the Bible) but also all ecclesiastical traditions handed over in written form.

It is clear that when he refers to divine writings as his
guide in the monastic life and practicing mental prayer he
has in mind not the Bible but the ascetic writings of the
Fathers beginning with the fourth century and ending with
the fourteenth, who were almost his contemporaries.

However, differing from Joseph of Volok and other con-

---

[4] Arkhangelski, letter no. 1.

temporaries, Nilus is aware of degrees in the authority of the writings. "Writings are many but not all are divine." The degrees of authority are indicated in the following personal confession: "Most of all I scrutinize the divine writings, first, the precepts of our Lord and their commentaries, and the traditions of the Apostles, also the doctrines of the Holy Fathers, and meditate on them. And *what agrees with my reason* I copy for myself and edify myself with it and hereon do I put my life and my breath." Far from holding human reason in contempt but still not setting it higher than Holy Scriptures, Nilus makes it an instrument for exploring the Scriptures. The concord between Scripture and reason is for him a necessary condition for behavior: "When I have something to do I first examine divine Scriptures, and if I do not find what agrees with my reason in beginning the matter, I delay until I find it."

St. Nilus also introduced critical methods into the Russian hagiography which was the object of his studies. Two manuscripts of the Lives of saints composed by him were preserved in the monasteries of St. Cyril and Holy Trinity. In the preface Nilus explains: "I was writing from different manuscripts, trying to find the correct ones; but I found many mistakes in these manuscripts and I corrected them so far as my weak reason was able to do so." He asks pardon from his reader in the event that there will appear in his work anything "inconsistent with the sense of truth." Unfortunately, the hagiographical works of Nilus have not yet been investigated, and one does not know whether his criticism had merely a philological or also an historical character. His disciple, Vassian, refutes with great energy ("you lie, Joseph") the charge of the famous abbot of Volokolamsk, Joseph, who said that the starets Nilus excluded miracles from holy books and did not believe in the Russian wonder-working saints, the thaumaturges. Thus were the first attempts of Nilus' critical thought greeted by the conservative school.

Nilus' personal freedom and broadmindedness marked him also in his role as a guide to the spiritual life. Here, too, the wise school of reason is needed. "Without wisdom even the good can be for evil if the law of time and measure is transgressed. But if wisdom establishes the measure and time to the good a wondrous benefit is gained . . . There is time for silence and time for tranquil conversation; there is time for perpetual prayer and for sincere service. Ahead of time do not dare too much . . . It is safe to go the middle way . . . In the middle way you will not fall." Yet, the esteem of measure, the proper time and the middle way, does not make the doctrine of Nilus spiritually mediocre or impoverished. On the contrary, no one in Russia excelled him in the theory of the spiritual way. Yet this way is determined by him as the movement toward a goal and not in a fixed amount of ascetic deeds. That is why not only time and measure are essential for him but also personal nature, personal calling. "Each of you ought to struggle in the order fitting him." It would be a delusion to think that Nilus leads his disciples by an easy way. His way is an ascetic one also.

His *Sketic* Rule is a classical work on ascetic life. Of its eleven chapters only half a chapter is dedicated to mental prayer, although in the preface the initiation to this prayer is declared the subject of the whole work. But Nilus is conscious of the danger of separating the mystical life from the ascetic. Incidentally, in Old Slavonic and Old Russian both Greek words "ascetic" and "mystical" were not incorporated nor were they translated adequately; "spiritual life" embraced both aspects in their inseparability.

The treatise of Nilus was the first Russian summary of the ascetic doctrine of the ancient Fathers. It is not original in ideas or in practical suggestions. Those who had read *The Ladder of Divine Ascent* by St. John Climacus,[5] which belonged to the early translated Slavonic fund of literature, would find little new in the ten and a half ascetic chapters of Nilus. However, Nilus is a free and creative translator. He tries to be clear and inspiring, never dull, even in the scholastic definitions of his Greek models. The only striking defect of his composition — and this is common to nearly all Russian authors of ancient times — is the lack of order or systematization. The mystical experience which is the summit of the spiritual life and for which asceticism is only a preparation and way ought, naturally, to be treated at the very end. Instead we find it in the second chapter, "Of our struggle," where this ultimate end is considered as one of the means in the ascetic struggle against sin. Thus, by the second chapter, Nilus has already disclosed his holy secret and all the subsequent exposition, which contains many excellent ascetic analyses and suggestions, is felt as a descent from the mystical Mount Tabor.

Let us consider some points of Nilus' ascetic doctrines which are classical both for Greek and Russian spirituality.

The first chapter, "On the different spiritual battles," gives a psychological analysis of sin from its origin in the human soul until it is completely overcome. From John Climacus (or, perhaps, Philotheus of Sinai) Nilus borrows the classification of five consequent stages of sin: the thought, the "conjunction" with it, its "acceptance," then enslavement, and finally "passion." For every stage he gives the Greek definition in translation, expressed in difficult philosophical terms and accompanies it by a clear explanation in common-sense language. For instance, the "conjunction" (*prosbole*) is defined, first, "scientifically" as a simple cogi-

---

[5] St. John Climacus, *The Ladder of Divine Ascent,* translated by Archimandrite Lazarus Moore, London, 1959.

tation or image of something which has newly entered the
heart and revealing itself to the mind . . . "that is, in
simple speech: any idea that comes into the mind of man."

Two features in this analysis immediately strike the
Western reader. First, Greek philosophical intellectualism
in the appreciation of the roots of sin. Sin begins with "cogitation" and not with desire (concupiscence) as for St. Augus-
tine and the Western ascetic school. The first stage is the
simple appearance of an idea. The second "conjunction"
(*prosbole*) is the meditation on it or "conversation" with it
by our free volition. Only in the third state does sinful desire appear, with an "acceptance" or inclination of
the soul and, of course, it remains in the last two stages,
different in that passion is not a temporary or occasional defeat by sin by an habitual state of soul.

The second trait, obviously connected with the first, is
an astonishing mildness in the judgment on the first stages
of sin. We must bear in mind that the original "cogitation"
is *any* idea (outside God) which comes into the mind, not
necessarily a sinful image. For a contemplative mystic, every
idea, even sinless in itself or useful and necessary to life,
becomes sinful if it comes between God and man. But by
itself it is sinless — because it does not depend on us. The
second stage also is "not necessarily sinful." Our conversation with the idea can "be praiseworthy when it occurs
piously," that is, when we strive to transfer it to the good.
Astonishing is the indulgence toward the third stage, doubt-
lessly sinful because here the soul is inclined to the cogitation
with pleasure — or lust. But all that Nilus has to say concerning the "acceptance" is: "If any one is advanced (on the
spiritual way) for him it is not sinless. If, however, a be-
ginner and a weak man consents to an evil cogitation but
immediately confesses before God . . . God pardons him."

Really heavy stages of sin begin "when man ceases to struggle against passion." But even the last one, which is the complete defeat of man by sin, does not mean his eternal damnation. As long as there is repentance there is hope. The state of habitual sin incurs either repentance in proportion to its gravity or future torment . . . and future torment will be incurred by our failure to repent and not by the fact that we have been assaulted by temptation. We must understand that the defeat in the struggle is not punished by itself. "Otherwise no one could receive forgiveness unless he were perfectly impossible," as Peter Damascene said.

The lenient tendency here is undeniable. If, instead of an idea, we place concupisence at the base of sin no stage in its development can be considered sinless.

Another chapter, of more theoretical or systematic content, is Chapter Five "On eight principal temptations." This is the well-known Eastern group: gluttony, fornication, covetousness, anger, sadness, accidie, vainglory, and pride. It corresponds to the Western seven deadly sins. Eastern theology does not know the division of mortal and venial sins, and the vices composing this group are generally not named sins but cogitations or spirits or evil spirits on the presumption that every passion has its presiding demon. The Western scheme (so-called *saligia*) lacks two of the sins (sloth and vainglory) but has one other, envy. But in this systematization of sin there is not strict line of demarcation. The Latin writer, John Cassian, introduced to the West the Eastern scheme which he learned during his long sojourn in Egypt. On the other hand, the most influential ascetic writer of the East, John Climacus, has the seven-member system probably borrowed from Pope Gregory the Great, whose disciple he seems to have been. The origin of both schemes has not yet been elucidated despite elaborate studies.

It is probable that the eight-cogitation system was created by Evagrius (Egypt, fourth century); the seven sins appear for the first time in Pope Gregory's works.

The Russian Nilus follows Evagrius, Nilus of Sinai, and the majority of the Greek Fathers. The enumeration of sins is followed by practical suggestions for fighting them. Accidie (we use this old English term for translating the Greek-Latin *akedia*) is a peculiarly monastic state of spiritual depression, loss of energy, and despair. A morbid state naturally produced by solitude and absence of work, it is exaggerated to a consciousness of being abandoned by God. Although accidie does not find its place in the Western scheme of sins it is often (more often than in the East) described as part of the mystical experience ("the dark night of the soul" in the term of St. John of the Cross). In the East accidie, also, is not treated as a simple sin. "God gives it even to the saints . . . from his love for the growth of virtues . . . Nothing is as profitable to a monk for gaining the crown as accidie if he unremittingly compels himself to divine works," the Russian Nilus quotes from Climacus.

From the other sins or cogitations we choose a few features in which the personality of Nilus reveals itself through the bulk of tradition. They are mostly connected with the "social" side of his doctrine; voluntary poverty or nonacquisition. In analyzing avarice he states — and this according to the ancient Fathers — that "this sickness is against nature" and therefore "the struggle against it is not difficult for those who occupy themselves with the fear of God." However, "when it is strengthened in us it becomes worst of all." And treating of pride (one would rather refer to it as vainglory) he speaks of the penchant for boasting among the monks of his own time and gives us a vivid picture taken from life. They boast of the name of their famous monastery and the multitudes of its brotherhood . . . or of the land-holdings, according to the newly prevailing custom . . . of the melodiousness of the church singing or eloquence of tongue. Others are elated by the skillfulness of their handicrafts . . . or boast of origin from parents noble in this world or if they themselves possess some dignities . . . And this is foolishness. All this has to be concealed . . . One must be ashamed of this rather than elated . . . Their glory is their infamy.

Among the most efficient weapons in combating sins or cogitations are the recollection of death and tears. Here St. Nilus already stands on common ground with all of Eastern and Russian Christianity: "As bread is the most necessary food, so the memory of death among the other virtues; it is impossible for a hungry man not to recall bread; likewise for the man striving to be saved, it is impossible not to recall death, as the fathers said." In practical suggestions for the exercise of this virtue Nilus repeats, sometimes literally, some chapters in Russian anthologies intended for the laity. Here, as in the doctrine of tears, all differences of social status or theological schools end in ancient Russia. "By weeping we are rescued from eternal fire." Where the difference of school is most marked is in the doctrine of obedience. From the time of Cyril of Belozersk, that is, ever since the founding of strong community life, obedience becomes more and more a central monastic virtue. St. Nilus very often quotes the old Palestinian Fathers John and Barsonophius (sixth century) who developed the doctrine of unconditional obedience up to its last (even immoral) limits. But this side of their doctrine is silently omitted by Nilus who never mentioned the necessity of turning to a starets in struggling against sins. In Chapter 10 he warns against prolonged or untimely conversations with friends and startsi.

This seclusion from the world of human beings, even

from one's fellows in the religious life is, perhaps, the most arduous part of Nilus' asceticism. Certainly he would never say with Ephrem the Syrian: "He who has become dead in heart to his nearest ones, for him the devil has become dead." Nilus retains in his heart a love, and a burning one, for his many spiritual sons and friends, but he prefers to curtail intercourse with them in order not to interrupt his intercourse with God. The most terrifying word issuing from his pen is a quotation from Simeon the New Theologian, where he speaks of the highest states of unity with God: "In this state man not only does not wish to quit his cell but he would like to hide himself in a pit dug out in the earth that there apart from the whole world he might see his immortal Lord and Creator."

In spite of Nilus' moderation in the bodily aspects of asceticism, his inward ascetic attitude toward the world is perhaps more stern and relentless than that of his disciplinarian rivals, Joseph of Volok and his disciples. As a teacher of bodily asceticism St. Nilus is particularly faithful to his canon of measure: "Concerning food and drink every one must hold the rules fitting to the strength of his body, still more his soul . . . The healthy and young have to fatigue their bodies with fasting, thirst, and labor as much as possible; the old and sick ought to give themselves a little rest." Nilus knows that "all natures cannot be embraced by one rule; for bodies have great differences in strength, like copper and iron differ from wax." His only advice concerning fasting is to be indifferent to the quality of food. Referring to St. Gregory of Sinai he counsels taking "a little from all courses offered even from the sweet ones." Acting in this way one can both escape pride and not show a contempt for a good creature of God.

These rules of Nilus, which appear puzzling to many, seem directed against the refectory rule of Joseph of Volok with its graduation of courses and the right of choice between them.

A form of asceticism particularly dear to Nilus is that of poverty. In the spiritual life poverty signifies not only the radical rejection of all acquisitiveness but also faithfulness to the humiliated (kenotic) Christ of the gospel. With Nilus poverty is not justified directly by the Gospel but is inwardly rooted in it. "Clear your cell and the scarcity of things will teach you abstinence. Love poverty, nonacquisition and humility." Poverty for St. Nilus is not only a personal ideal, or only a monastic (*sketic*) ideal, out of which the denial of monastic landownership follows directly — but it is a general Church ideal. St. Nilus, alone of the religious authors (though not, perhaps, of the saints) of ancient Russia, objects to beauty and splendor in the temple. "We ought not to possess golden and silver vessels, even the most sacred ones, as well as other superfluous things but offer only what is necessary for the Church." Citing St. John Chrysostom he advises those who bring ornaments as gifts to the Church to distribute them to the poor. He even recollects with sympathy an act of Pachomius the Great who destroyed on purpose the beautiful columns in his church, for "it is silly to admire the work of human hands."

Possessing no property, having no right to importune laymen with the requests for alms — in need, however, they were allowed "to take a few alms" — the monks ought to sustain themselves "with the righteous toil of their manual works." Unlike the cenobitic life which sustains itself chiefly on agricultural work, life in a *skete* requires work "under the roof" as less distracting from mental prayer.

To live by the labor of one's hands does not free one from entanglement in the economic life of society with its inherent sin. St. Nilus is perfectly conscious that every economic transaction is bound with the sin of self-interest. Knowing how difficult it is to calculate a "just price" he prefers to reverse the economic "law" of seeking one's profit and suggests seeking one's disadvantage. "In buying necessary things and in selling the objects of our work we ought not to harm our brother but rather to assume our own harm. Likewise we must not deprive of due reward those laymen who happen to work with us. It is not fitting for us to have anything superfluous." At this point there arises a large problem which in the time of Nilus troubled the Russian monastic world. How was one to preserve absolute poverty and still keep the precept of charity in the traditional form of alms-giving? This was the main objection of Joseph of Volok to the economic program of Nilus. That is why Nilus' argument at this point has a polemical sharpness: "As to the precept to give to those who ask and not to turn away those who borrow, this is ordered to evil persons; Basil the Great says: 'Whoever has no excess of necessary things is not obliged to make such gifts' . . . St. Isaac writes: 'Nonpossession is higher than such gifts.'" But then there are other forms of charity open to the poor themselves which take the place of alms-giving for them: "The alms of monks to help their brother with a word during his time of need and to relieve his sorrow with spiritual discourse, but even this is for those who are able. For the beginners to suffer sorrow, a wrong or blame from a brother is spiritual alms and this is higher than bodily alms, as the soul is higher than the body,' says St. Dorothy. If some wanderer comes we must give him comfort according to our power and, after that, if he is still in need, give him the blessing of bread and let him go."

This doctrine of Nilus became the economic program of the party of nonpossessors who generalized it, just as Nilus himself, requiring for the whole of Russian monasticism what was originally the rule of *skete*-dwellers or hermit colonies.

St. Nilus never forgets that the purpose of asceticism is but a preparation to the "doing of the heart," "mental guarding." Bodily action is merely the leaf, and the inner, that is, mental one, is the fruit. The first without the last is, according to Isaac the Syrian, "a barren womb and dry nipples." But inner asceticism is only a way to "mental prayer," the theory (hardly the practice) of which Nilus was the first to bring Russia from the mystics of Greece. The doctrine that was expounded by him, mainly in the words of Greek Hesychasts, is identical with that developed in modern mystical treatises. "Frank Tales of a Pilgrim" (a work of the nineteenth century), as far as is possible, helps the reader who has no personal experience to understand many points still obscure in the Rule of St. Nilus. The basis of this Greek method is the union of prayer with the physical rhythm of breathing and the heartbeat. The suspension of breath and the concentration of the inner imagination (mind) in the (anatomical) region of the heart are accompanied by perpetual rhythmical repetition of the Jesus prayer. Nilus is not afraid of the dangers of mystical ways and well aware of all their difficulties for many practitioners; he inspires novices with a description of the blissful states of contemplation.

This is, in a few words, the method of the Hesychasts as summarized by Nilus. At the beginning one must "make his heart silent and free from every cogitation." Having achieved complete inner silence the mind begins to look continually into the depth of the heart and says: "Lord Jesus Christ, Son of God, have mercy upon me." This prayer can be recited in abbreviated forms as well, especially by a novice. "And thus speak insistently, either standing or sitting or lying, closing your mind in the heart and restraining your breath, breathing as slowly as possible. The restraining of breath is very useful for the concentration of mind." It is remarkable that in this strain of inner prayer there is no place for visions, even those of the celestial world. "Do not accept in any way any images of dreams or visions lest you should be seduced." If cogitations overwhelm you, even good ones, you may abandon the "mental" (or spiritual) prayer to say prayers with your lips. Yet this is permitted only when "the mind, calling to God, succumbs and the body and the heart ache." Then "the singing," that is, the chanting of Psalms and liturgical services, is good as a "rest" and "relief." Yet one ought not to abandon prayer (that is, mental prayer) of his own will in order to stand for singing. "Leaving God within you to call to Him from without." This descent into the sphere of lower things (Psalms) Gregory of Sinai calls adultery of mind, a betrayal of the love of God.

Nilus, in the words of Isaac the Syrian, describes beautifully the divine joy of "mental" prayer. "There is truly kindled in you a joy and the tongue becomes silent . . . A certain joy is ever boiling up from the heart . . . and all your body is filled with an inebriating nectar and joy." This state is nothing other than "the kingdom of heaven." It is still more daringly depicted by Simeon the New Theologian:

> What tongue can express it? What words can describe it? This is formidable, indeed, formidable; it surpasses understanding. I behold a Light, which the world does not see, glowing in my cell as I sit on my couch. Within my own being I gaze upon the Creator of the world, and I converse with Him and love Him and feed on Him, am nourished only by the vision of God, and I unite myself with Him. And I rise above heaven; this I know surely and for certain. But where, at such a time, is the body? I do not know.

And further, speaking of God, Simeon the New Theologian says: "He loves me and receives me unto Himself and folds me in His embrace; while He is in heaven, He is at the same time in my heart, and I behold Him, here and there." And Simeon addresses God: "This, O Lord, shows me to be equal to the angels, and even above them, for Your substance is invisible to the angels, and our nature is inaccessible to them. Yet to me You are wholly visible, and Your substance is fused with my nature." It is this that St. Paul describes when he says that "eye hath not seen, nor ear heard." "In this state not only am I without any desire to leave my cell, but I long to hide in a pit deep in the earth, for there, removed from the whole world, I should gaze upon my immortal Lord and Creator."[6]

Nilus never speaks of his own experience in the higher forms of mystical prayer. He always quotes the Greek Fathers, citing them by name. A skeptical historian who might deny that Nilus knew mystical experience could hardly be refuted. However, such a supposition would be highly improbable. Russian literature of medieval times had a practical orientation. Nilus was a teacher of the spiritual life. And in this difficult science nobody can teach with the words of others. Besides, he is far from considering the mystical experience as the lot of a few elected saints. He protests energetically against this division of the ways of salvation. Mental prayer is fitting for all. "Woe to us who . . . say: 'This was fitting for saints of old but we do not need it, this is impossible for us.' But it is not true; it is not. If anyone exerts himself in the work of God, grace still more enlightens and helps him forever . . ."

The sad impossibility of dwelling perpetually on the heights of blissful prayer is explained by Nilus not only by the weakness of human nature but also by the economy of love: "We must have time to work for our brethren and to serve them with our word." This brotherly love though, on a lower spiritual level, represents another side of his soul turned toward the world which deprives his portrayal of sternness and imparts in him a great human charm. He finds for this love some striking words — not Greek ones but of

[6] Fedotov, *Treasury of Russian Spirituality*, pp. 104–105.

his own coining. "I cannot bear, my beloved," he writes to St. John Cassian, "that a mystery be kept under silence; but I become a madman and a fool for the sake of a brother." Astounding are the very addresses of his letters: "To the starets Germanus," "his own, his beloved one," "to my own brothers;" to an unknown person: "O my brother, beloved in Christ and dearest to God among all." The love of St. Nilus excludes the condemnation, even sprung from a zeal for virtue of anyone. Differing in this from Joseph of Volok he writes to his disciple Vassian who was in need of such instruction: "Guard yourself and do not try to blame or condemn anyone, even though something seems to you not right." It is clear that St. Nilus, in spite of all his abhorrence of heresies which is evidenced by his "confession of faith," could not approve the executions of heretics. Yet, the mild love of Nilus does not exclude a courageous adherence to the truth. "There is no good in the desire to please all men. You must choose what you like; either to care for truth and die for its sake, to live eternally or do what is sweet to people and be loved by them but hated by God." This readiness to witness to the truth destined Nilus and his disciples to a way of suffering and martyrdom.

X

ST. PAPHNUTIUS OF BOROVSK

*T*HE Northern monastic current radiating from the monasteries of Sergius and Cyril gave Russia most of her saints. Spiritually incomparably less rich but historically more influential was the Southern sphere of spirituality radiating from the Trinity monastery which spread new monasteries throughout the region of Moscow. Simonov, St. Savior-Andronikov monastery in Moscow itself, the monasteries in Serpukhov, Zvenigorod, Golutvin, and Borovsk surrounded Moscow with a ring of monastic colonies which were all offshoots of the Holy Trinity monastery. The anchorites of the North sought solitary contemplation. The Muscovite disciples of St. Sergius aimed at the realization of perfect communal life. Only St. Cyril of Belozersk was able to effect a happy balance between these two monastic ideals.

The observance of strict communal life was always accomplished in Russia only with great difficulty; it presupposed strict discipline and attention to the letter of the Rule. Both are found in the best Muscovite monasteries. Joseph of Volok, who visited a multitude of religious communities, assures us that such conditions were obtained in Simonov in Moscow and in the monastery of Savva in Tver. The following is a significant observation of the methods of Abbot Savva of Tver: sometimes he would beat with his staff, sometimes he would remain in seclusion; "he was cruel when there was need and merciful when it was meet." One cannot fail to notice in an abbot of this type some purely Muscovite features — good managing ability, practical sense, and great energy. These qualities seldom coincide with holiness. In the fifteenth century only two saints of this school are known, but the future belonged to them: Paphnutius, of Borovsk and Joseph of Volok.

The Life of St. Paphnutius (+ 1477) was written by
Vassian, the brother of Joseph.[1] The author was a disciple
and eyewitness. Paphnutius himself was a disciple of Nikita,
an abbot in Borovsk who, in turn, was a disciple of the great
Sergius. Thus, this genealogical line of Muscovite saints also
traced its origin to the starets of the Holy Trinity monastery.

We are told that Paphnutius was the grandson of a baptized Tatar *baskak* (collector of tribute). Perhaps this origin
was not without its influence on his character. At the age of
twelve he became a monk in the town of Borovsk where
Nikita had been abbot for some time. After a long period of
monastic life he himself became the abbot. His honest biographer does not say much about the years his subject spent in
the Borovsk monastery since he did not witness them himself. Prayer and labor seem to comprise the full content of
Paphnutius' life. He was already about fifty years old when
a crisis upset this peaceful existence. After a grave illness he
took the *skhema*, the highest degree of monastic initiation, and
ceased to celebrate divine services. Soon afterward he left his
monastery and retired to a forest not very far off, only two
versts from Borovsk, in the lands of another prince. We are
not told the reasons for his leaving Borovsk; it may have
been annoyance at lay visitors or a quarrel with the local
prince. At any rate, it was not a longing for contemplation
as is clear from all of Paphnutius' subsequent life. In the new
place he soon was followed by a group of his disciples and a
new monastery was started. The Prince of Borovsk persecuted
the fugitive and sent his servants to set fire to the new settlement. The servants did not dare, were terrified, and even
punished by divine wrath. Prince Basil himself, who later

---

[1] A. P. Kadlubovski, ed., *Zhitie sv. Pafnutiya* (Life of St. Paphnutius),
in *Sbornik Istoriko-Filologicheskago obshchestva pri Nezhinskom Institute*
(An Anthology of the Historical-Philological Society at the Nezhin Institute),
vol. II, Nezhin, 1898.

was taken prisoner by the Tatars, attributed his misfortune as well as his liberation to the prayers of Paphnutius.

The church in the new monastery was built in the honor of Our Lady and dedicated to her Nativity. At first it was a wooden church; later it was rebuilt in stone. This second building was painted by Metrophanes and Dionysius, the best architects of this time. This means that considerations of beauty in its ecclesiastical forms were not altogether alien to the severe abbot.

At this point begins the second Life of Paphnutius, the only one which is well known to us. However, his biographer did not present his facts in chronological or systematic order but composed the Life as a catalogue of miracles, from time to time interrupted by the sayings of the saint. In these, as well as in all other sources, the character of Paphnutius is clear and well-defined.

The first feature which strikes anyone who studies Paphnutius' life is his love for labor, for manual work — not as an ascetic exercise but for its economic advantage. Paphnutius was, first of all, an abbot-husbandman. During the building of the second church he prepared stones, carried water and bricks on his shoulders. When young Joseph Sanin, his future disciple, came to see him for the first time, he found the abbot in the forest, cutting wood. And the account of his death, composed by his favorite disciple Innocent, begins by telling how the starets had called him to a pond where the dam had been damaged and "taught him how to hold back the water." This was at the beginning of his last illness, a week before his death.

Part of his miracles correspond to his economic activities; for example, he made extraordinary rich catches of fish when the community was in need.

The second group of his miracles indicates the other dominant feature of Paphnutius' character, that is, the punitive miracles. They are more numerous than the usual, beneficial ones such as healings, expelling of demons, and so forth. It is true that in most cases the punishment pursues the aim of correction and improvement and indeed achieves it. But this is not always the case. Usually the punishment is not cruel; the main idea is that no sin should remain without punishment, and this produces the same effects as pardons and expressions of love do in the case of other Russian saints. In his severity, well-intentioned though he was, Paphnutius is a unique figure in Russian hagiography.

Let us note some examples.

An enormous flock of ravens nested around the monastery. Paphnutius was fond of these grim birds (one could see in this a temperamental sympathy) and forbade that any harm be done them. A son of the *voevod* of Borovsk shot a bird with his bow, whereupon his head was wrenched back. Paphnutius smiled — one of his rare smiles: "God has avenged the raven's blood." However, he consented to celebrate a *moleben,* a service of propitiation, and the youth was healed. Another hunter after ravens suffered too — the loss of his hawk.

The two following items evoke comparisons with analogous happenings in the Life of Sergius (and Theodosius). A servant sent by a prince with gifts for the monastery concealed part for himself. After a meal in the refectory he became paralyzed and dumb. Paphnutius denounced his sin but healed the servant.

A layman came to see Paphnutius and did not recognize him, probably because of the uncouthness of garb which he assumed like all other saints of ancient Russia. The man pulled him by his cassock and said: "Show me Paphnutius." The answer of the abbot was: "I think you are not sane but enslaved by the devil's pride." The other was naturally offended; in rage he mounted his horse and shouted: "I do not need his blessing! Despicable is he who was praised to me." On the homeward journey he almost drowned while crossing a river but was miraculously rescued by Paphnutius' prayers. Not the least punishment or even rebuke was ever inflicted by Sergius in similar cases.

The preceding were examples of minor transgressions. For grave sins Paphnutius saw no pardon, no way of repentance.

Once a man came to the monastery and expressed his intention of becoming a monk. But Paphnutius divined his wickedness. He ordered that he be given some food and sent away: "This man is a murderer for, while still a youth, he killed a monk, having struck him with his knife."

Another murderer came visiting dressed in monastic habit. He was a servant who had poisoned Prince Dimitri Shemyaka. Paphnutius said to the brethren: "Look at the man whom not even monastic consecration has purified from blood." It seems as if Paphnutius forgot that monastic life is a way of repentance, and that there is no limit to the grace of God.

The third case is likewise dubious from a theological point of view. Joseph, a disciple of Paphnutius, was sent to Prince Vorotynski and found him in great distress; his son had killed a pious man and for that crime himself had perished "by an evil death." When his mother ordered the celebration of Divine Liturgy for the deceased, the oven where the eucharistic breads (*prosphorae*) were baked became filled with blood. Learning of these tragic events Paphnutius simply recalled the scriptural text: "Vengeance is mine, I will repay, says the Lord." [2]

We have already seen the examples of Paphnutius' clairvoyancy which constitute the third group of miraculous stories in his Life. But even in his prophetic insights Paphnutius sees

---

[2] Hebrews 10:30, a quotation from Deuteronomy 32:35.

mainly the evil dwelling in man, as seen above in the stories of the murderers. He used to say that he could learn all from the expression of the eyes, the "cogitation." He knew, through a vision, that one of his spiritual sons outside the monastery had committed a sin of the flesh. Another youth sent to the market had looked sinfully at some women, who were forbidden access to the monastery. When he came back he found Paphnutius reading. The abbot looked at him and turned away saying: "This man is not the same as he was before."

Paphnutius' clairvoyance did not stop at the threshold of the invisible world. The numerous visions that he related to his disciples had a grim color which agreed with his outlook. Paphnutius was granted no celestial visions of Christ or Our Lady of the type which figure in Russian hagiography from the time of Sergius. Paphnutius told of demons and of souls in the other world. His demonology is that of the Kievan *Paterika*;[3] demons either scare their victims or seduce them. Thus, Paphnutius once dreamt of a demon who threw firebrands from the oven into the cell of two monks who had thought of leaving the monastery.

No wonder that this severe starets, from whom nothing was hidden, inspired fear even in his closest disciples and spiritual sons. To the latter belonged a young prince, George Vasilievich, who used to confess: "Every time when I go to confession to the starets my knees are bent from fear."

Along with sinners the wrath of Paphnutius fell upon all who manifested an unorthodox trend of mind; he expelled any such from his monastery. Unfortunately, we are not told what kind of deviations are meant. We know of no heresy that flourished during the life of Paphnutius, which would have had to occur between the heresies of the Strigolniks and the Judaizers. For other reasons he was almost as severe

---

[3] Fedotov, *RRM,* I, 150.

toward women; he did not even allow them to be mentioned in his presence. He was a great faster, abstaining from food entirely two days a week. Yet, strangely enough, they were not Friday and Wednesday, prescribed as fast days by the canon of the Eastern Church, but Friday and Monday; on Wednesday Paphnutius contented himself with *xerophagia*, noncooked vegetables. The Monday fast and the veneration of Monday itself indicates a certain mythological relic belonging to Russian popular religion, although there are several examples of the acceptance of this popular custom by ecclesiastical circles. The biographer praises Paphnutius for his excellent knowledge of Church canons. But he must have possessed and followed one of those "bad Nomocanons" which abounded in Russia from the earliest days of her conversion to Christianity.[4] Yet, Paphnutius displayed no particular canonical zeal at a very important turning-point in the history of the Russian Church. When in 1441 the council of Russian bishops elected a new Metropolitan without the consent of the Patriarch of Constantinople and implicitly, in a unilateral act, proclaimed the "autocephaly" (independence) of the Russian Church, Paphnutius did not construe this act as uncanonical and had to weather the wrath of the Metropolitan Jonas.

For a true appraisal of Russian piety one must keep in mind that even this saint of severely ascetical orientation considered almsgiving as absolutely necessary for salvation. He used to recount, probably from some ancient patericon, the revelation of the posthumous destiny of a merciful man; in order to help him cross the river of fire which separated him from paradise beggars constructed a bridge of their own bodies. And in his personal conduct Paphnutius was true to his teaching. We are told that during a famine he fed about one thousand people in his monastery.

[4] Fedotov, *RRM*, I, 180.

Another attractive feature, this one in full accord with his character, was the independence of his moral judgment before princes and other benefactors of his monastery. He was not neutral in politics. A tradition, not included in his Life, attributes to him many stories of the visionary-political type, where his partisanship is obvious. He told that in 1427, during a plague, a nun who had been half dead, coming to her senses related what she had seen in the other world. In paradise she saw the Great Prince Ivan Kalita of Moscow. He was rewarded for his charity to the poor. His surname Kalita, which means "bag," was interpreted, probably wrongly, as the bag with money which he used to distribute to the beggars. In this connection the following anecdote is told. Once the prince noticed that a beggar came to him in a line for alms for the third time. Ivan could not contain his indignation and, giving him alms for the third time, exclaimed: "Take away your insatiable eyes." "You are yourself insatiable eyes," replied the beggar, "You reign here and wish to reign in the next world." The contrasting figure in the tales of the nun is Vitovt, the King of Lithuania, who was seen in hell; a demon in the form of a terrifying black moor put in his mouth incandescent gold coins saying: "Eat your fill, you accursed." Yet even the demons themselves appear in the accounts about Paphnutius as wearing "coneshaped Lithuanian hats."

Yet, this Muscovite patriot reveals great courage and independence in judging the concrete acts of Muscovite politics. We have already seen some examples of this independence. The servant who had poisoned Prince Shemyaka was sent to the monastery in secret for this crime by the Prince of Moscow, which fact did not prevent Paphnutius from condemning him even in monastic habit.

The election of the Metropolitan Jonas was, certainly, an act of national and Muscovite policy, and the Great Prince

Basil II stood behind the council of bishops. Paphnutius refused to obey.

More examples of his independence and even of his
severity toward the princes of his time will be seen in the
following account which tells the story of his last days.

The memoir of Innocent on the last seven days of the
life of his teacher and starets, Paphnutius, is a unique document in Russian literature.[5] It is written in the simplest
possible style, matter-of-fact, without any hagiographical
ornamentation or any miraculous events. Obviously it was
written very soon after the death of Paphnutius when even
insignificant details were still fresh in the memory of the
author. And it gives such a vivid insight into both the character of Paphnutius and the everyday life of a Russian monastery of the fifteenth century that we have decided to print it
in abridged form, thus departing from our usual analytical
method of exposition.

In the year 6985 [1477] on Thursday of the third week after
Easter the starets called me to go with him out of the monastery.
When we went out he started to walk to the pond, which he had
made with great pains. When we came to the dam he saw a stream
of water flowing under the dam and began to teach me how to hold
back the flow of water. I told him: "I will return with the brethren
and you show us." But he replied: "I have no time to busy myself
with this work because I have another urgent work . . . After dinner I have a more necessary work." The starets returned to the
monastery; it was the time of the Divine Liturgy, after which he
walked to the refectory, following his custom, and partook of food.

At 6 [3] o'clock a disciple of the starets, young Barsonuphius, told
me: "Starets Paphnutius sent for you; go where he ordered you himself." I was troubled . . . [went to Paphnutius] and found the
starets sitting in the vestibule at the door on the bed . . . [I

---

[5] The text is published as an appendix to V. O. Klyuchevski, *Drevnerusskiya zhitiya sviatykh kak istoricheski istochnik* (Ancient Russian Lives
of Saints as an Historical Source), Moscow, 1871, pp. 439–453.

asked him]: "Why don't you go yourself, as you have no business?"
"I have business you don't know about because my union is going
to be dissolved." [Innocent goes with the brethren to the pond
but] has no success because of the great trouble of our souls . . . I
found the starets sitting in his cell. He said to me: "Send immediately to Prince Michael and tell him that he should neither ride
to me himself nor send anybody to me with any business for another work is in store for me."

[At Vespers he could not go to church and commanded] "Tomorrow morning all the brethren should be assembled before me
. . . On this same day, Thursday, I shall be liberated from my illness." [He commanded me to read Compline for him and go away
against my will]: "I could not find rest all the night and was without sleep." [During the night I often approached his cell] and
heard him not sleeping but praying. [His young disciple slept
soundly.] Friday after the hour of Matins I came, according to
custom, to wake him; he made me read Lauds and Matins and
listened sitting up. After Matins he allowed everybody to come to
him and he bade farewell to the brethren. A monk from St. Cyril's
monastery happened to be present there, a clockmaker by his art.
Dionysius implored the starets to give him his blessing with his own
hand, but Paphnutius would not even hear of it and was much annoyed. He said: "Why, my lord starets, do you ask a blessing and
help from me, a sinful man? I myself need many prayers and help at
this hour." [When Dionysius retired]: "What is in the mind of this
starets? I am sitting here, unable to help myself, and he asks for
my hand." [All the brethren were assembled, both the ill and the
strong, 95 in number. He let them go against their will.] Not for
the shortest time did I leave the starets and he kept complete silence,
only repeating the Jesus prayer incessantly.

[He went to the Divine Liturgy, though with difficulty, and
returned] leaning on his staff, resting for a while, but did not allow
brethren to lead or even touch him. [He lay down in his cell] but
did not mention food, simply ordering me to give him water a little
sweetened with honey because of his thirst. Since his illness he had
eaten nothing. [Prince Michael Andreevich sent to ask why he
could not be received.] I told him about the Prince's envoys, but he
answered nothing to the Prince, merely ordering that they be dismissed. [From Tver also letters and golden coins were sent], but
Paphnutius let the couriers and envoys in. I took the letters and

money, brought them into the cell of the starets . . . and said: "I will read the letters to you." The starets did not allow them to be read and ordered that they be returned to the couriers. I said: "Order me to take money for we need it." The starets became angry with me and forbade it . . . "Brother, Our Lady still possesses enough to give the brethren to drink and to eat; those people sent me not for my benefit's sake, but they demand from me, sinner that I am, prayers and forgiveness, and I, you see, am more in need of prayers and forgiveness at this time."

[For Vespers he goes to the church, in spite of his weakness.] In the church he joins the brethren [in singing] according to his custom. His custom was not to pass a single verse silent but he always sang with the brethren. [He would even have them repeat when he had not understood a word.]

[After Vespers they sang the *Panikhida* (the requiem service) as usual. The brethren wished to lead the sick abbot to his cell but he objected.] "I must hear it now more than ever because I shall not be able to hear it again."

[That night] I could hardly fall asleep because of many thoughts of the starets. But soon I awakened again, got up and went to the starets' cell. He was lying and saying prayers. *Saturday* [Paphnutius heard Matins and the Canonical Hours sitting in his bed but then prepared to go to the Divine Liturgy, refusing to drink.] Since the beginning of his sickness he had tasted nothing but water a little sweetened with honey . . . fermented mead (*kvas*) he did not touch. When I tried to force him to drink because of his illness he replied: "It is not only not useful but pernicious to die in drunkeness." [But he always ordered that the best mead be given to the brethren to drink . . .] "Let the brethren drink, after me laymen will drink it." I said to him: "Today taste of it yourself, for it is Saturday and the time of Pentecost." [6] The starets answered: "I know, too, that it is Saturday and Pentecost. But it is written in the canons — even if there is a great illness the sick must fast three days before the Communion of the Holy Mysteries . . . Tomorrow I wish to communicate . . ." This was his custom for many years; whenever he wished to communicate he would keep silence the whole week; he did not speak either with laymen or even with the brethren

---

[6] In the Eastern Church Saturday can never be a day of fast, with the sole exception of Easter Eve.

about necessary things. [He confessed his sins before Isaiah the priest, as always.] The priest was stricken with terror by the words of the starets as he himself told me.

[Prince Michael Andreevich sent the priest Ivan to beg that he be received] that the starets might bless and pardon him and his son, Prince Ivan. But the starets did not permit the priest Ivan to come to him. [Ivan entreated the brethren and finally Innocent to mediate.] Knowing the intentions of the starets and his firmness of character I did not dare even to speak of it. [Finally, Innocent yielded and transmitted the Prince's request.] As he kept silence I lost my boldness before the starets. After a while I wished to leave having made a low bow. But even then the holy man did not wish to dismiss me in sorrow: "I wonder about the Prince, what does he ask; bless my son, Prince Ivan; and Prince Basil, is he not his son? He is divided against himself, God knows where he can find peace and blessing . . ." [and about the priest Ivan]: "He has nothing to do with me even though he were the Prince himself." [Priest Ivan was not discouraged and tried to catch Paphnutius in the church at Vespers, but Paphnutius entered the sanctuary behind the iconostasis and did not come out until Ivan left the monastery.]

Soon after sunset Paphnutius himself called the brethren to the all-night service [before Sunday] . . . He was not weakened at all until the service was ended at the hour of dawn because the night was short.

Sunday . . . [Paphnutius attended the Divine Liturgy in the sanctuary and communicated. Innocent prepared the meal in his cell.] The starets did not wish to offend us; it was not that his nature desired food; he tasted a little and urged the brethren to eat from the dishes prepared for him. After that he took a short rest. [An envoy came from the Great Prince Ivan Vasilievich of Moscow, who had learned of the sickness of Paphnutius, and asked Innocent to announce him and deliver his letter. Innocent replied]: "No layman can enter the cell of the starets, not even the Prince" . . . [However he consented to deliver the letter.] The starets said to me: "Return this letter to him who brought it that he may carry it to the sender. I need nothing from this world anymore, nor desire any honor nor have any fear of this world." [Innocent is afraid]: "The Great Prince will be offended, do not anger him." But the starets said to me: "I tell you the truth, if you do not anger the One, the wrath of men will be powerless against you; but if you anger the One, the Christ, no one can help you; and a man, even though angered, will be appeased again." [The envoy went away unsuccessful in his mission; the same was true of the servants of the Great Princes Mary, the Prince's mother, and Sophia the Greek with money.] The starets permitted nothing to be taken from the gifts which were offered and was even annoyed at the many importunities. [There came] many other people, boyars and commoners from all sides. [Innocent does not dare even announce them] "because of my former experience."

I again entered the cell of the starets . . . : "Do you suffer much, my lord Paphnutius?" The starets answered: "Somehow or other. You see, brother, I have no strength any longer . . . but I feel nothing beyond my endurance of the illness."

He continued to eat nothing . . . [when food was brought to him he praised it and said]: "Do eat, and I will eat with you, because it is very tasty," but we knew that he, to say with Climacus, wished only to show himself the glutton.

His delight was always in pleasing the brethren; he himself always chose the worst, not only in food, but all the furnishings in his cell were poor. Also his vestments, mantle, cassock, sheepskin coat, and sandals were unfit even for a beggar. His conversation was always simple and sweet, not only with the brethren but also with laymen and pilgrims; he spoke not to please men but after the law of God . . . he never was impressed by any personage either prince or boyar . . . No one went away sorrowful after his conversation; to many he revealed in his conversation secrets of the heart . . . This wondrous man was in no virtue poorer than the saints of old; I have in mind Theodosius, Savvas [of Palestine], and other saints.

Monday. [Paphnutius attended the Divine Liturgy with difficulty. Innocent decided to ask him about the future of the monastery.] "My lord Paphnutius! While you are alive command that your will about the monastery's government be written down, how the brethren must live after you and whom you order to be *igumen*?" The starets kept silence.

After a while he began to speak with tears in his eyes: "Be careful of yourselves, brethren, and consider how you will keep the ecclesiastical order and the government in the monastery. Never change the singing rule, let candles burn, honor the priests as I did; do not deprive them of their remuneration that the divine services may not be impoverished . . . do not close the refectory to pilgrims, take care of alms; do not dismiss empty-handed those who ask for their own needs; avoid talking with people from the world, and labor in manual works. Keep your heart in all soberness from evil thoughts. After the prayers of Compline do not talk with one another; everyone must keep silence in his cell. Do not be absent from church services for any need except illness . . . If you do not scorn my precepts I believe that God Almighty and his purest Mother will not deprive this place of all benefits. But I know that after my departure from the monastery of the Holy Virgin there will come a rebel who will trouble my soul much and arouse a great riot among the brethren, but the purest Queen will appease the rioter and quell the tempest."

[To evidence his words Innocent refers to the eyewitnesses: Joseph, Arsenius, Barsonuphius.] Soon all this was realized; peace was kept one day only, Friday, when the starets was laid in the grave.

Tuesday. [Paphnutius reads the Psalter the whole day.] He ordered them not to disturb him [preparing for Communion on Wednesday . . .]

Wednesday. [He communicated in the sanctuary.] When he returned to his cell he stood in the vestibule and the brethren on both sides around him. He looked with his spiritual eye at the brethren and with his physical one at the icons of our Lord and the most pure Mother of God, the two holy icons which he possessed; he sighed, his eyes full of tears, and said: "Almighty God! Thou knowest all, thou examinest hearts and thoughts. If any one would mourn over me, a sinner, reward him a hundred times in this life and in the time to come of life eternal. If anybody will rejoice because of my death, the death of a sinner, do not accuse him of sin." For he saw both among the brethren. And we, hearing it, were terrified.

[Then, in his cell] he began to speak comforting words to the brethren with a glad countenance . . . And we thought, "he will feel better". [He regales some with mead.] "Drink, my sons, this cup; drink it as any last blessing, for I shall not drink or eat any more . . . Innocent, I have a vessel of mead, somebody sent me as a gift. I do not remember what his name is." The brethren said: "Kuzma." "Take it for yourself, I bless you because you have served me during my illness . . ."

[After dinner Innocent hastens to the starets to speak again about the monastery]. "My lord Paphnutius! You are not better, for all this week you have not touched any food. Why are you silent, my lord? What is your intention, to whom do you entrust the monastery, to the brethren or to the Great Prince? Why don't you speak?" He said: "To the Holy Virgin . . . who entrusted it to me. The most pure Queen herself deigned, or better, was pleased to glorify her name in this place and erected her temple . . . The Queen herself, as she began, so now will she perform what is useful for her house. You yourself know, this place was built not by princely power, not with the wealth of the strong, not with gold and silver . . . I put all my hope and confidence in the most pure Queen in all things . . . If now I also receive grace I will not discontinue offering prayers for you to the Lord. And so make progress, live in purity, not only as you lived with me but much better after my departure, working out your salvation with fear and trembling. That I may find rest because of your good works and those who will come after me will dwell in virtue . . . Every one shall remain where he is called; do not exceed, brethren, your measure for this is not only not profitable for you but even ruinous for your souls. Don't feel proud in the face of weak brethren; say nothing of your conduct, but you must be long-suffering with them as with your own limbs. Yes, my sons, do progress in virtue."

[Envoys come from Metropolitan Gerontius, the Great Prince, and the princesses for permission to see the starets] for they were much offended having no answer from the former envoys. But the starets was very angry with me and said to me: "What is in your mind? You do not give me, not for a single hour, rest from this world. You know that for sixty years I humored the world and worldly people, princes and boyars, hastened to meet them, joked with them, and hastened to see them off — why I do not even know. Now I have learned what benefit there was to me in all this . . . The Lord . . . gives me this day for repentance and again you do not give me quiet for a single hour; you lead laymen to me. Already I cannot go out of my cell lest they importune me."

Innocent, in dismay, dismisses the envoys [who pass the night in a neighboring village]. From that hour he did not dare annoy the starets in any way. [Paphnutius does not sleep the whole night, reading Psalms and saying the Jesus prayer.] This had been his custom for many years. After each customary set of prayers he never abandoned the Jesus prayer, holding the beads in his hands.

Thursday. [Paphnutius prepares to go to the Divine Liturgy]: "The day has come . . ." I asked him: "My lord Paphnutius! What day are you speaking of?" "The day of which I have spoken to you

before . . . Today is Thursday of which I told you before . . ."
[Joseph announced that a crowd of laymen and the governor of
Borovsk were standing by the church waiting for him.] The starets
returned unwillingly and became angry that they prevented him
from going to the church. He let the brethren go and sat himself in
the vestibule. The starets said: "Innocent alone is guilty; he ordered this." And I did not even dare tell him that I was not guilty
. . . One brother stayed with him, Arsenius. The starets himself
closed the door lest anyone enter . . . [After the Divine Liturgy]
I found the starets in his cell lying upon a bench beneath the front
window; the windows looked toward the monastery; he did not
allow them to be opened.

[All went to the refectory, Innocent remained alone with the
starets. Paphnutius asked to be brought to the other side of the cell]
"because there I shall have rest from this trouble, and I wish to go
to sleep, for I am fatigued." [Innocent understood] that the
starets would depart from this life. He asked him: "My lord Paphnutius! When you are departed, shall we call the archpriest from
the town to accompany you to your grave?" "By no means call him;
you wish to make a great riot for me; let nobody know until you
bury me." "Where do you order me to dig the grave for you?"
"Where you laid down Klim Gumennik, bury me with him, and do
not buy a coffin of oak — for its price of six *dengas* buy white loaves
and distribute them to the beggars. As for me, wrap me in bast and
making a hole low on one side, lay me there."

[The starets prays for his soul.] "In the hour of my end, O Virgin, rescue me from the devil's hands, from the Judgment and arguments and the terrible trial of bitter toll-houses and the cruel prince,
O Mother of God, and eternal damnation . . ."

[Innocent found the young disciple sleeping] and rebuked him
with angry words. But himself went out of the cell for refreshment's
sake and fell asleep. [He was awakened by singing.] I jumped up
with terror . . . I found the starets lying down. [The disciple says
that the starets was singing to himself the hymns of the requiem
service.] I said to him: "The starets is going to God." We fell
down and kissed his feet, inclined ourselves over his breast asking
for his blessing and final pardon . . . but the starets no longer
listened to our words . . . If he still spoke we could not understand what he was saying. [Paphnutius several times turned over
from the left side to the right which he had never done before. In-

nocent turned him back two or three times] but understood that
he beheld something unusual.

[They did not go to Vespers.] The starets lay in a seemly manner,
stretched his feet and laid his hands crosswise upon his breast. I
told his disciples: "Sit here, hold up the starets, and I will go and
see if the brethren have finished singing." I did not yet go up to the
window when the disciple of the starets shouted in horror: "Innocent, Innocent! — What do you see?" — The starets has sighed
— "I looked up, and lo! the starets breathed — lightly three times,
and in the three breathings gave up his holy soul into the hands of
God."

[Meanwhile the brethren came in, Innocent and the disciples
in tears.] The brethren made a great mourning over him . . . In
the morning, on Friday, at 1 [7] o'clock, the brethren dug up the
grave and we committed the body of the saint to the earth. None of
the laymen were present at that time. [After the interment people
and the clergy came but seeing that they were too late said]: "We
were unworthy to touch even the bed of such a servant of God."
[They prostrated themselves at the grave of the saint.]

An austere, awe-inspiring starets is vividly pictured in this
diary of his disciple. In spite of this other-worldly aloofness
(certainly accentuated by the approach of death) Paphnutius
enjoyed such veneration on the part of the laymen that gifts
of all kinds flowed abundantly into his monastery. His cult
in the palace of the Great Prince turned him into a family
saint of the princes of Moscow. Ivan the Terrible was believed to have been conceived through the posthumous prayers of St. Paphnutius and used to mention his name together
with those of the greatest Muscovite saints — Sergius and
Cyril. Paphnutius himself was fond of the princely line of
Moscow; he kept in his memory the traditions of Moscow's
past, of Kalita's virtues and shared them in the circle of his
disciples. The portrait of Joseph of Volok in its main features
is already seen in St. Paphnutius.

XI

ST. JOSEPH OF VOLOK

$\mathcal{W}$E know more of the life of Joseph of Volok than of any other Russian saint.[1] Three of his disciples wrote long biographies of their master; these disciples were Savva the Black, the saint's nephew, Dositheus Toporkov, and one whose name is unknown. Moreover, his own numerous works help us to reconstruct his spiritual life.

Joseph (1439–1515) was the successor to St. Paphnutius as abbot at Borovsk. At the age of twenty he had entered Borovsk where Paphnutius received him into his own cell and trained him in his stern school of "obedience without reasoning," which was just what Joseph had been seeking since childhood. Ivan Sanin (his lay name) came from a family of the gentry in Volok or Volokolamsk, with, we may say, a hereditary vocation for the monastic life. Among his ancestors and relatives we are acquainted with the names of eighteen monks and only with the name of one layman. Ivan learned the Psalter at the age of seven and at eight was able to read "all the divine books." The boy became a reader and singer in the church. From the divine books he derived "two fruits": "book wisdom and the desire for virtue." The latter he deemed attainable as the ideal of Christian perfection in monasticism. Together with one of his friends, Boris Kutuzov, he resolved to flee the world. "This short and fleeting life"

---

[1] All three Lives of St. Joseph of Volok have been published by K. Nevostruev in *Chteniya v Obshchestve Lyubitelei Dukhovnago Prosveshcheniya* (Readings in the Society of Lovers of Spiritual Enlightenment), Moscow, 1865. And the literature on Joseph of Volok has been enriched recently by the critical publication of his letters and monastic rule. For the letters see A. A. Zimin and Ya. S. Lur'e, eds., *Poslaniya Iosifa Volotskogo* (The Epistles of Joseph of Volok), Moscow, 1959. In the introduction the editors analyze the evolution of Joseph's political theories and provide an extensive bibliography. For the rule see the study by Thomas Špidlik, S. J., "Joseph de Volokolamsk: un chapitre de la spiritualité russe," *Orientalia Christiana Analecta*, vol. 146, Rome, 1956. J. M.

was not worth, in his eyes, that terrific "retribution" which awaits everyone when the soul departs the body. Ivan's parents did not object. The choice of a monastery was not easy; it depended on the choice of spiritual director, a starets. The more the future monk esteemed obedience the more important the personality of the starets. "To a man possessing reason it appears absurd to entrust himself, simply and at random, to an inexpert teacher." Ivan went first to Savva's monastery in Tver whither he was attracted by the fame of the starets, Barsonophius Neumoi. At the very outset of his new life he vowed never to transgress in any way whatsoever the precepts of his chosen starets. But the modest youth was at once repelled by the foul speech he heard in the refectory of the monastery where laymen dined. Ivan ran out of the refectory without eating: "He detested, from earliest child-hood, foul speech, blasphemy, and unruly laughter." Barsonophius understood the lad's difficulties; "It is unfitting that you dwell in the monastery of these parts," and he directed him to Borovsk, to Abbot Paphnutius.

We have mentioned in the preceding chapter the pictur-esque setting of their first meeting. The youth found the industrious abbot in the forest, felling trees and carrying off the trunks on his shoulders. Waiting until evening when the starets had completed these labors, Ivan fell at his feet and asked to be accepted as a novice. The initial reception was rather severe. After an exhaustive trial Paphnutius "ton-sured" Ivan changing, according to custom, his name to that of Joseph and requiring him to undergo all the usual "obedi-ences" of a novice: work in the bakery and in the kitchen, which was no light duty in a large monastic household with many hired workers and lay pilgrims. To emphasize the degree of Joseph's virtuousness, his biographers tell of his service as an attendant in the hospital. It is stated, quite as a matter of fact, that "sick brothers are oppressed by those who nurse them, for not all are able to serve neatly and to suffer meekly serious invalids . . . Joseph was ordered to perform this work, being patient in all things and loving obedience . . . zealous and alert . . . ready to turn to all who called upon him, giving them food and drink, raising them up and making their beds, refreshing and comforting . . . serving them as Christ himself." This personal kindness is a trait to be borne in mind, since it adds to and mitigates the portrait of the ruthless inquisitor of heresies he was to become. He received a personal reward for his work among the sick; the abbot permitted him to take into his own cell his invalid father, who had become a monk in the same monastery. Joseph cared for him for the fifteen years that remained of his father's life.

On his own deathbed Paphnutius selected Joseph as his successor, and the Great Prince Ivan III to whom Paphnutius entrusted his monastery confirmed this choice (1477).

The new abbot, however, soon came into difficulties with his brethren. Despite all the severity of Paphnutius in his monastery, the monks did not lead a completely communal life. In Russian monastic life the struggle against private property (or personal independence) proved far more difficult than that against the sins of the flesh. Joseph disclosed to the brethren his intention of establishing a regime of "unity and all common to all," but his plan did not meet with a favorable response. Only seven startsi supported Joseph, and two of them were Joseph's own brothers. In a secret council it was decided that Joseph should travel to all the monasteries in Russia and "choose in them what is of use." This was Joseph's second inspection of contemporary Russian monasteries. With him Joseph took as starets and companion a certain Gerasim the Black, concealing his abbatial dignity while traveling with him as though he were a "simple and ignorant monk, working at black (manual) labors." He was strongly impressed by the monastery of St. Cyril and by this monastery alone which was "cenobitical not in name only but in very fact." Apart from the strictness of community life he found there, Joseph was struck by the devotion and order both in church and refectory: "Everyone stood in his own place and dared not step out to another place."

Joseph spent seventeen months at St. Cyril's praying "in secret without books" — simulating illiteracy. He lived in a pen which was walled with wooden boards. On one occasion a brother came to his cell to call him for work and through a chink in the wall was able to eavesdrop on Joseph as he prayed; the strange monk was chanting psalms, reading the Epistles, the Gospels . . . The eavesdropper was not slow in spreading the news of this miracle; incidentally, from this we may conclude that neither literacy nor knowledge of the psalms from memory was at this time expected from the average monk. Joseph's incognito was revealed; he was dismissed from the bakery and given a private cell, but he did not remain at St. Cyril's.

Another incident, equally indicative of cultural conditions in the Russia of Joseph's time, occurred in Tver at the Savva monastery which has already been mentioned. During the "all-night service" the clerics slipped away, "as they were wont to do for refreshment." No one was left to chant, and the abbot could not utter a word for shame. Gerasim enjoined Joseph to take the book and read — not "spelling out the words by syllables as he wished to do, but to the full extent of his mastery of the art. And Joseph possessed clearness in tongue, swiftness in eyes, sweetness in voice and tenderness in reading; there was nowhere any other such man in those times." The abbot, amazed at Joseph's reading, sent to the Prince of Tver to tell him not to permit such an "artist" to escape from his realm. Our two travelers had to effect a narrow escape across the boundaries of the principality.

Meantime, the monks at Borovsk sought Joseph every-where and, presuming that he was dead, even petitioned the Prince of Moscow for a new abbot. However, Joseph re-turned suddenly, although he did not remain at Borovsk for long. He had not abandoned his plans for a perfect commu-nity life, and his heart "was burning with the flame of the Holy Spirit." Rallying his supporters, he left Borovsk again, this time for good. He returned to his own country to the forests of Volokolamsk, not to lead the life of a hermit but to found the ideal cenobitic community he had dreamed of for so long. Prince Boris Vasilievich of Volok, the brother of the Great Prince of Moscow, welcomed the abbot who was already known to him and granted him a tract of land twenty-eight versts from the town. To erect the first wooden church the prince himself and his boyars carried logs on their shoul-ders. This church, as had been the case with that of Borovsk, was dedicated to the "Dormition of the Mother of God" (1479). Seven years later a magnificent stone edifice was erected in its place, which was painted and decorated by "skillful artists," the famous Dionysius and his disciples. This church cost a thousand rubles, an enormous amount for the time; the stone church at St. Cyril's, which was built at the same time, cost only two hundred rubles. Its first "village" was presented to the monastery by the Prince of Volok in the very first year of its foundation, and from that time money and grants of land did not cease to accrue to the monastery. From the very beginning many boyars were numbered among its members. Although people of "simple stock" also joined, Joseph's foundation, like none other in Russia, at once took on an aristocratic character.

However, the aristocratic origins of the "elder brethren" in the time of Joseph did not diminish the ascetic severity of their common life; the abbot knew how to guide his flock in the discipline of the rule as well as through his own penitential zeal. The degree of Joseph's personal self-abnegation is shown in his relations with his own mother, when he refused, in the pattern of classical ascetic love, to see her on her visits to the monastery. In other respects his biographers characterize Joseph's personal holiness in the deeds of his select spiritual army; the teacher merges with his disciples. The Life speaks of them in the plural. "The Jesus prayer came from their lips ceaselessly, and they hurried to be on time for every service in the church . . . These sufferers for Christ tortured themselves, standing by night at prayer and by day running to their labors." What idle talk could take place among them, Savva the Black goes on to relate, when one monk never looked at his brother's face, "and tears flowed from their eyes . . . as the remembrance of death did not leave them for an hour . . . All in bast shoes and in mended garb, whether they come from a great house or from among the princes or boyars." This strict equality, however, did not necessarily apply to private prayers offered in one's cell and in particular to various ascetical acts which always required the abbot's permission and blessing: "One wore a mail-coat upon his naked body under his vestment; another, heavy chains; they made prostrations, some one thousand, some two thousand, or three thousand each day, some others slept sitting." In the cold church during the winter frosts, although frozen without fur clothing, they called to mind "the Tatar who did not get warm." The weak fled from the monastery: "Cruel is such a life; who can bear it in the present age?" But those who remained were fused into a strong battalion; for a long time after Joseph's death they continued their ascetical feats, accounts of which were collected in the original literature of Volokolamsk. In it we have been left a true Volokolamsk patericon, a unique patericon of Northern Russia, which unfortunately still remains unpublished.

In these ascetic exercises Joseph had to provide an example for his disciples; at any rate, the Lives tell us of "the uncouth and mended garb" of the abbot. Yet, at the same time, Joseph is depicted not as an emaciated ascetic but as a perfect embodiment of the Russian ideal of beauty: "He resembled in appearance the ancient Joseph 'the Beautiful' with his dark auburn hair, his rounded and not overly long beard." His healthy beauty corresponded to his taste for orderliness, for external beauty in life, particularly in the liturgical life. Aestheticism of ritual and custom was in complete harmony with Joseph's practical intelligence, with his sharp-sighted comprehension of the world about him, with his great talents as a manager and husbandman. Not only does he accept grants and gifts but is well able to make them accrue to the monastery, either as stipends for prayers in commemoration of the deceased, or as donations from novices of noble origin or as bequests from wills and final testaments. Why did he require all these riches? Joseph himself explains in his letter to a Russian princess: "We must acquire ecclesiastical belongings, holy icons, vessels, books and vestments; we must feed our brethren and give alms to the poor, to wanderers and passersby and feed them too." For all of this the annual expenditures, according to his calculations, amount to about 150 rubles (on another occasion he says 300 rubles) "apart from bread." On the other hand, in time of famine Joseph opens wide the granaries of his monastery; he feeds as many as 700 persons every day; he befriends over fifty children, abandoned by their parents, and founds an asylum to shelter them. When there is no grain he orders that it be purchased; when there is no money he orders that loans be negotiated and "bills signed" so that no one in the monastery, be he monk or guest, will go hungry. Monks complain: "We will starve ourselves and still be unable to sustain them." But Joseph persuades them to be patient, and, in accord with the classical pattern, it is the Great Prince who comes to the rescue and regales the starving community.

Joseph's charitable activities were evoked not only by famines and calamities. His monastery was always a source of economic aid for the neighboring population. When a peasant lost his scythe or thieves robbed him of his horse or cow, he came to the "father" and from him received "its price." "Then many peasants multiplied their ricks and increased their stores of rye." Since the majority of agricultural workers cultivated other people's lands in varying forms of legal dependency Joseph's financial aid to them was strengthened further by admonitions of a social nature addressed to the landlords. We possess a letter of Joseph to a boyar concerning "mercy toward the serfs." He has heard that the boyar's serfs "are wasted away with hunger and suffer from their nakedness." He persuades him to take care of his subjects, even if it be only for motives of his own interest. "How can an impoverished peasant yield the fruits of his fields? How can he pay his rents?" These practical, perhaps too practical considerations are corroborated by the threat of the Dread Judgment of God "when such [cruel] lords will be condemned to torments eternal." We are assured that Joseph's words had a practical influence on the social life of his country. "The peasants enjoyed a great indulgence from their lords due to his preaching." One of the biographers even writes, with a certain amount of exaggeration, that "then all the country of Volok was reformed to the good life."

As a practical man Joseph went so far as to resort to political measures in combating social evils. In a letter to the Prince of Dimitrov written during a famine Joseph demands that the prince fix the price of grain; otherwise general disaster cannot be averted. Yet, at the base of this social concern remains his abiding regard for the individual human soul,

"which the whole world cannot equal." Joseph's personal influence reached the upper classes more than it did the simple
folk, at least this fact is observed by his biographers and is
in accord with Joseph's political attitude. "Many of the
mighty often conversed with him and, obeying his words,
changed their savage customs to meekness and improved their
lives." With Joseph care for the soul of Dives or that of his
own brethren is emphasized more than mercy toward Lazarus; Joseph's social service springs not from compassion but
from the awareness of Christian duty.

The Lives of Joseph, rich as they are in valuable details
of a social character, are quite scanty in another respect; they
are silent about his inner spiritual life. Exterior ascetic deeds
and a wide range of activities take the place which in the
case of St. Nilus is devoted to mystical prayer. One vision
that is recounted by Savva, who otherwise does not mention
any miracles wrought by Joseph during his life, is quite indicative of Joseph's spirit. A certain monk, Vissarion by name,
a type of pure simpleton who was in disrepute with the
brethren, saw a dove on an icon of the Pietà which Joseph
was carrying. This dove inspires in Joseph himself the hope
that "God will not abandon this place." Thus, St. Sergius'
tongues of fire solidify into a white dove; the revelation of
mysteries, into quiet confidence.

There are admissions by Joseph himself of the spiritual
path chosen by him in his epistles and especially in his extensive Rule, called "the Spiritual Charter." Here we shall
find corroboration of impressions in the Lives.

Of the fourteen chapters of this Rule the first nine cover
its whole material content. They all deal with the external
life of the monastery and with ecclesiastical discipline; liturgical prayers, order in the refectory, silence after Compline,
monastic seclusion, various rituals, prohibition of alcoholic
beverages and of the visits of women and also of young boys.

These nine rules are given in four versions: a complete one, a brief form, a version for the special use of senior brethren, and one which is a short disciplinary code of "prohibitions." Joseph is indefatigable in giving details and in lavishly disseminating quotations and examples from the ancient Fathers and the Lives of the saints: on "dangerous" (cautious) sobriety, on the importance of even minute transgressions, and on the "dread and unmerciful" judgment which awaits the negligent. "Let us lay down our souls for a single jot of God's commandments." Joseph composed his Rule while death drew near. "Therefore I fear and tremble . . . For I believe that even the great luminaries, the pneumatophore fathers and holy martyrs did not pass the terrible hour of death without the trial of demonic 'toll houses.'" As the abbot must render account for the sins of all and the same duty of watching over souls is imposed on all, especially on "the great and seniors," so Joseph insists on the duty of being severe to sinners; in this case one is dispensed from the commandments of humility and nonjudging. "The abbot alone cannot cope with all . . . You must be more dreaded by the transgressor than the abbot . . . It is necessary to avenge lest together with the sinners, we incur the wrath of God."

However, the prevailing sentiment of fear does not render the Rule of Volokolamsk particularly severe. Punishments are not marked by cruelty: fifty to a hundred prostrations, a dry food diet, in extreme cases "iron chains"; neither are Joseph's demands on the brethren excessive. It is obvious that for Joseph the main thing is not the arduousness of asceticism but strictness in the observance of the Rule. He is himself convinced that the Rule is not difficult. "What misfortune is it not to be able to leave the monastery without permission? Or what pain not to talk after Compline? Is not the whole day enough for talk?" Only the absolute prohibition of beverages "which cause drunkenness" and of the access to the monastery on the part of women and "beardless youths" distinguished Volokolamsk from the average Russian monastery. It is particularly striking that Joseph, who in all his aspirations for the perfect community repeats many times that "food and drink are equal for all," creates, nonetheless, three categories of monks, according to the degrees of asceticism voluntarily embraced. These categories are differentiated in the refectory by the quantity of courses and elsewhere by the amount and type of clothing. The discreet leader takes into account the differences in natural capacities (and heavenly awards). For his monastery the practical abbot recruits the necessary bailiffs, managers for the monastery's vast estates, and especially a precious influx from the boyar class, only a few of whom are able to share in his labors and ascetic feats.

Some hints of his spiritual life can be drawn from the first chapter of the Rule which treats of liturgical prayer. The main idea here is the fear of God. Comparisons with the king and the court life of the palace recur at every step. The main emphasis is placed on external order in the church: "Everything has to be done decorously and in order." Joseph knows that it is required not only "to show bodily decency but also to concentrate the mind together with the heart's feeling." Yet, he indicates that the only way to this end is from the external to the internal: "First let us tend to bodily decency and orderliness and after that to the inner observance." Significant also is the stress laid upon concentration and firmness as well as the interdependence of bodily and spiritual tensions: "Press your hands together and join your feet, close your eyes, and concentrate your mind." This comprises the entire spiritual method of Josephism.

Inner concentration and the prevalent sentiment of fear are moderated in Joseph both by his practical common sense and a peculiar aestheticism of manner and custom. That is why his austere morality is expressed not so much in asceticism as, to use a phrase very fashionable in the modern Russian Orthodox world, in "life confession." With regard to laymen it was softened still more and took on the style of the Muscovite *kalokagathia*. The following is an instruction from Joseph's "Enlightener": "Let your gait be meek, your voice moderate, your word seemly, your food and drink undisturbing; look decent, talk decently, be sweet in your answers, not prolix in speech, conduct your conversation with a bright face that it may give joy to those conversing with you."

With his exceptional gifts, his erudition, and strength of will Joseph could not remain confined within the walls of his monastery. He took an active part in all the issues that agitated the eventful times in which he lived. More than anyone else he left his imprint on the style of the Muscovite tsardom and Muscovite religious life. All his political and ecclesiastical attitudes and activities followed, as a logical consequence, from his spiritual tendencies. The social work of his monastery was broadened into a large national service. An ardent patriot, loving the Russian land and her national shrines, Joseph contributed much to the transformation of the Prince of Moscow into the Orthodox tsar: "The tsar by nature is similar to all men; by his power he is similar to God on high." The autocracy satisfied his longing for social discipline and his belief that rulers owed a divine responsibility. In the ecclesiastical affairs of his time, Joseph's word was the decisive one. At the synod of 1503 he was victorious in defending the principle of monastic holdings against Nilus and Paisius. For thirty years he wrote and acted to combat the "judaizing" heretics and their protectors. Incited to this struggle by Gennadius, Archbishop of Novgorod, Joseph wrote letters to the bishops, persuading them to fight in the defense of Orthodoxy, and composed a large work of sixteen treatises against the heresy which have been collected under the title *Prosvetitel* (the Enlightener).[2] In the last years of Ivan III he personally influenced the Great Prince who had not been inclined to resort to harsh measures against heretics. Joseph's point of view is very radical. Tsars are obliged to send heretics into confinement or to deliver them up to cruel tortures. "It is all the same whether one kills a sinner and heretic with prayer or with one's own hands." One must not trust in their repentance; excommunication for life and confinement in prison must be the lot of even a repenting heretic. According to a Life of Joseph itself this harshness made many bishops and startsi rebel against Joseph. The epistles from the Transvolgan hermits indicate that the precepts of Christian mercy were still strong in Russia. But Joseph had the satisfaction of seeing his insistence overcome the religious scruples of the autocrat in Moscow itself. Basil III, the son of Ivan, gave the order: "Cut off the tongues of some heretics and deliver the others to fire!" Such victory over heresy, however, was the beginning of a painful cleavage in the religious mind of all of Orthodox society.

Severe to heretics, Joseph revealed the same harshness toward his other foes. Among them were numbered two canonized saints, Nilus Sorski and Serapion. The Archbishop of Novgorod, to whose diocese Volokolamsk belonged, excommunicated Joseph for the uncanonical transfer of his monastery to the jurisdiction of the Metropolitan of Moscow. However, the authority of Joseph at the royal palace was so great that the archbishop was deposed by a synod in Moscow and confined in the Holy Trinity monastery. Many of Joseph's friends were troubled. They urged him to beg the pardon of his former bishop. He refused, since he did not feel that he was guilty. In his letters he draws an extremely sharp picture of the archbishop in disgrace. The author of one

---

[2] Published by the Theological Academy of Kazan, 3 ed., Kazan, 1896.

Life tells that they were reconciled, whereas the author of Serapion's Life relates only that the archbishop pardoned Joseph without seeing him. In this conflict between saints, Moscow and Novgorod fought their last political contest. In his struggle with Nilus and his disciples Joseph destroyed the traditions of St. Sergius which had become too awkward and cumbersome as religious raiment for the resplendent Muscovite tsardom.

XII

THE HOLY FOOLS

"*T*HE fools for Christ's sake" constitute a particular order of canonized saints in the Eastern Orthodox
Church.[1] This radical manifestation of Christian kenoticism,
a form of ascetic life unknown in ancient Kievan Russia, made
its first appearance in the fourteenth century. Its climax came
in the sixteenth century, and it has never since been abandoned
by the Russian people. Chronologically the holy fools are
distributed as follows: In the fourteenth century there were
four, in the fifteenth eleven, in the sixteenth fourteen, and
in the seventeenth seven. At this point the Church authorities
discontinued the canonization of the holy fools and even
forbade this kind of life because many abuses and impostures
had become connected with it. "Holy foolishness," however,
resisted official disapproval. Its representatives are not canonized any more, but continue, as before, to enjoy popular
veneration. Ivan Bunin, the novelist, in a short essay, recollects all the "holy fools" he knew in his life (he holds all of
them as impostors); the number is about thirty. We have
evidence that even now under the Soviet regime this type
of ascetic life still exists.

It is a widespread opinion that this religious phenomenon
is an exclusive characteristic of the Russian religious mind.
This is not true, or at least, it is an exaggeration. The Greek
Church has canonized six holy fools (*saloi*). Two of them,
Simeon (sixth century) and Andrew (probably ninth century), are written about in extensive and very interesting
biographies, which were known in ancient Russia and called
for imitation. The Russians particularly appreciated the Life
of St. Andrew,[2] who was even considered a Slav, for the

---

[1] I. Kovalevski, *Yurodstvo o Khriste: Khrista radi* (Foolishness in
Christ: For the Sake of Christ), Moscow, 1895; 3 ed., Moscow, 1902.

[2] *Acta Sanctorum, Maii,* VI.

eschatological revelations that it contained. But not all the forms of ascetic life of the Greek Church were imitated in Russia — certainly not with equal zeal. Stylitism, for instance, left the Russians rather cold. The reason for this was not the seemingly superhuman hardship of this form of asceticism as the different fortune of the *salos* on Russian soil proves. Even the physical aspects of their life did not yield to stylitism in asperity. And, yet, the "holy foolishness" became in Russia the most popular, a truly national form of ascetic life.

In approaching it for study, however, we find ourselves in an unhappy situation. Our sources, the Russian Lives of the canonized "fools" are very inadequate. Their biographies are rare and still rarer are any composed by contemporaries. Furthermore, the latter are appalling in terms of their paleness and commonplace rhetoric. The lack of literary skill, the tradition of hagiographic clichés, does not explain the strangeness of this fact. Russian monks found their true biographies sometimes very picturesque ones. The contrast with the lives of the Greek *saloi* is amazing. The first Greek "fool," Simeon, received his "life" at the pen of a very gifted and original writer, Leontius of Neapolis.[3] Leontius gave up the solemn, semi-liturgical manner of hagiographers. In his two large biographies of saints he gave vivid human portraits sketched in a low style, not even in a literary Greek, but in the language spoken by the people. This style fitted perfectly the life of a popular, strange, and shocking saint like Simeon. Leontius did not try to cover with a veil of decency the frenzy of his actions. Perhaps he even exaggerated them. Now, in the example of Simeon, one sees that the paradox of Christian foolishness embraces not only the rational but the moral side of the personality as well. A feigned madness is accompanied by a feigned immorality. The saint commits indecent and preposterous deeds all the time, causes scandal

---

[3] *PG,* vol. 93, cols. 1669–1798.

in a church, publicly eats sausages on Good Friday, destroys merchandise in the market, dances with prostitutes and spends nights in their houses. Of course, all these acts have a hidden, beneficent sense. They serve to convert sinners, but the external scandal is great and this effect is precisely what was aimed at. The Russian lives of holy fools do not tell of anything like that. To feign madness is good enough for them. They are afraid of a bad example or, perhaps, their awe and veneration for the saints keeps them from mentioning such abominations. They are not needed for the glorification of the saints. Posterity can forget about what scandalized the contemporaries. Whether it was Russian common sense (moral orientation) or devotional scruples the literary figures of Russian "fools" are devoid of the colorful paradox of the Greek Simeon. On the other hand, the same anecdotes, derived from the life of Simeon, were told in Moscow about its greatest "fool," St. Basil "the Innocent." Unfortunately, these popular stories were written down only in the nineteenth century. They did not find their place in the official Life of the saint, a very dull production of the sixteenth century. The meager features mentioned in old chronicles and, especially, the numerous examples of modern "fools" are, rather, in the style of Simeon. Although, concerning the modern "fools," one must keep in mind that, having been refused the blessing of the Church since the seventeenth century, this way of life had necessarily degenerated. Thus, one is uncertain about the true character of medieval "foolishness for Christ's sake" in Russia. The stereotyped Russian words *yurod* and *pokhab* modestly covered the scandalous side of their lives. These words are to be translated as "foolish" and "shameful" and seem to express the two sides of the outrage of "normal" human nature — both rational and moral.

Since the Russian Lives of the holy fools do not reveal to us what we need to know to understand the religious sense of their paradoxical behavior, and since the scope of the present work does not permit us to analyze the Greek sources at length, we have to fall back on another method. We shall try to extract from a Greek hagiographic document some of the fundamental principles upon which the holy *salia* is based. In our opinion they are the following:

1) First, we must note the ascetic repression of vainglory which is always a great danger for monastic asceticism. In this very simple sense *salia* is a feigned madness with the aim of provoking vilification from men. Even now this continues to be the most common official explanation of *salia* in the Orthodox world. This also is an adequate reason for its beginnings. Indeed, it originated in monasticism where it was not a particular way of life but a subsidiary means of struggling against pride. Pride (and vainglory) was considered the most diabolical sin; it threatened precisely the most advanced ascetic, the wonder-working and venerated starets. Thus, one meets in Egyptian patericons tales of feigned insanity, temporarily adopted by the monks before lay visitors or after miraculous manifestations. But, at least once, in the patericon of Palladius, we read of a perpetual feigning. A nun at Tabennisi in a monastery of Pachomius was considered insane by all the sisters, who insulted her at every step until a starets Pitirim saw in a vision the diadem upon her head.[4]

The first true *salos*, Simeon, also passed through the monastic school. Only after he with his friend John had spent many years in the desert and achieved a great degree of perfection did he decide to radically change his life and go to the city (Emessa). However, in his case the motive was not a flight from vainglory. He was not disturbed by admiring visitors in his solitude.

---

[4] Palladius, *Historia Lausiaca*, in J. A. Robinson, ed., *Texts and Studies: Contributions to Biblical and Patristic Literature*, 5 vols., Cambridge, Eng., 1891–1904, V, 98.

2) The second principle in *salia,* strange though it may seem, is service to the world in a special mission, not by word or beneficent action but through the power of the Spirit which works through the disguise of madness but is manifested in clairvoyance and prophecy.

These are the words of Simeon at the parting with his monk friends: "Of what use are we living in the desert? Listen to me, let us go, let us gain others for salvation."

He really achieves this goal through a very complicated ploy. He takes a full measure of outrage for his foolish conduct but this is his private affair. Yet, in his very acts of madness, in his jokes (like the fools of medieval kings), he manages to teach people the bitter truth of their inner selves, and through these strange lessons confirmed by miracles and, particularly, by fulfilled prophecies some people are converted. But then his incognito is partially lifted. New friends begin to adore the new man of God, and he requires absolute silence from them, even punishing the loquacious. One cannot help but see a vital contradiction between the two purposes of the *salia;* the radical form of humility and the mission of salvation. The ascetic repression of one's own vainglory is bought at the price of leading one's fellow man into the sin of rash judgment or even of cruelty. St. Andrew of Constantinople prayed to God to pardon people whom he gave the occasion of persecuting him. But the act of saving souls provokes gratitude and veneration which nullifies the ascetic motive of the *salia.* That is why the life of a holy fool is a perpetual oscillation between moral acts of saving men and immoral acts of insulting them.

3) Living in cities among men, the *saloi* manage to bring asceticism to a radicalism undreamed of by the hermits of the desert. The hermits did not give up, at least, a hut (or cave) and some garb. Some *saloi* walked naked or half naked and had no roof over their heads. To the usual ascetic forms of

abstinence from food and sleep was added suffering from cold and other climatic afflictions. The winter in Constantinople was severe; in Northern Russia it was horrid for a naked body. Although the ascetic side of the *salia* is not the most essential one it is interesting to observe the difference between the motives and forms of their asceticism and those of classical monasticism. For a monk *askesis* is a means of battling against sensuality. For a *salos* it is a radical form of destitution, of contempt for the world and all the conditions of ordinary human existence. Thus, nakedness is a radical form of the rejection of human culture. In this respect *salia* is akin to the life of ancient cynics, yet transformed by the idea of following the humiliation and kenosis of Christ. In fact, the *salia* is the most radical form of Christian kenoticism. That is why it became so popular on Russian soil.

4) All that have preceded are practical, morally religious purposes of *salia*. But even taken together they do not explain conclusively the paradox of this form of life. *Salia* always remains irrational — a disinterested impetus to madness which claims a religious motivation. This motivation is free from all practical and moral considerations. We find it, in a deep and paradoxical form, in St. Paul's First Epistle to the Corinthians:

> For the word of the cross is to them that perish *foolishness,* but unto us who are saved it is the power of God (1:18).
> It was God's good pleasure through the *foolishness* of the preaching to save those who believe (1:21).
> If any man thinketh that he is wise among you in this world, *let him become a fool,* that he may become wise (3:18).
> We are *fools* for Christ's sake (4:10).

What Paul means, in the first place, is the paradox of faith in the crucified Messiah. Foolish, in the eyes of the world is our faith. Yet, were the Orthodox holy fools really fools to accept literally the invitation of Paul: "Let him become a fool"? This is the opinion of a scholarly Bollandist: "It is an aberration and almost sacrilegious interpretation of the word of St. Paul." [5] We are so accustomed to the paradox of Christianity that we hardly see in the tremendous words of Paul anything but a rhetorical exaggeration. But Paul insists here upon the radical irreconcilability of the two orders — that of the world and that of God. In the kingdom of God reigns a complete inversion of our earthly values. "The wisdom of this world is foolishness with God" (I Cor. 3:18) and vice versa: "The foolishness of God is wiser than men's" (I Cor. 1:25). These are deep and dangerous words. Out of their spirit springs Tertullian's *Credo quia absurdum* and the whole irrationalist current of Christian thought, including Kierkegaard and the moderns.

Not upon the theological but upon the ethical plan *salia* was an attempt at a literal realization of Paul's precept: derision of the world. At all times certain Christians feel the mighty need to challenge the world, to emphasize their belonging to another order of life. The connection with the doctrine of St. Paul is evidenced by the very appellation of these strange saints — "fools for Christ's sake." Many other ascetic or caritative motives come into play in order to justify a paradoxical way of life from the point of view of Christian ethics, but the unethical and irrational root remains. It is essentially the need to lay bare the radical contradiction between the Christian truth and both the common sense and the moral sense of the world in the act of ridiculing the world.

Now this Christian idea of the incompatibility of the two worlds finds its parallel in most pagan religions in the religious veneration of madness. This is not a simple search for historical analogies because not only Christian elements may

---

[5] See the anonymous "Bulletin de publications hagiographiques," *Analecta Bollandiana* 16:91 (1897).

exist in the widespread appreciation of "holy foolishness" in Russia. Many primitive and even highly cultivated peoples consider the state of madness as a possession by demonic powers, good or evil, divine or satanic. The ancient Greeks venerated sacred *mania* in the cult of Dionysius and even Apollo, who seized the soul of his priestess, inspiring her with the spirit of unintelligible prophetism. In the Gospels madness is possession by evil spirits but in the early Church some manifestations of the Spirit (the Holy Spirit) border on abnormal states of mind (glossolalia, *extasis*). That religious *extasis*, among many Christian sects of old and modern times took morbid, mad, and foolish forms, is well known.

Returning to the holy fools of the Greek and Russian Church it is not a chance coincidence that all these "fools" are possessed with a prophetic spirit and live in continuous communication with the invisible world (divine and demonic). The opening of one's spiritual eyes, a higher sensibility and penetration are the price for the suppression of the human reason; on the other hand the gift of healing is nearly always connected with bodily asceticism, with the power over the matter of one's own flesh.

We are far removed from our starting point, feigned madness. Indeed, from a certain point of view a real madness or foolishness or a mental deficiency is no obstacle for Christian holiness. As physical or nervous disease is compatible with higher mystical states (St. Teresa) so mental deficiency can exist with purity of heart and the spirit of charity. The ambiguity of the word "innocent" (in Russian it has its correspondent in *blazhenny*, which also means "blessed") in many modern languages is a proof for our contention. Most Western scholars see in all Orthodox holy fools pure mental cases. Such is the attitude of Heinrich Gelzer toward Simeon of Emessa whose life he studied carefully.[6] I believe that in this case his distrust is unjustified. But in many others one is at a loss and cannot decide whether he faces real or fake madness. The Church, when canonizing a holy fool always presumes the mask, the disguise, because the point of departure of this kind of life is monastic and ascetical. But for lay people, especially for the Russian people, the difficulty does not exist. Sincere or feigned, a madman with religious charisma (prophecy, clearsightedness, and so forth) is always a saint, perhaps the most beloved saint in Russia.

The beginnings of the *salia* in Russia were not dissimilar to those of Greece. In the Kievan period it was a supplementary ascetic device with which to pursue the aim of self-humiliation. It was a temporary stage of monastic life sometimes within the fence of the cloister. The first Russian "holy fool" was Isaac of the Kievan Caves monastery,[7] who began his spiritual career unwarily, as a recluse in the subterranean cave and was seduced by the demon. As a result of his spiritual experience he temporarily lost his reason. In his case, as in many others, the exact boundary between natural and feigned madness is difficult to draw. At first his foolishness manifested itself in his strange manners. He worked in the kitchen where he was a general object of mockery. Once, following the order of the sorcerers, he caught a raven with his hands and the brethren, in an astonishing reaction, began to consider him as a thaumaturge. After that his foolishness became quite voluntary. "Avoiding human glory he began to feign foolishness and to make trouble now for the abbot, now for brethren." He wandered outside the monastery and assembling children in the cave played monks with them.

---

[6] Heinrich Gelzer, "Ein griechischer Volksschriftsteller des 7 Jahrhunderts," *Historische Zeitschrift* 61:1–38 (1889).

[7] Fedotov, *RRM*, I, 147–148.

For this he was sometimes beaten by the abbot. At the end of his life he won his battle with the demons who acknowledged their impotence.

St. Abraham of Smolensk in the twelfth century, as a youth, distributed his property to the poor and put on "uncouth garb" (like St. Theodosius): "He walked as one of the beggars and imposed foolishness upon himself." No details of this period of his life are given. It is quite possible that his biographer calls "foolishness" the very beggarly and vagabond life of the saint. In this case Abraham cannot be listed among the "fools." Later on he became a monk and an abbot and a very scholarly one. His social self-humiliation was then a kenotic feature attesting to the influence of St. Theodosius.[8]

In the Mongol period, a temporary *salia* is assigned to the great Cyril of Belozersk. As a young monk in the Simonov monastery in Moscow (fourteenth century) he adopted "foolishness" for "the purpose of concealing his virtue." We do not know what the actions of "derision and raillery" were for which his abbot condemned him to a diet of bread and water for six months.[9] With Cyril this was a short, transient exercise in humility.

So far we have no example of an ascetic for whom the "foolishness for Christ's sake" was the main trait of his life and the title for his canonization. The first true Russian *salos* was Procopius of Ustyug. Unfortunately, his Life was composed in the sixteenth century, many generations after his death that it gives as 1302.[10] Yet, single events of his

---

[8] *Ibid.,* p. 159.

[9] For Cyril's Life see V. Yablonski, ed., *Pakhomi Serb i ego agiograficheskie pisaniya* (Pachomius Serb and His Hagiographical Writings), St. Petersburg, 1908.

[10] V. O. Klyuchevski, *Drevnerusskiya zhitiya sviatykh kak istoricheski istochnik* (Ancient Russian Lives of Saints as an Historical Source), Moscow, 1871, p. 277.

life are anachronistically located in the twelfth, fourteenth, and fifteenth centuries. Thus, the historical value of his Life is not great. Many episodes are borrowed from the Greek legend of St. Andrew the *Salos*. But, having no better source material from the Middle Ages, we cite some features of this Life after which many legends of later holy fools were shaped. St. Procopius is the ancestor and example of all Russian *saloi*.

From the very beginning of his Life one is faced with a puzzle. The Russian saint is said to be "of the Western countries, of the Latin tongue, of the German land." In old Russia this meant that he was a foreigner and Roman Catholic. A rich merchant, he came to Novgorod with his companions for trade and here he remained, being converted to Orthodoxy. How are we to interpret this astonishing information?

We know one of the Russian holy fools whose foreign origin seems to be very probable. But he lived in the sixteenth century (+ 1581) in Rostov and had the nickname Ivan the Hairy. Until recent times upon his sepulchre a Latin psalter was to be seen. On one of its pages one could read the following inscription from the beginning of the eighteenth century: "Since the time of the death of blessed Ivan the Hairy and Merciful down to our days upon his sepulchre there was this book, a very old one, the Psalter of David, in Latin dialect which the saint of God used to read in praying." The Catholic West did not know "foolishness for Christ's sake" as a particular way of life. Strange as it may seem, the choice of such a life by a foreigner converted to Orthodoxy is not known but the experience of modern times reveals many examples of Germans who, becoming Orthodox, display both a particularly Russian nationalism and religious zeal. The case of the German "fool" Ivan in Rostov could be a genuine one. But another *salos* of Rostov,

Isidore (+ 1424) is assigned the same foreign origin in his later and untrustworthy biography. Its author simply quotes the passage of the Life of Procopius transferring it to his hero. Thus, one deals with a typical hagiographical scheme in the stories of Russian *saloi*. Their supposed foreign origin could be the expression of their strangeness to the surrounding life, of their wanderer status on the earth. The repudiation of one's mother country is an ascetic virtue particularly connected with "foolishness for Christ's sake."

The motive for the conversion to Orthodoxy of the German merchant as it is cited in the Life of Procopius is very interesting. "He saw in Great Novgorod the true Orthodox Christian faith because it shone in the world like the sun, the rich ornaments of the churches, the veneration of holy icons and the great chime of bells, the holy singing and the reading of holy books in numerous monasteries around Novgorod . . ." For the Russian author the most efficient or, perhaps, the only proof of the true faith is not dogmatic truth but the richness of cult and its aesthetical framing. Let us not forget that the author belongs to the Muscovite period, although this is a constant feature of Russian devotional life in all ages, from Prince Vladimir the Saint, through Andrew of Vladimir (twelfth century) and Stephen of Perm (fourteenth century), down to the great *raskol* (schism) of the seventeenth century.

The Life of Procopius has the young "German" come to St. Barlaam (twelfth century — an anachronism) to be baptized by him and dwell in his monastery. Whether he took monastic vows or remained a layman we are not told. In later times most of the Russian holy fools were laymen. When rumors of his saintly life spread in Novgorod, citizens began to venerate him, and this was the reason for his feigned "foolishness." With this was connected, however, in Procopius' case an ascetic call for wandering, so typical of the later

Russian religious trend. "I do not wish this corruptible glory, I wish to go wandering to Eastern countries," he declared to his starets Barlaam, who demanded from him a more conventional life in strict monastic seclusion. Yet, "seeing him immovable and inflexible in heart, he blessed him to go where the Holy Spirit commanded him to be." Here, the moment of disobedience, the break of discipline, is alluded to as typical of *salia*.

Having left Novgorod, Procopius "passed through many towns and villages, impervious forests and swamps, seeking the ancient lost fatherland . . ." Assuming foolishness he suffered "many annoyances and insults, beating and pushing by senseless people . . ." The saint prayed for them: "Lord, do not impute it to them as sin for they do not know what they do." The ordeals of winter frost and summer heat are already mentioned in connection with this wandering life.

All this is but a completely unhistorical prologue to the Ustyug Life of Procopius of which some local traditions could be preserved. Ustyug, which is known to us as the native town of St. Stephen, was not an insignificant center in the Russian North. Characteristically, the Life lets Procopius settle down in this town because of "the beauty of its churches." Yet, far from being "great and glorious" in the fourteenth century, the presumed age of Procopius, Ustyug had not even a stone cathedral at that time, as we are informed by the same source.

The manner of his life is typical of later Russian fools, taking its pattern from that of St. Andrew of Constantinople. By day Procopius strolled along the streets, half-naked, persecuted with mockeries and blows which he received "as in a strange body and even with thanks." By night he made the rounds of all the churches praying "for the welfare of the town and the people." He slept in streets, on dung hills, or in a dilapidated, roofless hut — in his later years on the

porch of the Cathedral Church dedicated to Our Lady. He
accepted some food as alms from some pious people but not
every day and "never from the rich."

The only mark of his "foolishness" is mentioned in his
Life. Procopius used to carry three pokers in his left hand all
the time. Later, when his prophetic wisdom was recognized,
the citizens paid attention to the direction in which the tops
of the pokers were turned: toward the sky or parallel to the
ground. This was a forecast for a good or bad harvest that
year.

Not foolishness but inhuman ascetic sufferings and humiliations are offered as the reader's pious meditations. In a
drastic and picturesque way they are pictured in the chapter
on "the great winter frost."

One year the frost was extraordinarily cruel. Houses
were buried under snow, men and cattle perished of cold.
"All flying birds died since they had nothing to eat." Particularly miserable was the fate of beggars and wanderers.
Their frozen bodies were picked up on roads and thrown
into huge common graves or pits to be buried with summary
church prayers in the spring, according to the Russian custom.

All this terrible time the saint spent on the porch of the
church. After two weeks of this experience he came to a certain Simeon, a pious man who pitied Procopius, and asked a
meal from him. To this friend of his Procopius told the
story of his pains and his salvation:

At first I could not endure it and was in despair for my life . . .
By night I descended from the porch . . . and came to a small hut
in front of the cathedral where beggars were living . . . wishing
to find some rest. But they . . . coming out with sticks chased me
away as a dog, being disgusted by me . . . and they shouted to me:
"Go away from here, you fool" . . . Then I came to an empty hut
and found there dogs lying in a corner. I lay down by them wishing

to be warmed by them. But those dogs got up and fled out of the hut and from me . . . Do you see, my lord and honorable father Simeon, what a sinner I am. Beggars and dogs are disgusted by me.

A miraculous vision saved the saint from imminent death. When he returned to his porch and cowed down expecting the end, he felt, all of a sudden, a strange warmth and saw a beautiful youth with a branch of celestial flowers. The angel tapped him on his face with the branch . . . "and immediately the scent of flowers entered my heart."

The description of the frost, of saints seeking refuge with dogs and their disgusted departure as well as the self-humiliating reflections on this occasion, are all derived from the Greek Life of St. Andrew. To dissemble his source the author assumes the fiction of the confidence of Procopius to his friend Simeon, who is supposed to have written down the posthumous relation of his friendship with the saint. The figure of a confidant plays a great role in the Greek Life of St. Simeon, and it seems necessary in order to reveal the inner life of a *salos* so dissimilar to his external appearance.

As a "fool for Christ's sake," Procopius possessed a prophetic grace (no healings are assigned to him). Two of his prophecies are related to details in his Life. As a fellow-countryman of the great St. Stephen of Perm, who was born in Ustyug, Procopius had to be brought into the closest relations with the latter saint. According to the Life he became the friend of his father. He also prophesied to his mother Mary the future of her still unborn son. To make the miracle still more wondrous she is represented as a three-year-old child. One evening, at the time of Vespers, she passed with her parents by the cathedral outside which "a great many people stood listening to the Vesper Songs" (unworthy to enter). Procopius descended from the porch, his usual place of abode, and making a prostration before the little girl said before all the people that "This is the Virgin Mary, the mother of the great father Stephen, the Archbishop and the teacher of Perm."

But the most famous prophecy and the miracle connected with the memory of Procopius was that of the "flaming cloud" and the salvation of the town of Ustyug. Once, after Matins, Procopius came to the cathedral and declared to the priest and the whole congregation the revelation granted to him: "Brethren, repent of your many sins. If you don't you will perish a cruel death, by fire and water, and all your town." Nobody believed the fool, in spite of his tears and sobs. He walked through the town, like Jonah in Nineveh, repeating his revelation but with no success. "On the second Sunday at noon a dark cloud appeared suddenly — and it became like night. From all the four points arose large clouds; lightning flashed incessantly; the thunder was so terrific that no one could hear each other. Even the earth trembled . . . and the heat was extreme." Then the people understood the imminent perdition. They gathered in cathedrals, prostrated in prayers to God and Our Lady before her icon. A fountain of oil, miraculously sprung from the icon, was the sign of the divine pardon. The cloud was emptied by a hail of stones about thirteen miles from the town in a wood where fallen trees, even in the sixteenth century, witnessed to the old terror. Besides the Life of Procopius the story of the stone hail in Ustyug is told in manuscripts of the fifteenth century, and an annual ecclesiastical procession from the town to the wood commemorated until our time the miracle of Procopius . . . The stones still lying on the spot were identified as the splits of a meteorite. This was, obviously, the historical core of the legend.

The death of Procopius is described as a worthy conclusion of his life. Having received a revelation of his approaching demise, he comes by night to the gate of a monastery (probably unsuccessfully asking for entry). After prayer he lay down "at the end of the bridge" with his hands crossed upon his breast. "Of a sudden a tempest arose with snow; a snow over two palms deep covered the town of Uglich and its surroundings and destroyed all the vegetable and grain harvests." The clergy looked for three days for Procopius, not seeing him in the church, and only on the fourth was he found buried under a huge snow drift. He was interred, according to his own will, not in the cemetery, or near a church, but at the bank of the river where he liked to spend his time looking at the boats. Kenotic humiliation accompanies all the details of the story. To appreciate the miraculous element in his death one is reminded of its date, the eighth of July, when the great Greek martyr, Procopius of Cesaria, is commemorated. It is a common device of martyrologists to assign the day of little and unknown saints after their illustrious namesakes. Thus, even the day of the death of St. Procopius was unknown in Ustyug.

Still less is known about the other "fools for Christ's sake" of the Russian Middle Ages. At the end of the fifteenth century (+ 1494) in the same Uglich lived another *salos*, Ivan. The traits of asceticism from his youth are derived from the Life of St. Sergius. The main feature of his legend is the same as Procopius', the frost. He lives in a church cabin at the cathedral, half-naked, enduring all kinds of insults. A new miraculous motive, occurring also in the ancient Kievan *paterikon* — is his sleep in an oven on live coals. A priest who saw this performance of his told the story. His insensibility toward cold is, thus, complemented by one toward heat in this portrait of a Christian "Cynic". A witness of the saint's miraculous power, like his confidant, is a necessary figure in this branch of hagiography. General social contempt would have made his posthumous canonization impossible.

It is not without significance that the legend of St. Procopius has the first Russian holy fool come from Novgorod. This great city was the cradle of Russian *saloi*. All the saints of this school of the fourteenth and the beginning of the fifteenth century are connected with Novgorod, directly or indirectly. This does not mean that kenotic humility was the outstanding feature of the rich merchant city. Perhaps the opposite is true. But Novgorod, to a greater degree than the princely states, expressed the stamp of Russian popular life and mind. Religious life here was more spontaneous and less traditional. If "foolishness for Christ's sake" is a particular mark of the Russian religious mind, it was bound to manifest itself earlier and stronger in Novgorod than elsewhere. Here flourished in the fourteenth century Nicholas (Kochanov) and Theodore, of whom we know from local chronicles. By their fighting they parodied the bloody battles of the political parties in Novgorod. Nicholas lived on the side of the river called "Sophia bank" (where the cathedral was located), Theodore on the opposite or "Commerce" bank. They insulted and threw stones at each other across the Volkhov river. As soon as one tried to cross the bridge the other drove him back shouting, "Don't come to my bank, live on your own." The legend adds that after some of these battles the innocents returned to their quarters not over the bridge but straight across the water as though they were walking on dry land.

Another miracle was told about Nicholas. Once he was invited to the banquet of the mayor who, obviously, belonged to his admirers. But the servants did not wish to admit the fool. Then all the vessels of wine in the house became empty and remained so until the misunderstanding was cleared up and the saint received his satisfaction.

Exactly the same miraculous episode occurs in the Life of the *salos* Isidore of Rostov (died 1474). Klyuchevski has noted that many of the Rostov legends are copied from the patterns of Novgorod.[11] Another miracle of Isidore is derived from the famous epic song of Sadko, the rich merchant of Novgorod. This Sadko, thrown overboard into the sea by his companions as the propitiating victim to the Sea King, was saved by the intervention of the great St. Nicholas, the Lord of the waters. In an analogous situation a merchant of Rostov has a vision of the *salos* Isidore who saves his life. From the legend of Procopius, as we have seen, derives the notice of the "German" (that is, foreign) origin of Isidore.

We cannot help mentioning here a contemporary of Isidore, a strange saint of Novgorod, who was only half a *salos*, half a monk, gifted with a prophetic insight. This is Michael of the Klop Trinity monastery in the neighborhood of Novgorod (+ 1453).[12] He has the nickname of *Salos* (and the word even appears in its Greek form), although in none of the three known versions of his Life is there any feature of holy foolishness in the proper sense: nakedness, nomadic life, humiliations, and so on. St. Michael of Klop is a seer and his Lives are collections of "prophesies," which were probably written down in his monastery, whose residents surrounded the saint with much veneration during his entire life which, of course, destroys the main significance of the "foolishness for Christ's sake." Only the strangeness of his manners, the theatrical symbolism of his gestures could be interpreted as *salia*. At most, his "foolishness" is expressed in the beginning of his Life which relates not his origin, which remained unknown, but his unusual appearance in the monastery of Klop.

On the eve of St. John's day (in 1409), during the all-

---

[11] *Ibid.*, p. 281.

[12] See "Povest o Mikhaile Klopskom," N. Kostomarov, ed., *Pamyatniki starinnoi russkoi literatury* (Monuments of Ancient Russian Literature), vol. IV, St. Petersburg, 1862, pp. 36–51.

night service, in the closed cell of one of the monks, was found an unknown old man. "Before him a candle was burning, and he was sitting and writing a copy of the Acts of the Apostles." He answered all the questions of the abbot by a literal repetition of his words. At first he was taken for a devil and incense was burnt before him as a means of exorcism, but the old man, though "covered by the incense smoke," kept praying and making the sign of the cross. Both in the church and in the refectory he behaved orderly and according to the rites; moreover he displayed the not very usual art of "sweet reading." But he did not wish to reveal his name. The abbot liked him and allowed him to remain in the monastery. It is not said whether he was tonsured or where. He was an exemplary monk, obedient in all things to the abbot, spending his days in praying and fasting. His life was "very cruel." In his cell he had neither a bed nor pillow but used to lie "on sand," heated his cell with dung and ate nothing but bread and water.

His name and noble birth were disclosed during the visit to the monastery by a Prince of Uglich, Constantine, the son of Dimitri Donskoi. In the refectory the Prince stared at the old man, who was reading the Book of Job, and said: "This is Michael, son of Maxim . . . The starets is connected with us (the princes of the Moscow dynasty) with the ties of parentage." The monk neither denied nor confirmed this statement, but upon the abbot's insistence confessed that Michael was his real name. As no Russian had the name of Maxim, the parentage-in-law had to be made, and Michael himself could not be of princely blood.

After this visit Michael's renown in the monastery was naturally enhanced and his attemps at *salia*, whatever they were, could not damage his fame. Princes and bishops conversed with him, asked his blessings and frequently received his very ominous prophecies. Under the Abbot Theodosius he is described by his side as the co-administrator of the monastery. Now he points to a spot where a well is to be dug; now he predicts a famine and orders that the starving be fed with the rye belonging to the community in spite of the murmur of the brethren. Severe to the mighty of this world, he forecasts the illness of a mayor who wronged the monastery, the death of Prince Shemyaka and of Archbishop Euthymius I of Novgorod. In these prophecies of Michael there is an element of pro-Muscovite politics which puts him in opposition to the boyars of Novgorod. Later legends ascribe to him the prophecies of the birth of Prince Ivan III of Moscow and the ruin of the freedom of Novgorod.

In all this one sees no real foolishness but a quaintness of form which is striking to the imagination. Foretelling the death of Shemyaka he strokes his head, and promising Euthymius, the archbishop-elect, his ordination in Lithuania, he takes a handkerchief from his hands and puts it on his head. He follows the coffin of a deceased abbot accompanied by a domesticated deer whom he lures with a piece of moss from his hands. One could say that only the general esteem of holy foolishness in Novgorod at that time imposes the nimbus of *salia* on this severe ascetic and seer.

There is a particular feature in the Life of Michael that draws our attention. It is the stress put on his disguised high· social rank. Simple boyars were not very rare among Russian monks, but here we have almost a prince. The secret shrouding of his origin tickles the curiosity and enhances the devotional awe before his humility. Greatness in voluntary humiliation is an aspect of Russian kenotic religion akin to foolishness for Christ's sake but not identical with it. Michael of Klop is, perhaps, the first historical manifestation of this Russian religious trend; to seek and to guess greatness hidden in a humble appearance. This is a religious background for political "imposture" marking Russian history of the seventeenth and eighteenth centuries. The people fervently acclaimed false tsars and political pretenders who arose from the lower classes. Even more recently, many people, both simple and educated, including some scholars, saw and still see the Emperor Alexander I in the disguise of the starets Theodore Kuzmich living in Siberia after his supposed death in 1825.

The first of the Muscovite holy fools was Maxim (+ 1433) who was canonized at the church council of 1547. His official life has not been preserved. The sixteenth century gave Moscow Basil the Blessed and Ivan, nicknamed "Big Cap." The wordy, florid official Life of St. Basil gives us no indication of his special characteristics as a holy fool. His image is preserved in a popular Moscow legend, which is also known to us from later notes. It is full of historical impossibilities, chronological incongruities, and, in places, direct borrowings from the Greek Life of St. Simeon. Yet this is the only source which acquaints us with the popular Russian ideal of the "Blessed One." To what extent it corresponds to the sixteenth century saint of Moscow we cannot tell, however.

According to popular legend, Basil was apprenticed to a shoemaker as a child, and even then revealed his gift of foresight when he laughed and wept at a merchant who had ordered a pair of boots, the merchant dying shortly afterward. When he left the shoemaker, Basil began to lead a wandering life, walking naked (like St. Maxim) through Moscow, and lodging with a widowed noblewoman. Like the Syrian holy fool, he destroyed wares, such as bread and *kvas* in the market in order to punish dishonest tradesmen. Behind all his paradoxical acts there lay a lesson in truth and justice which could be clearly discerned; these acts were not committed because of the ascetic desire of a holy fool for self-humiliation. Basil hurled stones at the houses of the virtuous and kissed the stones ("the corners") of the houses where "blasphemies" were committed; the devils he had expelled clung to the former, while angels wept in the latter. He gave the gold he received from the tsar not to beggars but to a well-dressed merchant, because the merchant had lost all his property and although he was starving he had not ventured to go begging. The drink the tsar gave Basil he poured out of the window, in order to put out the fire in distant Novgorod. Most terrifying of all, he smashed with a stone the miraculous icon of the Virgin at the Barbarian gates, because a devil was drawn of the board underneath the holy picture. He could always discern the devil in every form, and he pursued him everywhere. Once he recognized him in a beggar who was collecting a lot of money and granting the donors in return "temporary happiness." In his reprisal against the devil beggar there is a moral which is directed sharply against "well-intentioned self-interest": "When you collect Christian souls by the promise of happiness you turn them to the love of silver."

Several times the Blessed One is presented as an accuser, although a meek one, of Ivan the Terrible. Once he reproached the tsar for letting his mind wander while he was in church to the Swallow Hills where his palace was being constructed. As he died around 1550, St. Basil did not witness the terror of Ivan's *oprichniki*, but the legend assures us that he went to Novgorod during the executions and destruction of the city (1570). Here in a cave under the Volkhov Bridge, he summoned Ivan and offered him fresh blood and meat. In reply to the tsar's refusal, he embraced him with one arm, and with the other pointed to the souls of the innocent martyrs rising up to heaven. The tsar in horror waved a handkerchief, ordering the executions to stop, and the terrible offerings turned into wine and sweet watermelon.

Evidence of the respect accorded St. Basil, who was canonized in 1588, lay in the churches dedicated to him as early as the sixteenth century. Also the name of the Pokrov (and Trinity) Cathedral in Moscow, where he was buried, was changed by the people to the Cathedral of Basil the Blessed.

During the reign of Tsar Theodore Ivanovich, another holy fool, nicknamed "Big Cap" was active in Moscow. He was not native to Moscow. He had come down from the Vologda regions and had worked in the Northern saltworks as a water carrier. When he moved to Rostov (actually he is a saint of Rostov), Ivan built himself a cell by the church and took refuge there, hanging chains and heavy rings on his body. When he went out into the street he put on his cap, that is, his clothing with a hood, as is clearly explained in his official life and as was painted in the ancient icons. Pushkin, in *Boris Godunov*, was among the first to call this cap "iron." A special feature of Ivan's religious feat, it was said, was his penchant for looking directly at the sun for long periods as he thought about the "truthful and just sun." Children and madmen mocked him (weak echoes of real holy foolishness), but he did not punish them, as Basil the Blessed had done, and he predicted the future with a smile. Just before his death the Blessed One moved to Moscow, but we know nothing of his life there. He died in a bathhouse, and during his funeral, in the same Pokrov Cathedral where Basil was buried, a "sign" appeared; a terrible thunderstorm which caused much suffering. The Englishman Fletcher tells us that during this period "they have one [holy fool] at Mosko that walketh naked about the streets and inveyeth commonly against the state and government, especially against the Godonoes [Godunovs] that are thought at this time to be great oppressours of that commonwealth." [13] This holy fool is usually identified with Ivan, although his nakedness would seem to contradict the clothing of the "Cap."

By the sixteenth century accusations against the tsars and the strong of this world had already become an inseparable characteristic of the holy fool. The clearest evidence for this appears in the chronicle tale of the conversation between the holy fool of Pskov, St. Nicholas, and Ivan the Terrible. When the fate of Novgorod in 1570 threatened Pskov, the holy fool and the local governor, Prince Yuri Tokmakov, ordered tables set up along the streets with bread and salt, and saw that the tsar was met with low bows. When the tsar went to Nicholas for a blessing after the service, Nicholas warned him "with terrible words to stop this great bloodshed." When Ivan, despite the warning, ordered the bell removed from Holy Trinity, that same instant his best horse fell down, "as the saint had prophesied," the Pskov chronicler writes. A well-known legend adds that Nicholas offered the tsar raw meat, despite [its being] Lent, and when Ivan refused with the words: "I am a Christian and do not eat meat in Lent," he objected, "But you drink Christian blood?" This gory hospitality of the holy fool of Pskov was, of course, reflected in the popular legend of Basil of Moscow.

For understandable reasons, foreign travelers paid more attention to the political role of the holy fools than did the Russian hagiographers. Fletcher wrote in 1588:

> They have certeyne eremites [whom they call holy men] . . . This maketh the people to like well of them, because they are as Pasquils, to note their great mens faults that no man els dare speake of. Yet it falleth out sometime, that for this rude libertie which they take upon them, after a counterfeite manner, by imitation of prophets, they are made away with in secret; as was one or two of them in the last emperours time, for beying over bold in speaking against the government.[14]

---

[14] *Ibid.,* p. 119.

Fletcher tells of Basil the Blessed that "he would take upon him to reproove the olde emperour for all his cruelty and oppressions done toward his people." He also tells of the great respect that the Russians had for the holy fools at that time:

They use to go starke naked, save a clout about their middle, with their haire hanging long and wildly about their shoulders, and many of them with an iron coller or chaine about their neckes and middes, even in the very extremity of winter. These they take as prophets and men of great holines, giving them a liberty to speak what they list without any controulment, though it be of the very highest himselfe. So that if he reprove any openly, in what sort soever, they answere nothing but that it is *pro graecum,* that is, for their sinnes. And if any of them take some piece of sale ware from anie mans shop, as he passeth by, to give where he list, hee thinketh himselfe much beloved of God, and much beholden to the holy man for taking it in that sort.[15]

From these descriptions by foreigners we may conclude, first, that the holy fools in Moscow were numerous, composing a special class, and that the Church canonized very few of the total number. It is extremely difficult, by the way, to draw up an accurate list of the canonized saints in this category, since these Blessed Ones were revered almost exclusively by the people. Secondly, the general respect accorded them, even though they were occasionally mocked by children or pranksters, and the chains which they wore openly, completely altered the meaning of the ancient Christian holy fool in Russia. This was least of all a test of humility. At this period holy foolishness was a form of prophetic service, in the ancient Jewish sense, combined with extreme asceticism. The only specifically "foolish" quality which was retained was mockery of the world. It was no longer the world which abused the Blessed One, but the Blessed Ones who abused the world.

---

[15] *Ibid.,* pp. 117–118.

It was no coincidence that the prophetic service of the
holy fools had social and even political meaning in the sixteenth century. In this period the Josephite hierarchy grew
slack in their duty of sympathy for those in disfavor and in
the exposure of injustice. The holy fools assumed the task
of the ancient Church leaders and holy men. This lay form
of sainthood filled as well the vacancy left in the Church
after the period of the sainted princes. The change in the
nature of the state resulted in completely contrasting forms
of service to the nation. The sainted princes built the state
and strove to realize in it the principles of justice. The Moscow princes built a strong and stable state, which existed by
force of compulsion and demanded obligatory service; it no
longer required the princes to sacrifice themselves for it. The
Church had transferred the structure of the state wholly to
the tsar, but the injustice which triumphed in the world and
in the state demanded the corrective of a Christian conscience.
This conscience could pronounce its judgment the more
freely and authoritatively, the less it was connected with the
world, the more radically it denied the world. The holy fool
and the prince entered the Church as defenders of Christ's
truth in public life.

The general decline of spiritual life after the middle of
the sixteenth century inevitably was reflected by the holy
fools. In the seventeenth century there were fewer holy fools,
and no more from Moscow were canonized by the Church.
The holy fools, like the sainted monks, were confined to the
North, returning to their Novgorod homeland. Vologda,
Totma, Kargopol, Arkhangel, and Vyatka are the cities of
the last ones canonized. The authorities of the state and of
the Church in Moscow began to be suspicious of the Blessed
Ones. They noted the presence among them of false holy
fools, of the genuinely insane, or of deceivers. Even the
Church feastdays of the saints already canonized, such as

Basil the Blessed, were given less importance. The Synod stopped canonizing holy fools completely. Deprived of the spiritual support of the intellectual leaders of the Church and persecuted by the police, the holy fools went into a decline and the movement degenerated.

XIII

ART AND RELIGION

*I*N speaking of religious life in medieval Russia we must
not fail to consider the religious art of the period.
This was Russia's greatest and most original creation. The
fifteenth century, which we have called the golden age of
Russian sanctity or spiritual life, can, with as much right,
be called the golden age of Russian art. For painting, at
least, one can venture to say that neither the nineteenth nor
the twentieth centuries have produced a genius equal to that
of Andrei Rublev, the icon painter. In comparing medieval
art with contemporary spirituality, the modern student will
see that it clearly had certain advantages. Ancient Russia
had no theology worthy of the name. The written word in
the best literary documents, the Lives of saints like Sergius
or Stephen, was awkward and powerless to render the
higher mystical states of prayer. In these vague accounts
we can only surmise the spiritual life of Russia's greatest
saints. But in art such handicaps as the lack of classical learning and literary skill did not exist. Without any obstacles,
such as those of language, the Russian artist went directly to
the school of the Greek painters and in time (about the fifteenth century) was able to even equal these masters.

In Kiev Russian mosaicists and painters were but modest
disciples. In spite of their early successes they lacked originality, and the surest means of distinguishing Russian works
from their Byzantine models is their second-rate quality.
Even when this criterion fails us and the difference in quality
becomes almost imperceptible, the spirit of Kievan art remains Greek and very little can be inferred from its characteristics as to the tendencies of the Russian religious mind.

This is no longer the case in Mongol or medieval Russia. Greek traditions have not died; Greek artists still work

in Russia and form schools of Russian disciples; and yet an original national genius is unmistakable. Russian religious art belongs to the great world of Byzantium, but within it it already has its own definite sphere. Not all its features originated in Greece. A great deal must be attributed to national traditions, and something to Oriental influences.

This national school of Russian art is far from uniform. It shows rapid development in time and is differentiated into local schools. Now we can even detect the brushes of individual painters and in many cases ascribe them to definite names. This is the brilliant achievement of a recent school of Russian research which began in the first years of this century. It was the work of one generation of Russian scholars in art history, and a few words on the methods of their work should precede the exposition of their achievement. Otherwise we might overlook the fragmentary nature of our knowledge of ancient Russian art and the enormous difficulties that still obstruct any general synthesis.

While ancient churches have always been accessible to the eyes of admirers and students of architecture, medieval painting in wall frescoes as well as in icons has been practically inaccessible and unobservable until quite recent times. Because of bad conditions of preservation, particularly from the smoke of lamps and candles, ancient icons used to be painted over practically every fifty years. Frescoes were also restored or painted anew in quite different styles. The nineteenth century proved particularly fatal for Russian art, and worst of all were the ignorant attempts of its first restorers. Only in our own time has a respect for ancient art, a growing understanding of its principles, and a new technique in restoration revealed to us the authentic works of Russian medieval art.

This new technique consists mainly in an extremely painstaking and scrupulous removal of all the successive layers of painting that cover the original work. It is a procedure of uncovering and cleaning rather than one of repainting. The results have been almost miraculous. Dark sacred figures, hidden in massive silver "vestments" have reappeared, shining in fresh and vivid colors. It was only at this point, in the second decade of this century, that research in Russian art became possible. The new method of "restoration" is a very slow and painstaking procedure. Many years of hard labor are needed for the "uncovering" of a single icon.[1] The 1917 revolution did not end all this valuable work. It was continued for the most part by the same expert scholars; however, publications gradually petered out until in about 1930 they stopped almost completely. In the thirties more churches were razed than restored. The vandalism in the cities of Moscow and Kiev was particularly destructive. Then came the second war with its fresh destruction at the hands of both the Germans and the Russians. No wonder that our knowledge of the ancient masters and their disciples is so fragmentary and that the experts still argue about many fundamental issues.[2] One of them is the problem of the local schools.

What is beyond any doubt is the original and national character of the art of Novgorod.[3] The city of Novgorod and its territory has yielded by far the greatest numbers of artistic monuments in architecture as well as in painting. The cultural predominance of this city-state is clearly reflected in

---

[1] I. E. Grabar, *Voprosy restavratsii* (Problems of Restoration), 2 vols., Moscow, 1926–1928; A. I. Anisimov, *Les anciennes icones et leur contribution à l'histoire de la peinture russe,* Paris, 1929.

[2] The restoration of monuments of medieval Russian art has been underway again in the Soviet Union since 1950. For current achievements consult principally the monumental *Istoriya russkogo iskusstva* (A History of Russian Art), I. E. Grabar, V. N. Lagarev, and V. S. Kemenov, eds., 5 vols., Moscow, 1953–1954. J. M.

[3] V. N. Lazarev, *Iskusstvo Novgoroda* (The Art of Novgorod), Moscow, 1947.

this fact. The hand of some Greek masters and their followers is also recognizable. More questionable is the existence of an ancient and independent school at Suzdal (or Vladimir). Despite the great authority of the chief proponent of the Suzdal school, Professor Igor Grabar, its existence has not been completely established; local qualities presumed to be present in its works can be explained as the contribution of Greek and other foreign artists whose activities in this province are richly documented. Still less is known of other local centers such as Tver, Rostov, or Ustyug. Up to now the work of the modern restorer has not reached many provincial towns. And we must leave it to future investigations to decide as to the degree of their artistic independence.

One old prejudice has been dispelled once and for all in the course of recent research: that of the anonymity of medieval art. Certainly, icons were not signed. But ancient monastic inventories and even political chronicles mention the names of famous painters and their works. Individual manners or styles were always distinguished although as time passed they were very often confused. Thus modern research is confronted by the not impossible, though not always easy task, of attributing existing works of art to individual artists or, at least, to their schools. In many cases, as in Novgorod, the shroud of anonymity has not been lifted. This is even more the case with architectural monuments.

In dealing with medieval art in the present chapter we are not concerned with purely artistic, formal problems. Our concern is the reflection of religious life in art and art's significance for spirituality. This does not mean that our only preoccupation is with the subject matter of iconography. Both form and content (subject) are treated only in their interdependence upon devotional life.[4] In view of the restrictions

---

[4] The work by L. Ouspensky and V. Lossky, *The Meaning of Icons,* Boston, 1952, is a good introduction to the role of religious art in Orthodox theology and spirituality. J. M.

of space we cannot acquaint the reader with the monuments of Russian art and we shall assume that he has some familiarity with them. For those who have none, and, for that matter, to all our readers, we suggest that they consult several available textbooks, such as those of D. R. Buxton, P. P. Muratov, T. Talbot Rice and others.[5]

Let us begin with architecture. In Russia it was not, certainly, a great art in the sense that Byzantine or Western medieval architecture were. While Russian icon-painting can claim universal importance, Russian church buildings remain delightful monuments of a local, sometimes provincial, art. This art is by no means barbarous. It pleases in its harmony, its sense of proportion, and its great decorative mastery. But one would look here in vain for the grandeur or majesty of Hagia Sophia or the cathedrals of Naumburg or Rheims.

Architecture in medieval Russia is a continuation and development (at least in Novgorod) of the style created by Kievan Russia. It was, indeed, a new creation and not a transplanting of Byzantine forms. Of course, all Russian churches were, like the Byzantine, central buildings upon a quadrangular base and crowned with a dome. Not a single basilica, or elongated rectangular church was built in ancient Russia, but here the similarity with the Byzantine church ends. Buildings with large domes (or cupolas) were, perhaps, technically too arduous a task for Russian masons. The dome embracing the whole building to symbolize heaven descending to earth gives place to a more modest dome that can be interpreted, at best, as a vista to heaven. Russian churches in the Kievan period and later were rather small in periphery and tended to develop into a dimension of height. The general form is that of an elevated cube with

[5] D. R. Buxton, *Russian Medieval Architecture*, Cambridge, Eng., 1934; P. P. Muratov, *Les icones russes*, Paris, 1927; T. Talbot Rice, *Russian Art*, Harmondsworth, 1949.

three (or one) apses on the eastern side. The uniformity of high walls is dispelled by narrow windows and a system of horizontal and vertical ornamental lines. The whole building is crowned not with one but with many, usually five, small cupolas which are low cylindrical towers covered by rounded tops (in Russia called "heads"). With the exception of the central cupola other domes have purely decorative value, and no spheric excavations in the ceiling correspond to them within the building. Simplicity and elegance are the main features of ancient Russian churches. Elegance attains an extraordinary refinement of external ornamentation in the churches of Vladimir and its province in northeastern Russia.

Different theories were proposed as to the origin of the particular type of architecture. There is a striking similarity between the small, high stone Russian churches and those of Armenian and Georgian origin in the Caucasus. An Eastern origin for this type would seem very probable. The similarity to the Western Romanesque (Norman) architecture has also been noted; but it pertains only to ornamental details, which is not surprising since the presence of Western workmen, at least in Vladimir, is attested by the Chronicles. A purely Russian origin for this stone architecture is out of the question since the Eastern Slavs had experienced only wooden construction.

The storm of the Mongol invasion proved fatal to the full flowering of this art in northeastern (Vladimir) Russia. For generations stone building was stopped. When it was revived, it was limited to the imitation of old forms on a minor scale. The lowering of technical skill can be seen in the custom of commissioning the more important works by masons from outside, particularly from Novgorod and Pskov.

Only in Novgorod, which did not suffer an invasion, did ecclesiastical architecture continue without interruption.

However, very little was built even in Novgorod during the thirteenth century. The ancient type remained for the most part in simplified form. In Novgorod one can still see many of these small churches with only one apse and practically no external ornamentation, which are not devoid, however, of a certain esthetic charm. But in the second half of the fourteenth century a new development sets in. There begins to be erected bigger churches with rich ornamentation and more complicated structure but without abandoning the ancient pattern. These two types of churches, rich and modest, coexisted in Novgorod side by side until the end of the city's independence. And yet no new work could rival the venerable and ancient cathedral, St. Sophia, which remained forever the strongest link with Byzantium and its artistic traditions.

Yet, in the domain of architecture another tradition gradually became apparent: the national, the old Russian one. It was not noticeable in Kiev; now, in the North, it makes its presence felt. The Russians, in the whole forest zone of the North, built in wood, as they do even now, and achieved great mastery in this art. The Novgorodians particularly were famous as skillful carpenters. Their artistic skill, especially in the decorative carving of detail, deserves our admiration all the more when we reflect that the saw as a carpenter's tool was unknown in Russia until the seventeenth century and all this fine carving was hewed with an ax.

The first church in Novgorod erected after its conversion to Christianity at the end of the tenth century was a wooden one. Nearly all the innumerable churches in small towns and villages for centuries were also wooden and, likewise, the first churches of forest hermitages and even famous monasteries like those of St. Sergius, Cyril, or Ferapont before they were rebuilt in stone. The first stone church in

Moscow, the cathedral of the Dormition, was founded only in 1328. The Chronicles never fail to mention the foundations and consecrations of stone churches as great ecclesiastical events. Because of their fragility none of the wooden churches of the Middle Ages have survived. They suffered from the incessant fires which seem to consume each Russian town at least once in every century. We do not even possess pictorial representations or detailed descriptions of the oldest wooden churches. The oldest existing wooden buildings belong to the seventeenth century and even these are very rare. But the construction of wooden churches has continued in the North even in recent times, and thus we possess some patterns for this ancient Russian art. Assuming the conservative nature of every popular art one can imagine similar forms of construction in existence throughout the Middle Ages. These are their outstanding features: construction from horizontal logs, small dimensions, crowning towers with octagonal pyramidal tops (so-called "tents"), sometimes many cupolas or "heads" of a very elegant shape. Rich porches and galleries often supply sufficient external ornamentation, but even in their simplest form the charm of these modest chapels, lost in the forests in the Northern villages, is undeniable.

There was an abundance of these wooden chapels in Novgorod despite the great number of stone churches. One can get a surprising picture of their great number by looking into the so-called "Chronicles of the Churches of God," a large volume which registers the construction throughout the centuries of churches in Novgorod alone.[6] The number of churches is partly explained by their small size. But still another religious motive was present in the endless multiplication of small chapels. This motive is revealed by the

---

[6] *Novgorodskaya letopis; Letopisets novgorodski* (The Novgorodian Chronicler), Moscow, 1781; St. Petersburg, 1879.

curious custom of "one-day churches" (*obydennye*), which was well-known not only in Novgorod but also in other medieval towns. During a plague or some general disaster, citizens would vow to build a church in a single day to propitiate the angered Godhead. The desire to obtain immediate results probably accounts for the strikingly short period of construction. Involuntarily one thinks, by way of contrast, of Western cathedrals also built by the whole community and sometimes also in consequence of a vow requiring centuries for their completion. The monumental, the grandiose is absent in medieval Russia. Yet it does not follow that these one-day churches are necessarily ugly. Whether wood or stone, material of modest constructive forms admitted fine decorative possibilities.

Russian medieval churches still lacked bell-towers. They were replaced by so-called bell-galleries (*zvonnitsy*), elevated arcades under the free arches on which the bells were suspended. These bell-galleries, whether joined to the church or standing separately, are sometimes very attractive as are the various porches and parvises surrounding the main body. In these additional parts one can see the influence of wooden construction which is also generally accepted as the source of the original development of Russian domes.

The external dome or cupola in Byzantium was a small segment of a large sphere as may still be seen in Hagia Sophia. It corresponded exactly to the inner appearance of the dome with its idea of a vault of sky. In Russia the external "heads" over their cylindrical "necks" or drums became more and more independent of their inner structure.[7] The metal-covered and gilded "heads" had grown in height and become more rounded and pointed. The form of the

---

[7] A similar development in a somewhat different decorative setting became common in Byzantium after the ninth century. It was on this Byzantine basis that the original Russian architectural school developed. J. M.

most ancient "heads" in Novgorod is not known to us since they were rebuilt according to later tastes. A typical Novgorodian "head" of the fourteenth and fifteenth centuries has the form of a military helmet crowned by a cross. The latest development, particularly in Muscovite time, enlarged the head still more and sharpened its top, even transforming the helmet into an "onion" (the technical term). In many wooden as well as stone churches in the North the "onion" is not so squat as in Moscow, and its elongated and narrowed form is very slender and elegant. It reminds one of the flame of a candle, so cherished in Russian devotion, and thus it evokes, more than any other architectural form, the sense of "tenderness," the Russian *umilenie* in all the complexity of religious associations connected with this word.[8]

The opposite direction was followed by the church builders in Pskov, an important frontier republic dependent on Novgorod. The noble architectural type of Novgorod underwent a provincial deformation. The typical church in Pskov is low, but its cupola, generally a single one of large "onion" form, has grown out of all proportion. It attains in some cases half the size of the church itself. The general impression is far from elegant but has its own charm: cozy, homey, intimate. All the majesty of Byzantium has completely evaporated in this popular democratic world.

In our imagination, let us enter one of these medieval Russian churches. At first glance you are amazed by the multitude of people, mostly women, but also young bachelors, who fill the large parvises during the service. These are the people who are forbidden to enter the church: the excommunicated, or, better, penitents under *epitimia*. Passing the main door you step into the church itself and find yourself in a high, semi-obscure space illuminated by an occasional ray of sunlight from the narrow windows and number-

---

[8] Fedotov, *RRM*, I, 393.

less suspended lamps and candelabra standing before the icons. If it is a stone church of some size, in the middle you see four wide columns supporting the cupola. Its vaults end in a rather narrow "drum" lighted by small openings. But you look in vain for the Western apse. It is invisible, cut off from the main body of the church by a high wooden wall, called the iconostasis. This wall is completely covered, or rather it consists of nothing but icons in horizontal ranges, one above the other, up to the ceiling or almost that high. Three doors (the principal one, known as the "royal gate," is richly ornamented and gilded) when opened permit a glance into the sanctuary with its gorgeously vested altar. But most of the time the doors are closed and the architectural view is truncated. The church looks foreshortened at the eastern, the most sacred side. This organic formal defect is concealed and partly compensated for by the richness of the inner decoration, the carvings in wood, mostly gilded, the reflection of lights and, above all, by wonderful paintings covering not only the iconstasis but the whole church from top to bottom, its walls, the central columns, and the cupola itself. The general impression is always vivid and awe-inspiring. But this is a quite different impression from that of a Byzantine cathedral, not to mention a western basilica.

The small size of the Russian churches results not only from a lack of technical skill and from climatic conditions, in virtue of which the churches were most difficult to heat during the very severe Russian winter. It was also, in part, a requirement of Russian religious taste, at least in the medieval and later Muscovite periods. This concerns particularly the iconostasis. Byzantium took the first step toward its creation, by placing one range of small icons upon the grille separating the sanctuary from the main body of the church. One does not see, however, that this structure changed much in the general aspect of the church. Both

Byzantine medieval churches and those in Kiev left an open view of the apse with the monumental Madonna and other important mosaics or frescoes. It is presumed that the decisive step toward the creation of a plain iconostasis was made sometime during the fourteenth century throughout the entire Christian East. We still possess many old iconostases from the fifteenth century, or at least royal doors, which pierced the iconostasis in the center, of great beauty. The loss of the architectural vista was, apparently, unnoticed or overlooked.

At a later date we have striking evidence of this Russian taste for confined spaces. When Tsar Ivan IV built the famous cathedral, generally named after St. Basil, in the Red Square in Moscow, he, or his Russian builders, divided the whole space of the church with stone walls into nine small compartments so that they had nine small churches instead of one great one.

What is the religious idea, then, which underlies this artistic taste? Living in the atmosphere of the Russian medieval churches and comparing this esthetic experience with the devotional life of the Russian people one must draw a conclusion. Russian liturgical feeling is, perhaps, as far removed from Byzantium as it is from the Catholic West. We have neither "heaven descending upon earth" nor earth longing for heaven, as in a Gothic basilica, neither the assembly of both the heavenly and the earthly Church as it is expressed so powerfully in the liturgical hymns of Byzantium, nor the assembly of the earthly Church before the sacrificial altar, as in the Church of Rome. In the ancient Russian Church the divine is felt to dwell not above, in heaven, but right there present in the shrine in all the holy objects that fill it, in icons, crosses, relics, in the chalice and the golden book of the Gospels, in all these things that are kissed and worshiped. The complete incarnation of the spiritual in the material is one of the essential tendencies of the Russian religious mind.

In the light of this experience it is clear that the church exists not so much for men as for God. The church is the "house of God" in a favorite Russian saying. Not the place of assembly but rather a treasure chest, a shrine for holy things which embody the presence of God. Men enter it with fear and trembling as they enter a holy place of pilgrimage, or, feeling unworthy, pray from without in the parvis.

If the whole church is a shrine, the sanctuary is a shrine within the shrine. No one except a priest can pass through the royal doors, and the closing of these doors creates a high wall which separates the Holy of Holies from the place of prayer for the laity and emphasizes the dreadful ominousness of the mysteries. But what are these mysteries? Of course, the Holy Eucharist, the core of the Christian liturgy, the core of the church life. And yet, the creation of the iconostasis veiled the mystery so deeply that for many it ceased to be understood or even perceived. The origins of this development are also found in Byzantium. At first the veil on the chancel during the solemn prayers of the consecration (*anaphora*), then the low, inaudible pronunciation of the *anaphora* as well as the other prayers, wrongly called "secret" (in Greek "mystic"). Despite the protest of Justinian in the sixth century this practice prevailed and thus the Greek liturgy lost for the laity most of its meaning. On Slavic and Russian soil, the correct understanding of the liturgy was also made difficult by a series of philological misunderstandings. The word *altar*, precisely in this Latin form, was used by the Slavonic translators for the whole sanctuary, and not for the sacred table. As for the altar in the proper sense it was not even rendered by the word "table," as in Greek (*trapeza*) but by the Slavic-Russian word meaning *throne* (*prestol*). At the beginning prestol meant precisely table with the prefix of excellency "pre," "the most sacred table." But since in Russian the one word *stol* was used for both table and chair (or throne), in the course of time prestol retained in Russia only its second meaning, so that the altar was and is referred to by Russians with the word meaning throne. This produced a complete deformation of the idea of the sacrificial altar in the popular mind. In some Russian religious songs the Mother of God is depicted sitting in the sanctuary upon the altar instead of a throne. In other songs this position is even occupied by a saint whose body is venerated in a particular church.[9] For most of the laity the time of consecration is lost and the solemn procession with the prepared "gifts" (bread and wine), known as the Great Entrance (which occurs at the beginning of the Liturgy of the Faithful and begins with the singing of the Cherubikon), was considered as the climax of the Liturgy.[10] As we have seen in previous chapters the centuries of Mongol domination witnessed the gradual decline of frequent Communion, and that meant a decrease of interest in the Eucharistic significance of the Liturgy. And then the iconostasis was developed in such a way that it secluded the sanctuary and the Eucharistic mystery from the congregation still more. The religious attention and veneration of the latter was concentrated or lavished upon the holy icons which were kissed and worshiped before which candles were placed by everyone on entering the church, and what transpired beyond the sacred wall of icons remained unnoticed. Icons gained what the Eucharist lost.

Russian art was the winner. Painting profited by the extraordinary growth of icon veneration and, unlike architecture, elevated Russian medieval creations of the brush to a

---

[9] G. P. Fedotov, *Stikhi Dukhovnye* (Spiritual Poems), Paris, 1935, pp. 52–53, 63–64.

[10] Compare the prophetic episode in the Life of St. Sergius, above, pp. 218–219.

height never since attained. Religious and artistic motives, mystical contemplation of the celestial world and the purely human joy in color, composition, and design united in a harmonic whole, not, however, without the accidental prevalence of one of these trends of interest.

Did theological thought find an adequate role in this synthesis? A modern Russian thinker has claimed high theoretical value for the Russian icon calling it a "philosophy in colors." [11] In the first half of the sixteenth century Russian iconography did, indeed, create a series of quite new types of subjects illustrating dogmatic ideas or ecclesiastical hymns. For the Middle Ages one knew little about any such new Russian creations. Byzantine models were followed, though not in a slavish way. Numerous Russian saints, Russian costumes and even historical events found their way into the icons but no new theological ideas.

The invention of the iconostasis required a new distribution of the classical iconographic types. The wall fresco had to yield its importance to the icon on wood; the mosaic disappeared completely during the Mongol period, probably because of lack of technical skill. And the majestic apse, which has become invisible except to the celebrating clergy, retreats before the icon wall.

The first row of icons (called "local") of a greater height and size are the most important. On either side of the central royal doors one always sees Christ (to the right of the observer) and the Mother of God to the left. Both are knee-length figures. The Savior is represented as holding the book of the Gospels in one hand and blessing with the other. Two types, a mild and a severe one, were reproduced.

---

[11] E. N. Trubetskoi, *Umozrenie v kraskakh: vopros o smysle zhizni v drevne-russkoi religioznoi zhivopisi* (Speculation in Colors: The Question of the Meaning of Life in Ancient Russian Religious Painting), Moscow, 1916, new edition, Paris, YMCA Press, 1965; translated as *Die religiöse Weltanschauung der altrussischen Ikonenmalerei*, Paderborn, 1927.

Sometimes the last was called by a technical name, "Savior-ardent Eye." The same can be said of the Virgin. The two predominant types bequeathed by Byzantium were *Hodegetria* and *Eleousa;* both held the divine Child but in different positions and with different expressions. In the *Hodegetria* type the heads of the Mother and Child are straight and parallel, not related to one another. The Child looks before him with omniscient unchildlike eyes. The Mother with the same countenance is the ideal of the Heavenly Queen. Unlike Greece, Russia favored the type of *Eleousa,* *umilenie* (tenderness). Here the Child presses his cheek to that of his Mother whose expression is one of love rather than majesty. In Novgorod a third type of Madonna was venerated which also derived from Greece. In Byzantium it was called *Emmanuel.* Mary was represented as the *Orante* with raised hands, and a medallion on her bosom contains an image of the divine Infant, before his birth. In Russia this icon has always been called by the word *Znameniy* (Sign), in commemoration of a famous political event of the year 1169. The victory of the Republican army of Novgorod over the coalition of the northeastern princes under the leadership of Andrei of Vladimir was attributed to this image of Our Lady which became the Palladium of the City.

The other "local" icons on the iconostasis were dedicated to the saint or the feast in whose name the particular church was dedicated and to other highly venerated saints among whom St. Nicholas was seldom absent. The side doors usually were painted with the images of the two archangels, Michael and Gabriel, often of great beauty, in Hellenistic style. The royal door with two carved or grilled wooden folds also bore small images, usually six in number, two central icons of the Annunciation and at the four corners figures of the Evangelists or the Church Fathers.

The second, a small row of icons, represented the

"twelve" principal feasts ("holy days") of the Church calendar which often outnumbered this prescribed and sacred amount. The number of rows varied in different churches. Usually one row was dedicated to the Prophets with Our Lady sitting in their midst, another to the Apostles surrounding a central group called in Russian *Deisus*, a deformation of the Greek *deesis* (praying). This represented Christ sitting as Judge between Mary and St. John the Baptist. John was painted in his haircloth and with wings symbolizing his ascetic, angelic perfection. He and Mary both bowed before the enthroned Judge beseeching him on behalf of sinful mankind. These three central figures (*Deesis* in the proper sense) were followed by two archangels; the twelve Apostles headed by Peter and Paul completed this highly important row. All the faces were turned toward Christ, and thus the whole composition, though consisting of separate icons, represented one single whole, the heavenly participants in the Last Judgment.

Besides the iconostasis separate icons were hung on the walls, particularly on the four central columns; they lay on lecterns and sometimes were even placed outside the church over the entrance or on the great apse. For Russian devotion there were never enough icons. Yet, frescoes also retained their place. In most cases only a few fragments are preserved from ancient times. But where the whole painting has been preserved under layers of later successive "restorations" we see that the whole surface of the walls was covered by painting, either separate figures or groups or scenes. Little or nothing remained of merely decorative patterns.

The Pantocrator, a breast-figure of rather severe countenance, with the fingers of the hand contracted, not blessing, maintained his place in the cupola. This hand holds the whole universe. In Novgorod a legend was told of the Pantocrator in the dome of St. Sophia. It was supposed that the Christ held the city of Novgorod in his hand; the day that the hand opened Novgorod would perish.

Beneath the Pantocrator in the four triangles which connected the drum of the cupola with the four columns were the four Evangelists. The western wall, as in Western basilicas, was occupied by a grandiose depiction of the Last Judgment. This general scheme is the same as in the West. Sometimes this picture is broken into separate groups which cover even the neighboring parts of the northern and southern walls. In the decoration of these walls a freer choice by the artists or their patrons prevails. In the famous frescoes of St. Ferapont the walls are painted in three rows of pictures; the upper one illustrates the particular songs of the Akathistos to Our Lady, the middle one contains (a rare subject in medieval Russia) the stories of the Gospels, taken, however, from the liturgical readings of the Lenten and Paschal periods (*Triodia*). Below, or in the central columns the space is reserved for the martyrs, represented in their Roman armor as soldiers of Christ.

The apse of the sanctuary, although invisible from the main body of the church, did not remain unadorned. Mary as the *Orante* and the Communion of the Apostles — both common subjects in ancient Byzantine churches — grew gradually rarer until they disappeared completely. Their place was taken, however, by figures and scenes of no less interest to dogmatic theology. Many have a symbolic relation to the Eucharistic mystery or the liturgy in general. Such were those in St. Ferapont which depicted a legend taken from the *Leimonarion* (the "Spiritual Meadow" — in Greek, an ancient hagiographical collection) representing an angel concelebrating the Liturgy with a priest[12] or the "Service of the Holy Fathers." In the last icon Christ is portrayed with white hair as the Ancient of Days (Dan. 7) in a tricolored

---

[12] Compare the visions in the Life of St. Sergius, above, pp. 218–219.

circle. On the right stands the altar with the naked Infant upon it; on the left, the Table of the Offerings with the chalice and paten (*diskos*), which has great importance in the Orthodox liturgy for the preparation of the Eucharistic species. Eight saint-hierarchs face either the altar or the table of the offerings; these are the liturgical theologians of the Eastern Church.

The great artist Dionysius who painted this church displayed great freedom in the choice of subject matter. One of his most interesting compositions is "The Teaching of the Three Hierarchs." The three most venerated Fathers of the Eastern Church (all of them supposed liturgists), St. Basil, St. Gregory and St. John Chrysostom, are represented as seated and writing. From them streams of salutary waters flow in all directions and are quaffed by their disciples and the faithful.

And now let us turn from subject matter to style. There is a widespread idea that the formal art of the icon was in principle opposed to "picture" painting. The adherents of this thesis attempt to characterize the features which distinguish icon painting from secular art in bimensural space vision, in the idealized "transfigured" countenance, in the abstract landscape and still life. Of course, an icon never was a realistic portrait or genre scene. It ignored realistic perspective; it was conventional in representing landscapes, buildings, and details. It presented an idealized reality, in approximation of the medieval vision of the Kingdom of God. But it did so with the means of contemporary technique. It did not differ in form from the secular painting of its age but differed greatly from iconographic devices of other times or countries.

For the Russian Middle Ages one must proceed from the fundamental fact that, although Greek influence continued, it now was of another school than Kievan Byzantinism.

Russian Chronicles tell us of various Greek masters coming
to Novgorod and other towns and working there, at times
with the help of Russian assistants. A certain Isaiah the
Greek was painting in Novgorod in 1338; some Greeks were
in Moscow in 1343 and 1344. Their artistic identity has not
been determined, unlike the later and greater master, Theophanes the Greek, whose work is well known to art historians.[13]

What was the tradition and style that these newcomers
brought? Byzantium at this time, after the eclipse of the
thirteenth century, had entered a last flowering of its culture.
This period is known as the Renaissance of the Paleologues.
It has, indeed, some common features with the very early
religious period of the Italian Renaissance. Various Byzantine
and Russian icons remind one of Duccio or Cimabue, if one
does not adhere too closely to the parallel. This similarity
was so striking for some Russian scholars (Likhachev,
Kondakov) that they assumed the direct impact of Italian
art upon the East through the medium of a conjectural
"Italo-Cretan school." Now the balance of the opinion has
turned in the opposite direction, and historians are inclined
to acknowledge the debt of the Italian Renaissance to Greece
in the domain of art as it has long been recognized for
philology and philosophy.

The frescoes of Paleologan Greece are better known than
her contemporary wood icons: (the frescoes of Mistra,
Kahrie-Jami). What one sees in their figures and scenes is
different from the art of the Macedonian and Comnenian
dynasties (tenth to twelfth centuries). A new revival of
Hellenistic forms is undeniable. Human beauty, tenderness,
and elegance replace the hieratic majesty and severity of old.
Slender, elongated figures are the most striking external note.
Some critics even find a new realism and interest in nature

---

[13] V. N. Lazarev, *Feofan Grek i ego shkola*, Moscow-Leningrad, 1961.

but these elements should not be exaggerated. We remain, as before, in the sphere of the ideal, the otherworldly, but its air has changed. It is freer, more human and at the same time more spiritual.

From the purely formal point of view, two styles exist or vie with one another: the pictorial and the graphic. This implies the struggle of space against line, modeling against design, three dimensions against two. The first technique is used more frequently in wall painting; the second, in icons. The medieval Greek coined two different terms for these two techniques, *zographia* and *ikonographia*. Both arts undergo a mutual influence, but not in equal measure, however. The influence of the icon prevailed, so that line triumphs over space in the fifteenth century. The full development can be studied more easily in Russian models. Yet the linear style is typical for the art of the Quattrocento in Italy and for the whole of Europe. I would even include Chinese painting of the fifteenth century in the parallel although I am incompetent to explain the striking similarity.

The few existing frescoes of the fourteenth century in Russia, all in Novgorod, are good examples of Paleologan art. In the Church of Volotovo (about 1352) the modeling of the figures is in such relief, and the contrast of light and shadow is so strong that one is tempted to speak of the technique of impressionism. The whole impression is earnest and profound. This church is believed to have been painted by the Russian disciples of a Greek master. More perfect in execution but essentially in the same style are the frescoes in the Church of St. Theodore Stratilates (about 1370) in Novgorod. They are attributed by one of the competent scholars to Theophanes the Greek himself, the famous *zographos*, whose work in Russia we are able to follow until the beginning of the succeeding century. In 1405 he painted the Church of the Annunciation in Moscow together with

Andrei Rublev, the greatest Russian painter of all time. Thus, Theophanes represents a living link between the full flourishing of medieval art in Byzantium and its climax in Russia.

Andrei Rublev was tonsured a monk at the Holy Trinity soon after the death of the great Sergius. He must have imbibed the mystical piety of the great saint and probably learned the rudiments of his sacred art under the guidance of an older monk, Daniel, together with whom he achieved many wonderful works of art in various towns. At first we see both iconographers in Moscow, living at and painting the monastery of St. Savior, which was headed by one of the disciples of Sergius. At that time Theophanes also worked in the Church of the Annunciation together with Rublev. Here Rublev had full opportunity to study the manner of Theophanes. Moreover, his teacher Daniel seems himself to have passed, directly or indirectly, under the influence of Theophanes. Such, at least, is the opinion of Professor Igor Grabar, who has made an ingenious attempt to identify the individual contributions of Daniel and Andrei in the frescoes of Vladimir which are known to be the result of the joint effort of the old and the young master. This already indicates that the style of Rublev was different from that of both his teachers, the Russian and the Greek. Indeed, Rublev preferred linear to spatial art and thus initiated the new style, that of the Russian Quattrocento which, perhaps, was more in harmony with Russian artistic feeling. Rublev's design has nothing violent or overly expressive in it but it achieves a perfect harmony, particularly in the composition. With his mastery of design Rublev combines an incomparable sense of color. He graduated their particular nuances, avoiding blatant isolated patches or contrasted juxtapositions. The following is an adequate appreciation of Rublev's artistic qualities by Grabar: "A sense of rhythm, a sense of coloristic harmony,

an extraordinary spirituality of conception."[14] Indeed, for
Andrei, a monk and saint, formal perfection was only a means
of expressing his heavenly visions. This was clear to his contemporaries and succeeding generations. No less a personage
than Joseph of Volok writes of him and his teacher Daniel
that they "always elevate mind and spirit to the immaterial
divine light."[15] The best known icon by the hand of Rublev
is the image of the Holy Trinity in the monastery of Sergius.
It is "the summit of theological conception" in the opinion
of a connoisseur of modern art, I. A. Olsupev. Since its "uncovering" in 1904, it has been recognized without question,
as the most sublime work of Russian art.

The composition of this icon was established by tradition.
The Holy Trinity in the Eastern Church was represented
only symbolically in the guise of the three angels who appeared to Abraham. Three celestial guests are sitting about
a table set with modest food offered by the patriarch. They
are resplendent with superhuman beauty. The Hellenistic
type of angel-genius has been transfigured into a mystic glory
as never before or since in Christian art. The angels differ in
the colors of their tunics (light blue, light purple, and light
green) and slightly in the expressions of their meditative,
otherworldly faces. In their hands they hold long and very
thin staffs, also symbolical, as the sign of being wanderers.
The interplay of their heads inclined to one another and of
their arms with their staffs communicates a quasi-invisible
movement and life to the composition, which is perfect in the
triangular form, so dear to classical Italian art.

In his "Trinity" Rublev leads one through beauty to
the vision of the divine life, the aim of all mystical con-

---

[14] I. E. Grabar, *Die Freskomalerei der Dimitrij Kathedrale in Wladimir,*
Berlin, 1925.

[15] Quoted in *Voprosy restavratsii,* I, 12. The literature on Rublev is
steadily growing: M. Alpatov, *Andrei Rublev,* Moscow, 1959; V. N. Lazarev,
Andrei Rublev, Moscow, 1960. J. M.

templation. Among his other icons, the most sublime are, perhaps, a monumental, majestic figure of St. Paul from a *deesis* and the Savior, almost miraculously saved from destruction in Zvenigorod. It was found by Grabar's commission in a shed for firewood, split in two and obviously ready for the stove. The vertical split does not disfigure the unforgettable face. This is, perhaps, in its spiritual essence, the best image of Christ in the history of art. Traditional in the general pose and features, it has lost all the severity of the Greek Pantocrator without sinking to the merely human or divine, a unique solution of this dogmatic crux which has been realized by artistic intuition.

The Byzantine background of Rublev's art, namely the Paleologue Renaissance, is obvious although one can accept Muratov's judgment expressed in a somewhat too general form: "At this time (the fifteenth century) the artists of Russia far surpassed the Byzantine masters who had once taught them." [16] But where are the sources of the original Russian features of Rublev's art? Here Russian historians are in complete disagreement. Muratov derives them, without any justification, from Novgorod; Grabar, with insufficient justification, from the conjectural ancient school of Suzdal. The problem is insoluble in the present state of our research, as far as formal artistic and technical elements are concerned. As to Rublev's spirituality neither Novgorod, Suzdal, nor Moscow, her successor, can account for it. Rublev's spirituality could spring only from the new mystical movement, that of the monastery of the Holy Trinity which was both Rublev's monastic cradle and the site of his finest creation. For the most part he worked in the South, in Moscow, Vladimir, Zvenigorod, but he could not have found the source of his religious inspiration there. He must have brought it with him from the Holy Trinity monastery.

[16] Muratov, p. 189.

Though all comparisons are deceptive they can facilitate the comprehension of an art so remote and of which no reproductions give an adequate idea. (The chromos of the Trinity's colors are not to be trusted on reproductions.) In his life and in the religious attitude to his art Rublev must remind a stranger of Fra Angelico. But he lacks completely all the naïveté and primitiveness of the Italian saint. Rublev's art is mature and confident, a fulfillment rather than a first groping or beautiful survival. Remaining on Italian soil one could find the next parallel to Rublev in Duccio, the tender mystical painter who was just beginning to free himself from the same Byzantine tradition that trained the Russian artist.

As Rublev ennobled the beginning of the fifteenth century, so Dionysius was the venerated master of its close: "Famous among all his art . . . not only iconographer but, what is more, a *zoographer* (*zhivopisets*)," says one of his younger contemporaries.[17] Of his life nothing is known except his Russian origin. In the eighties one finds him working in Borovsk, in the monastery of St. Paphnutius. As his name is mentioned together with but after the name of a certain Metrophanes he must have been a younger painter, perhaps the disciple of the former. We know many churches where he worked in the South (Volokolamsk) and the North (St. Savior on the Rock and St. Ferapont). The ancient inventory at Volokolamsk even preserved the number of icons painted by Dionysius in the monastery (87) together with those by Rublev — an indication of his great glory. All his work has been destroyed either by the ravages of time or vandalism. The only exception is the monastery of St. Ferapont. This church was painted in 1500 and 1501 by Dionysius and his two sons. The subjects of the frescoes have already been

---

[17] Savva, Bishop of Krutitsa, in a Life of St. Joseph of Volok, is quoted in B. T. Georgievski, *Freski Ferapontova Monastyrya* (Frescoes of the Ferapont Monastery), St. Petersburg, 1911, p. 26.

analyzed. As to their style, Muratov emphasizes the almost "feminine elegance" that softens all features of severe asceticism.[18] Georgievski, the author of the monograph on these frescoes, speaks of the "aerial, greenish-blue tone of their colors."[19] Yet he admits a lack of expression and movement "as compared with Mistra and Serbia." And Muratov remarks that the style here triumphs over "content." Neither mystically deepened nor humanly moving, beauty is here almost an end in itself, quiet, reposing and self-sufficient.

Muratov suggests that Dionysius "grew out of the icons of Novgorod." This is not so certain in view of his "aerial" colors. A tie with Rublev is also possible though we do not know the intermediary links. At any rate Dionysius represents the last phase of the short life of great art in Russia. With his sons, who worked alone after the death of their father, we see, quite evidently, the point of decline into the dry manner of the sixteenth century.

The fifteenth is the century of the icon, not of the fresco. At least it is known to us thus far under this aspect. The best Russian icons date from this time. Many of them have now entered foreign collections and have thus made the Russian icon widely appreciated outside Russia.

Many of those icons once belonged to old iconostases but a number of them were painted to be hung separately in the church or even in private homes. They were obscure and uncommunicative until they were cleaned and uncovered. Now they sparkle with vivid colors and seem newly born. As I have already mentioned, most of them originated in the political and artistic domain of Novgorod.

As is natural, most of the icons represent single figures; the Savior, Our Lady, the favorite saints. These are the same

---

[18] P. P. Muratov, *L'ancienne peinture russe*, Prague and Rome, 1925, p. 126.

[19] Georgievski, pp. 48-50.

whose legends entered deeply into Russian folklore having
struck the popular imagination. They were not always those
whose veneration was prompted by the liturgy of the Church.
Ascetic saints are rare in Russian icons. The most popular are:
St. Nicholas in his two aspects: as a kind, merciful protector
of the distressed or as a severe avenger of evildoers sometimes even depicted with a drawn sword in his hand; St.
Theodore, or rather the two St. Theodores, Tyron (the re-
cruit) and Stratilates (the General); St. George, the dragon-
killer; the prophet Elias represented on his chariot of fire
ascending to heaven; among the Russian saints — Boris and
Gleb, the martyr princes. Only one of the women saints,
St. Paraskeve, had the privilege of being represented as a
single figure on icons.[20] Her traditional depiction is striking.
Clad all in scarlet with a thin cross in hand she is resplendent with a severe beauty which recalls that of an archangel,
a Christian parallel to Athene. St. Sergius was not honored
by the veneration of the Church in Novgorod until the fall
of the democracy, and thus his icons are rare. Very frequent,
on the other hand, are the icons of St. Floros and St. Lavros
in their role as the patrons of horses. These, however, are not
two-figure icons like those of Boris and Gleb, but a very
complicated composition. The two saints occupy the upper
plane. Under them one sees a landscape with a lake, and
three horsemen ride, obviously, to water their steeds. Their
strange hippic names are written over their heads; Speusip-
pus, Melasippus, Eleusippus. Students of comparative religion see in them survivals of the pre-Christian cults of Asia
Minor. It is remarkable that in the opposite corner of Europe,
in Langre, an ancient city of France, there existed the cult of
the same saints better known as the "Twins of Langres."

Coming back to Russian icons we find numerous types

---

[20] See Fedotov, *RRM*, I, 362, 389.

which are not single figures but compositions, sometimes very complicated and always artful and harmonious. Among them are the so-called twelve great feasts (holy days) with the episodes from the lives of Jesus and Mary, the first based upon the canonical Gospels, the second, as in the West, in the apocryphal Gospel of James. Among the "feasts" we also see the Crucifixion of a quiet Eastern type and the *Pietà*, where the display of grief sometimes finds a pathetic eloquence in the gestures of the mourning women.

Picturesquely, one of the most interesting feast-icons is that of the Transfiguration. The transfigured Christ, all in white, is encompassed by a circle or by an almond-shaped segment of all the rainbow colors. The terror-stricken Apostles lie on the ground. There is some mystical significance in this subject, although it is treated in Novgorod with a richness and a joy in the sensuous that seems to be a true characteristic of Russian popular art. In the whole Russian North, under Novgorod's influence (even in Tver and Pereyaslavl), cathedrals were dedicated to the Savior in the name of his Transfiguration. The results of this are to be seen in the frequency of this subject in the extant icons of the fifteenth century.

A particular, and, perhaps, the most beautiful group of compositions are those dedicated to Our Lady, where Mary is represented surrounded by angels or saints. These are: the "Ascension of Christ," where Mary beholds her Son rising amidst the gathering of the celestial and earthly Church, the "Veil" or "Protection" of the Mother of God where she stands in the air in a church of Constantinople spreading out her veil over the people as the sign of her patronage, the so-called *synaxis* (in Russian *sobor*) of Our Lady where she is surrounded by the angelic "orders", finally, the beautiful composition called by the initial words of a hymn: "All creatures rejoice in thee, full of grace." Here angels and human saints are followed, on the lower plane, by the animal world amidst trees and flowers, all praising the holy Virgin.

As to the formal values of medieval icons we have mentioned already fine linear design, a faultless rhythmical composition, especially remarkable in the arrangement of groups and mass scenes, and — colorism. In no sense is it a naïve or primitive art but one in full possession of its formal means. As to the colorist's tonality, in the school of Novgorod one observes a quite different taste from that of Rublev and Dionysius. Here we see a definite predilection for warm sensual tones. Blue, or greenish blue, is notable by its absence. Red and yellow predominate. Amber yellow are the backgrounds, scarlet are the chariot and the horses of Elias, the flying mantle of St. George riding his fabulous white steed, the shields of Boris and Gleb, and the whole vesture of Paraskeve. Green, especially in the icons of the Transfiguration, is of a deep tone, that of summer foliage. If green is the color of earth, scarlet, to our astonishment, in this school is the sign of celestial visions. The great exception is the holy Virgin who preserved her traditional Byzantine appearance. Her mantle, or omophorion, is in a dark wine red shading into purple. This dark red, contrasted with the snow white vestments and the wings of the angels who escort the Virgin, create a most noble coloristic gamut.

But, in general, the Novgorod coloristic taste bears witness to a robust popular art, conscious of its strength and the joy of life. The same bright and rich colors, with the predominance of red, are observed among the modern Russian peasantry, in their costumes, in popular art, in children's toys. This means that in Novgorod one finds not merely a local taste but rather a reflection of the artistic feeling of all Northern or Great Russia.

Insofar as it is possible to follow chronologically the development of the icon of Novgorod, one can notice toward the end of the fifteenth century the change from a popular to a more elegant and refined style. It finds its expression in the elongation of the figures, in more complicated and pathetic gestures, in softened coloristic tones. The old republic felt more aristocratic toward the end of her political life. And this refined art Novgorod bequeathed to Moscow, her conqueror and the inheritor of her cultural tradition.

Another feature of this development is the growing trend toward the decorative, a perpetual danger for Russian art. Russians are, certainly, gifted with a sense of rhythm and decorative values and with a degree of spiritual energy. This always constitutes a threat of superficiality. If many of the icons of the fifteenth century maintain the ideal balance between the spiritual and the sensuous, religious content and formal expression, in others one feels the joy of art for its own sake, the play of forms and colors. Still later on, the icon will become purely ornamental. As strange as it sounds, aestheticism and refinement were the same temptation for the Russian medieval artist that they were for the artist of the Western Renaissance.

If we follow Professor Igor Grabar, this school of Novgorod was of old opposed by that of Suzdal (in the larger sense), that is of the Great-Russian Center: Suzdal, Vladimir, Tver, Moscow. Theirs was from the beginning an aristocratic art "astonishing in its harmony, refinement and elegance," and "a wondrous sense of measure." "Its general tone is always rather cold, severely in contrast to the painting in Novgorod."

We could easily accept this theory which easily fits our frame of cultural zones; it would fill the field of feudal Russia. Unfortunately, it is built on too frail a base; perhaps one or two early icons of the pre-Mongol period could be attributed to the central region. Pending further investigation, we must content ourselves with the two clearly defined schools: that of Novgorod and the other, whose activities were localized in the center of the Russian state but which must be more fairly called the school of Rublev after the greatest of its masters. In the larger sense, the first is the expression of the national Great Russian artistic temperament, the second, a reflection of mystical spirituality that originated with St. Sergius. Both have their roots in the soil of Byzantium but they develop in opposite directions; one toward the national, the other toward the celestial.

A question which requires a more precise answer is the relation of the "Rublev school" to the two monastic currents which have been studied above: the Transvolgans and the Josephites. It is obvious that in its spiritual content the icon of Rublev is much nearer the mystical hermits of the North than the social, ritualistic and ascetic monasticism of Muscovy. And yet, we have seen that Rublev and Dionysius as well worked both in the North and the South, Rublev even for the most part in the South. The severe Paphnutius himself called Dionysius to paint his new church, and the number of icons by the hand of Rublev and Dionysius in the monastery of Joseph was extremely great.[21] How then explain this apparent indifference in the relations between the trends of art and spiritual life?

The answer is, perhaps, not so difficult to find. The artist is dependent on the patron; he goes where he is called. But in the North he had a more limited field of activity. Great monasteries like St. Cyril, St. Ferapont, or St. Savior on the Rock were rare. The mystics were lovers of poverty and prayed in small wooden chapels. They did not need external means of art from which to draw their religious inspiration. Some of them even rejected art as luxury and vanity. St.

---

[21] This can be seen in an inventory of the monastery treasurer that dates from the middle of the sixteenth century. The text is in Georgievski, appendix.

Nilus, at least, is not far from iconoclasm in some of his
radical sayings. On the other hand, in the South, princes
and abbots were building new sumptuous monasteries and
churches that needed much work from icon and fresco painters. Liturgical beauty was welcomed here as one of the foundations of spiritual life. The school of Paphnutius and Joseph
was unable, because of their severe ascetic spirit, to produce
its own style of art. Did it perceive the heterogeneous-
ness, the strangeness of the Northern iconographers? I do
not think so. Even the severest ascetic knows his moments of
umilenie (tenderness) and is warmed by visions of celestial
beauty. However, he does not lay this experience at the foundation of his religious and moral life. He leaves his celestial
vision, as well as that of liturgical beauty, behind him when
he crosses the threshold of the church. Such has been the experience of the Russian ritualists at all periods of history.
This fact gives a clue to many contradictions within the
Russian religious mind.

A brief postscript on a third aspect of religious art. It is
generally believed that sculpture has no place in the Orthodox cult. This is undoubtedly true for the present state of
things but it is not so as far as the past is concerned. In the
Middle Ages sculpture had a place, though a modest one,
among the sacred arts. Even Byzantium knew icons in bas-
relief such as can be seen in San Marco in Venice. Relief
images in stone existed in Kiev and Vladimir though their
place was on the outer walls of the church. In the Mongol
period we find images, carved of wood, in relief or full figure.
They are rare but they are often among those most venerated
by the people. Two saints, in particular, admitted this unusual
form of representation: St. Nicholas and St. Paraskeve, both
on the very borderline of the mythological. Perhaps this gives
the key to the riddle. It has been maintained that carved icons
penetrated into Russia from the West and, indeed, they are

found mostly in the western regions, Novgorod and Pskov. Yet the famous Nicholas of Mozhaisk is close to Moscow.

The reasons for the Byzantine rejection of statues are not known; at any rate they are not of a dogmatic nature. It is generally accepted that three-dimensional images more easily evoke memories of paganism and are more apt to be guilty of a sensual misrepresentation of the spiritual. Their rejection, thus, is considered as a concession to defeated iconoclasm. Then, Slavic religious sensualism together with the reminiscences of pre-Christian cults could be a reason for their reappearance in Russia but only in the cases of the most popular and mythologized saints. This is, of course, a hypothetical opinion. The fact is that carved icons existed through all the medieval and Muscovite periods of Russia and were forbidden only by the Holy Synod in the eighteenth century when they began their migration from churches to archeological museums.

XIV

THE TRAGEDY OF OLD RUSSIAN SPIRITUALITY

*T*HE contrast between the Transvolgan nonpossessors, disciples of Nilus Sorski, and the Josephites was truly great, in the direction of their spiritual life and in its social consequences as well.[1] One group proceeded from love, the other from fear, the fear of God, of course; one group displayed meekness and forgiveness of all, the other sternness to the sinner. In organizing monastic life, one side was almost anarchic, whereas the other maintained strict discipline. The spiritual life of the Transvolgans stemmed from selfless contemplation and mental prayer; the Josephites loved ceremonial piety and prayer according to regulation. The Transvolgans defended spiritual freedom and interceded for persecuted heretics, while the Josephites put them to death. The nonpossessors preferred labor in poverty to property or even to donations, while the Josephites sought riches for the sake of organized public charity. The Transvolgans, although unquestionably thoroughly Russian in origin, stemming from St. Sergius and St. Cyril, were nourished by spiritual streams of the Orthodox East, whereas the Josephites displayed striking religious nationalism. Finally, the Transvolgans cherished their independence from secular power, while the Josephites worked to reinforce the autocracy and voluntarily placed their monasteries and the whole Russian Church under its protection. The principles of spiritual freedom and a mystical life were contrasted with social organization and regulated piety.

---

[1] Soviet historians have recently devoted several studies to the controversy between the "possessors" and the "nonpossessors." The last general work devoted to the subject is by Ya. S. Lur'e, *Ideologicheskaya borba v russkoi publitsistike kontsa XV–nachala XVI veka* (Ideological Struggle in Russian Publishing from the End of the 15th to the Beginning of the 16th Centuries), Moscow, 1960. J. M.

The contradiction between these spiritual tendencies did not necessitate conflict between them *per se*, but the practical results of their attitudes toward monastic property and heretics made conflict inevitable. St. Nilus himself refrained from polemical messages as he did from any participation in political life. His disciples, especially Vassian Patrikeev, called also *Kosoi* (the squinter), wrote with great ardor on his behalf.[2] Joseph, who lived longer than Nilus, proved to be a tireless polemicist. Both sides sought the support of the government authorities. Ivan the Third was not disposed to execute heretics, and both he and his successor had thought of secularizing the monastery lands; this explains the protection that Basil III extended for a long time to Vassian, who lived in Moscow at the Simonov monastery and, as a result of his high princely descent, had entry to the palace. The Josephites did not achieve victory easily, but the prospect of losing property aroused the greater part of the Russian Church, not only the Josephite faction against the Transvolgans. The Grand Prince could not oppose this predominant attitude; in the end he sacrificed Vassian, who was condemned at the Church Council of 1531 on accusations of theological blunders which were interpreted as heresies. Even before Vassian, a monk from Mt. Athos, an Orthodox humanist and writer, Maxim the Greek, was condemned in 1525. He raised the possibility of reviving in Russia the Orthodox culture which had perished in Byzantium, and this hope died out with his condemnation. Maxim was accused of inaccuracies in his translations; behind these accusations lay a desire for revenge against a man who had shared the views of the nonpossessors and had condemned the external, ceremonial tendency of Russian piety. After thirty years of seclusion in various Russian monasteries,

---

[2] A monograph on Vassian was published in 1960 by N. A. Kazakova, *Vassian Patrikeev i ego sochineniya* (Vassian Patrikeev and His Works), Moscow and Leningrad, 1960.

Maxim died in the Holy Trinity monastery of St. Sergius, where he was venerated locally as a saint for the sufferings he had innocently borne.[3]

Metropolitan Daniel, who had condemned Maxim and Vassian, had been himself one of the abbots of the Volokolamsk monastery and one of the disciples of St. Joseph. By his devotion to the Grand Prince and unconditional defense of the Prince's interests, even to the extent of violating the canons and his moral obligations, he was able to make himself essential. During his time, the Josephite tendency became more firmly established in Moscow. The Volokolamsk monastery became the source of bishops for all Russia, like the ancient Kievan Monastery of the Caves and St. Sergius' monastery. The victory of Josephism was of course a result not only of economic interests, of the ownership of lands by the Church, but of the general similarity and harmony between this trend and the state of Moscow with its stern discipline, the effort required of all elements in society, and the bondage of all to taxes and service.

The Transvolgans underwent a crushing blow about twenty years after the first attack. This time they were paying for their attitude toward heresy, not toward property. Even at the beginning of the century, they had granted refuge to persecuted heretics, motivated, of course, by reluctance to participate in bloodshed, not by sympathy for their doctrines. The heresy of the Judaizers set in motion waves of rationalism. Many who were suspected of this heresy sinned only in free thinking or in holding a critical attitude of mind. Even Nilus himself had been accused of this. His disciples had no desire to conduct an ecclesiastical court, and they re-

---

[3] On the very important figure of Maxim, see V. S. Ikonnikov, *Maksim Grek i ego vremya* (Maxim the Greek and His Times), 2 ed., Kiev, 1915, and E. Denissoff, *Maxime le Grec et l'Occident,* Paris and Louvain, 1943. Denissoff has identified Maxim with Michael Trivolis, a former Dominican monk and disciple of Savonarola.

ceived all who came to their monasteries. In the fifties a nest of heresy was discovered in the Transvolgan region. Among the monks accused there was one real heretic, Theodosius Kosoi. The others were guilty of free thinking in various forms. Among those condemned was the Abbot of Holy Trinity, Artemius, who, when he escaped to Lithuania, revealed himself as a staunch fighter for Orthodoxy. Theodoritus, the missionary to the Lapps, was also called to account; Prince Kurbski, his spiritual son, undoubtedly an Orthodox believer, composed a real saint's Life about him. Under Metropolitan Macarius in 1553–1554 many Transvolgans were condemned to seclusion in monasteries along with two real heretics, Bashkin and Kosoi. For several years searches proceeded through the Northern monasteries. We must suppose that as a result many startsi wandered out over the Vologda and maritime wilderness, and the old dwellings of hermits around the monastery of St. Cyril grew empty. This was a crushing blow to a whole spiritual trend, which had in any case been suppressed by the ecclesiastical victory of the Josephites.

The history of the posthumous veneration accorded the founders of both trends is also instructive. St. Joseph was canonized three times at the end of the sixteenth century for local and general (1591) veneration. His authority stood unquestionably high, even in the middle of the century. He was venerated by the Muscovites more highly than all the other "modern" miracle workers, and in the seventeenth century he occupied a position immediately after St. Sergius and St. Cyril in the Moscow heavenly hierarchy.

Nilus Sorski was not canonized at all in Moscow, although the construction of a stone church in his *skete*, an idea of Ivan the Terrible, was a sign of respect for him. We do not know at all exactly when his local canonization took place, whether at the end of the eighteenth or in the nineteenth century.

He was canonized quietly as a token of the growing respect for him in modern times, and his canonization was sanctioned by the Synod in the *Verny Mesyatseslov* (Calendar of Russian Saints) in 1903.

Both trends of Church life in the sixteenth century were reflected in the official Lives of saints of that period. These have been by no means completely studied or published, but Kadlubovski's[4] research enables us to trace into the sixteenth century the same two types of Russian saintliness that we have observed in the fifteenth. In several cases, however, we cannot place a saint in a definite school, either because his biography lacks concreteness or because the saint chose to follow a moderate course between the two tendencies. We may make one observation; the tendency which triumphed in the life and hierarchical structure of the Russian Church was far from triumphing in the person of her saints. Here it was the opposite trend which was victorious. Among the saints who were Josephite in tendency, we may include with assurance only Daniel of Pereyaslavl and Gerasim of Boldin.

None of the immediate disciples of St. Joseph were canonized. Daniel (+1540) was tonsured in the Borovsk monastery by Paphnutius and consequently participated with Joseph in his spiritual school.[5] He was also a teacher of Gerasim of Boldin. Daniel's official Life, which is rich in factual content, depicts the saint as dedicated from his youth to stern asceticism. In imitation of Simeon Stylites the boy tied a rope tightly around his body under his clothing; his parents could not understand the reason for their son's illness

---

[4] A. P. Kadlubovski, "Ocherki po istorii drevne-russkoi literatury zhiti svyatykh" (Essays on the History of the Ancient Russian Literature on the Lives of the Saints), *Russki Filologicheski Vestnik* (Russian Philological Messenger), vol. 18, Warsaw, 1902.

[5] An important monograph was devoted to Daniel by V. Zhmakin, *Mitropolit Daniil i ego sochineniya: Issledovanie* (Metropolitan Daniel and His Works: A Study), Moscow, 1881.

·until they discovered "a stink and rotting flesh." Another of his characteristics, also inspired by ancient ascetic literature, was that no one could persuade him to wash in the baths. The saint showed the same strict attitude toward baths later in his monastery when he was abbot there. After twelve years in Borovsk, Daniel returned to Pereyaslavl and lived there in various monasteries, taking upon himself a special task, the burial of those who died unexpectedly. When he founded his own Trinity monastery, he showed himself to be a strict abbot, very attentive to the arrangement of monastic life. The ascetic severity of his youth was considerably modified, however. Like Joseph he made his monastery closely dependent on the Moscow grand princes, who are called "tsars" in the official Life of the saint. Even the founding of a new monastery is explained as in accordance with the tsar's wish for which Daniel had practical reasons as well: "If the Church is not in the name of the tsar, nothing will lie ahead for us but impoverishment." Basil III appointed a successor for him in his old age and made him godfather of his sons.

Gerasim of Boldin (+1554) was tonsured at the age of thirteen by Daniel and was his devout disciple for twenty years. His official Life described his ascetic feats in strong language, his fasting (he ate only every two or three days), his "prayer beneficially extended" all through the night until Matins, his endurance of heat and cold with which he burdened "the violent wild beast, his flesh." Then, with his abbot's blessing he went into the desert, not to the Transvolga but into the regions of Smolensk, where he lived in a wilderness, enduring much from devils and evil men. We are told of a "basket" which the saint hung by the roadside, where passersby might leave donations for the unknown hermit. It was guarded from wild beasts by a crow, the favorite bird, incidentally, of Paphnutius of Borovsk. Two years later Gerasim founded his monastery in a new place, in

Boldin, fifteen versts from Dorogobuzh, and when he went begging to the "tsar" Basil III, he received a generous donation from him. Although Gerasim had apparently been attracted in his youth to a hermit's life, he subsequently emerged as a tireless builder of monasteries and an organizer of cenobitic communities. He built four monasteries in all, in Boldin, Vyazma, Zhizdra, and Sverkov on the Dneiper, all headed by his disciples. His biographer, the *igumen* Antony, has reported his dying precepts to the monks, which coincide completely with the "Law" or testament which the saint left after him. These admonitions and this "Law" referred to monastic discipline and maintained the spirit of Joseph's last will. Gerasim had borrowed from Joseph the institution of an assembly of twelve elders with whom the *igumen* shares his authority.

An important place in the official Life and in the posthumous miracles of Gerasim is occupied by the punishments of those who offended the monastery or of the detractors of the saint. In almost every case, however, the saint forgave the repentants and healed them. The sternest punishment was allotted to peasants who set their dogs on passing monks; Gerasim predicted the death of cattle in this village for "humiliating the monastic calling."

Let us now turn from saints of Joseph's or, more precisely, Paphnutius' school, to the disciples of St. Nilus and the Transvolgans. Two of Nilus' disciples were canonized, Cassian Uchemski and Innocent of Komel. The first (+1504 or 1509) was Greek by birth, Prince Mankupski in the world; he was tonsured in the Ferapont monastery on the White Lake and founded his own Uchemski monastery fifteen versts from Uglich. Innocent Okhlyabinin was Nilus' favorite disciple, his companion in his wandering through the holy places of Greece. When he left St. Nilus' *skete*, he withdrew into the Komel forest in the Vologda Government, where after a long period as a hermit he founded a monastery for his disciples. He copied with his own hand Nilus' Rule, adding his own "Preface" and "Appendix." He died long before his teacher, in 1491. A detailed Life of Innocent was destroyed, as was the Life of Nilus, during the Tatar ravages of 1538, but even in its shorter version we see in him a true disciple of Nilus: "Humble in disposition and meek in appearance, he studied the holy scriptures diligently and *examined them with his whole mind.*"

The second great religious leader of Komel, Cornelius (+1537), combined in his Rule and his life features of the piety of Nilus and of Joseph, with Nilus' influence predominant. We might speak of his tendency toward eclecticism, if his official Life did not portray him as an integral and original personality. Born in Rostov, he went with his uncles at the age of twelve to St. Cyril's monastery, where he was tonsured. Chains and heavy labor ("Who does not know the threshing floors of St. Cyril's?") did not prevent him from engaging in copying books. All his life he showed reverent respect for St. Cyril and for his monastery.

A spiritual pilgrimage, which Cornelius was one of the first in Russia to undertake, brought him first to Novgorod to Archbishop Gennadius, Joseph's friend, and later to the Komel forest via the monasteries of Tver. Only in the sixtieth year of his life, after many labors and dangers, did the hermit build his first church, "The Presentation of the Virgin," for his disciples. Cornelius founded a cenobitic community, not a *skete*, in his old age with strict rules for common living. He did not seek villages and property for his community; he himself and his monks tirelessly dug out roots and plowed the virgin forest. His feats of labor recall the situation of Russian monasteries in the fourteenth century; some episodes reported, such as the fallen tree and the fire in the brushwood, are deliberately copied straight from the life of

St. Cyril. Grand Prince Basil Ivanovich obliged him almost forcibly to accept property in land and villages. During a famine the monastery might feed the needy and even bring up abandoned babies, like the Volok monastery, but Cornelius would not contribute to the needy in the Josephite, economical way. He would give two or three times on the same occasion to any beggars who tried to deceive him. His disciples protested, but Antony the Great, the patron of one of the monastery churches, appearing to him in a dream, approved his impractical generosity. The official Life tells of quite a number of cases of misdemeanors and even crimes by monks and laymen. Cornelius was never strict in his punishments. When he ordered loaves of bread baked without a blessing to be thrown out onto the road, he was only following St. Theodosius of the Caves Monastery. He forgave bandits and even two of his own monks who ambushed him to kill him: "The 'Blessed One' reproved them . . . consoled them and forgave them their sin." Although a builder of a monastery, he longed for silence, and he left his monastery several times to take refuge in the Kostroma forests with his disciple Gennadius, and there he undertook to build a new *skete*. He also withdrew to St. Cyril's, planning to end his days in his native monastery, but the monks of Komel found a powerful hand to raise against their fugitive abbot. Each time they appealed to the Grand Prince, who would oblige the saint to return to his monastery; Cornelius referred to his age and weakness and tried to escape secretly, all in vain. He died in the Komel monastery to which he left his famous Rule. The Rule, consisting of fifteen chapters, tells in the preface of his two sources of inspiration, Nilus and Joseph. Beginning with Nilus' words, that he was writing for his "peers and brothers," not for his disciples, "for we have only one teacher," he ended with Joseph's words on the strict responsibility of the abbot for those under his authority and the ordeals after death which await everyone. The chapters in the Rule to a great extent repeat the instructions of Joseph in referring to the order of church prayer, of meals, and of life in the cells. Cornelius added the last chapters on the novices from his own experience, and throughout the Rule he maintained his main idea of nonpossession. His instructive admonitions, which are inserted in his official Life, are permeated through and through with the spirit of the hermit of Sora. Take for example his discussion of the question of his disciples: "What is love, and what commandment do you say to keep?" Cornelius answered according to the Gospels about the love of God and of one's neighbors. Behind his meekness and love there lay a profound understanding of spiritual life, as it had been developed by the Transvolgan school. He taught that "the heart should be kept by mental prayer from vile thoughts." Incidentally, we do not have positive information about mystical tendencies in St. Cornelius. Apparently in his effort to combine Nilus' spiritual ideal with Joseph's social ideal, Cornelius returned to the remote example of St. Cyril, restoring the wholeness and harmony of his work and enriching it by the two forms of experience in later monastic life.

St. Cornelius' broad-minded attitude considerably increased the influence of his monastery and his Rule. Even during his lifetime, six of his disciples founded monasteries in the Russian North, and a seventh did so after his death. Most of them reached the rank of saints. One of them, Gennadius (+1565), labored with Cornelius to found the monastery of Kostroma and Lyubimograd. St. Cornelius might be said to have bequeathed him his meekness. Gennadius loved to chat with peasants in the fields, and he would spend the night in their huts, never wearying of instructing them; this was an unusual feature in a Russian saint's life. Another, Cyril Novoezerski (+1532), inherited from Cornelius his love for pilgrimages. He wandered through

Northern Russia, through its forests and cities, for twenty years, barefoot and in rags, never spending a night under a roof, but usually on church porches. Later he founded his monastery on an island in the middle of Novoezersk, thirty versts from Belozersk. According to his official Life, he appears to have been somewhat stricter than his teacher. Numerous miracles, some of which were recorded even in the seventeenth century, bear witness to the widespread popular reverence for him. Ivan the Terrible also venerated him; he is supposed to have predicted the miseries of the Time of Troubles. In the nineteenth century he overshadowed the ancient Cyril in popular veneration.

The Novgorod region in the sixteenth century continued to provide great religious leaders, many of whom went to the maritime North. For the majority of them we cannot define the trend of their spiritual lives. St. Alexander Svirski, tonsured at Valaamo, founded his monastery near the Svir river. We know that he was on terms of spiritual love with Cornelius of Komel to whom he sent one of his disciples. Nilus Stolbenski (+1555), tonsured by the Pskov abbot, St. Savva Krypetski, chose the feat of complete solitude. For thirty years he concealed himself in the Rzhev forests until the influx of people forced him to move to Stolbenski Island in Seliger Lake, which gave him his surname. For twenty-seven years he took refuge in his cell without any disciples. He did not even build a chapel, a very rare case among Russian religious leaders. He prayed before the icon of the Mother of God and censed her icon. In his cell two crutches were erected on which he leaned as he slept; he never used a bed. This was all that was told of him by his neighbors from whom he endured much malice. Twice they even burned down the pine wood on the island in order to drive out the hermit. Only after many years was a monastery founded on the island. The Life of St. Nilus was written down at the request of the Stolbenski monks in St. Gerasim's Boldin monastery; perhaps this may explain a certain sternness which is attributed to the mysterious hermit of Seliger. One exceptional feature in the veneration shown him by the devout seems to fit the unique qualities of his religious devotion. At the Stolbenski Monastery, up to recent times, little wooden statues of the saint were sold to pilgrims; this custom survived the general synodal prohibition against carved icons.

Nikander of Pskov (+1582) also took refuge in a hermit's hut and did not found a monastery. He began his life in the forest even before he was tonsured, when he was extremely young. His solitude was broken by years as a novice in the Savva Krypetski monastery, where he was tonsured, but he left it twice because of his disagreements with the envious monks, who were dissatisfied with the strict discipline.

The image of St. Antony Siiski (+1558) has come down to us more vividly than that of many others. A peasant of Novgorod, he left the world as a widower, when he was already mature. He did not go to a famous monastery to be tonsured, but he received the tonsure in one of the Northern Kargopol monasteries. Wandering through the wild North, amid swamps and lakes near the Arctic coast, he finally founded his monastery on the Sii River in the Kholmogory district. He was a tireless laborer and sweated hard over the meager, unfertile Northern soil. He also liked to fish in solitude, letting the swamp mosquitoes bite him; this had been one of the ordeals undertaken by St. Theodosius, whose cult had been revived in the North by St. Alexander Svirski. St. Antony loved the wilderness, and he left his monastery in the care of the *igumen* whom he had appointed, but he was obliged to return just before his death at the insistence of the brothers. This hermit, who had wandered into such remote regions, was still obliged to enter into relations with

Moscow, and he sent to ask Basil III's permission to build on state land. He urged his monks to pray that an heir be granted the Grand Prince, and before his death he instructed them to pray for Tsar Ivan Vasilievich and for all the leaders of the Russian land. He also did not refuse to own villages. In the teachings, which are reported in his official Life, and in his own testament, which has been preserved, he insists both on the observance of the regulations for common life (here are borrowings from Cornelius of Komel) and especially on brotherly love and meekness. He showed this meekness and humility in his own life; "he held low his pastoral rod in his hand." His testament, perhaps intentionally, borrows heavily from a decree of St. Cyril's.

However obscure the images of these Northern sixteenth-century saints may be for us, some general observations may be noted. We can see features of the piety of both Joseph and Nilus, and an effacement of their sharper, distinguishing traits, such as Joseph's sternness and Nilus' mental prayer. By stressing brotherly love and a moderate strictness in regulations for monastic life, the last ancient Russian saints were returning to their original source, to Cyril's monastery on Belozersk. It was Cyril who made the deepest impression on the Northern Russian cenobites, not St. Sergius, who differed from him in the degree of his humility and his strictness. Yet, after the mystical profundity in the legacy of St. Sergius, this return to St. Cyril forces us to conclude that their spiritual resources had been somewhat exhausted. In the quality which composes the heart in the life of the Church, in the presence of holiness, the sixteenth century must unquestionably defer to the fifteenth.

To those who find this judgment subjective and unconvincing, let us propose another criterion, a statistical one, however odd it may seem to use statistics for religion. Real holiness cannot be calculated in statistical terms, but ecclesiastical canonizations can. There is some correspondence, however approximate, between these magnitudes. In the period after Metropolitan Macarius, there was no change in the policies of canonization by the Russian hierarchy until the eighteenth century. Canonizations of modern as well as ancient saints were frequently and readily performed. If we scan the lists of canonized saints in the sixteenth and seventeenth centuries, we may observe a visible "drying up" of sainthood. Take for example Golubinski's lists.[6] They are far from complete, but we may judge the relative figures by them. If we choose from the lists only the names of canonized monks, placing them in different periods by the year of their death, we will see that twenty-two saints appear in the first half of the sixteenth century, eight in the second, eleven in the first half of the seventeenth century and two in the second half. The decrease is steep and regular in the seventeenth century; there are seven saints in the first quarter, four in the second, two in the third, and none in the fourth. When we turn from figures to personalities, we must observe that, except for Dionysius, the Archimandrite of Trinity, who was famous in the political and cultural life of Russia, the names of the last saints in ancient Russia mean nothing to us. They are all locally venerated holy men, the official Lives of most of whom are not even extant. They all lived and were active in the North in remote areas and were no longer connected in any way with Moscow, which, before the midsixteenth century had constantly seen wandering holy men within her walls and palaces. Basil III and even Ivan the Terrible were able to talk with saints; the pious Alexis Mikhailovich could only go on pilgrimage to their tombs. There were no canonized monks in the last century before Peter the Great. Actu-

---

[6] E. E. Golubinski, *Istoriya kanonizatsii svyatykh v russkoi tserkvi* (The History of the Canonization of Saints in the Russian Church), Moscow, 1894.

ally Russia's brief sacred history (*philotheos historia*) came to an end toward the end of the sixteenth century.

The midsixteenth century became a crucial landmark. There are great spiritual resources even in the second quarter of the century (nine saints in the first quarter, thirteen in the second), but by the middle of the century, the generation of the disciples of St. Nilus and Joseph were already dead. The Transvolgan monasteries were destroyed in the fifties, and with them perished the mystical tendency in Russian monasticism. Josephitism celebrated its complete victory in the Russian Church, but it obviously created an unfavorable climate for the development of spiritual life. Among St. Joseph's disciples we may find many hierarchs but not a single saint. The year 1547, the date of Ivan the Terrible's coronation, divided Russian spiritual life into two spheres, the era of Holy Russia from the era of the Orthodox empire. Josephitism rendered great national service to the Russian state, as the activities of Metropolitan Macarius demonstrated, but Macarius' Church Council of the *Stoglav* (1551) also revealed the somber aspects of this victorious tendency.

The domination of regulated piety, of "ceremonial confessionalism," was established for a long time in the religious life of Russia. This was striking to all foreigners, and even the Orthodox Greeks found it oppressive, despite their admiration for it. The life which accompanied this piety, in the family and in society, became more and more oppressive. Ivan the Terrible found the most zealous ceremonial piety compatible with refined cruelty and his *oprichniki* were conceived as a monastic order. In Russia as a whole, cruelty, dissoluteness, and sensuality accompanied strict ceremonial piety without strain. The negative aspects of Russian social life, which have been regarded as signs of the influence of the Tatars, developed mostly after the sixteenth century. Compared to the sixteenth century, the fifteenth was an era of freedom, spiritual relief, and inspiration, as is so eloquently expressed in the Novgorod and early Moscow icons, in comparison to later ones.

Today it is clear that the basic road of Muscovite piety led straight to the Old Believers. The schismatics cherished the *Stoglav* for good reason, and Joseph of Volok became their main saint. With the schism, a great, though narrow, religious force left the Russian Church, bleeding it white a second time. We must not forget that the first great spiritual bloodletting took place a hundred and fifty years previously. At that time the great thread leading from St. Sergius was broken; with Avvakum, St. Joseph's school left the Russian Church. The complete absence of saints in the last quarter of the seventeenth century, during Peter the Great's youth, bears witness to the stultification of Russian life, the soul of which had fled. At the dawn of her existence, Ancient Russia had preferred the road of holiness to the road of culture. In the last century, it proudly asserted that it was holy and the only Christian land, but living holiness had abandoned it. Peter the Great destroyed only the outworn shell of Holy Russia. For that reason his violence against this Ancient Russia met only insignificant opposition from the clergy.

XV

CONCLUSION

*H*OWEVER, the centuries of the empire, which created a break, or rather a chill, between the hierarchical Church and popular religion did not destroy sanctity entirely. However strange it might seem at first glance, it was in bureaucratic Russia, Western in its culture, that Russian sanctity was aroused from the lethargy of the seventeenth century. It seemed as if the stifling hothouse which was created when Orthodox piety reached into every aspect of daily life was a less favorable climate for sanctity than the cold frost of the St. Petersburg winters. Far from the protective surveillance of the authorities, unnoticed by the intellectuals or even by the Church hierarchy, spiritual life glowed on in the monasteries, in the *sketes,* and in the lay world. The Russian monastery of recent times had been far from the spiritual ideal. Toward the end of the Synodal period, decadence, sometimes taking very serious and disgraceful forms, could be observed in the great majority of the monasteries. Yet even in the most dissolute of them, a small forest retreat or a recluse's cell might sometimes be found where prayer never stopped. In the cities, among the laymen, in the capitals, amid the noise and rumble of civilization, as well as in the remote provinces, holy fools, blessed ones, pilgrims, the pure in heart, the penniless, performers of works of love, passed on their way. The people in their love noticed them. In their grief they streamed to an elder in the wilderness, or to the hovel of a blessed one, thirsting for a miracle which would transform their wretched lives. In an age of enlightened disbelief, the legend of ancient centuries came alive, and it was not only a legend but a living miracle. The rich spiritual gifts which St. Seraphim (1795–1833) radiated were striking, and not only unenlightened, dull-witted Russia found its way to him. St. Seraphim unsealed the seal which the Synod had placed on Russian sainthood, and he alone of all recent holy men reached the rank of sainthood. Our generation reveres him as the greatest of all the saints of Russia, ancient and modern. The very emergence of Seraphim in the surroundings of the eighteenth and nineteenth centuries presumes the restoration of the mystical tradition, which had been stifled in Muscovite Russia. In fact, at the beginning of the eighteenth century, the Elder Paisius Velichkovski (1722–1794), persecuted by the police like the heretics, went abroad to Rumania, and with the help of the manuscripts of Nilus Sorski founded there a living school of mental prayer. Paisius Velichkovski became the father of the Russian elders. Optina Pustyn and Sarov, which were directly connected with him, became two centers of spiritual life, two bonfires at which frozen Russia warmed herself. *The Way of a Pilgrim* (circa 1860)[1] was a nameless witness to the practice of mental prayer in the middle of the nineteenth century outside the monastery walls, among the pilgrims and solitary hermits.

The rebirth of spiritual life in Russia not only brought to life the experience of ancient times, but it produced completely new forms of sainthood in Russia as well. The institution of the elder (the starets) must be considered in this way, as a special channel that passed on spiritual gifts and service to the world. The elder combined the spiritual activity of a monk with the life of a layman and the sanctification of a priest, nourished by the mystical experience of the Eucharist.

St. Seraphim combined deeply traditional qualities with

---

[1] For the *Way of a Pilgrim* see the translation by R. M. French, published together with *The Pilgrim Continues His Way*, London, 1954. See also pp. 280–345 in G. P. Fedotov, *A Treasury of Russian Spirituality*, New York and London, 1950; Harper Torchbook (TB 303), New York, 1965. J. M.

a bold, prophetic gift that appeals to the modern mind. A traditional hermit, who lived with a bear of the forest, who defined the meaning of his spiritual endeavor in the words of Macarius of Egypt, he still bore witness to a new spiritual era by his white clothing, his Easter greeting, and his invitation to participate in the joy which has already been revealed in the flesh by the bright mystery of the Incarnation.

Although it surpassed in many ways the spiritual experience of ancient Russia, this modern sainthood was inferior to it in one respect. It had almost no connections with the life of the Russian nation and its culture. To an unprecedented extent in the Christian world, the recluse's cell and the monastic retreat were cut off from the world, even though they were open to those who came from it. Never was the influence of Mt. Athos on Russian spiritual life felt so strongly as in the last two centuries. The broken Russian spiritual tradition was replaced by the ancient Eastern school of the *Philocalia.*

The sins of Russia were burned in the flame of the Revolution, and it produced an unprecedented flowering of sainthood, that of martyrs, confessors, and lay spiritual heroes. The small persecuted flock of the Russian Church has now been driven out from the work of creating Russian life and its new culture. It cannot assume responsibility for the society created by "the enemy." But the time will come when the Russian Church must again face the task of rechristening a Russia deprived of God. Then she will be responsible for the fate of the national life as well. Then her renunciation of society and culture, which has lasted two centuries, will end. Then the experience of service to society by the saints of Ancient Russia will be seen as surprisingly contemporary and will inspire the Church to new cultural feats.

INDEX